S0-BCS-888

MARINAOMI

TURNING JAPANESE

2DCLOUD • MINNEAPOLIS, MINNESOTA

TURNING JAPANESE

MARINAOMI

marinaomi.com

Cover Design: Vincent Stall

Production / Back Cover / Interior Design: Will Dinski

Published by 2dcloud
PO BOX 6281, Minneapolis, Minnesota 55406
2DCLOUD.COM

DISTRIBUTED TO THE TRADE in the U.S. by Consortium Book Sales
& Distribution | www.cbsd.com | In Canada by Publishers Group
Canada | www.pgcbooks.ca | Orders: (800) 283-3572

First Edition, May 2016
10 9 8 7 6 5 4 3 2 1

© 2016 MariNaomi

All rights reserved.

No part of this book (except small portions for review purposes)
may be reproduced in any form without expressed written consent
from the author and 2dcloud.

Library of Congress Control Number: 2015934609

ISBN: 978-1-937541-16-3

Printed in Korea

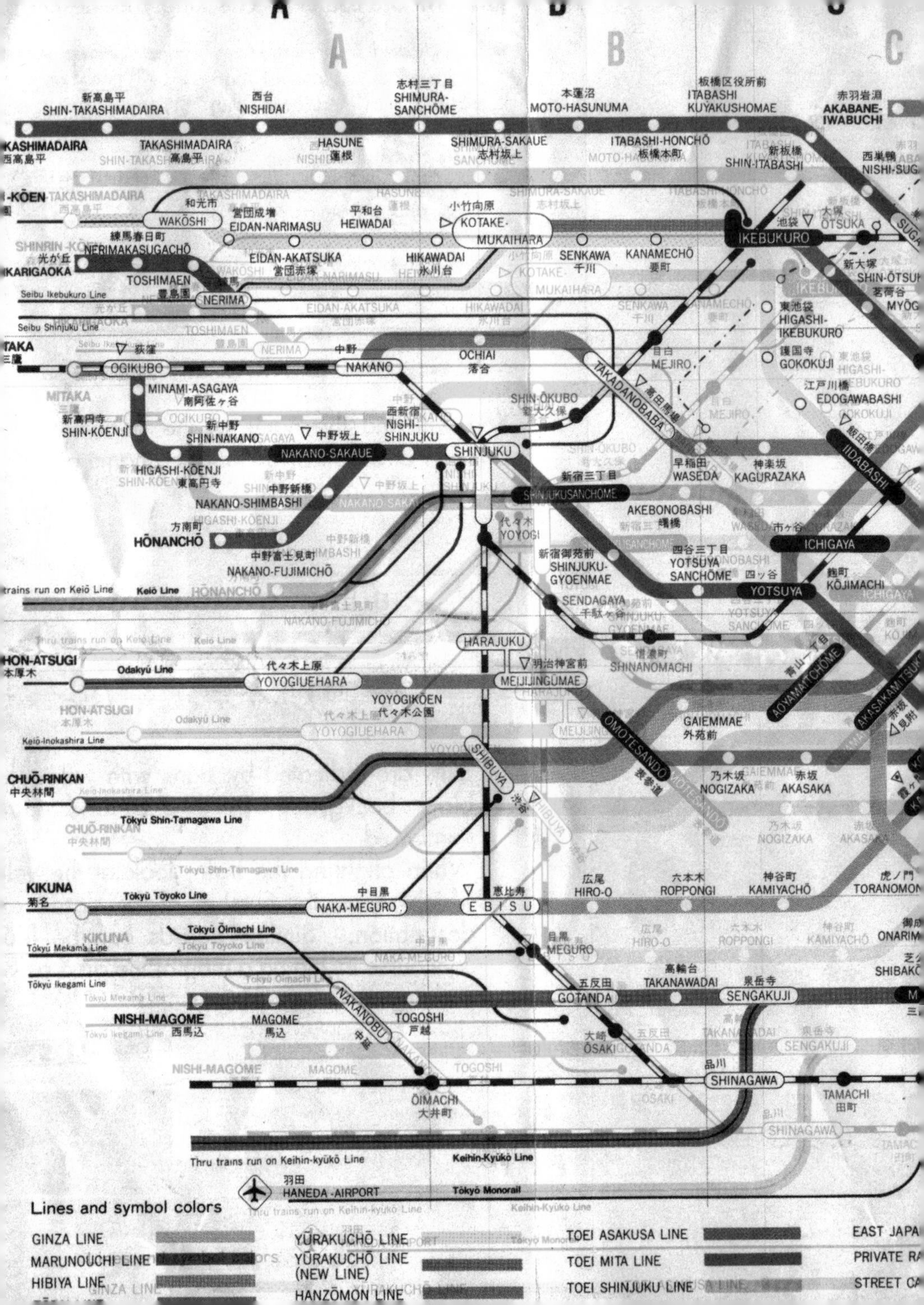

A
B
C
新高島平
SHIN-TAKASHIMADAIRA
西台
NISHIDAI
志村三丁目
SHIMURA-SANCHŌME
本蓮沼
MOTO-HASUNUMA
板橋区役所前
ITABASHI KUYAKUSHOMAE
赤羽岩淵
AKABANE-IWABUCHI
TAKASHIMADAIRA
西高島平
高島平
HASUNE
蓮根
SHIMURA-SAKAUE
志村坂上
ITABASHI-HONCHŌ
板橋本町
新板橋
SHIN-ITABASHI
西巣鴨
和光市
WAKŌSHI
営団成増
EIDAN-NARIMASU
平和台
HEIWADAI
小竹向原
KOTAKE-MUKAIHARA
池袋
IKEBUKURO
大塚
ŌTSUKA
練馬春日町
NERIMAKASUGACHŌ
光が丘
EIDAN-AKATSUKA
営団赤塚
HIKAWADAI
氷川台
SENKAWA
千川
KANAMECHŌ
要町
新大塚
SHIN-ŌTSUKA
茗荷谷
MYŌGA
TOSHIMAEN
豊島園
NERIMA
Seibu Ikebukuro Line
Seibu Shinjuku Line
東池袋
HIGASHI-IKEBUKURO
荻窪
OGIKUBO
中野
NAKANO
OCHIAI
落合
目白
MEJIRO
護国寺
GOKOKUJI
三鷹
MINAMI-ASAGAYA
南阿佐ヶ谷
TAKADANOBABA
高田馬場
江戸川橋
EDOGAWABASHI
新高円寺
SHIN-KŌENJI
新中野
SHIN-NAKANO
中野坂上
NAKANO-SAKAUE
西新宿
NISHI-SHINJUKU
SHINJUKU
SHIN-ŌKUBO
新大久保
飯田橋
IIDABASHI
HIGASHI-KŌENJI
東高円寺
中野新橋
NAKANO-SHIMBASHI
新宿三丁目
SHINJUKUSANCHŌME
早稲田
WASEDA
神楽坂
KAGURAZAKA
方南町
HŌNANCHŌ
代々木
YOYOGI
AKEBONOBASHI
曙橋
市ヶ谷
ICHIGAYA
中野富士見町
NAKANO-FUJIMICHŌ
新宿御苑前
SHINJUKU-GYOENMAE
四谷三丁目
YOTSUYA SANCHŌME
四ッ谷
YOTSUYA
麹町
KŌJIMACHI
trains run on Keiō Line
Keiō Line
SENDAGAYA
千駄ヶ谷
信濃町
SHINANOMACHI
HARAJUKU
明治神宮前
MEIJIJINGŪMAE
青山一丁目
AOYAMAITCHŌME
AKASAKAMITSUKE
赤坂見附
HON-ATSUGI
本厚木
Odakyū Line
代々木上原
YOYOGIUEHARA
YOYOGIKŌEN
代々木公園
GAIEMMAE
外苑前
Keiō-Inokashira Line
SHIBUYA
渋谷
OMOTESANDŌ
表参道
乃木坂
NOGIZAKA
赤坂
AKASAKA
CHŪŌ-RINKAN
中央林間
Tōkyū Shin-Tamagawa Line
KIKUNA
菊名
Tōkyū Tōyoko Line
中目黒
NAKA-MEGURO
恵比寿
EBISU
広尾
HIRO-O
六本木
ROPPONGI
神谷町
KAMIYACHŌ
虎ノ門
TORANOMON
ONARIMON
Tōkyū Ōimachi Line
Tōkyū Mekama Line
目黒
MEGURO
高輪台
TAKANAWADAI
SHIBAKŌEN
Tōkyū Ikegami Line
五反田
GOTANDA
泉岳寺
SENGAKUJI
NISHI-MAGOME
西馬込
MAGOME
馬込
NAKANOBU
中延
TOGOSHI
戸越
大崎
ŌSAKI
品川
SHINAGAWA
ŌIMACHI
大井町
TAMACHI
田町
Thru trains run on Keihin-kyūkō Line
Keihin-Kyūkō Line
羽田
HANEDA-AIRPORT
Tōkyō Monorail
Lines and symbol colors
GINZA LINE
MARUNOUCHI LINE
HIBIYA LINE
YŪRAKUCHŌ LINE
YŪRAKUCHŌ LINE (NEW LINE)
HANZŌMON LINE
TOEI ASAKUSA LINE
TOEI MITA LINE
TOEI SHINJUKU LINE
EAST JAPA
PRIVATE RA
STREET CA

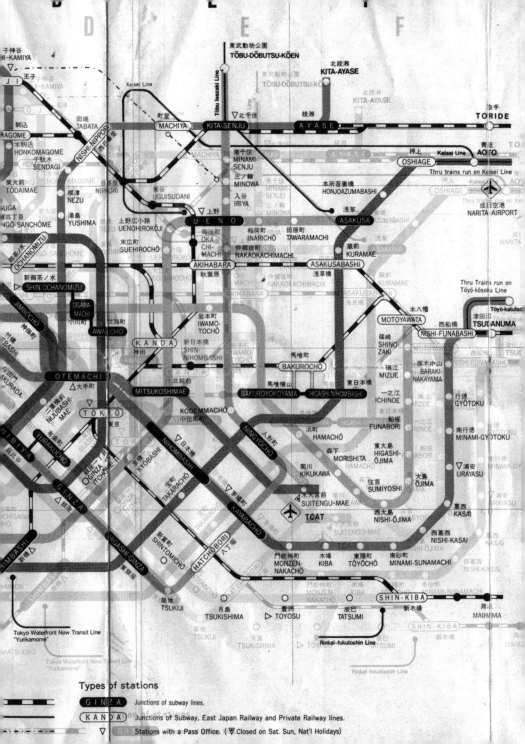

Types of stations

▬▬		Junctions of subway lines.
GINZA		Junctions of subway lines.
KANDA		Junctions of Subway, East Japan Railway and Private Railway lines.
▽		Stations with a Pass Office. (▽ Closed on Sat. Sun, Nat'l Holidays)

for Sabrina ♡

BOOK ONE

THE YEAR WAS 1995 AND I WAS TWENTY-TWO YEARS OLD.

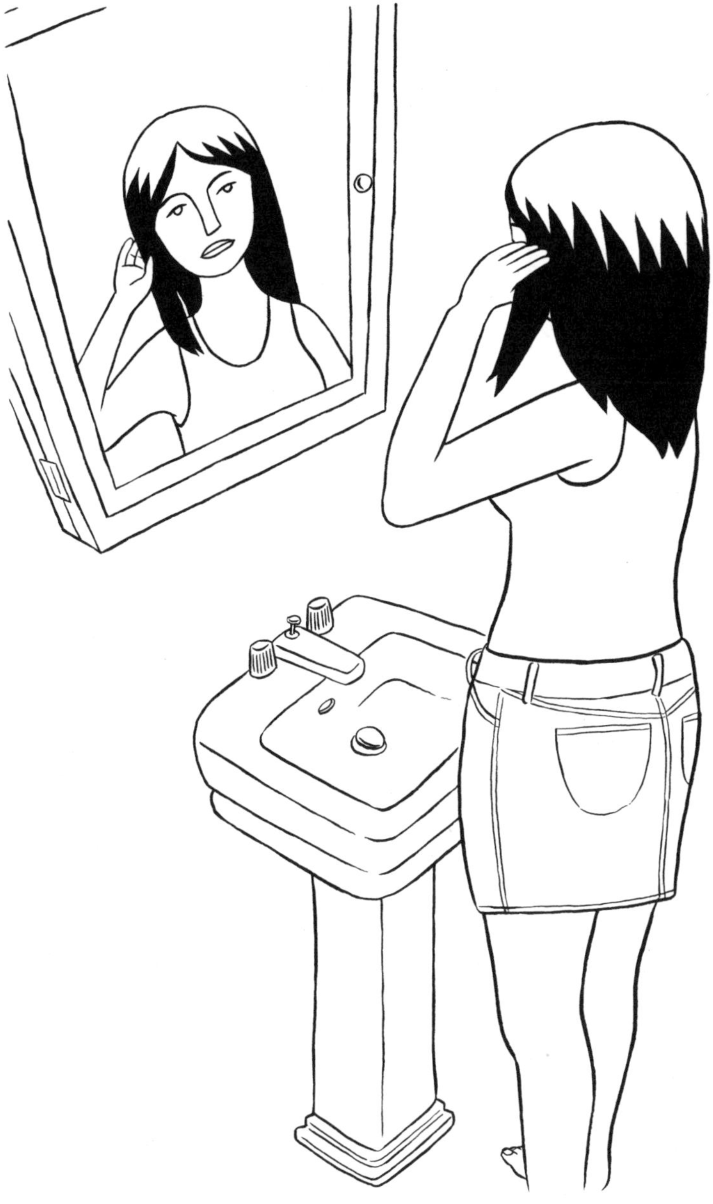

I HAD RECENTLY GONE THROUGH A BREAKUP WITH FRANCIS, MY BOY-FRIEND OF FIVE SWEET, SAVORY AND TURBULENT LONG YEARS.

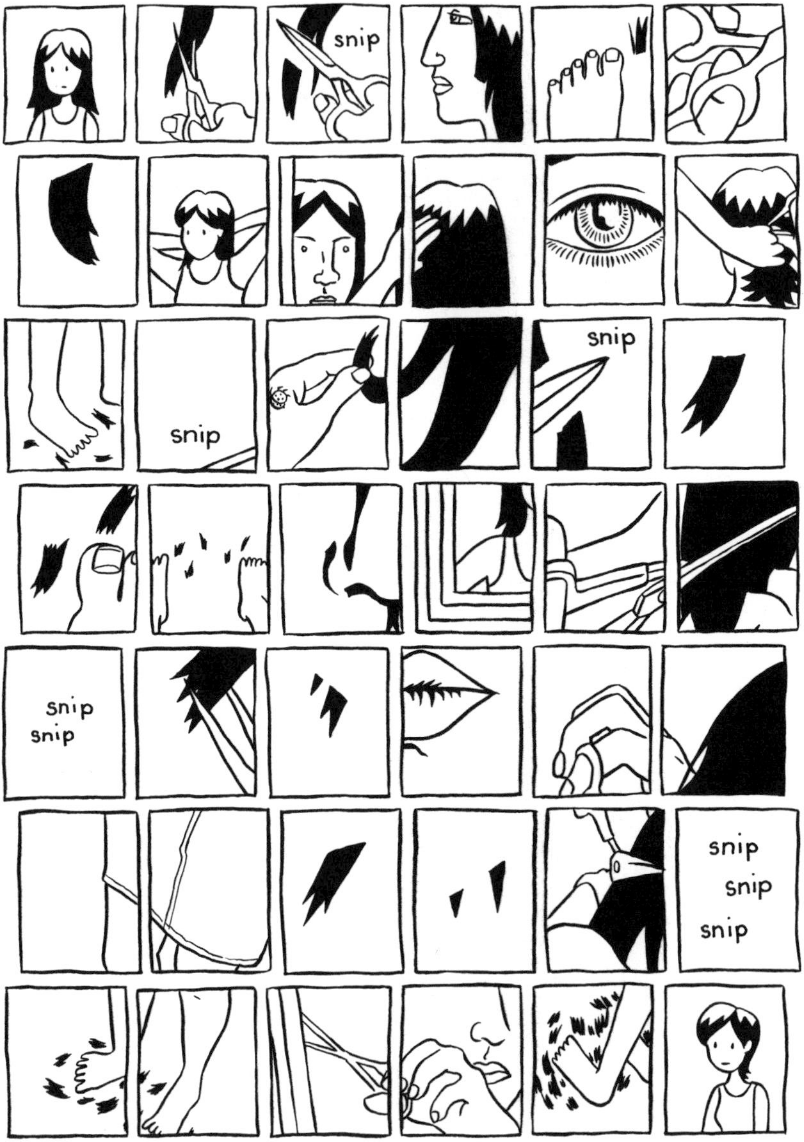
snip
snip
snip
snip
snip
snip
snip
snip

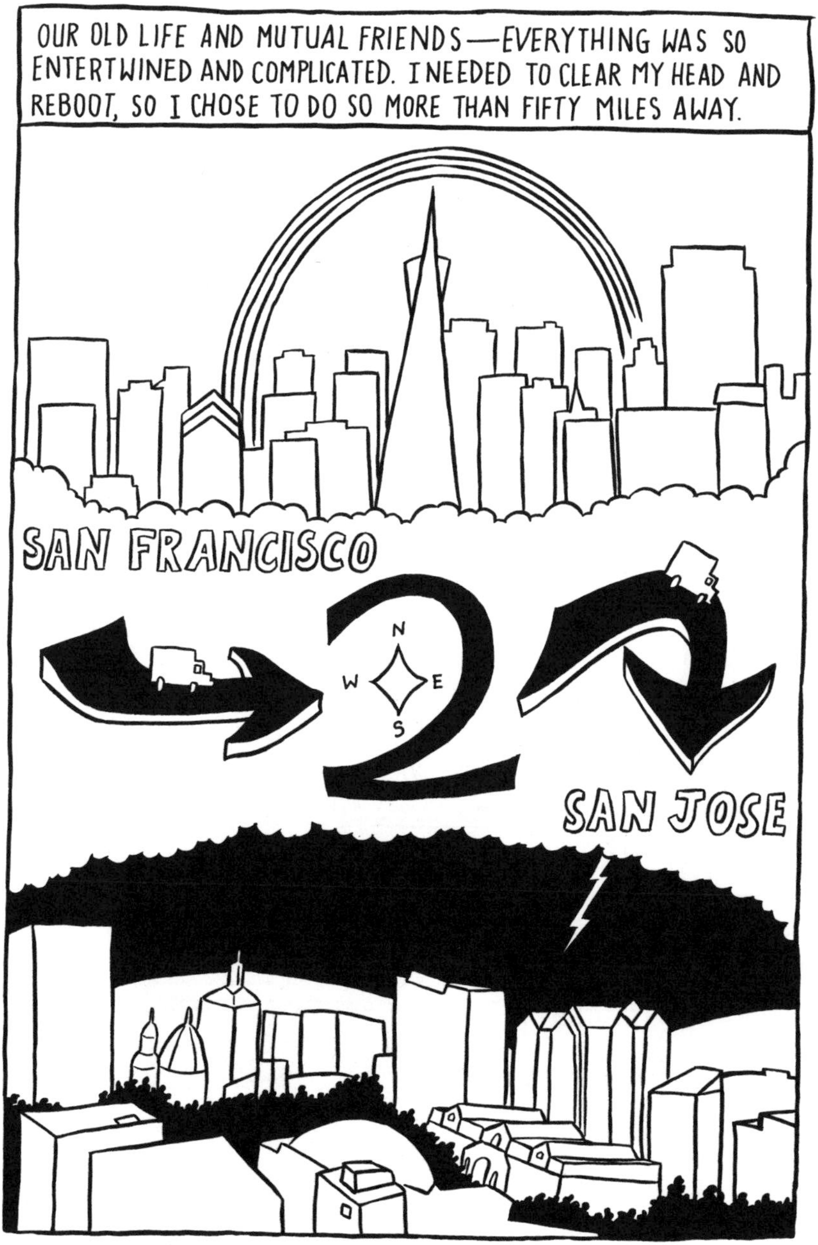
OUR OLD LIFE AND MUTUAL FRIENDS—EVERYTHING WAS SO ENTERTWINED AND COMPLICATED. I NEEDED TO CLEAR MY HEAD AND REBOOT, SO I CHOSE TO DO SO MORE THAN FIFTY MILES AWAY.
SAN FRANCISCO
2
N
W
E
S
SAN JOSE

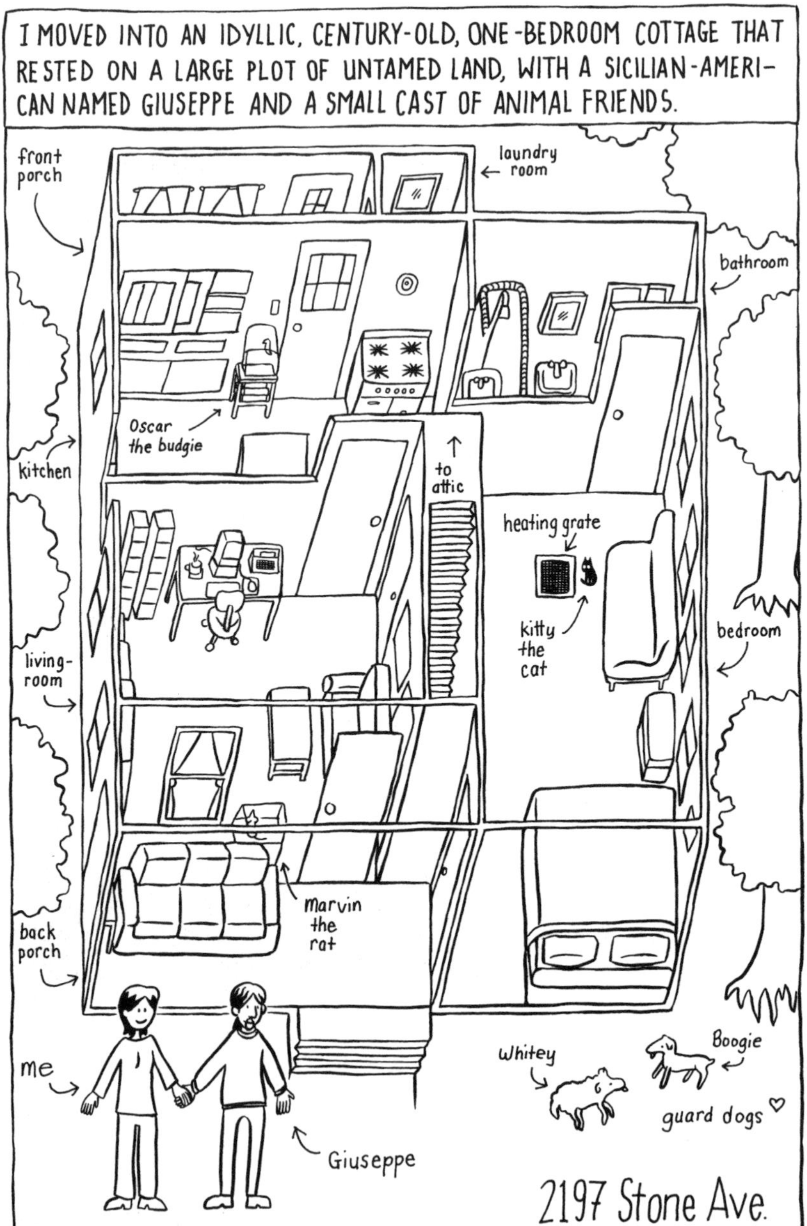
I MOVED INTO AN IDYLLIC, CENTURY-OLD, ONE-BEDROOM COTTAGE THAT RESTED ON A LARGE PLOT OF UNTAMED LAND, WITH A SICILIAN-AMERICAN NAMED GIUSEPPE AND A SMALL CAST OF ANIMAL FRIENDS.
front porch
laundry room
bathroom
Oscar the budgie
kitchen
to attic
heating grate
kitty the cat
bedroom
living-room
marvin the rat
back porch
me
Giuseppe
Whitey
Boogie
guard dogs ♡
2197 Stone Ave.

IN THE DISTANCE YOU COULD HEAR COWS LOWING. IT WAS ALMOST BUCOLIC...

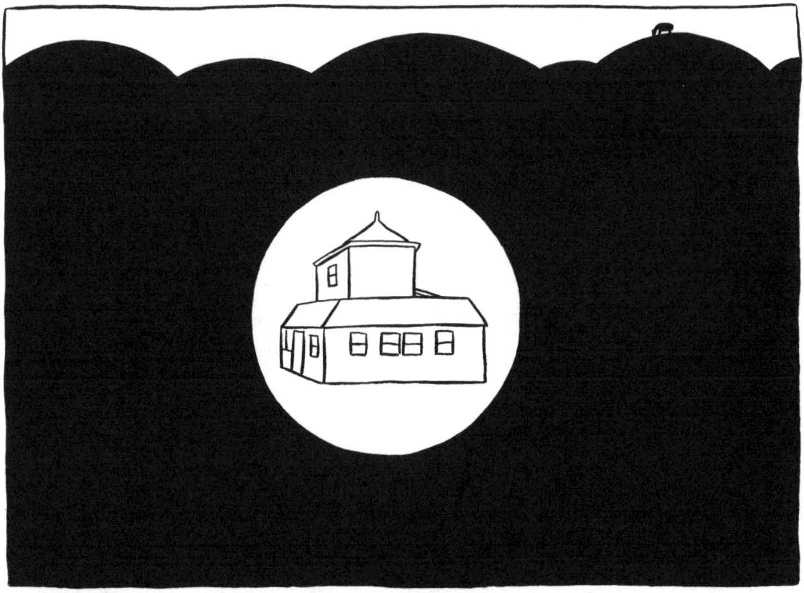

...IF IT WEREN'T FOR THE FREEWAYS SURROUNDING US.*

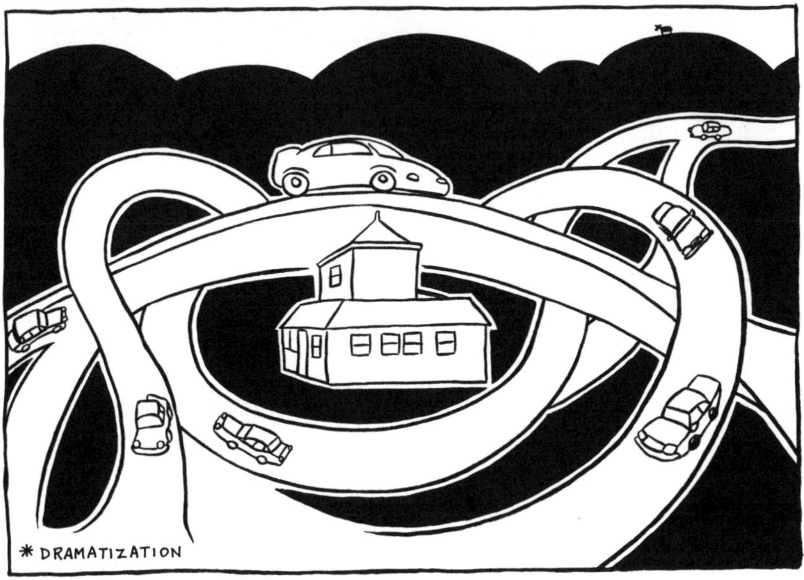
* DRAMATIZATION

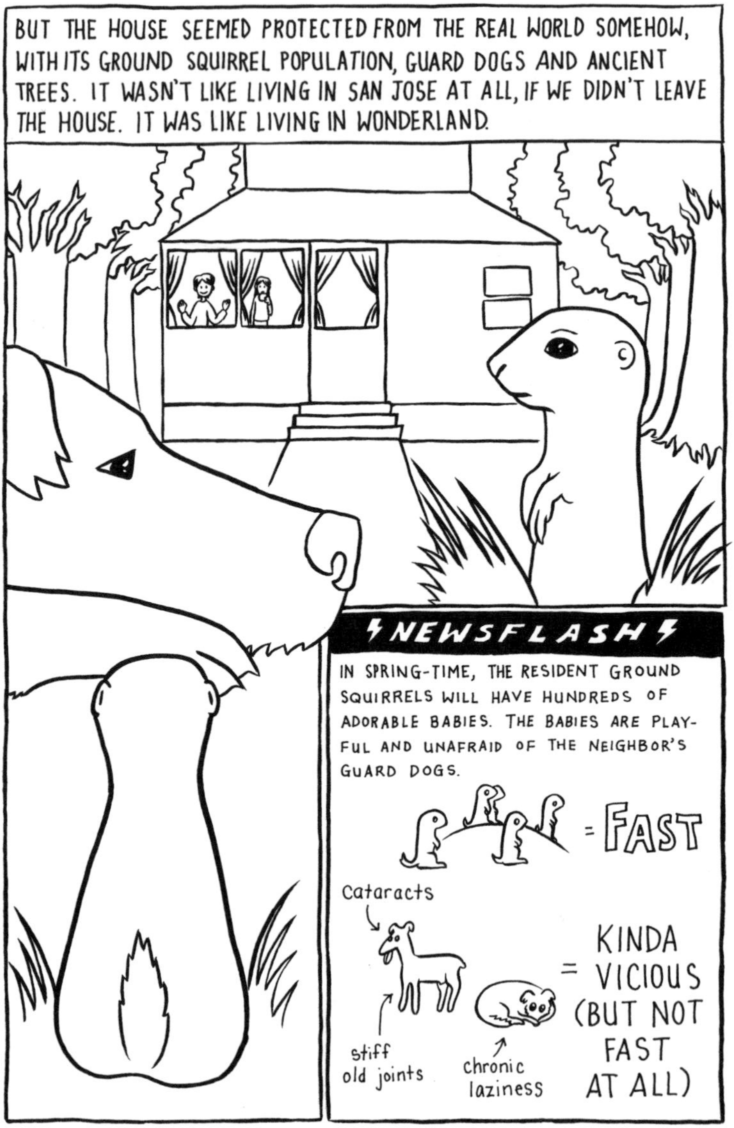
BUT THE HOUSE SEEMED PROTECTED FROM THE REAL WORLD SOMEHOW, WITH ITS GROUND SQUIRREL POPULATION, GUARD DOGS AND ANCIENT TREES. IT WASN'T LIKE LIVING IN SAN JOSE AT ALL, IF WE DIDN'T LEAVE THE HOUSE. IT WAS LIKE LIVING IN WONDERLAND.
NEWSFLASH
IN SPRING-TIME, THE RESIDENT GROUND SQUIRRELS WILL HAVE HUNDREDS OF ADORABLE BABIES. THE BABIES ARE PLAYFUL AND UNAFRAID OF THE NEIGHBOR'S GUARD DOGS.
= FAST
Cataracts
stiff old joints
chronic laziness
= KINDA VICIOUS (BUT NOT FAST AT ALL)

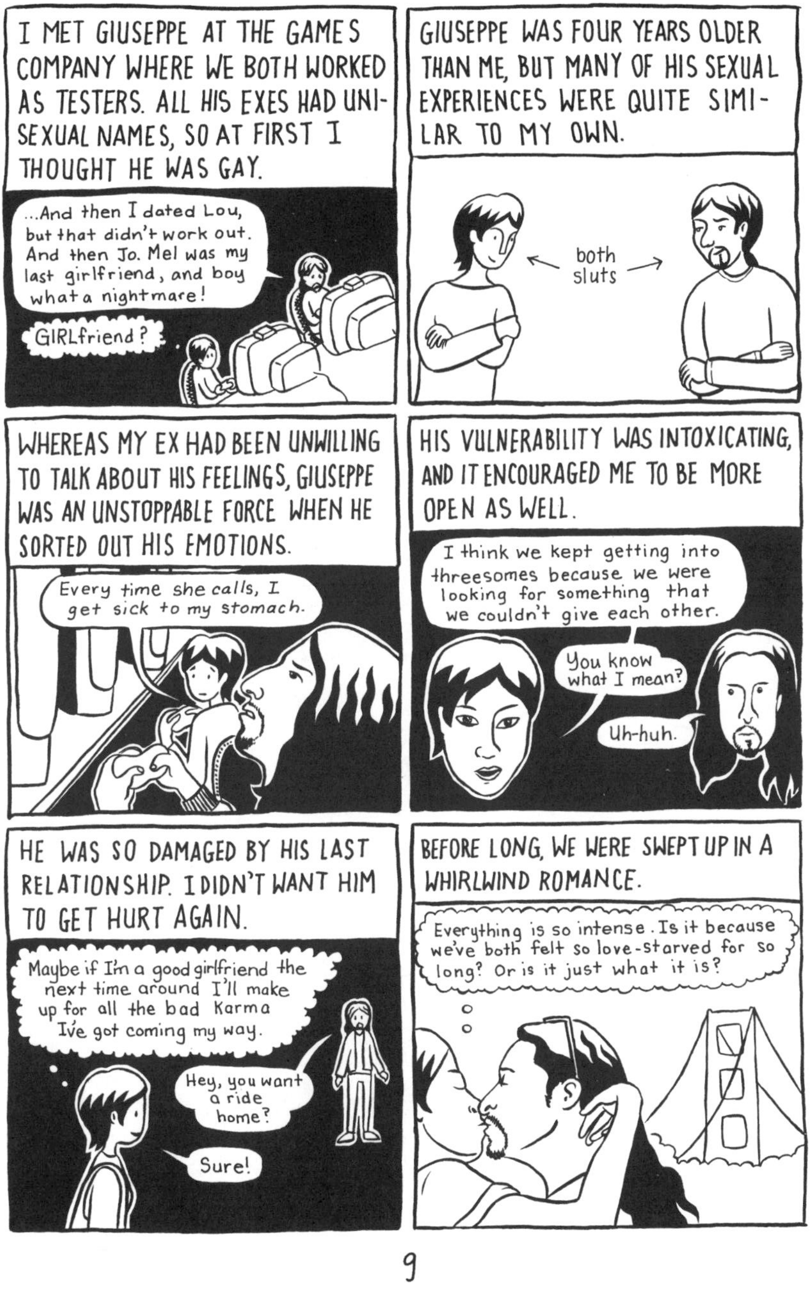
I MET GIUSEPPE AT THE GAMES COMPANY WHERE WE BOTH WORKED AS TESTERS. ALL HIS EXES HAD UNISEXUAL NAMES, SO AT FIRST I THOUGHT HE WAS GAY.
...And then I dated Lou, but that didn't work out. And then Jo. Mel was my last girlfriend, and boy what a nightmare!
GIRLfriend?
GIUSEPPE WAS FOUR YEARS OLDER THAN ME, BUT MANY OF HIS SEXUAL EXPERIENCES WERE QUITE SIMILAR TO MY OWN.
both sluts
WHEREAS MY EX HAD BEEN UNWILLING TO TALK ABOUT HIS FEELINGS, GIUSEPPE WAS AN UNSTOPPABLE FORCE WHEN HE SORTED OUT HIS EMOTIONS.
Every time she calls, I get sick to my stomach.
HIS VULNERABILITY WAS INTOXICATING, AND IT ENCOURAGED ME TO BE MORE OPEN AS WELL.
I think we kept getting into threesomes because we were looking for something that we couldn't give each other.
You know what I mean?
Uh-huh.
HE WAS SO DAMAGED BY HIS LAST RELATIONSHIP. I DIDN'T WANT HIM TO GET HURT AGAIN.
Maybe if I'm a good girlfriend the next time around I'll make up for all the bad Karma I've got coming my way.
Hey, you want a ride home?
Sure!
BEFORE LONG, WE WERE SWEPT UP IN A WHIRLWIND ROMANCE.
Everything is so intense. Is it because we've both felt so love-starved for so long? Or is it just what it is?

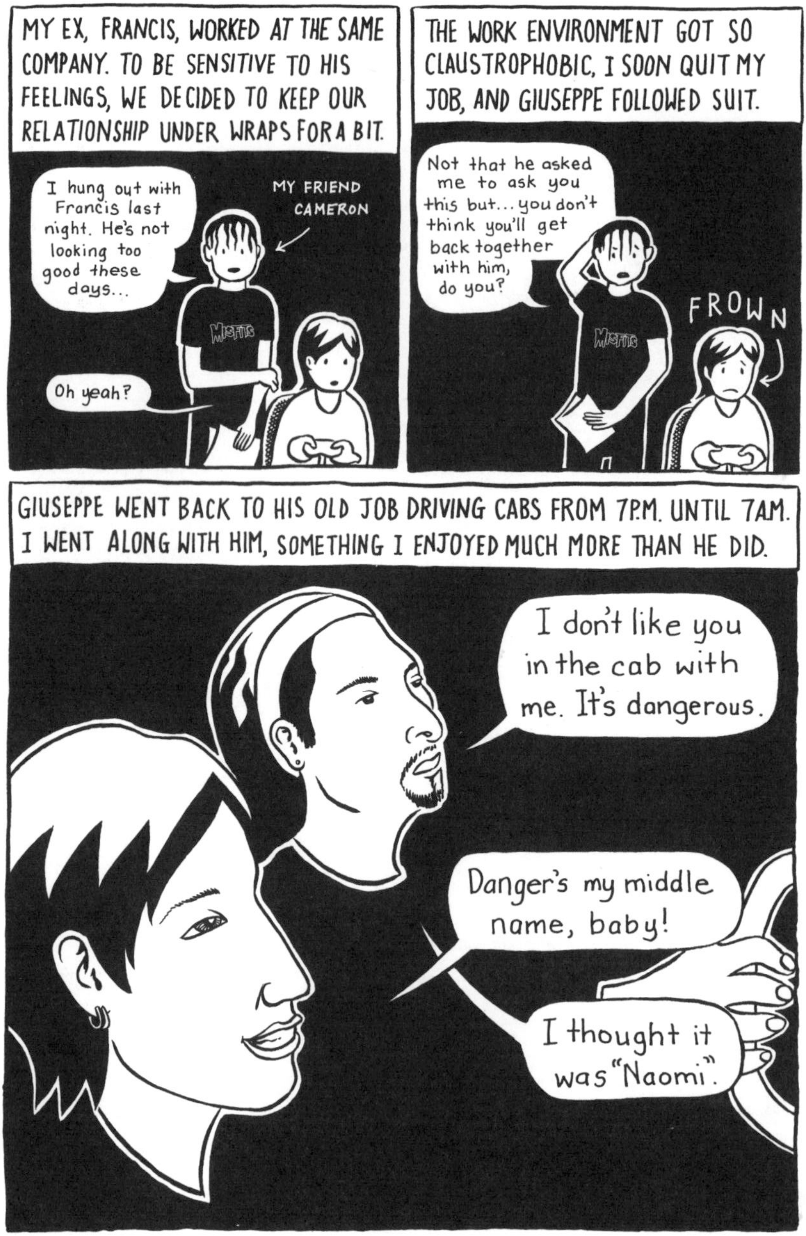
MY EX, FRANCIS, WORKED AT THE SAME COMPANY. TO BE SENSITIVE TO HIS FEELINGS, WE DECIDED TO KEEP OUR RELATIONSHIP UNDER WRAPS FOR A BIT.
I hung out with Francis last night. He's not looking too good these days...
MY FRIEND CAMERON
MISFITS
Oh yeah?
THE WORK ENVIRONMENT GOT SO CLAUSTROPHOBIC, I SOON QUIT MY JOB, AND GIUSEPPE FOLLOWED SUIT.
Not that he asked me to ask you this but... you don't think you'll get back together with him, do you?
MISFITS
FROWN
GIUSEPPE WENT BACK TO HIS OLD JOB DRIVING CABS FROM 7P.M. UNTIL 7A.M. I WENT ALONG WITH HIM, SOMETHING I ENJOYED MUCH MORE THAN HE DID.
I don't like you in the cab with me. It's dangerous.
Danger's my middle name, baby!
I thought it was "Naomi".

DURING THESE TWELVE-HOUR RIDES, WE HAD HOURS OF ALONE TIME WHERE WE GOT TO KNOW ALL ABOUT EACH OTHER.

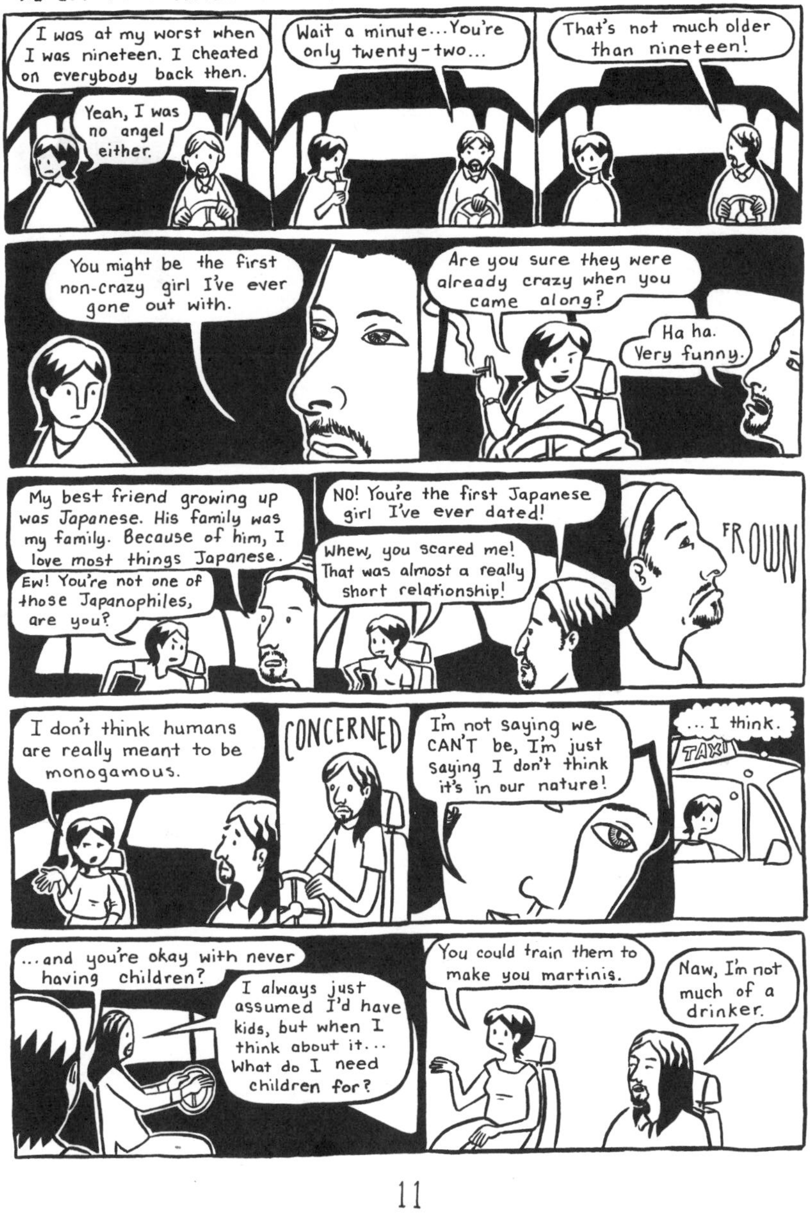

I was at my worst when I was nineteen. I cheated on everybody back then.
Yeah, I was no angel either.
Wait a minute...You're only twenty-two...
That's not much older than nineteen!
You might be the first non-crazy girl I've ever gone out with.
Are you sure they were already crazy when you came along?
Ha ha. Very funny.
My best friend growing up was Japanese. His family was my family. Because of him, I love most things Japanese.
Ew! You're not one of those Japanophiles, are you?
NO! You're the first Japanese girl I've ever dated!
Whew, you scared me! That was almost a really short relationship!
FROWN
I don't think humans are really meant to be monogamous.
CONCERNED
I'm not saying we CAN'T be, I'm just saying I don't think it's in our nature!
...I think.
TAXI
...and you're okay with never having children?
I always just assumed I'd have kids, but when I think about it... What do I need children for?
You could train them to make you martinis.
Naw, I'm not much of a drinker.

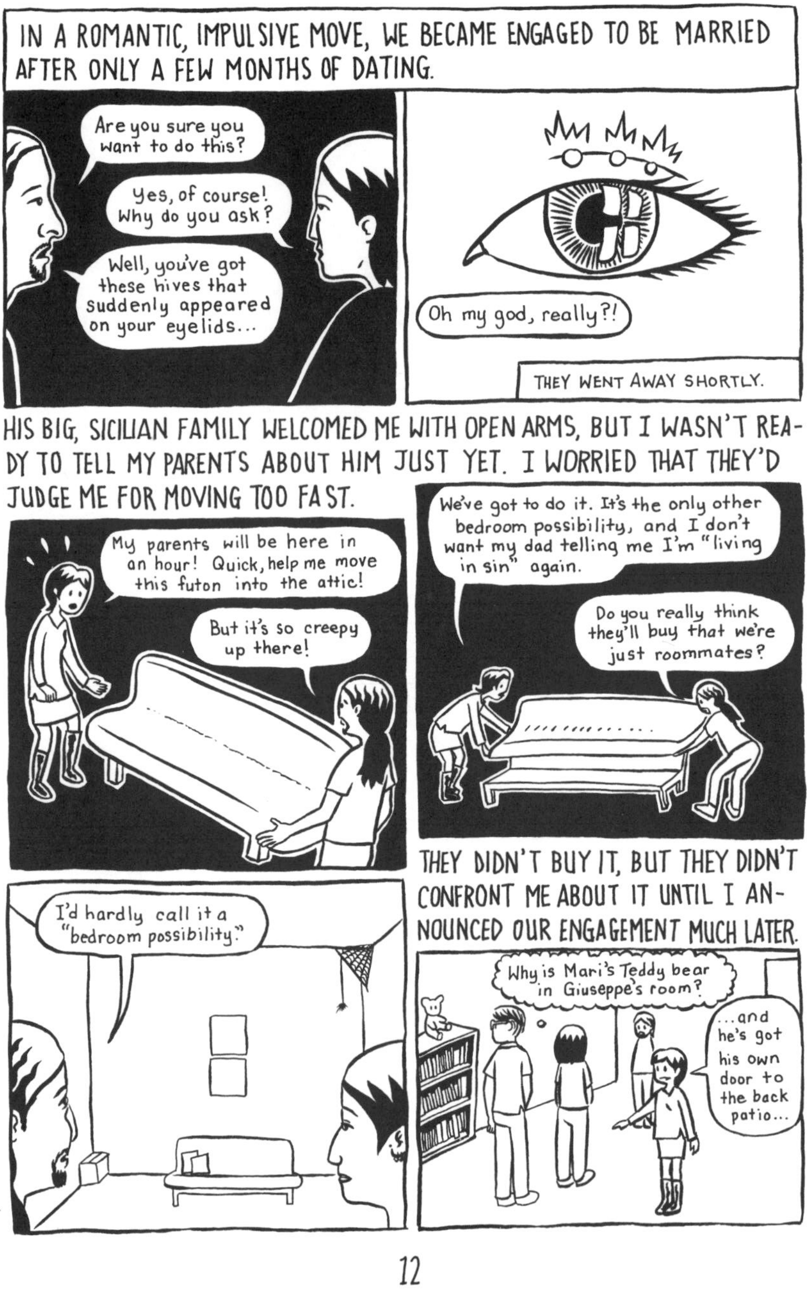
IN A ROMANTIC, IMPULSIVE MOVE, WE BECAME ENGAGED TO BE MARRIED AFTER ONLY A FEW MONTHS OF DATING.
Are you sure you want to do this?
Yes, of course! Why do you ask?
Well, you've got these hives that suddenly appeared on your eyelids...
Oh my god, really?!
THEY WENT AWAY SHORTLY.
HIS BIG, SICILIAN FAMILY WELCOMED ME WITH OPEN ARMS, BUT I WASN'T READY TO TELL MY PARENTS ABOUT HIM JUST YET. I WORRIED THAT THEY'D JUDGE ME FOR MOVING TOO FAST.
My parents will be here in an hour! Quick, help me move this futon into the attic!
But it's so creepy up there!
We've got to do it. It's the only other bedroom possibility, and I don't want my dad telling me I'm "living in sin" again.
Do you really think they'll buy that we're just roommates?
I'd hardly call it a "bedroom possibility."
THEY DIDN'T BUY IT, BUT THEY DIDN'T CONFRONT ME ABOUT IT UNTIL I ANNOUNCED OUR ENGAGEMENT MUCH LATER.
Why is Mari's Teddy bear in Giuseppe's room?
...and he's got his own door to the back patio...

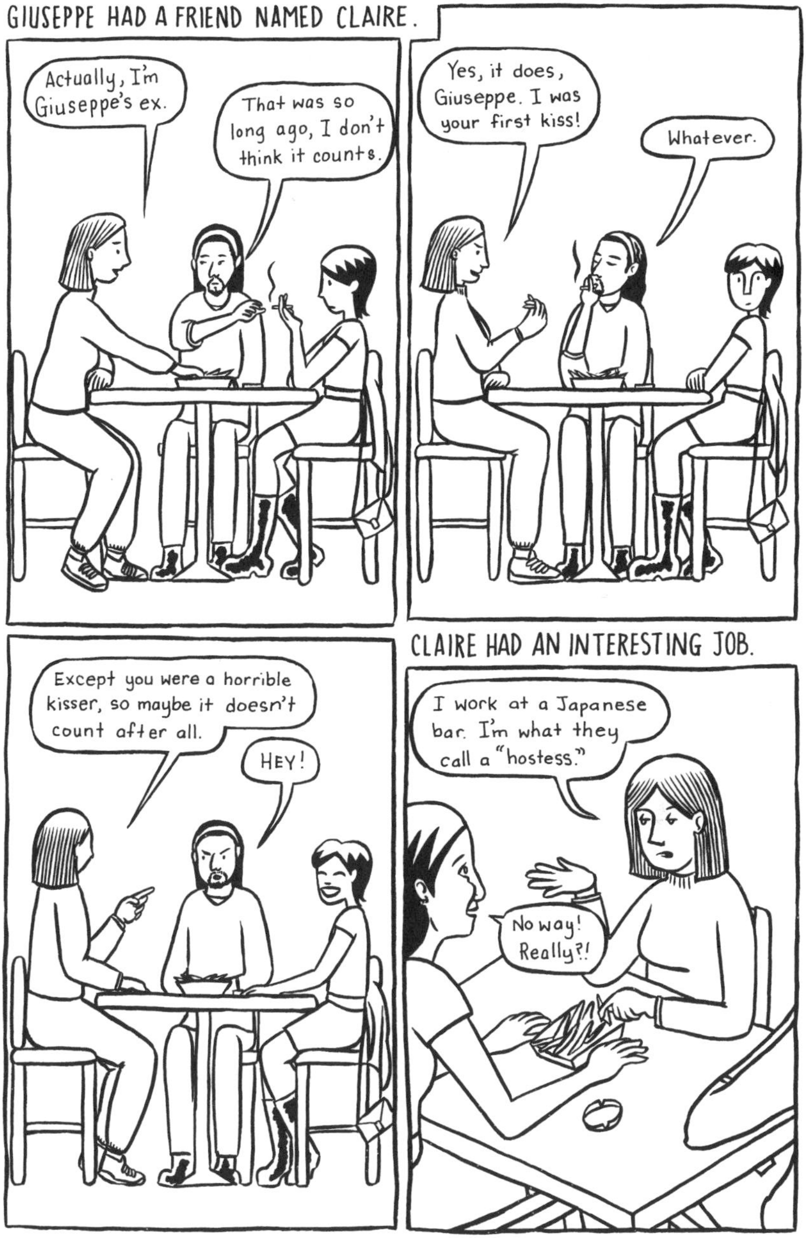
GIUSEPPE HAD A FRIEND NAMED CLAIRE.
Actually, I'm Giuseppe's ex.
That was so long ago, I don't think it counts.
Yes, it does, Giuseppe. I was your first kiss!
Whatever.
Except you were a horrible kisser, so maybe it doesn't count after all.
HEY!
CLAIRE HAD AN INTERESTING JOB.
I work at a Japanese bar. I'm what they call a "hostess."
No way! Really?!

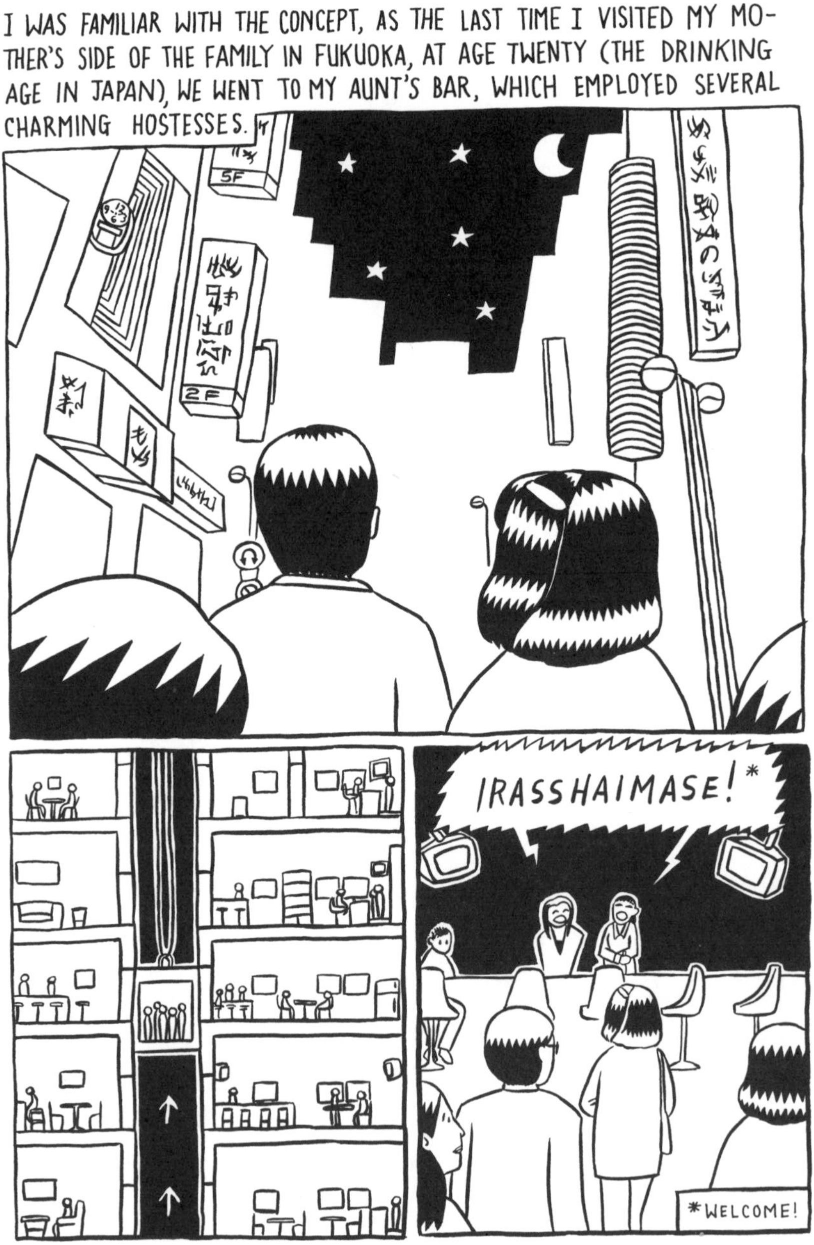
I WAS FAMILIAR WITH THE CONCEPT, AS THE LAST TIME I VISITED MY MOTHER'S SIDE OF THE FAMILY IN FUKUOKA, AT AGE TWENTY (THE DRINKING AGE IN JAPAN), WE WENT TO MY AUNT'S BAR, WHICH EMPLOYED SEVERAL CHARMING HOSTESSES.
5F
2F
IRASSHAIMASE!*
*WELCOME!

BAR HOSTESSES WERE KIND OF LIKE BARTENDERS...

...ONLY THEY MADE MORE OF AN EF-FORT TO BE SOCIAL WITH THE PATRONS,

I-I-I will always love

Ayi-aayi- I will always love yooooou...

AND PARTICIPATED IN THE REVELRY MORE THAN REGULAR BARTENDERS.

CLAP

CLAP

CLAP

THEIR PRIMARY ROLE WAS TO EN-COURAGE YOU TO DRINK.

#,すに

Er, no, thanks.

Mom, tell her I don't wanna sing.

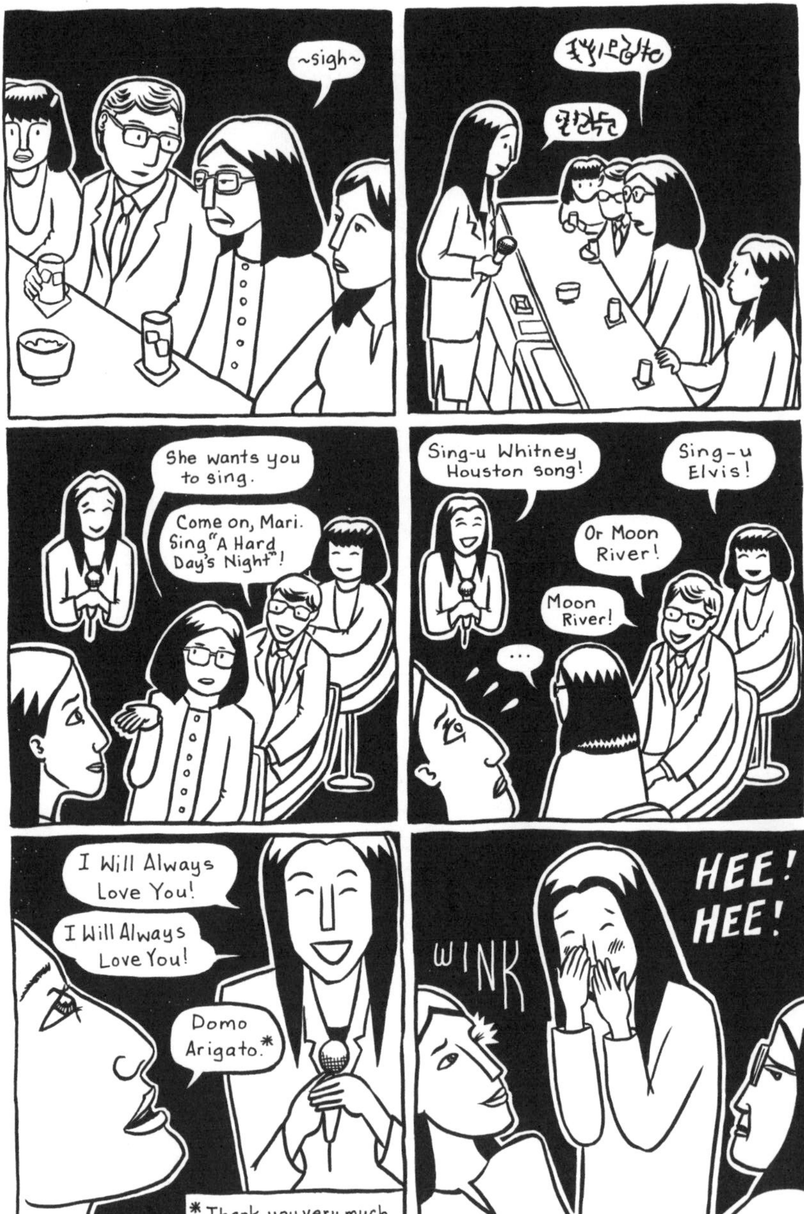
~sigh~
She wants you to sing.
Come on, Mari. Sing "A Hard Day's Night"!
Sing-u Whitney Houston song!
Sing-u Elvis!
Or Moon River!
Moon River!
...
I Will Always Love You!
I Will Always Love You!
Domo Arigato.*
* Thank you very much.
WINK
HEE! HEE!

I WAS INTRIGUED BY THE IDEA OF ONE OF THESE BARS EXISTING IN THE STATES, A HOME AWAY FROM HOME FOR EXPAT JAPANESE BUSINESSMEN IN BLAND SILICON VALLEY. I GRILLED CLAIRE ABOUT HER JOB FOR HOURS.

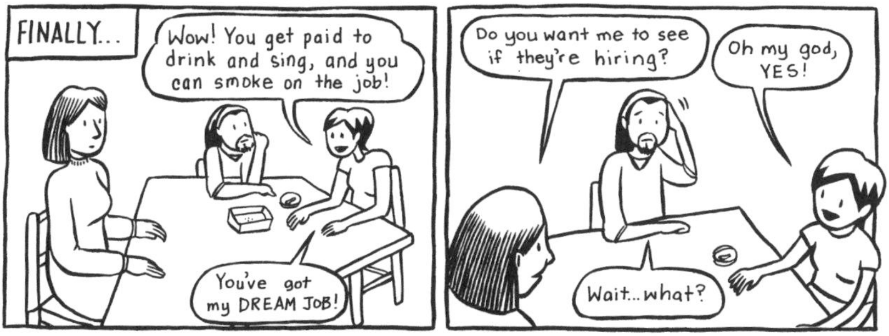
FINALLY...
Wow! You get paid to drink and sing, and you can smoke on the job!
You've got my DREAM JOB!
Do you want me to see if they're hiring?
Oh my god, YES!
Wait...what?

I LEFT THAT CONVERSATION WITH A LIGHT HEART. THE PROSPECT OF STUMBLING INTO SUCH AN UNUSUAL OPPORTUNITY ABOLISHED ALL OF MY HOMESICKNESS FOR SAN FRANCISCO IN ONE FELL SWOOP. I WAS HEADY WITH POSSIBILITY.

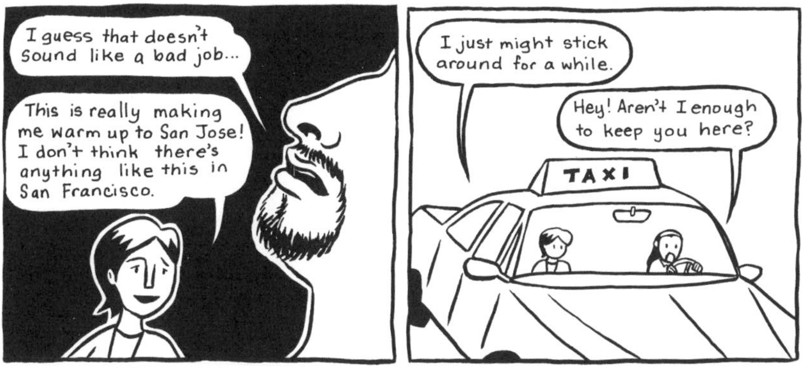
I guess that doesn't sound like a bad job...
This is really making me warm up to San Jose! I don't think there's anything like this in San Francisco.
I just might stick around for a while.
Hey! Aren't I enough to keep you here?
TAXI

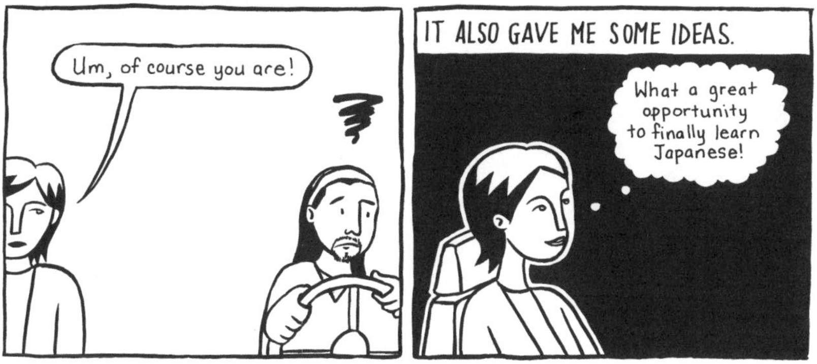
Um, of course you are!
IT ALSO GAVE ME SOME IDEAS.
What a great opportunity to finally learn Japanese!

MY RELATIONSHIP WITH THE JAPANESE LANGUAGE WAS A ROCKY ONE. MY MOM, WHO MOVED TO AMERICA FROM JAPAN WHEN SHE WAS NINETEEN YEARS OLD, NEVER SPOKE JAPANESE AROUND THE HOUSE UNLESS SHE WAS ON THE PHONE WITH HER FAMILY OR JAPANESE FRIENDS.

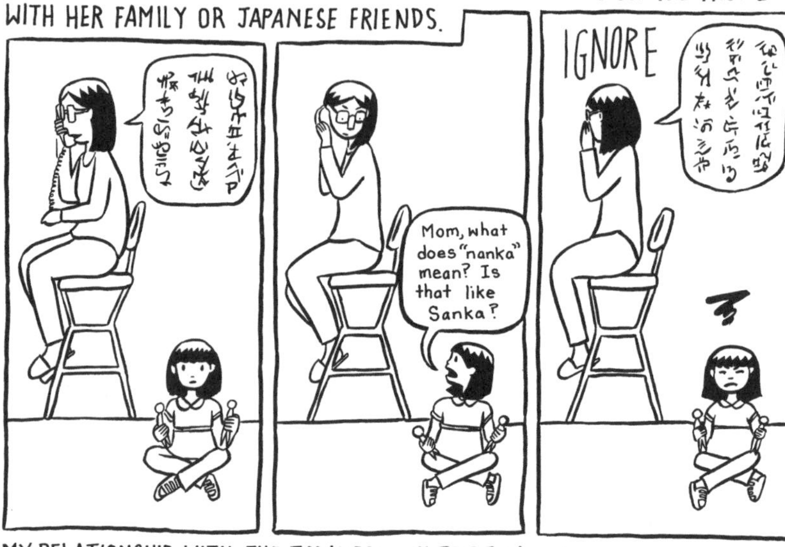
Mom, what does "nanka" mean? Is that like Sanka?
IGNORE

MY RELATIONSHIP WITH THE JAPANESE CULTURE WAS JUST AS NEBULOUS AND WAS USUALLY RELEGATED TO FOOD. I SUSPECT I WASN'T THE ONLY HAPA KID WHO LIVED IN SUCH LIMBO.

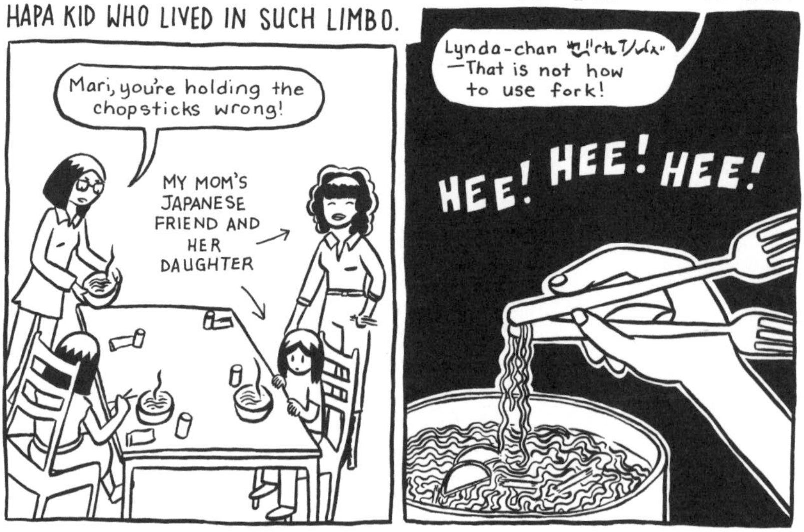
Mari, you're holding the chopsticks wrong!
MY MOM'S JAPANESE FRIEND AND HER DAUGHTER
Lynda-chan
—That is not how to use fork!
HEE! HEE! HEE!

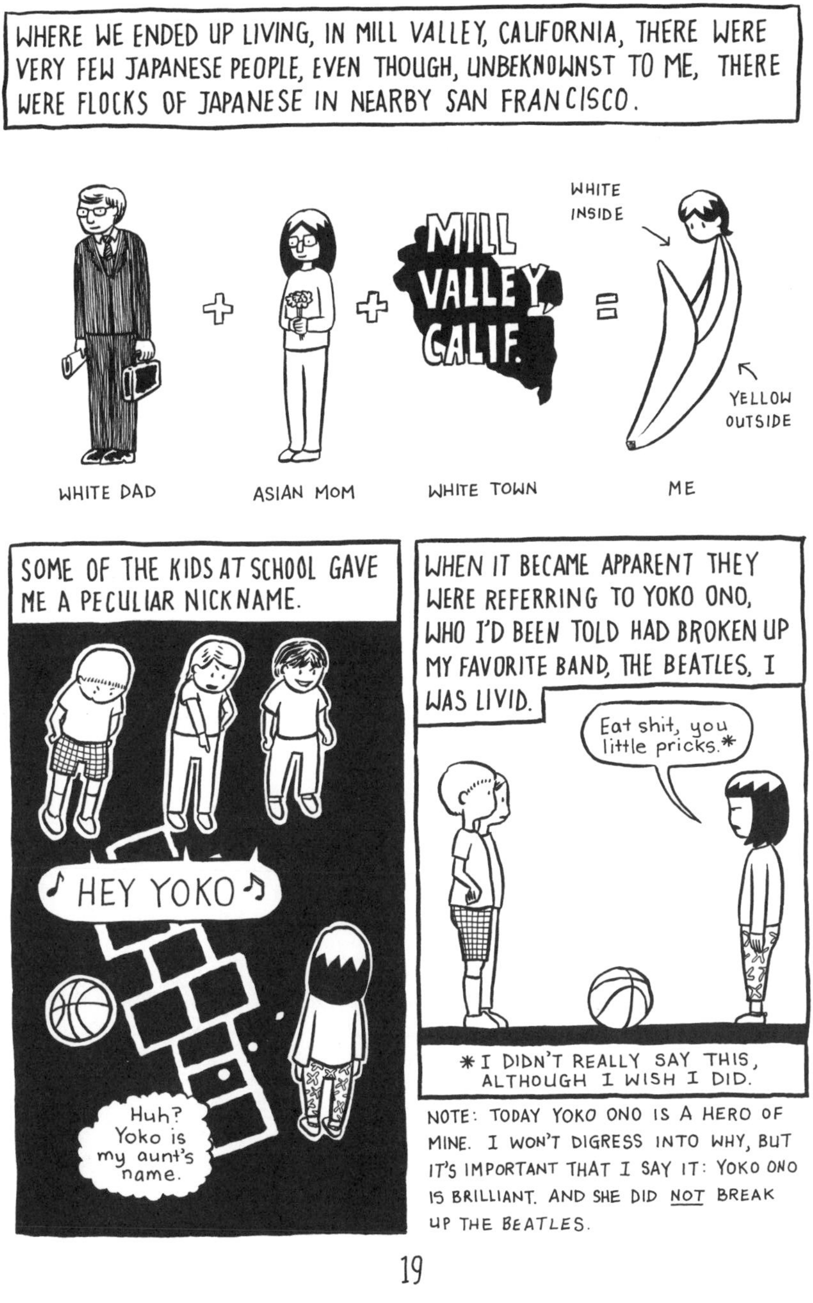
WHERE WE ENDED UP LIVING, IN MILL VALLEY, CALIFORNIA, THERE WERE VERY FEW JAPANESE PEOPLE, EVEN THOUGH, UNBEKNOWNST TO ME, THERE WERE FLOCKS OF JAPANESE IN NEARBY SAN FRANCISCO.
MILL VALLEY, CALIF.
WHITE INSIDE
YELLOW OUTSIDE
WHITE DAD
ASIAN MOM
WHITE TOWN
ME
SOME OF THE KIDS AT SCHOOL GAVE ME A PECULIAR NICKNAME.
♪ HEY YOKO ♫
Huh? Yoko is my aunt's name.
WHEN IT BECAME APPARENT THEY WERE REFERRING TO YOKO ONO, WHO I'D BEEN TOLD HAD BROKEN UP MY FAVORITE BAND, THE BEATLES, I WAS LIVID.
Eat shit, you little pricks.*
* I DIDN'T REALLY SAY THIS, ALTHOUGH I WISH I DID.
NOTE: TODAY YOKO ONO IS A HERO OF MINE. I WON'T DIGRESS INTO WHY, BUT IT'S IMPORTANT THAT I SAY IT: YOKO ONO IS BRILLIANT. AND SHE DID NOT BREAK UP THE BEATLES.

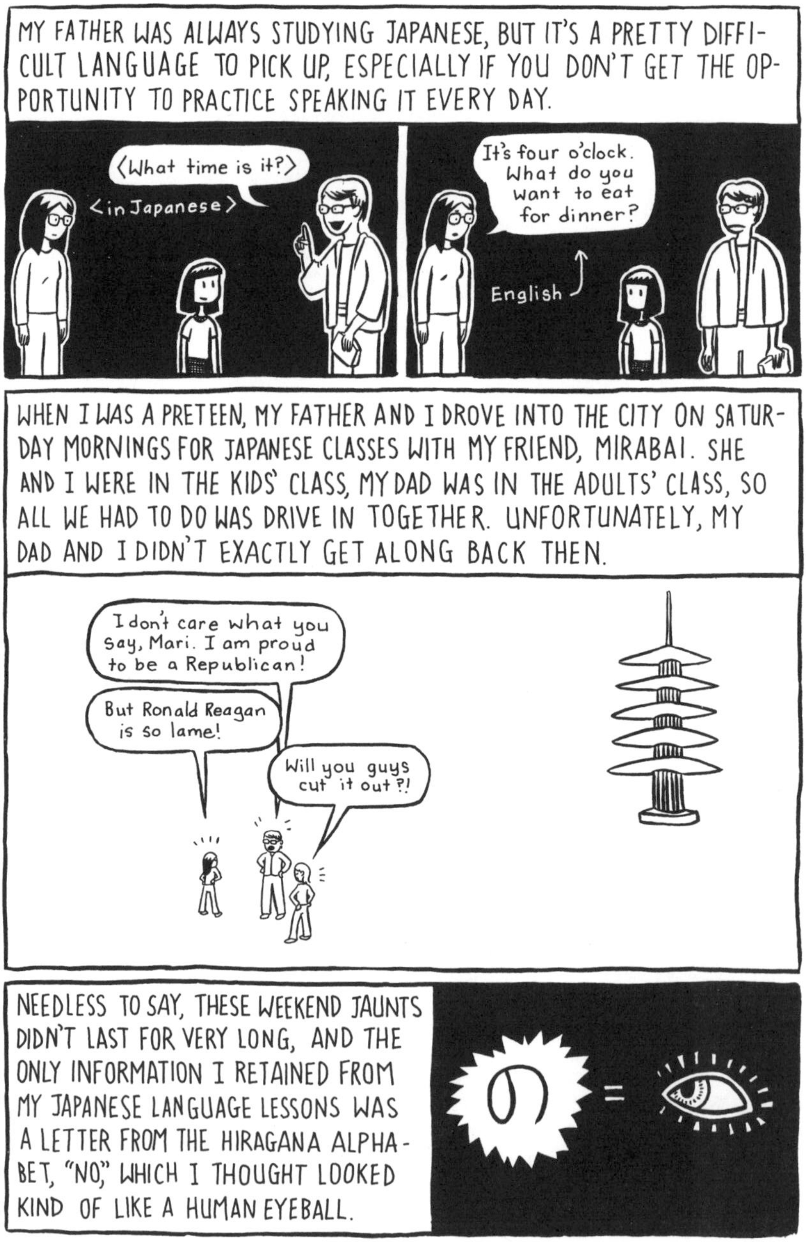
MY FATHER WAS ALWAYS STUDYING JAPANESE, BUT IT'S A PRETTY DIFFICULT LANGUAGE TO PICK UP, ESPECIALLY IF YOU DON'T GET THE OPPORTUNITY TO PRACTICE SPEAKING IT EVERY DAY.
⟨What time is it?⟩
<in Japanese>
It's four o'clock. What do you want to eat for dinner?
English
WHEN I WAS A PRETEEN, MY FATHER AND I DROVE INTO THE CITY ON SATURDAY MORNINGS FOR JAPANESE CLASSES WITH MY FRIEND, MIRABAI. SHE AND I WERE IN THE KIDS' CLASS, MY DAD WAS IN THE ADULTS' CLASS, SO ALL WE HAD TO DO WAS DRIVE IN TOGETHER. UNFORTUNATELY, MY DAD AND I DIDN'T EXACTLY GET ALONG BACK THEN.
I don't care what you say, Mari. I am proud to be a Republican!
But Ronald Reagan is so lame!
Will you guys cut it out?!
NEEDLESS TO SAY, THESE WEEKEND JAUNTS DIDN'T LAST FOR VERY LONG, AND THE ONLY INFORMATION I RETAINED FROM MY JAPANESE LANGUAGE LESSONS WAS A LETTER FROM THE HIRAGANA ALPHABET, "NO," WHICH I THOUGHT LOOKED KIND OF LIKE A HUMAN EYEBALL.

IN PRESENT DAY, I HAD HIGH HOPES OF FINALLY CONNECTING WITH ASIAN PEOPLE AND SEEING WHAT THEY WERE LIKE BEYOND THE STEREOTYPES I HAD ENDURED IN HOLLYWOOD MOVIES AND ON TV.

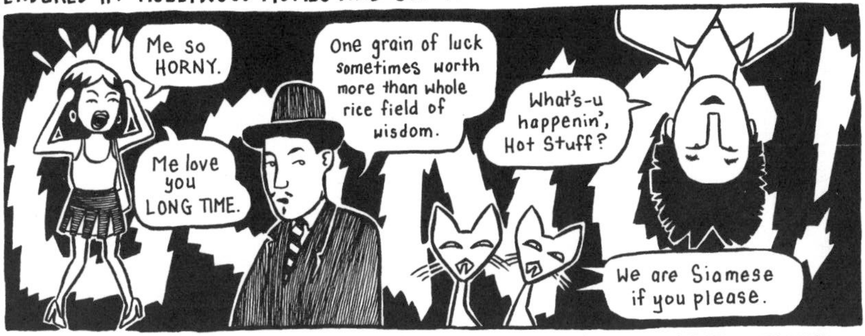

Me so HORNY.
Me love you LONG TIME.
One grain of luck sometimes worth more than whole rice field of wisdom.
What's-u happenin', Hot Stuff?
We are Siamese if you please.

BUT WHEN I GOT THE HOSTESSING JOB, THINKING I'D FINALLY GET IN TOUCH WITH A CULTURE I'D ONLY BEEN AT THE VERY FRINGES OF FOR MY ENTIRE LIFE, MY FEELINGS OF ALIENATION ACTUALLY WORSENED.

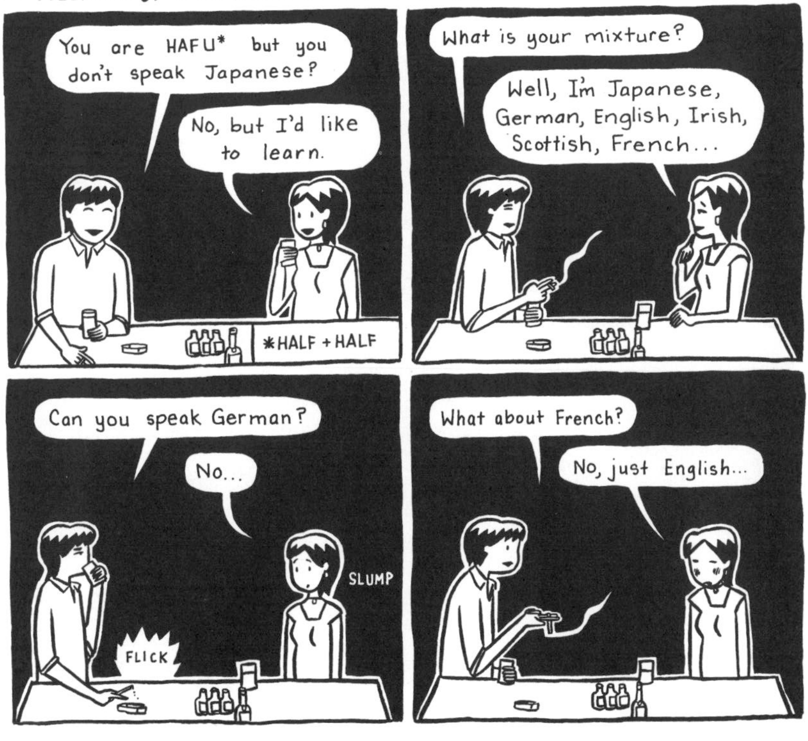

You are HAFU* but you don't speak Japanese?
No, but I'd like to learn.
*HALF + HALF
What is your mixture?
Well, I'm Japanese, German, English, Irish, Scottish, French...
Can you speak German?
No...
FLICK
SLUMP
What about French?
No, just English...

I BORROWED A GREAT BOOK ON HOW TO LEARN JAPANESE FROM CLAIRE, AND
GOT TO WORK LEARNING THE JAPANESE ALPHABET* ON MY OWN.

あ AH	へ HEH	サ SA	ラ RAH	な NA	ウ OOH	マ MA	す SUE
い EE	ほ HO	シ SHE	リ REE	に KNEE	エ EH	ミ ME	せ SEH
う OOH	ま MA	ス SUE	ル ROO	ぬ NEW	オ OH	ム MOO	そ SO
え EH	み ME	セ SEH	レ RE	ね NE	カ	メ MEH	た TA
お OH	む MOO	ソ SO	ロ ROE	の NO		TOE	ち CHI
か KA	め MEH	タ TA	ワ WA	は HA		A	つ TSU
き KEY	も MOE	チ CHI	ヲ OH	ひ HE		YOU	て TEH
く KOO	や YA	ツ TSU	ン N	ふ FOO		YO	と TOE
け KEH	ゆ YOU	テ TEH	あ AH			ラ RAH	な NA
こ KO	よ YO	ト TOE	い EE			リ REE	に KNEE
さ SA	ら RAH	ナ NA	う OOH			ル ROO	ぬ NEW
し SHE	り REE	ニ KNEE	え EH			レ RE	ね NE
す SUE	る ROO	ヌ NEW	お OH			ロ ROE	の NO
せ SEH	れ RE	ネ NE	か KA			ワ WA	は HA
そ SO	ろ ROE	ノ NO	き KEY	CHI		ヲ OH	ひ HE
た TA	わ WA	ハ HA	く KOO	ツ TSU	ン N	ふ FU
ち CHI	を OH	ヒ HE	け KEH	ゆ YOU	テ TEH	あ AH	へ HEH
つ TSU	ん N	フ FOO	こ KOH	よ YO	ト TOE	い EE	ほ HO
て TEH	ア AH	ヘ HEH	さ SA	ら RAH	ナ NA	う OOH	ま MA
と TOE	イ EE	ホ HO	し SHE	り REE	ニ KNEE	え EH	み ME
な NA	ウ OOH	マ MA	す SUE	ろ ROO	ヌ NEW	お OH	む MOO

* OVER THE COURSE OF MY STUDIES, I MANAGED TO MEMORIZE ALL
NINETY-SIX CHARACTERS IN THE PHONETIC KANA (HIRAGANA AND
KATAKANA) ALPHABETS. OF THE 60,000+ KANJI CHARACTERS (CHINESE
SYMBOLS THAT REPRESENT COMPLETE OR PARTIAL WORDS), I ONLY
LEARNED ABOUT FORTY.

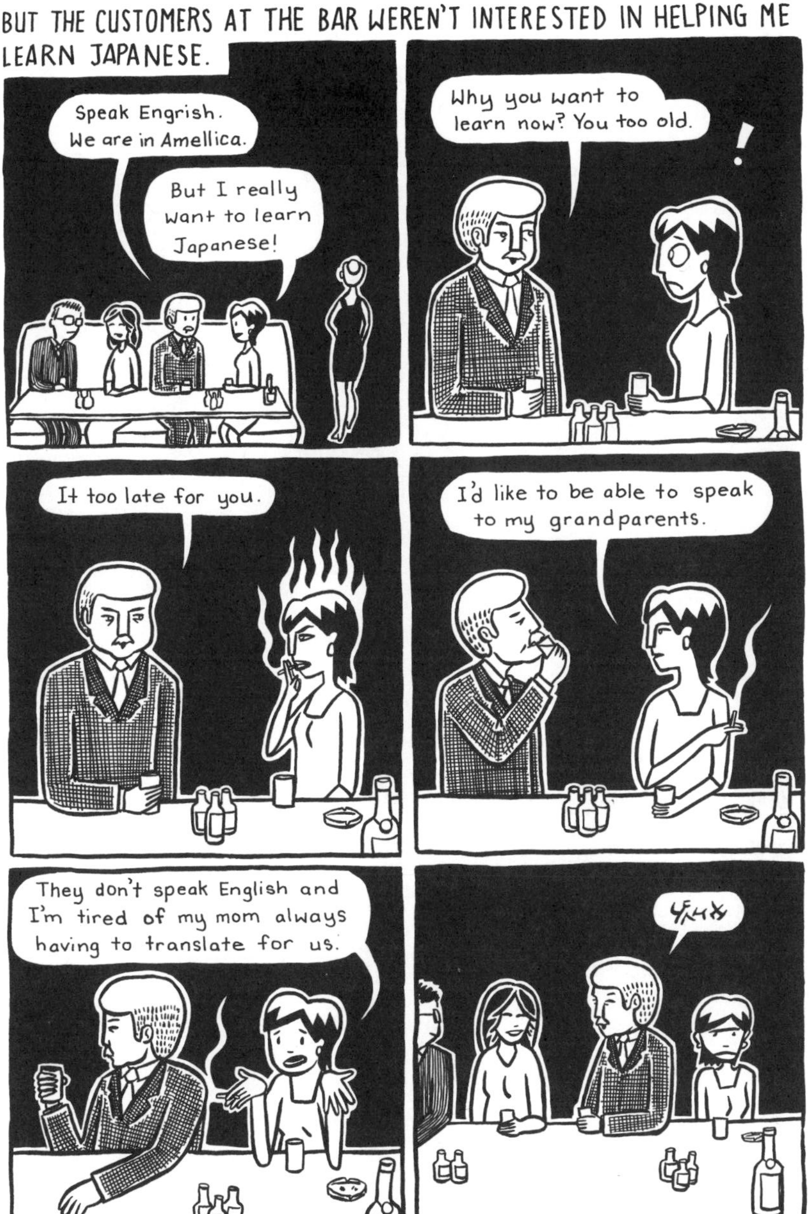
BUT THE CUSTOMERS AT THE BAR WEREN'T INTERESTED IN HELPING ME LEARN JAPANESE.
Speak Engrish. We are in Amellica.
But I really want to learn Japanese!
Why you want to learn now? You too old.
!
It too late for you.
I'd like to be able to speak to my grandparents.
They don't speak English and I'm tired of my mom always having to translate for us.

REGARDLESS OF THE CAVALIER ATTITUDE THE CUSTOMERS TOOK TO MY NEW PASSION, I HAD NO INTENTION OF LETTING GO, AND I HAD SOME PRETTY GOOD REASONS. FOR EXAMPLE, ON MY LAST VISIT TO JAPAN, I STARTED TO NOTICE SOME PECULIAR ACTIVITY WHEN IT CAME TO MY MOTHER TRANSLATING FOR ME.

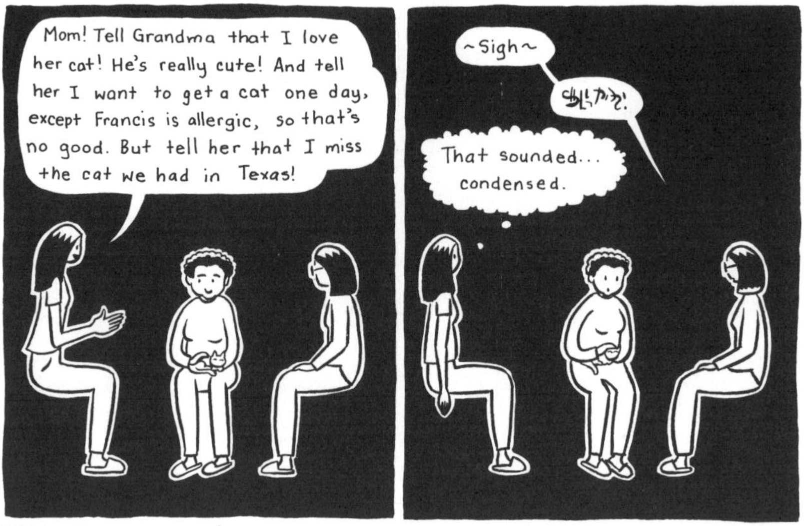
Mom! Tell Grandma that I love her cat! He's really cute! And tell her I want to get a cat one day, except Francis is allergic, so that's no good. But tell her that I miss the cat we had in Texas!
~Sigh~
That sounded... condensed.

STILL, IT WAS A LITTLE DISHEARTENING WHEN NOBODY TOOK ME SERIOUSLY, SO I DECIDED TO GIVE MYSELF SOMETHING TO LOOK FORWARD TO.

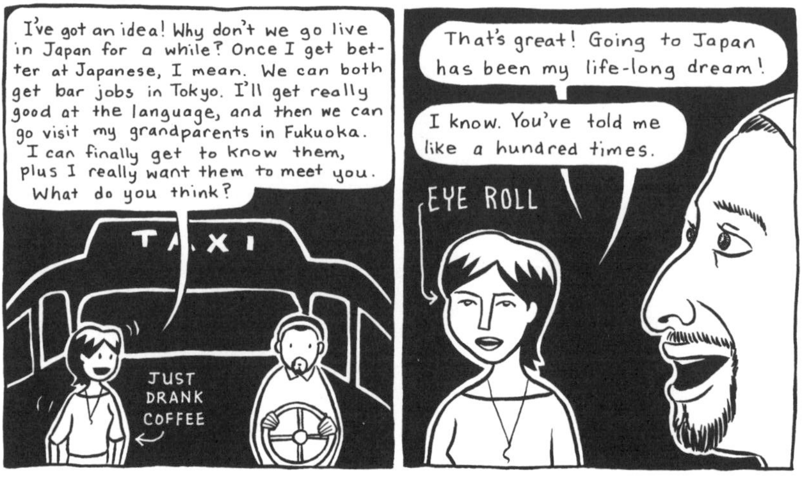
I've got an idea! Why don't we go live in Japan for a while? Once I get better at Japanese, I mean. We can both get bar jobs in Tokyo. I'll get really good at the language, and then we can go visit my grandparents in Fukuoka. I can finally get to know them, plus I really want them to meet you. What do you think?
TAXI
JUST DRANK COFFEE
That's great! Going to Japan has been my life-long dream!
I know. You've told me like a hundred times.
EYE ROLL

MARI VISITS HER MOM

MY BAR CLIENTS WEREN'T THE ONLY ONES NOT TAKING MY LANGUAGE LEARNING SERIOUSLY.

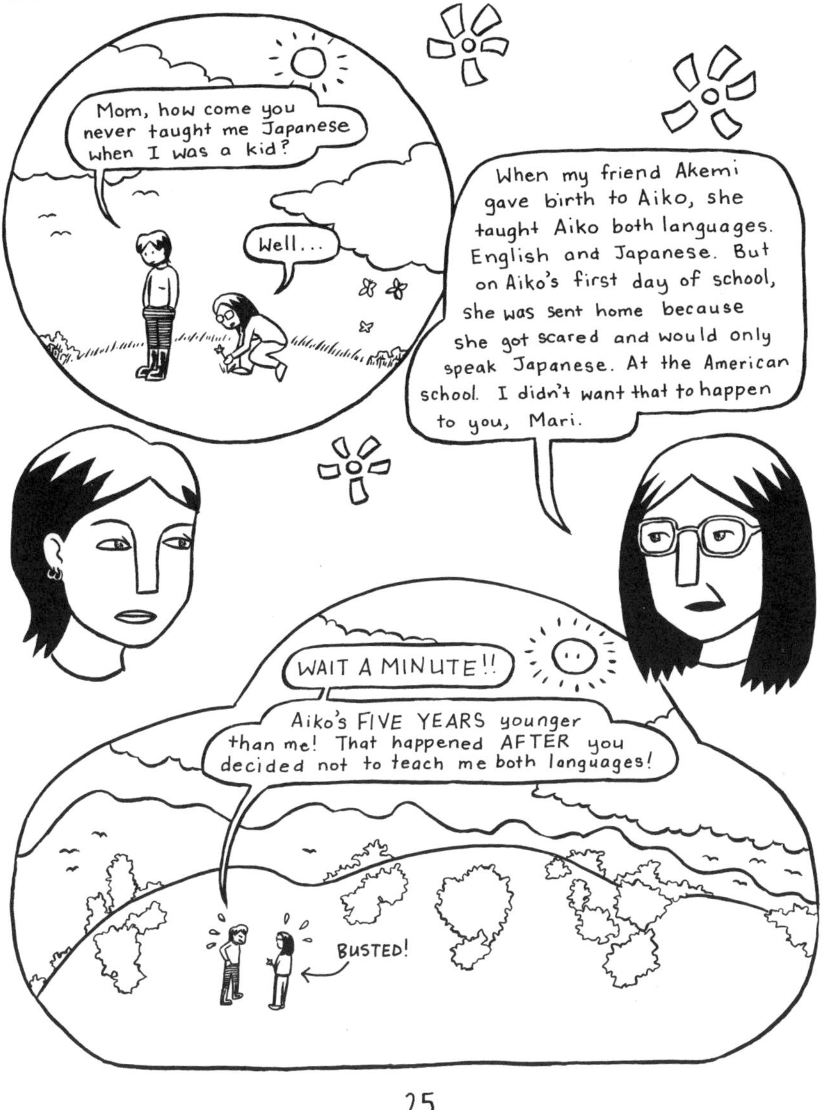
Mom, how come you never taught me Japanese when I was a kid?
Well...
When my friend Akemi gave birth to Aiko, she taught Aiko both languages. English and Japanese. But on Aiko's first day of school, she was sent home because she got scared and would only speak Japanese. At the American school. I didn't want that to happen to you, Mari.
WAIT A MINUTE!!
Aiko's FIVE YEARS younger than me! That happened AFTER you decided not to teach me both languages!
BUSTED!

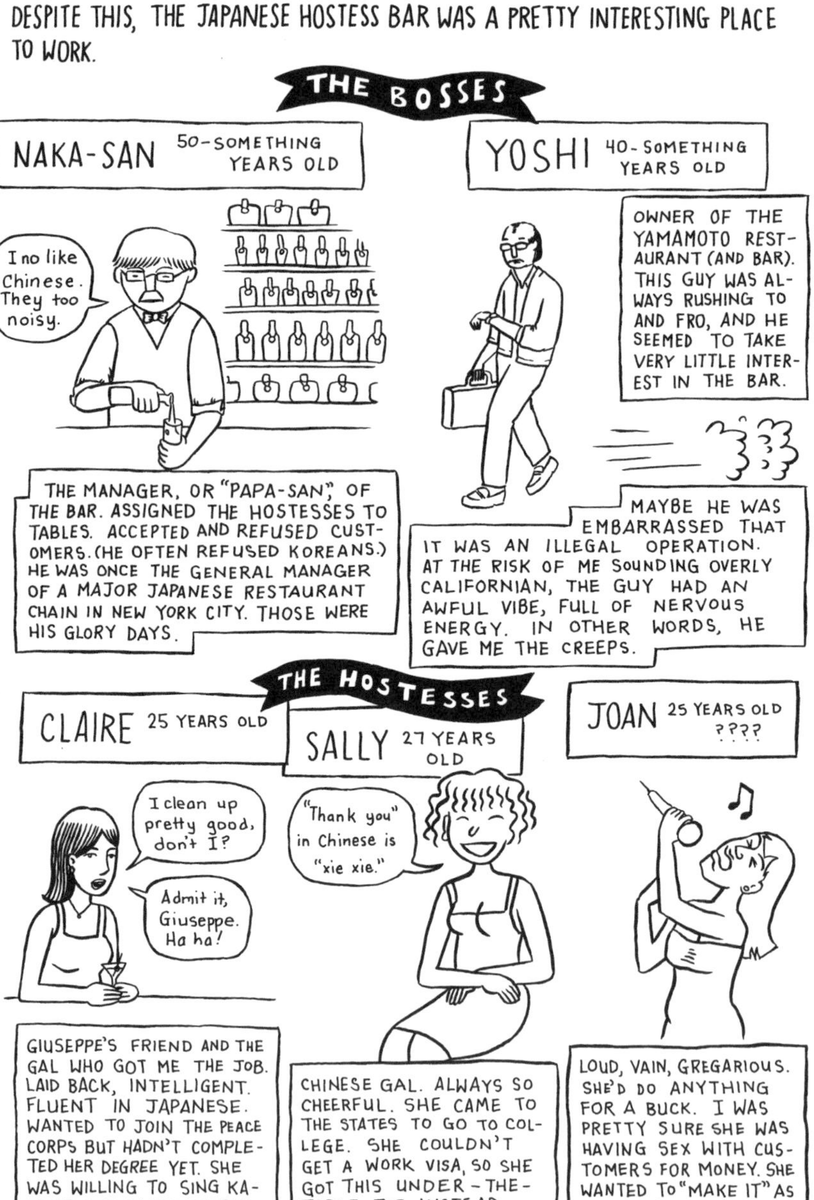
DESPITE THIS, THE JAPANESE HOSTESS BAR WAS A PRETTY INTERESTING PLACE TO WORK.
THE BOSSES
NAKA-SAN 50-SOMETHING YEARS OLD
I no like Chinese. They too noisy.
THE MANAGER, OR "PAPA-SAN," OF THE BAR. ASSIGNED THE HOSTESSES TO TABLES. ACCEPTED AND REFUSED CUSTOMERS. (HE OFTEN REFUSED KOREANS.) HE WAS ONCE THE GENERAL MANAGER OF A MAJOR JAPANESE RESTAURANT CHAIN IN NEW YORK CITY. THOSE WERE HIS GLORY DAYS.
YOSHI 40-SOMETHING YEARS OLD
OWNER OF THE YAMAMOTO RESTAURANT (AND BAR). THIS GUY WAS ALWAYS RUSHING TO AND FRO, AND HE SEEMED TO TAKE VERY LITTLE INTEREST IN THE BAR.
MAYBE HE WAS EMBARRASSED THAT IT WAS AN ILLEGAL OPERATION. AT THE RISK OF ME SOUNDING OVERLY CALIFORNIAN, THE GUY HAD AN AWFUL VIBE, FULL OF NERVOUS ENERGY. IN OTHER WORDS, HE GAVE ME THE CREEPS.
THE HOSTESSES
CLAIRE 25 YEARS OLD
I clean up pretty good, don't I?
Admit it, Giuseppe. Ha ha!
GIUSEPPE'S FRIEND AND THE GAL WHO GOT ME THE JOB. LAID BACK, INTELLIGENT. FLUENT IN JAPANESE. WANTED TO JOIN THE PEACE CORPS BUT HADN'T COMPLETED HER DEGREE YET. SHE WAS WILLING TO SING KARAOKE, BUT LACKLUSTERLY.
SALLY 27 YEARS OLD
"Thank you" in Chinese is "xie xie."
CHINESE GAL. ALWAYS SO CHEERFUL. SHE CAME TO THE STATES TO GO TO COLLEGE. SHE COULDN'T GET A WORK VISA, SO SHE GOT THIS UNDER-THE-TABLE JOB INSTEAD.
JOAN 25 YEARS OLD ????
LOUD, VAIN, GREGARIOUS. SHE'D DO ANYTHING FOR A BUCK. I WAS PRETTY SURE SHE WAS HAVING SEX WITH CUSTOMERS FOR MONEY. SHE WANTED TO "MAKE IT" AS A ROCK'N'ROLL SINGER.

EMIKO	and	AKIKO	NORIKO
19 YEARS OLD		18 YEARS OLD	33 YEARS OLD

Kampai!

THESE TWO WERE BFFs SINCE CHILDHOOD. THEY WERE PRO-
MISED LUCRATIVE WAITRESSING JOBS BY YOSHI, WHO WAS
FRIENDS WITH THEIR FATHERS. THEY WERE TOO ASHAMED TO
TELL THEIR DADS WHAT JOBS YOSHI REALLY GAVE THEM.
EMIKO WAS SWEET/PERKY, AND AKIKO WAS SHY/AWKWARD.

PARTY GIRL, TRUST FUND
KID, JET SETTER. NORIKO
GOT THIS JOB SO SHE COULD
HANG OUT WITH HER PAL
AND ROOMMATE, RYOKO.

RYOKO 32 YEARS OLD   SUE ANNE 27 YEARS OLD

heart on
her sleeve

A DIE-HARD ROMANTIC. SHE KNEW SOME
ENGLISH, SO SHE OFTEN TRANSLATED
FOR THE AMERICAN GIRLS. A WILD
CHILD WITH LOTS OF MANIC ENERGY,
SHE HAD BEEN A MAIL-ORDER
BRIDE WHO HAD SCARED OFF HER
MEEK SILICON VALLEY HUSBAND.
SHE LOVED YORKSHIRE TERRIERS,
AND SHE OWNED HALF A DOZEN.

AMATEUR BODY BUILDER, PROFESSION-
AL MODEL. SOUTHERN BELLE, BLEACH-
BLONDE HAIR, ACRYLIC-TIPPED NAILS,
BREAST IMPLANTS. KNEW HOW TO
SUBTLY WORK A TABLE. WOULDN'T
SING KARAOKE BUT SHE WAS WILLING
TO SLOW-DANCE WITH CUSTOMERS. SHE
AND CLAIRE WERE FRIENDS.

27

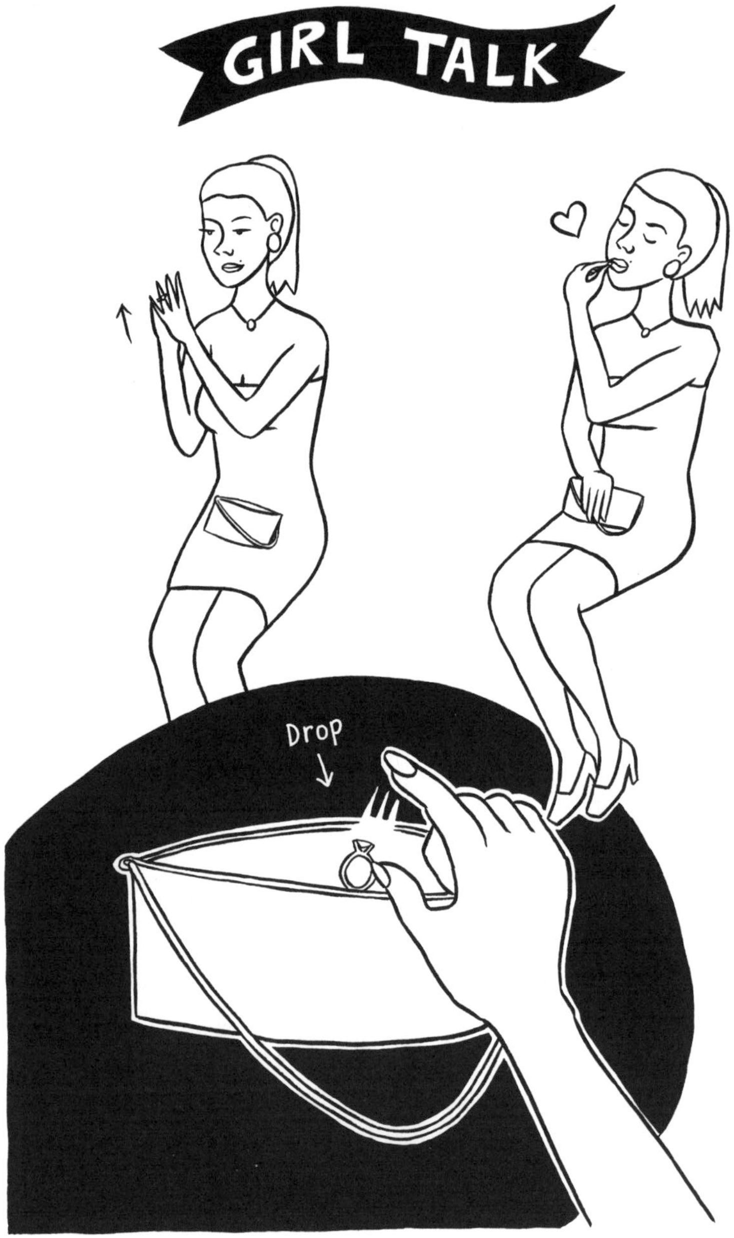
GIRL TALK
Drop

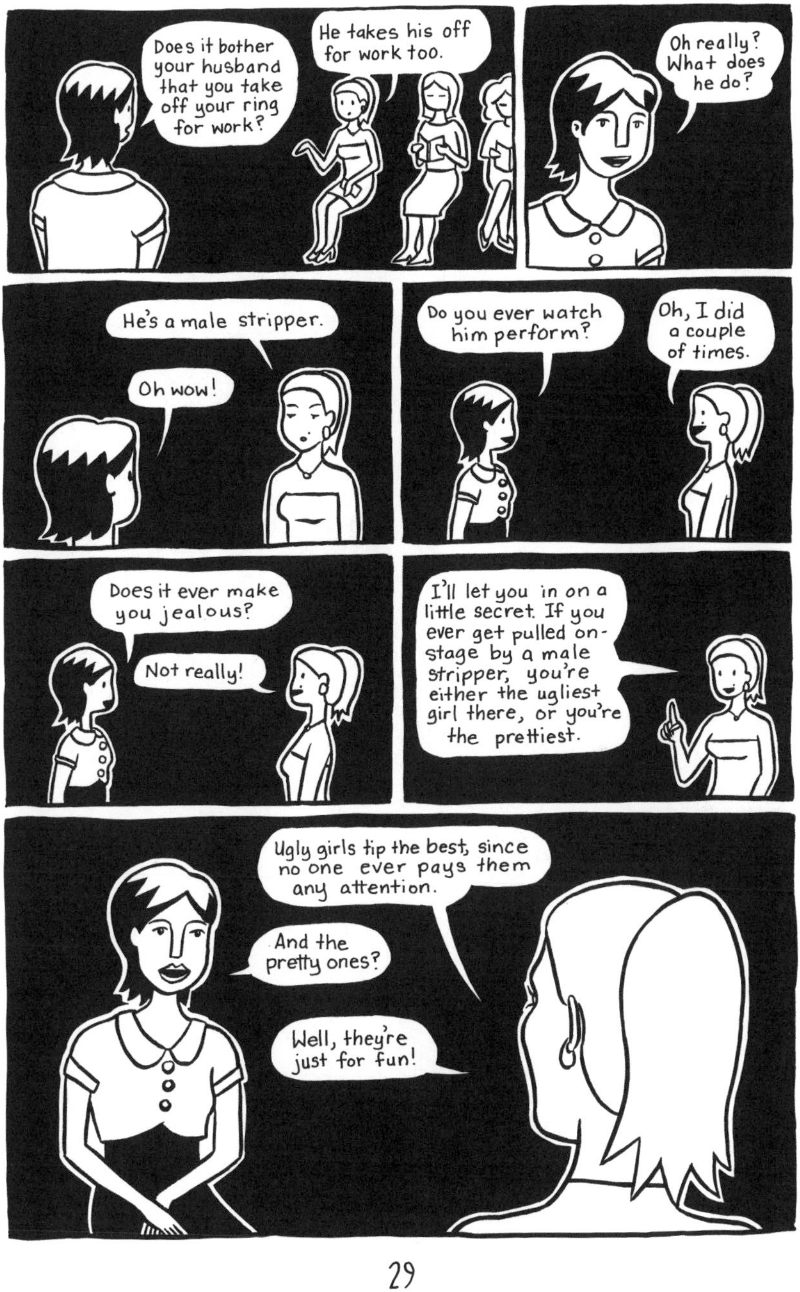
Does it bother your husband that you take off your ring for work?
He takes his off for work too.
Oh really? What does he do?
He's a male stripper.
Oh wow!
Do you ever watch him perform?
Oh, I did a couple of times.
Does it ever make you jealous?
Not really!
I'll let you in on a little secret. If you ever get pulled on-stage by a male stripper, you're either the ugliest girl there, or you're the prettiest.
Ugly girls tip the best, since no one ever pays them any attention.
And the pretty ones?
Well, they're just for fun!

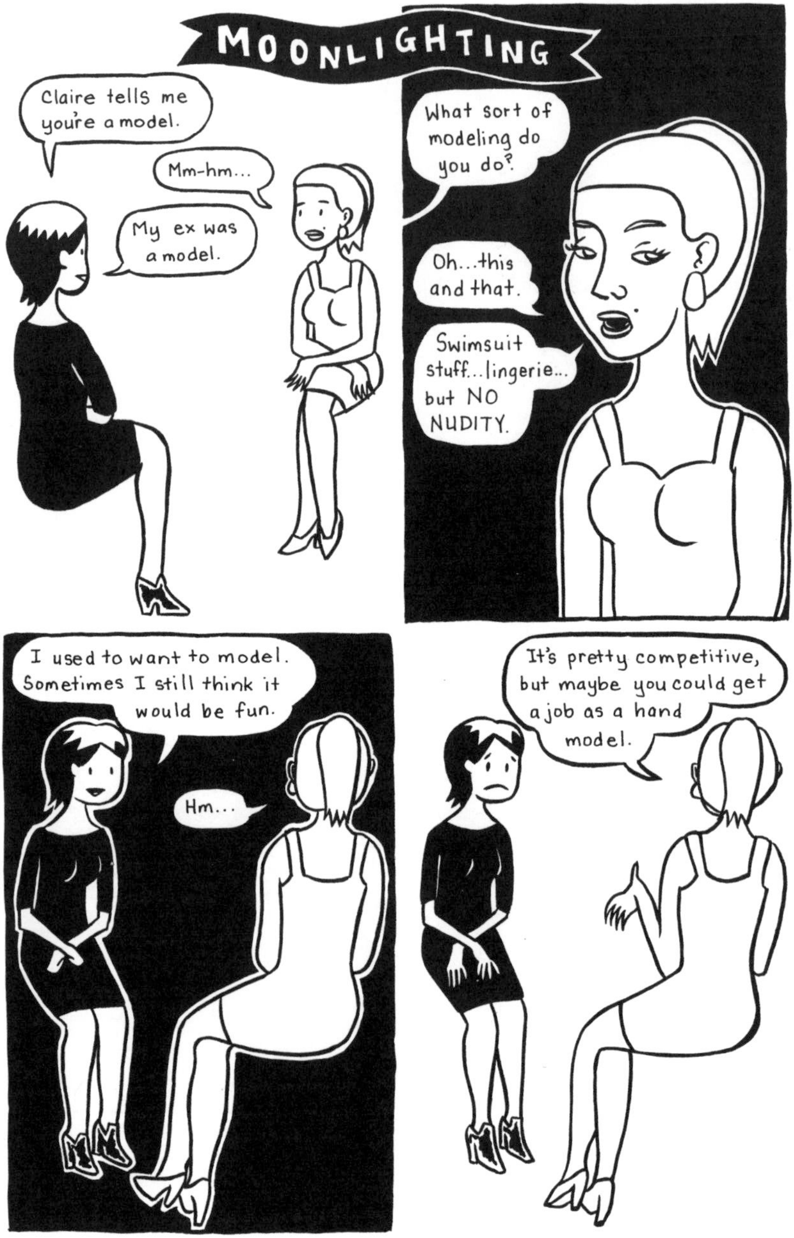
MOONLIGHTING
Claire tells me you're a model.
Mm-hm...
My ex was a model.
What sort of modeling do you do?
Oh...this and that.
Swimsuit stuff...lingerie... but NO NUDITY.
I used to want to model. Sometimes I still think it would be fun.
Hm...
It's pretty competitive, but maybe you could get a job as a hand model.

KINDNESS OR CRUELTY?

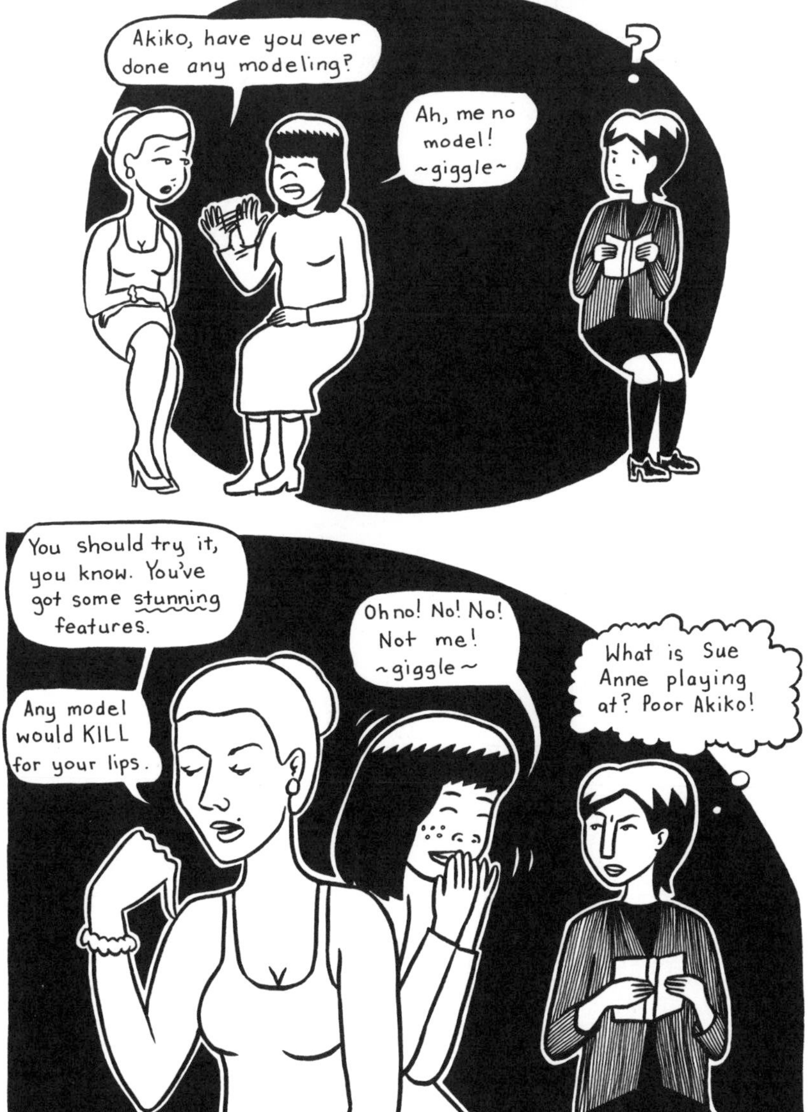
Akiko, have you ever done any modeling?
Ah, me no model! ~giggle~
?
You should try it, you know. You've got some stunning features.
Any model would KILL for your lips.
Oh no! No! No! Not me! ~giggle~
What is Sue Anne playing at? Poor Akiko!

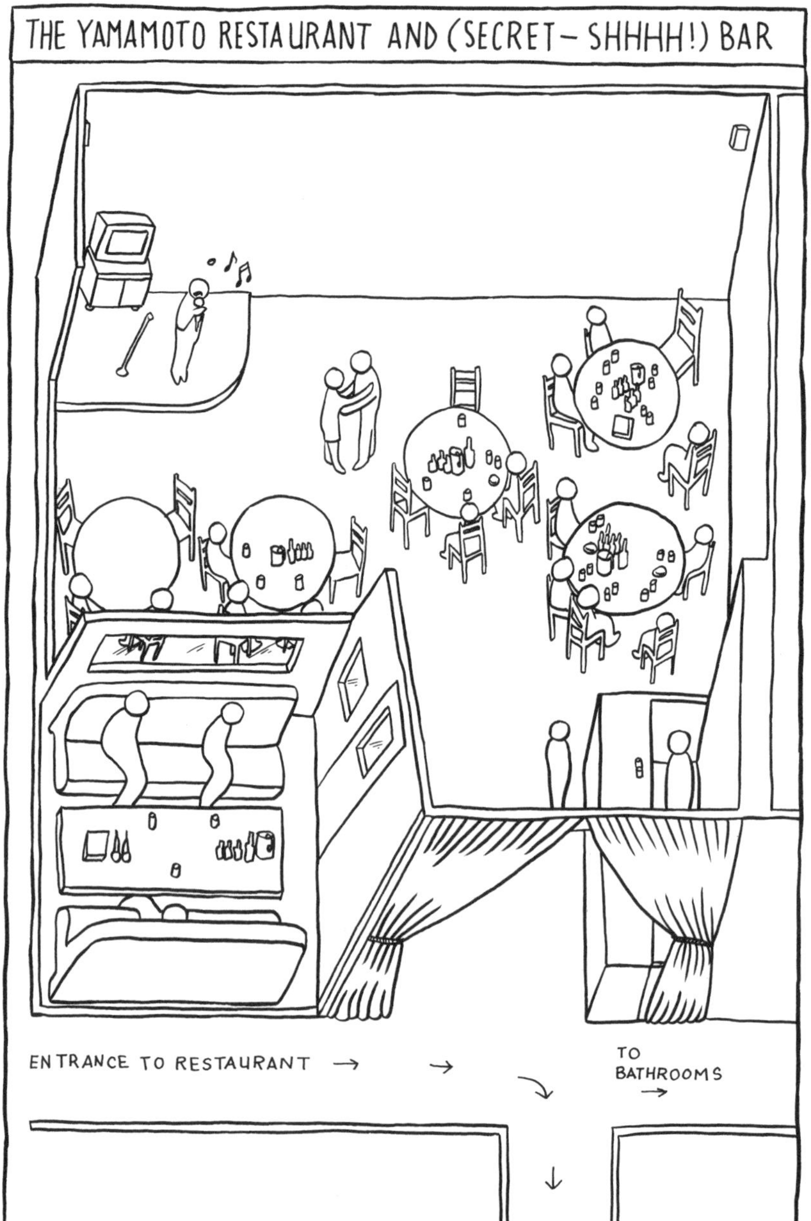
THE YAMAMOTO RESTAURANT AND (SECRET– SHHHH!) BAR
ENTRANCE TO RESTAURANT →
TO BATHROOMS →

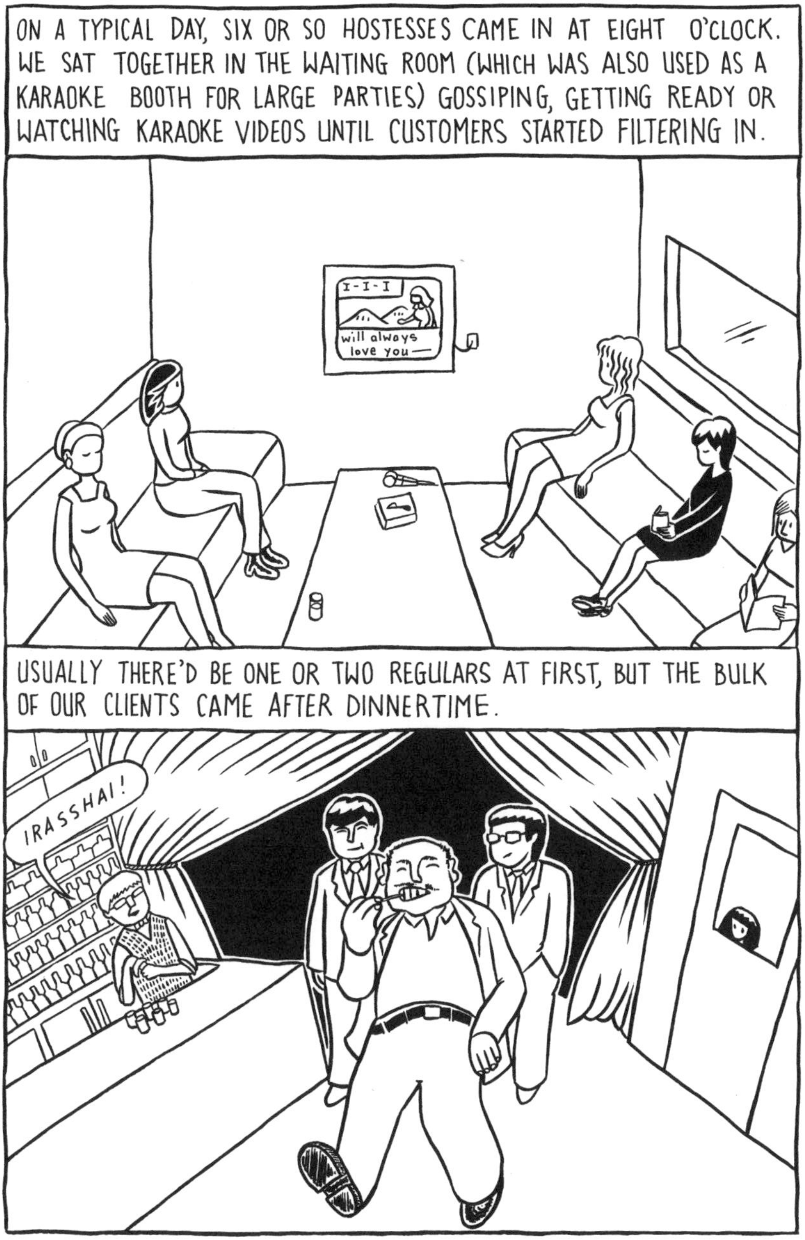
ON A TYPICAL DAY, SIX OR SO HOSTESSES CAME IN AT EIGHT O'CLOCK. WE SAT TOGETHER IN THE WAITING ROOM (WHICH WAS ALSO USED AS A KARAOKE BOOTH FOR LARGE PARTIES) GOSSIPING, GETTING READY OR WATCHING KARAOKE VIDEOS UNTIL CUSTOMERS STARTED FILTERING IN.
I-I-I
will always love you—
USUALLY THERE'D BE ONE OR TWO REGULARS AT FIRST, BUT THE BULK OF OUR CLIENTS CAME AFTER DINNERTIME.
IRASSHAI!

NAKA-SAN ASSIGNED HOSTESSES TO THE TABLES. IF A JAPANESE-SPEAKING CLIENT CAME IN, HE'D PLACE A JAPANESE GIRL WITH THEM. IF THEY WERE ENGLISH-SPEAKING, THEY WOULD GET AN AMERICAN.

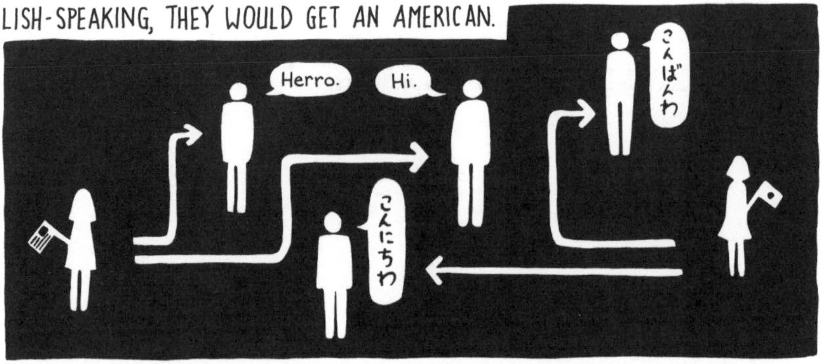
Herro.
Hi.
こんばんわ
こんにちわ

MANY OF THE HOSTESSES HAD REGULARS THEY'D DEVELOPED RELATIONSHIPS WITH OVER TIME, SO THE REGULARS WOULD BE SEATED WITH THEIR FAVORITE HOSTESS.

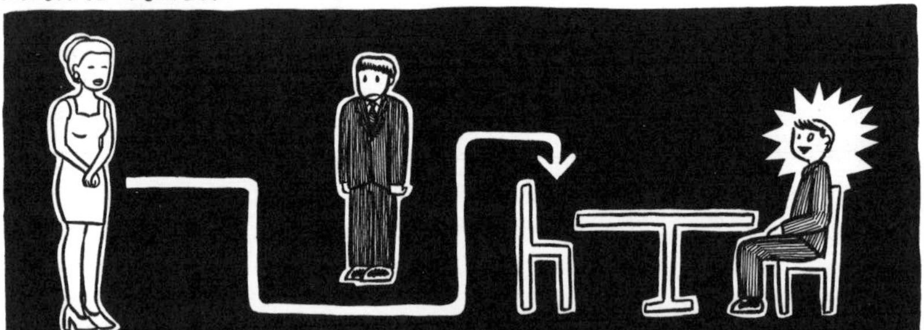

AT TIMES, A HOSTESS WOULD HAVE MULTIPLE REGULARS SHOW UP AT THE SAME TIME. WHEN THAT HAPPENED, NAKA-SAN WOULD SEAT THE GIRL WITH THE MOST GENEROUS (OR WELL-TO-DO) CLIENT, AND THE OTHER MEN WOULD HAVE TO WAIT THEIR TURNS, OFTEN IN THE PRESENCE OF A HOSTESS WHOM THEY FOUND LESS DESIREABLE. THIS WAS, OF COURSE, NO FUN FOR ANYBODY.

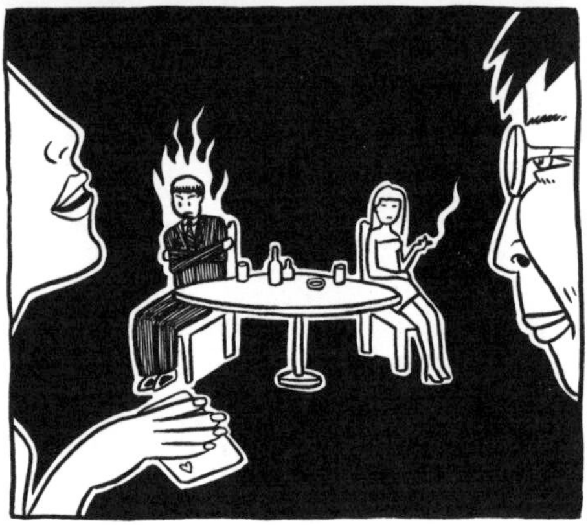

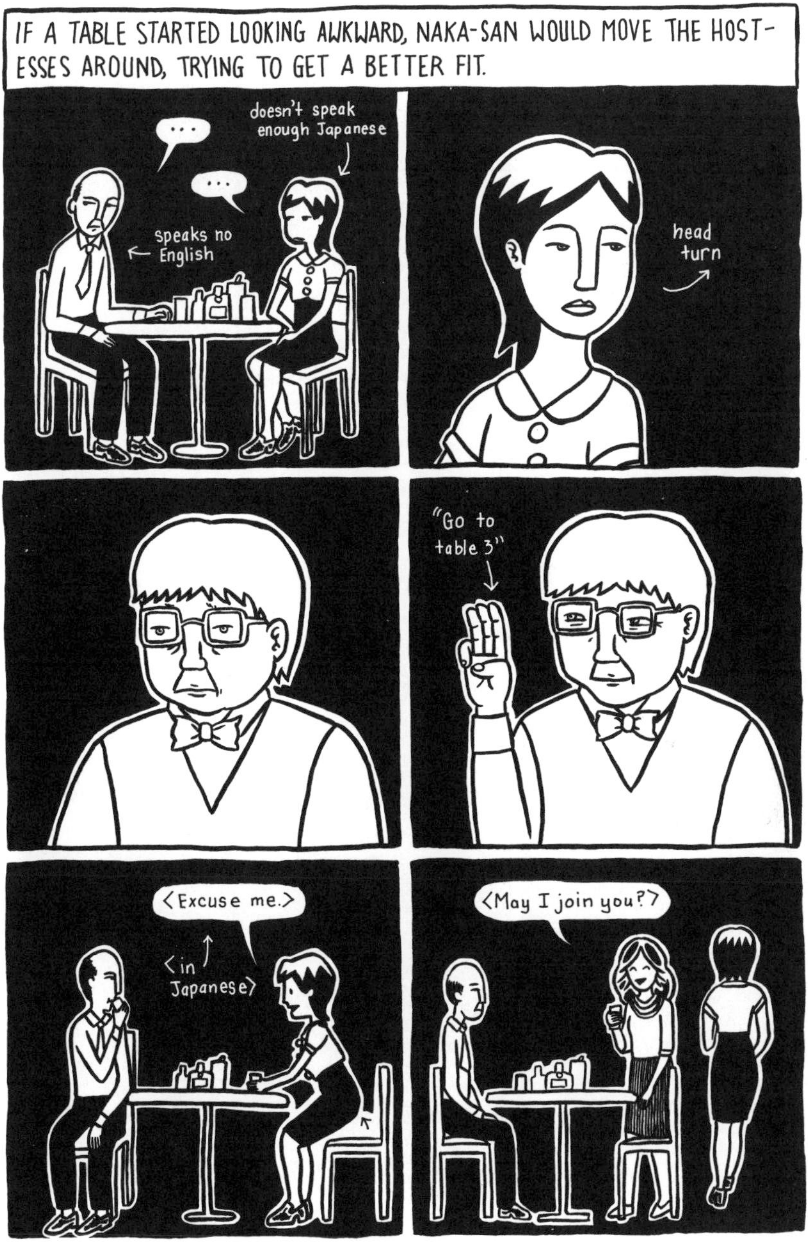
IF A TABLE STARTED LOOKING AWKWARD, NAKA-SAN WOULD MOVE THE HOSTESSES AROUND, TRYING TO GET A BETTER FIT.
...
...
doesn't speak enough Japanese
speaks no English
head turn
"Go to table 3"
<Excuse me.>
<in Japanese>
<May I join you?>

CLIENTS WOULD ORDER SUSHI FROM THE RESTAURANT NEXT DOOR. SOMETIMES THEY'D EVEN SHARE. ONCE, I CAME IN HUNGRY, SO I WAS RELIEVED WHEN THE MEN AT MY TABLE ORDERED A GIANT PLATTER AND DIDN'T SEEM TO BE TOUCHING IT.

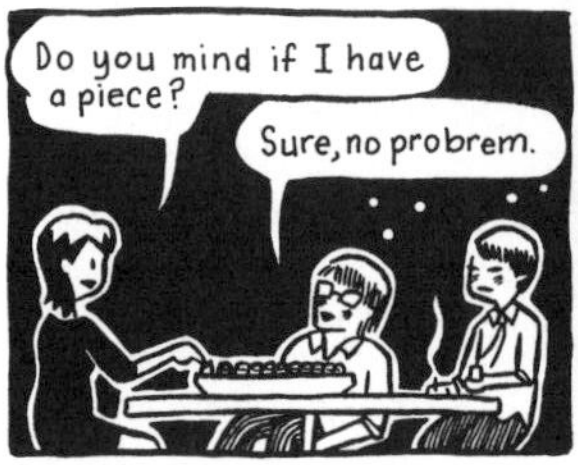
Do you mind if I have a piece?
Sure, no probrem.

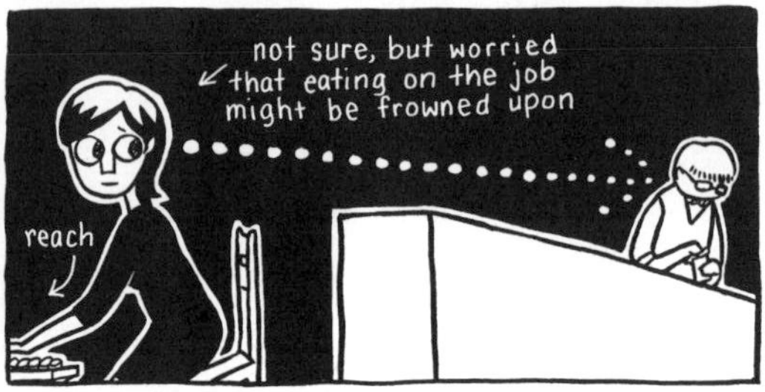
not sure, but worried that eating on the job might be frowned upon
reach

WHEN I LOOKED DOWN AT THE SUSHI PLATTER, I NOTICED SOMETHING ODD.

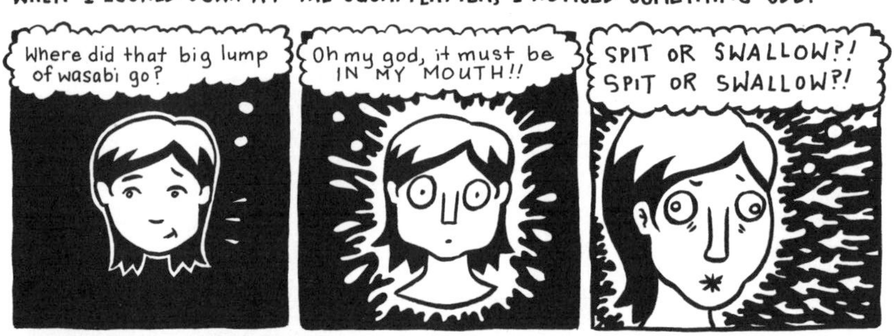
Where did that big lump of wasabi go?
Oh my god, it must be IN MY MOUTH!!
SPIT OR SWALLOW?! SPIT OR SWALLOW?!

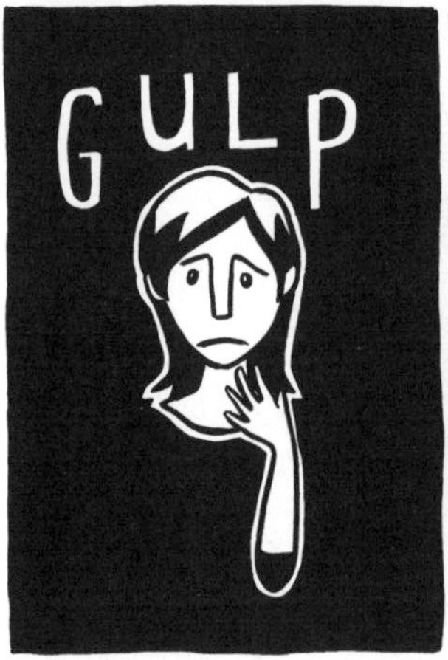
GULP

WITHIN MOMENTS I HAD WHAT CAN ONLY BE DESCRIBED AS AN ADRENALINE RUSH.

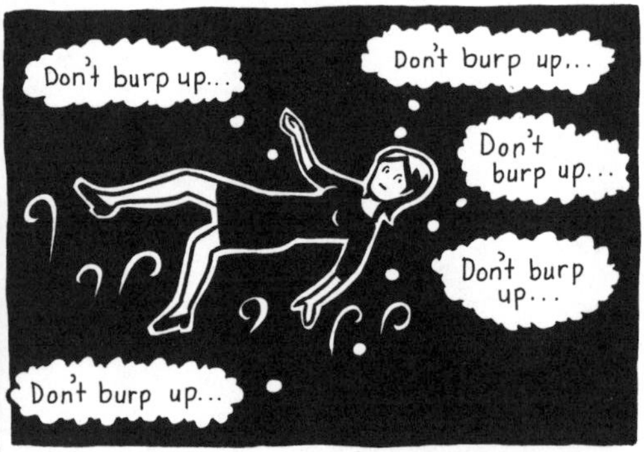
Don't burp up...
Don't burp up...
Don't burp up...
Don't burp up...
Don't burp up...

AFTER THAT INCIDENT, I NEVER HAD ANY PROBLEMS EATING WASABI AGAIN. IT WAS ALMOST AS IF I HAD BEEN INJECTED WITH WASABI ANTIBODIES, AND ALL OF A SUDDEN I WAS IMMUNE TO ITS SPICINESS.

AS A HOSTESS, I WAS EXPECTED TO:

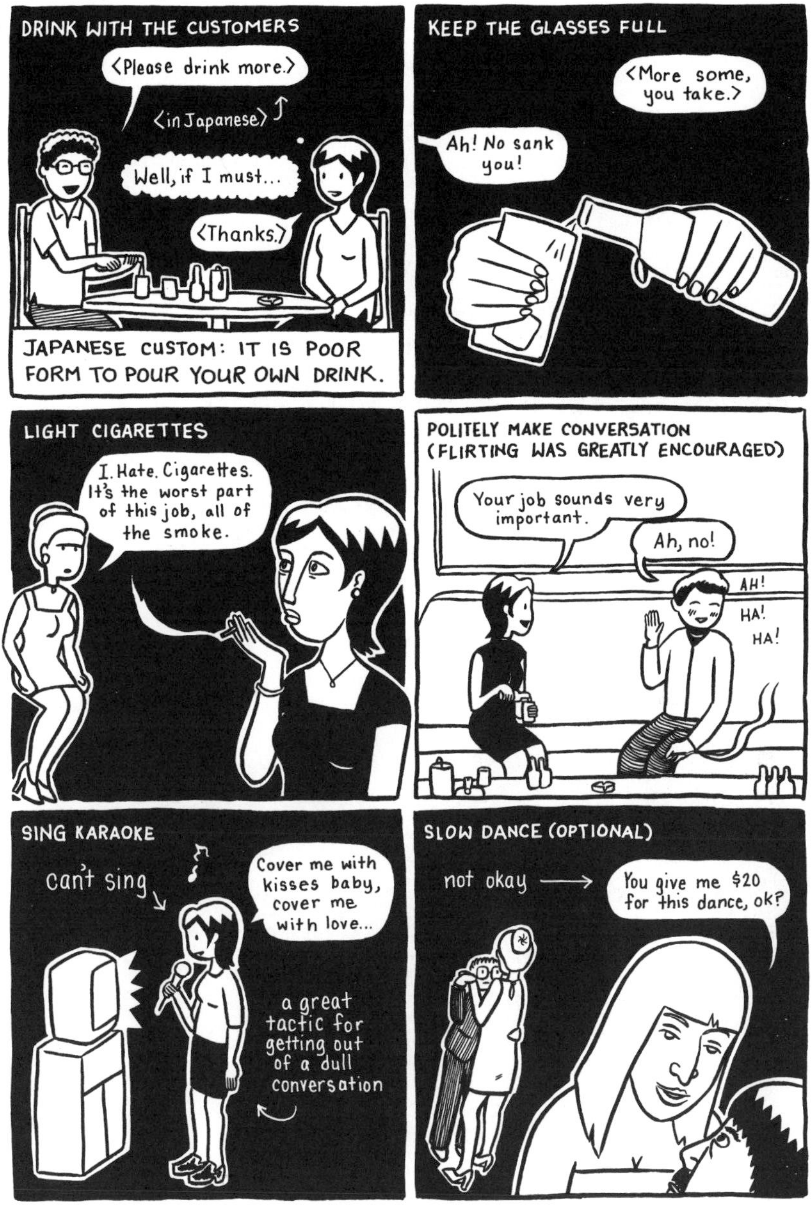
DRINK WITH THE CUSTOMERS
<Please drink more.>
<in Japanese>
Well, if I must...
<Thanks.>
JAPANESE CUSTOM: IT IS POOR FORM TO POUR YOUR OWN DRINK.
KEEP THE GLASSES FULL
<More some, you take.>
Ah! No sank you!
LIGHT CIGARETTES
I. Hate. Cigarettes. It's the worst part of this job, all of the smoke.
POLITELY MAKE CONVERSATION (FLIRTING WAS GREATLY ENCOURAGED)
Your job sounds very important.
Ah, no!
AH! HA! HA!
SING KARAOKE
can't sing
Cover me with kisses baby, cover me with love...
a great tactic for getting out of a dull conversation
SLOW DANCE (OPTIONAL)
not okay
You give me $20 for this dance, ok?

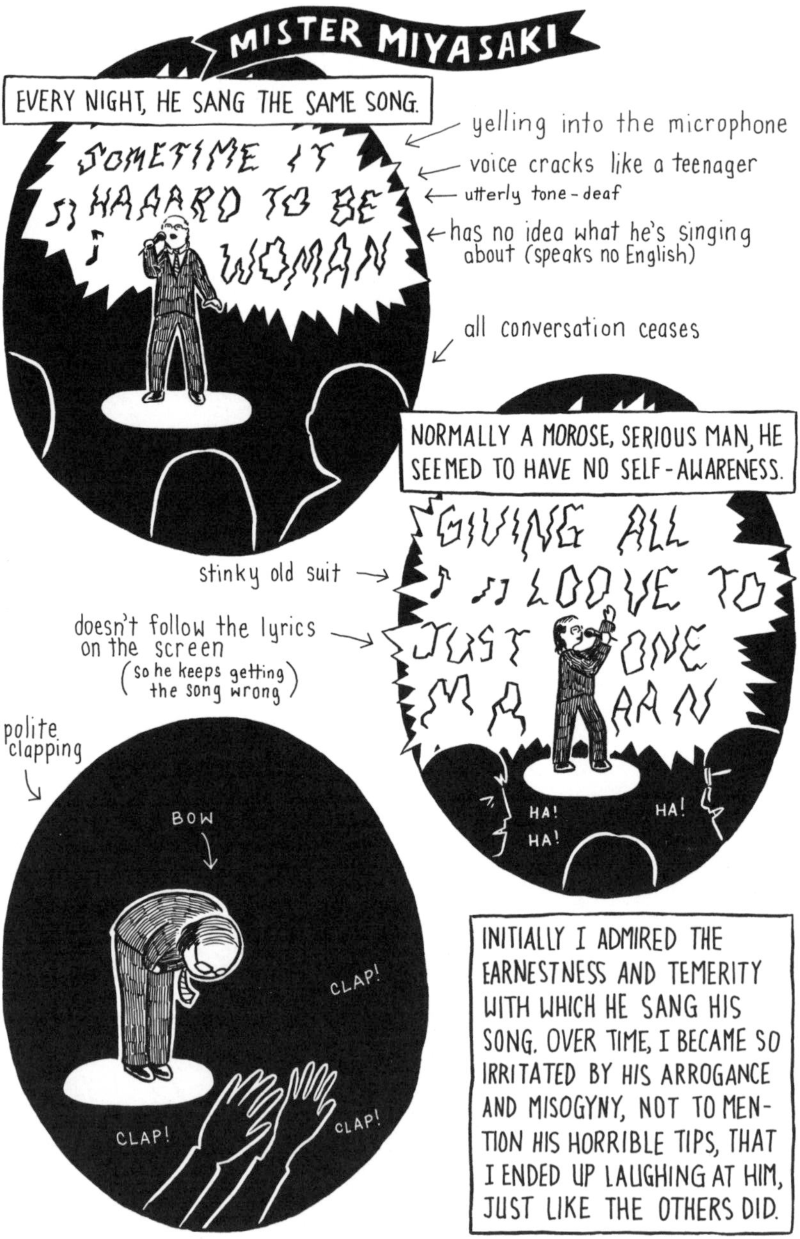
MISTER MIYASAKI
EVERY NIGHT, HE SANG THE SAME SONG.
SOMETIME IT HAAARD TO BE WOMAN
yelling into the microphone
voice cracks like a teenager
utterly tone-deaf
has no idea what he's singing about (speaks no English)
all conversation ceases
NORMALLY A MOROSE, SERIOUS MAN, HE SEEMED TO HAVE NO SELF-AWARENESS.
GIVING ALL LOOVE TO JUST ONE MAAAN
stinky old suit
doesn't follow the lyrics on the screen
(so he keeps getting the song wrong)
HA! HA!
HA!
polite clapping
BOW
CLAP!
CLAP!
CLAP!
INITIALLY I ADMIRED THE EARNESTNESS AND TEMERITY WITH WHICH HE SANG HIS SONG. OVER TIME, I BECAME SO IRRITATED BY HIS ARROGANCE AND MISOGYNY, NOT TO MENTION HIS HORRIBLE TIPS, THAT I ENDED UP LAUGHING AT HIM, JUST LIKE THE OTHERS DID.

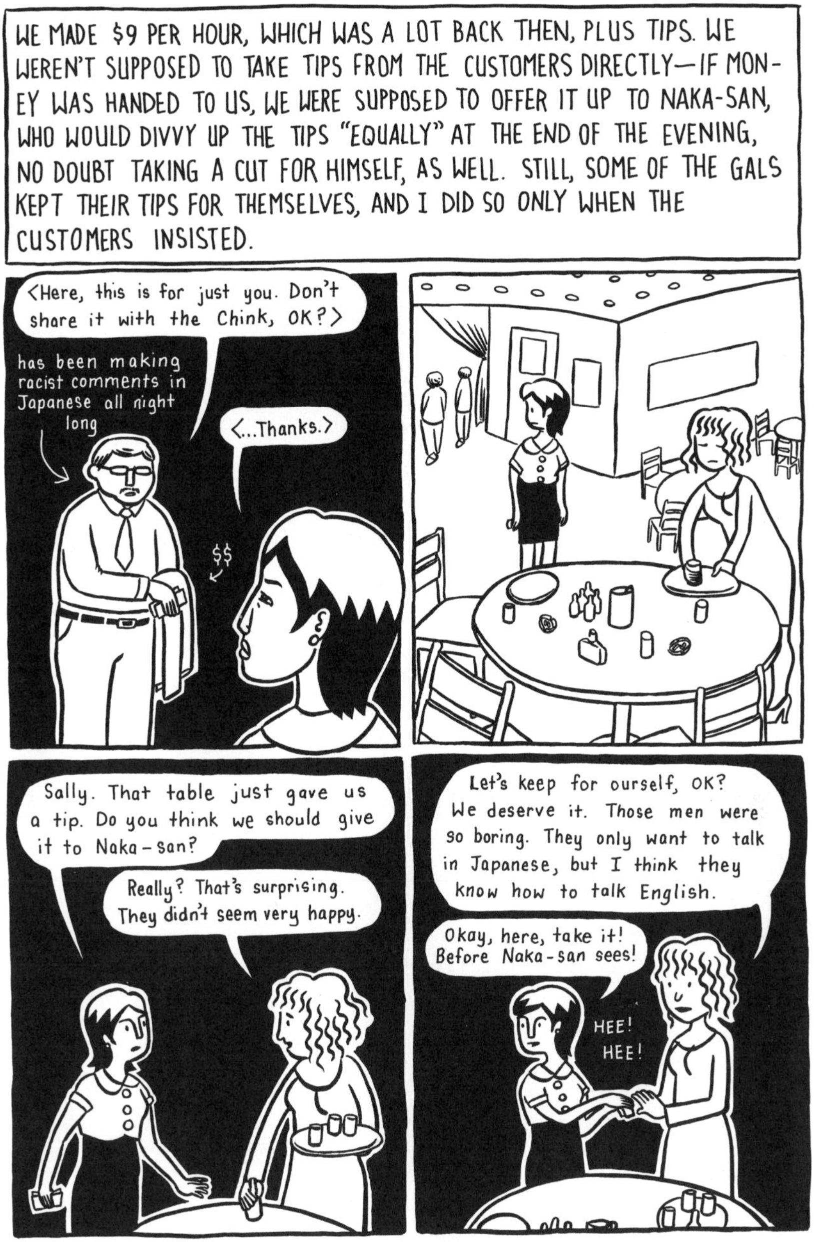
WE MADE $9 PER HOUR, WHICH WAS A LOT BACK THEN, PLUS TIPS. WE WEREN'T SUPPOSED TO TAKE TIPS FROM THE CUSTOMERS DIRECTLY—IF MONEY WAS HANDED TO US, WE WERE SUPPOSED TO OFFER IT UP TO NAKA-SAN, WHO WOULD DIVVY UP THE TIPS "EQUALLY" AT THE END OF THE EVENING, NO DOUBT TAKING A CUT FOR HIMSELF, AS WELL. STILL, SOME OF THE GALS KEPT THEIR TIPS FOR THEMSELVES, AND I DID SO ONLY WHEN THE CUSTOMERS INSISTED.
<Here, this is for just you. Don't share it with the Chink, OK?>
has been making racist comments in Japanese all night long
<...Thanks.>
$$
Sally. That table just gave us a tip. Do you think we should give it to Naka-san?
Really? That's surprising. They didn't seem very happy.
Let's keep for ourself, OK? We deserve it. Those men were so boring. They only want to talk in Japanese, but I think they know how to talk English.
Okay, here, take it! Before Naka-san sees!
HEE! HEE!

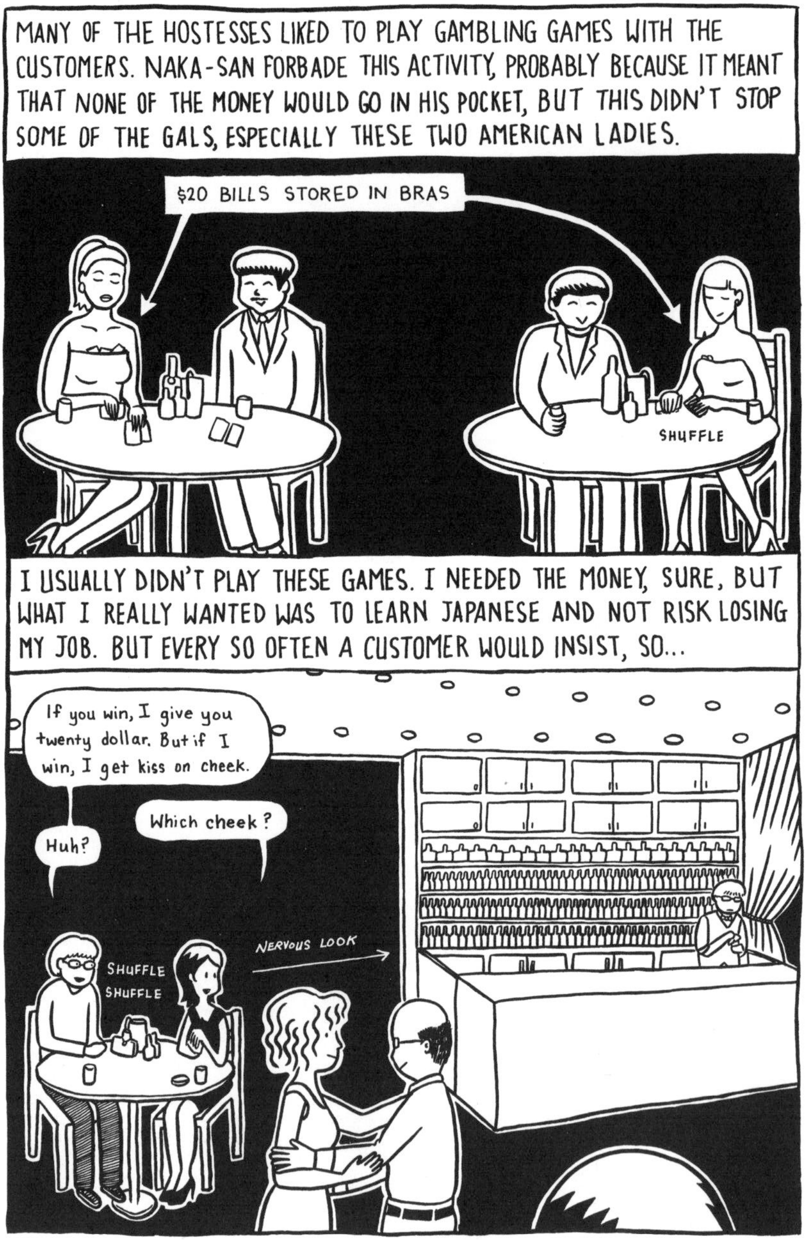
MANY OF THE HOSTESSES LIKED TO PLAY GAMBLING GAMES WITH THE CUSTOMERS. NAKA-SAN FORBADE THIS ACTIVITY, PROBABLY BECAUSE IT MEANT THAT NONE OF THE MONEY WOULD GO IN HIS POCKET, BUT THIS DIDN'T STOP SOME OF THE GALS, ESPECIALLY THESE TWO AMERICAN LADIES.
$20 BILLS STORED IN BRAS
SHUFFLE
I USUALLY DIDN'T PLAY THESE GAMES. I NEEDED THE MONEY, SURE, BUT WHAT I REALLY WANTED WAS TO LEARN JAPANESE AND NOT RISK LOSING MY JOB. BUT EVERY SO OFTEN A CUSTOMER WOULD INSIST, SO...
If you win, I give you twenty dollar. But if I win, I get kiss on cheek.
Huh?
Which cheek?
SHUFFLE SHUFFLE
NERVOUS LOOK

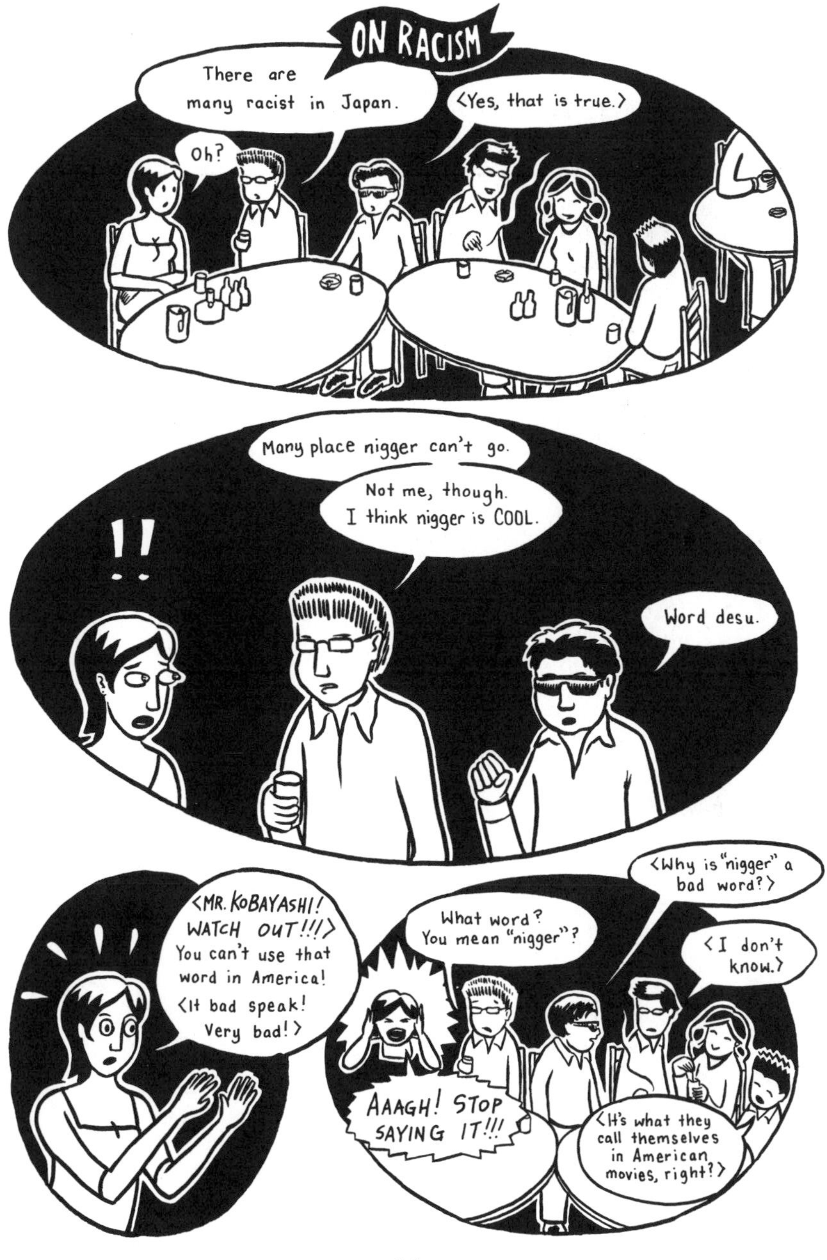
ON RACISM
There are many racist in Japan.
Oh?
<Yes, that is true.>
Many place nigger can't go.
Not me, though. I think nigger is COOL.
!!
Word desu.
<MR. KOBAYASHI! WATCH OUT!!!> You can't use that word in America! <It bad speak! Very bad!>
What word? You mean "nigger"?
AAAGH! STOP SAYING IT!!!
<Why is "nigger" a bad word?>
<I don't know.>
<It's what they call themselves in American movies, right?>

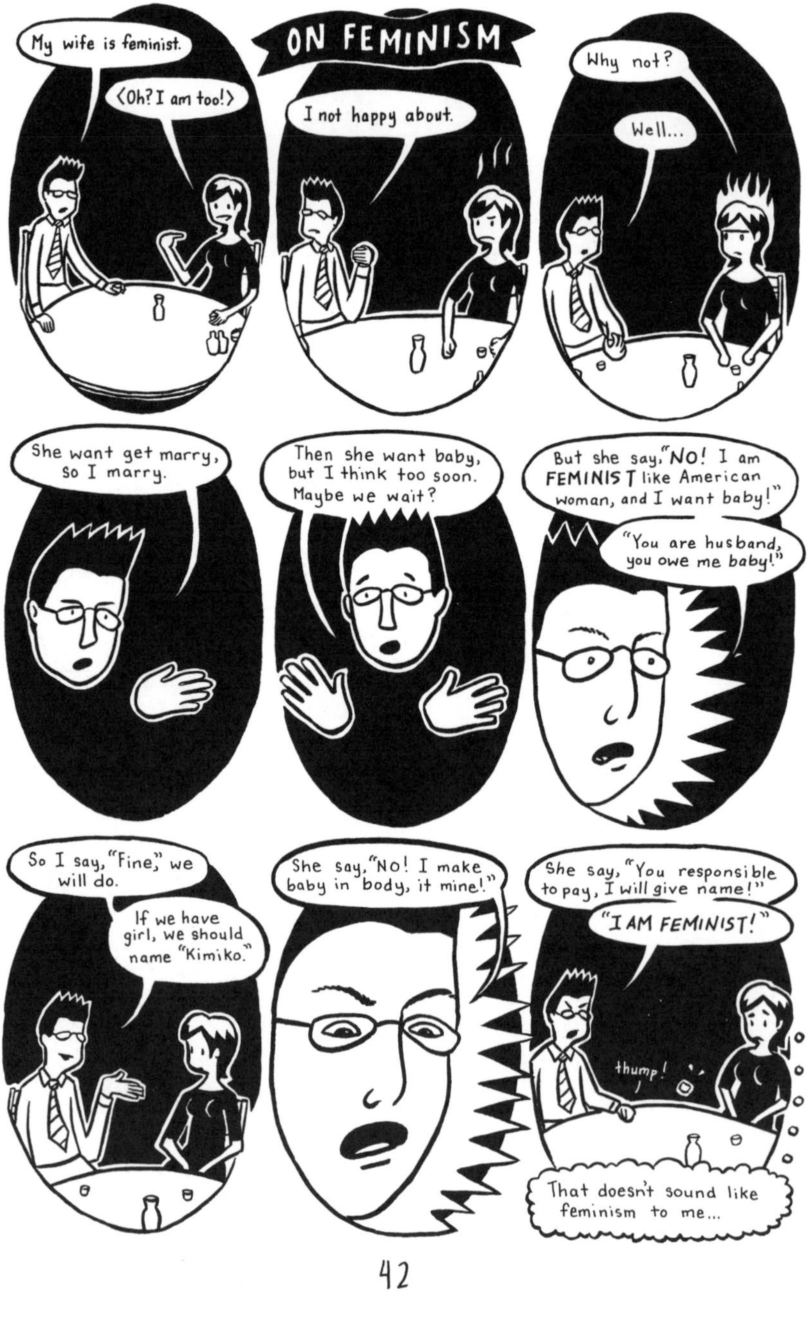
ON FEMINISM
My wife is feminist.
<Oh? I am too!>
I not happy about.
Why not?
Well...
She want get marry, so I marry.
Then she want baby, but I think too soon. Maybe we wait?
But she say, "NO! I am FEMINIST like American woman, and I want baby!"
"You are husband, you owe me baby!"
So I say, "Fine," we will do.
If we have girl, we should name "Kimiko."
She say, "No! I make baby in body, it mine!"
She say, "You responsible to pay, I will give name!"
"I AM FEMINIST!"
thump!
That doesn't sound like feminism to me...

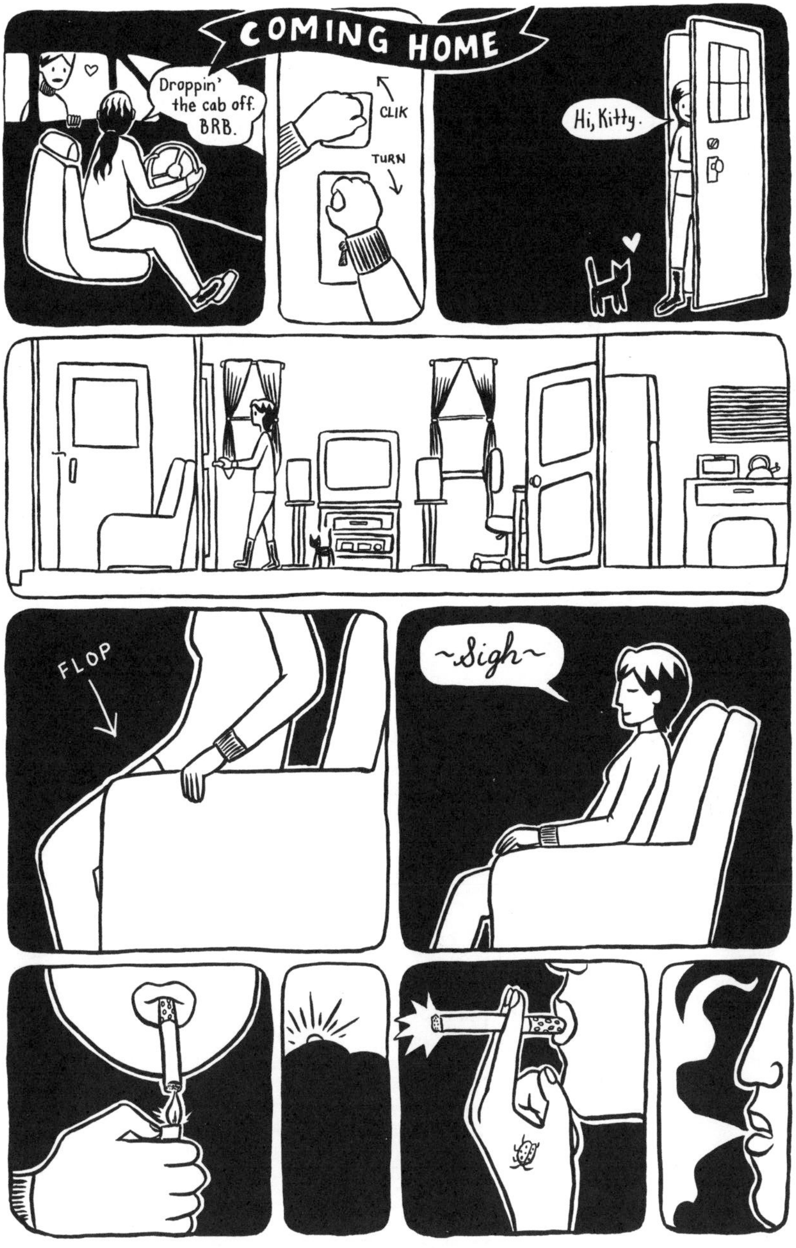
COMING HOME
Droppin' the cab off. BRB.
CLIK
TURN
Hi, Kitty.
FLOP
~Sigh~

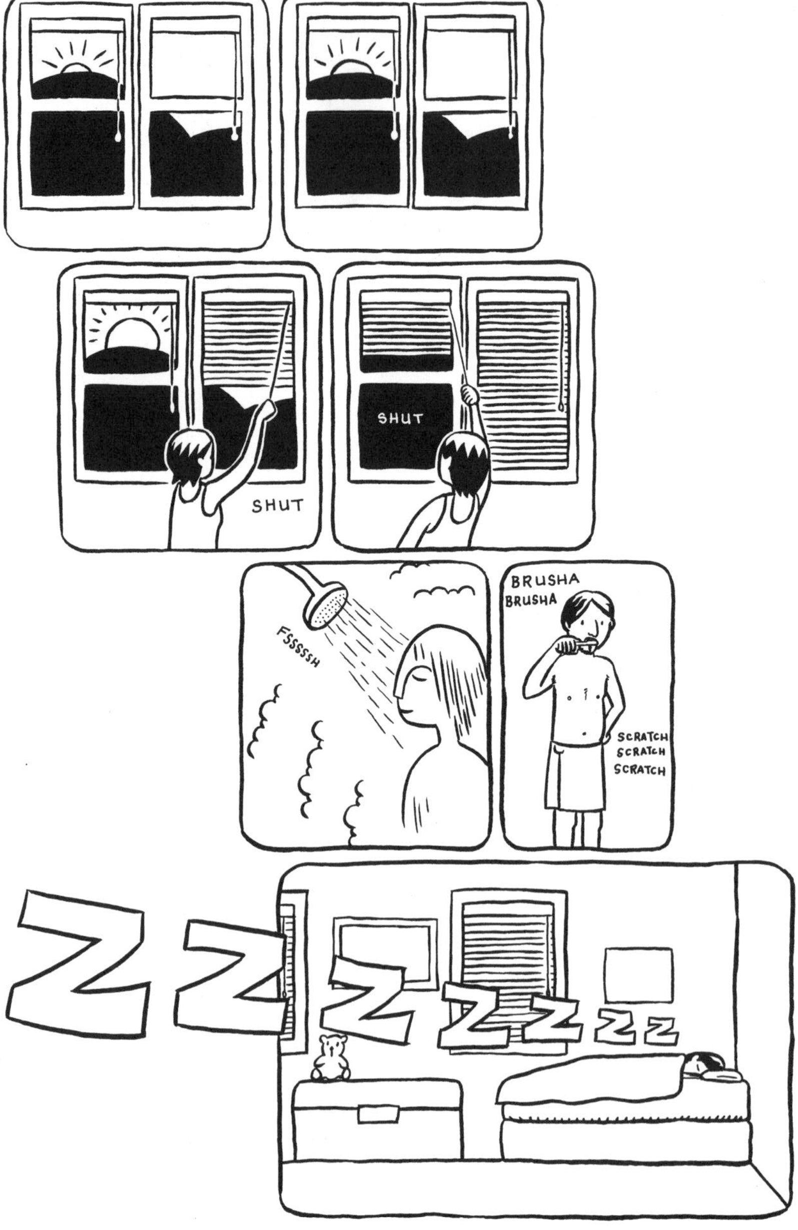
SHUT
SHUT
FSSSSSH
BRUSHA
BRUSHA
SCRATCH
SCRATCH
SCRATCH
ZZZZZZZZ

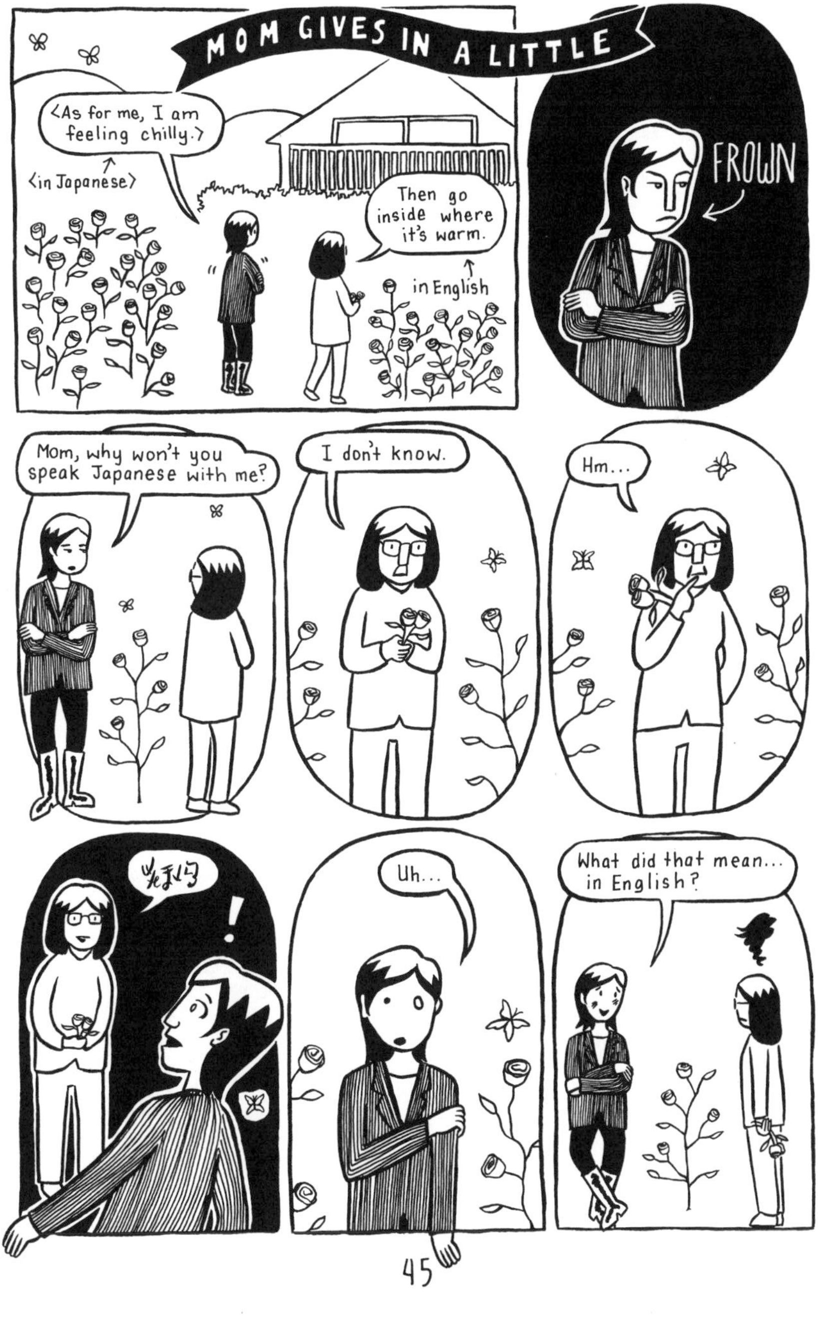
MOM GIVES IN A LITTLE
<As for me, I am feeling chilly.>
<in Japanese>
Then go inside where it's warm.
in English
FROWN
Mom, why won't you speak Japanese with me?
I don't know.
Hm...
!
Uh...
What did that mean... in English?

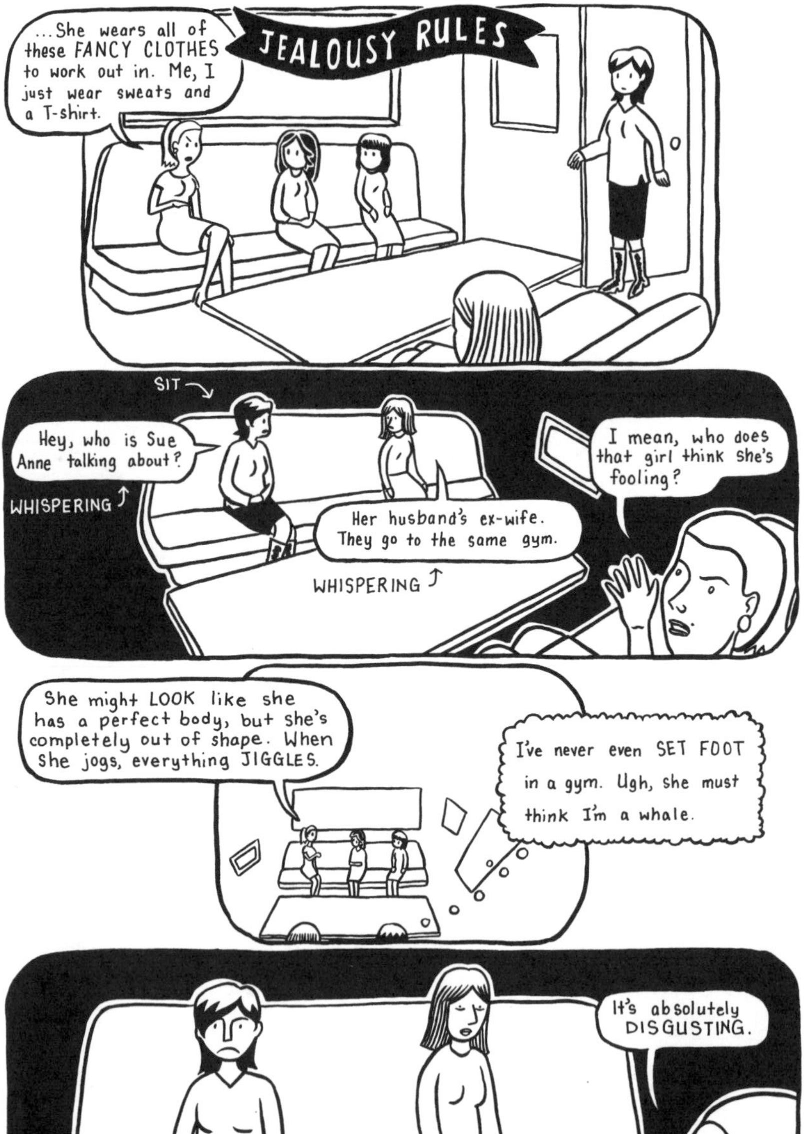
JEALOUSY RULES
...She wears all of these FANCY CLOTHES to work out in. Me, I just wear sweats and a T-shirt.
SIT
Hey, who is Sue Anne talking about?
WHISPERING
Her husband's ex-wife. They go to the same gym.
WHISPERING
I mean, who does that girl think she's fooling?
She might LOOK like she has a perfect body, but she's completely out of shape. When she jogs, everything JIGGLES.
I've never even SET FOOT in a gym. Ugh, she must think I'm a whale.
It's absolutely DISGUSTING.

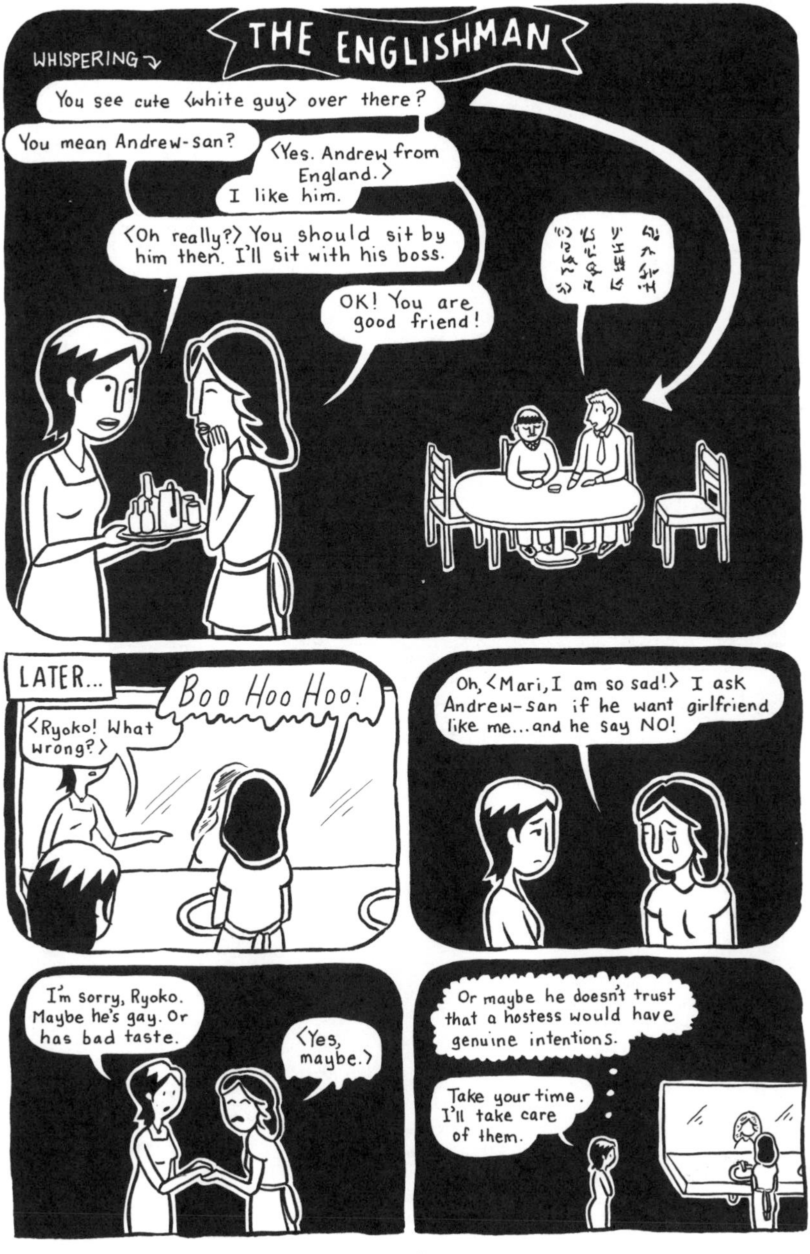
THE ENGLISHMAN
WHISPERING
You see cute <white guy> over there?
You mean Andrew-san?
<Yes. Andrew from England.> I like him.
<Oh really?> You should sit by him then. I'll sit with his boss.
OK! You are good friend!
LATER...
<Ryoko! What wrong?>
Boo Hoo Hoo!
Oh, <Mari, I am so sad!> I ask Andrew-san if he want girlfriend like me...and he say NO!
I'm sorry, Ryoko. Maybe he's gay. Or has bad taste.
<Yes, maybe.>
Or maybe he doesn't trust that a hostess would have genuine intentions.
Take your time. I'll take care of them.

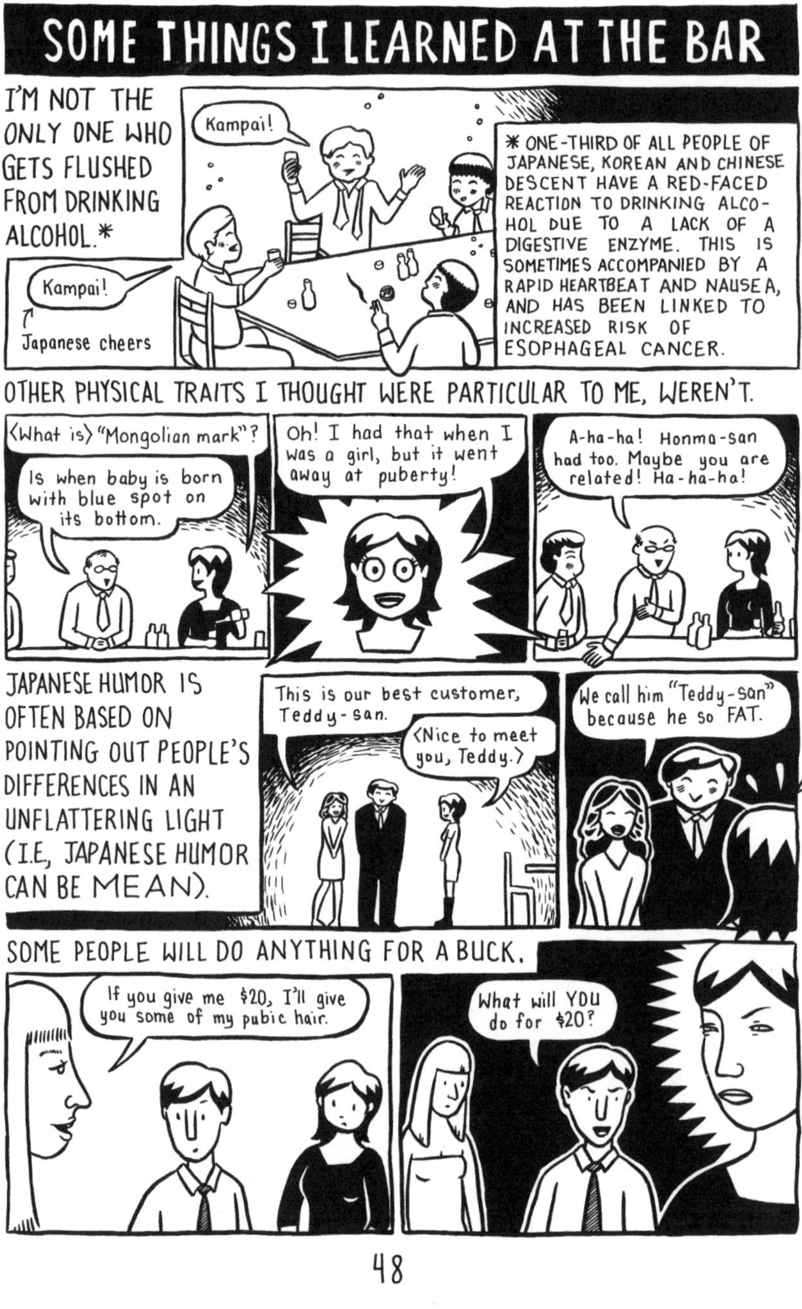
SOME THINGS I LEARNED AT THE BAR
I'M NOT THE ONLY ONE WHO GETS FLUSHED FROM DRINKING ALCOHOL.*
Kampai!
Kampai!
Japanese cheers
* ONE-THIRD OF ALL PEOPLE OF JAPANESE, KOREAN AND CHINESE DESCENT HAVE A RED-FACED REACTION TO DRINKING ALCOHOL DUE TO A LACK OF A DIGESTIVE ENZYME. THIS IS SOMETIMES ACCOMPANIED BY A RAPID HEARTBEAT AND NAUSEA, AND HAS BEEN LINKED TO INCREASED RISK OF ESOPHAGEAL CANCER.
OTHER PHYSICAL TRAITS I THOUGHT WERE PARTICULAR TO ME, WEREN'T.
〈What is〉 "Mongolian mark"?
Is when baby is born with blue spot on its bottom.
Oh! I had that when I was a girl, but it went away at puberty!
A-ha-ha! Honma-san had too. Maybe you are related! Ha-ha-ha!
JAPANESE HUMOR IS OFTEN BASED ON POINTING OUT PEOPLE'S DIFFERENCES IN AN UNFLATTERING LIGHT (I.E., JAPANESE HUMOR CAN BE MEAN).
This is our best customer, Teddy-san.
〈Nice to meet you, Teddy.〉
We call him "Teddy-san" because he so FAT.
SOME PEOPLE WILL DO ANYTHING FOR A BUCK.
If you give me $20, I'll give you some of my pubic hair.
What will YOU do for $20?

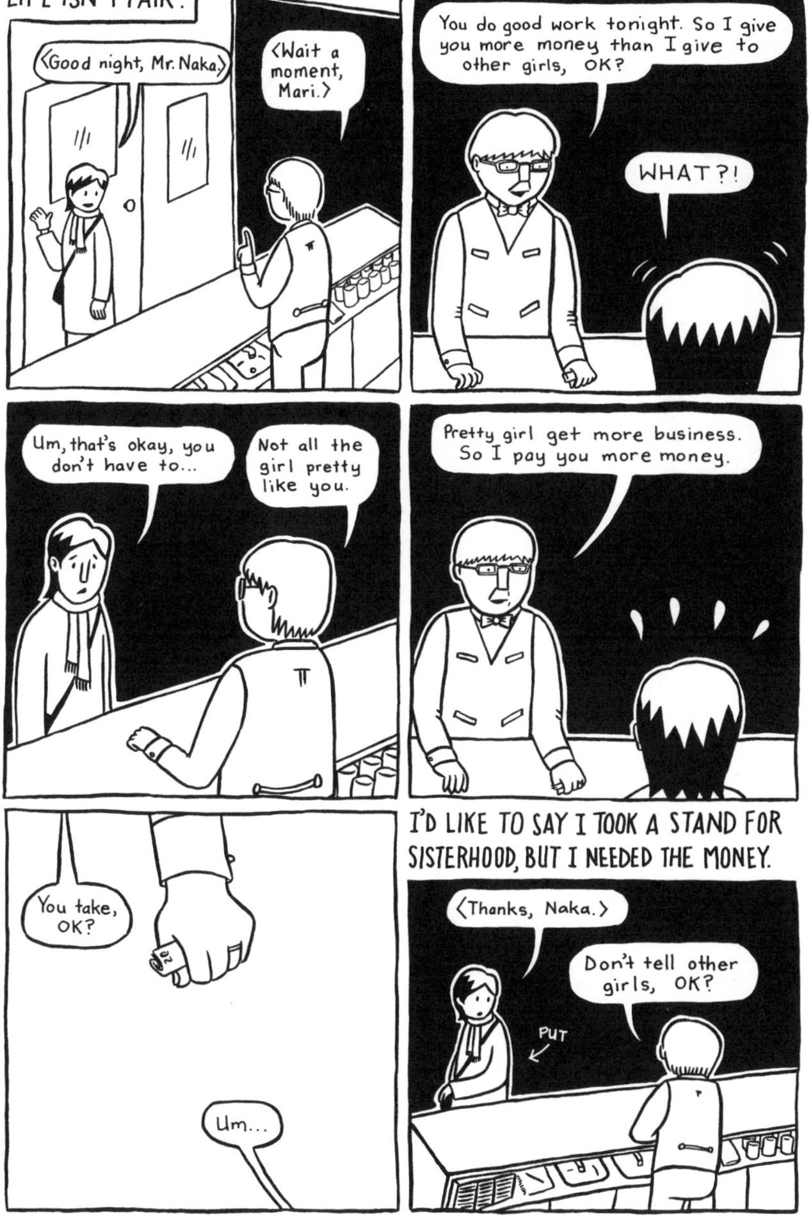
LIFE ISN'T FAIR.
⟨Good night, Mr. Naka.⟩
⟨Wait a moment, Mari.⟩
You do good work tonight. So I give you more money than I give to other girls, OK?
WHAT?!
Um, that's okay, you don't have to...
Not all the girl pretty like you.
Pretty girl get more business. So I pay you more money.
You take, OK?
Um...
I'D LIKE TO SAY I TOOK A STAND FOR SISTERHOOD, BUT I NEEDED THE MONEY.
⟨Thanks, Naka.⟩
Don't tell other girls, OK?
PUT

EVEN THE MOST BEAUTIFUL PEOPLE CAN BE INSECURE.

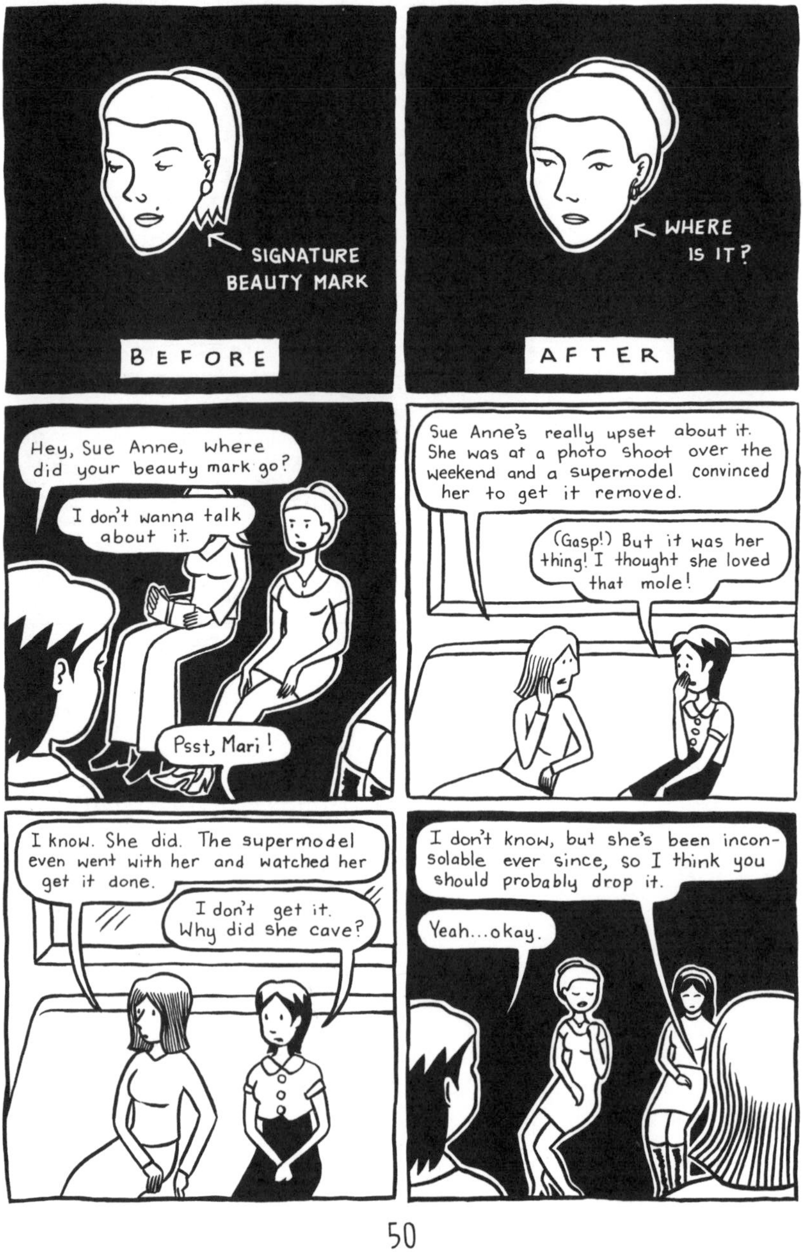

SIGNATURE BEAUTY MARK
BEFORE
WHERE IS IT?
AFTER
Hey, Sue Anne, where did your beauty mark go?
I don't wanna talk about it.
Psst, Mari!
Sue Anne's really upset about it. She was at a photo shoot over the weekend and a supermodel convinced her to get it removed.
(Gasp!) But it was her thing! I thought she loved that mole!
I know. She did. The supermodel even went with her and watched her get it done.
I don't get it. Why did she cave?
I don't know, but she's been inconsolable ever since, so I think you should probably drop it.
Yeah...okay.

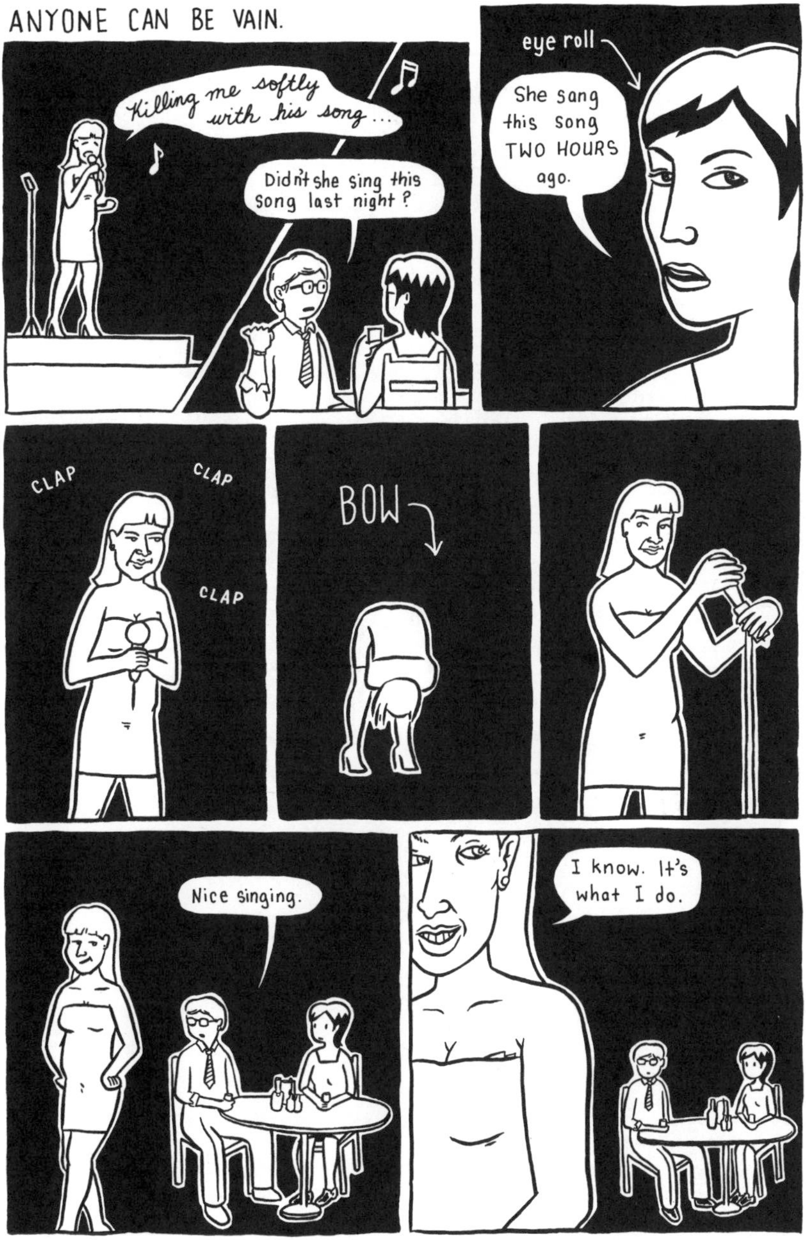
ANYONE CAN BE VAIN.
Killing me softly with his song...
Didn't she sing this song last night?
eye roll
She sang this song TWO HOURS ago.
CLAP
CLAP
CLAP
BOW
Nice singing.
I know. It's what I do.

YOU NEVER KNOW WHAT YOU'RE GETTING.

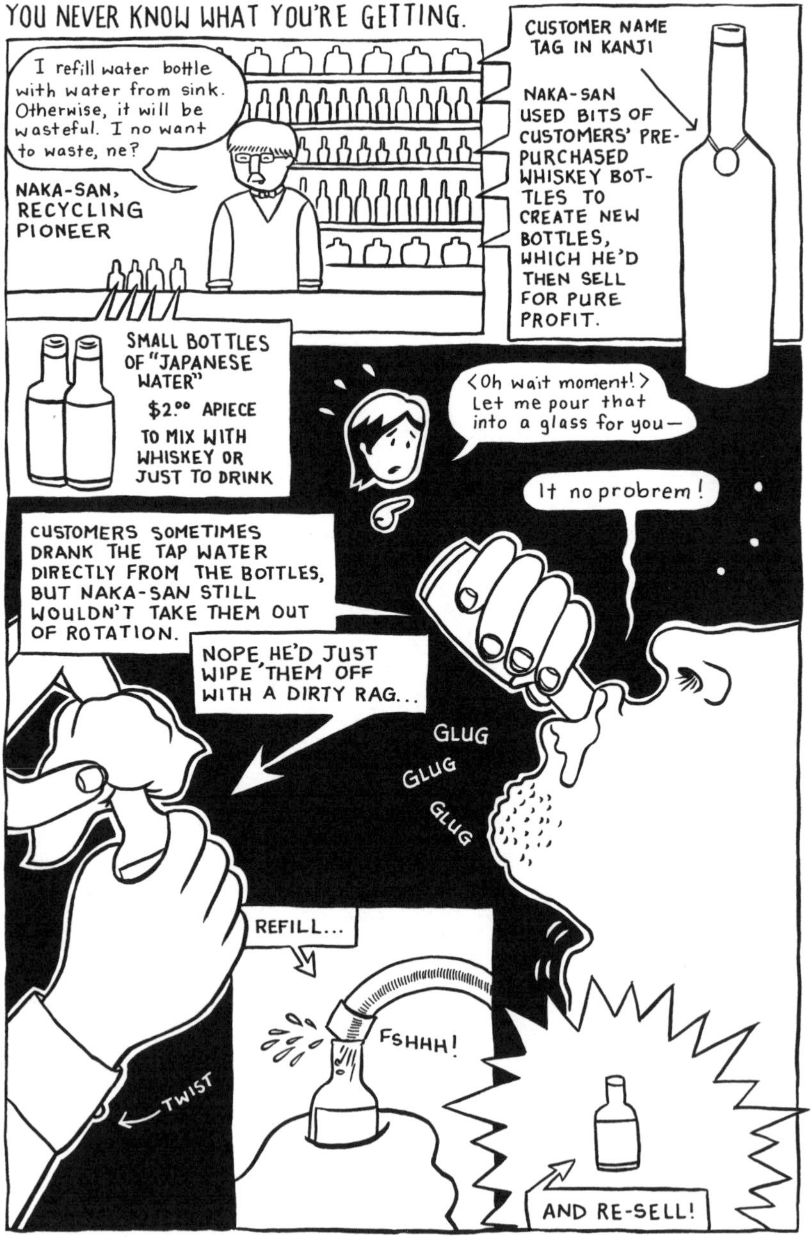

I refill water bottle with water from sink. Otherwise, it will be wasteful. I no want to waste, ne?
NAKA-SAN, RECYCLING PIONEER
CUSTOMER NAME TAG IN KANJI
NAKA-SAN USED BITS OF CUSTOMERS' PRE-PURCHASED WHISKEY BOTTLES TO CREATE NEW BOTTLES, WHICH HE'D THEN SELL FOR PURE PROFIT.
SMALL BOTTLES OF "JAPANESE WATER"
$2.00 APIECE
TO MIX WITH WHISKEY OR JUST TO DRINK
<Oh wait moment!> Let me pour that into a glass for you—
It no probrem!
CUSTOMERS SOMETIMES DRANK THE TAP WATER DIRECTLY FROM THE BOTTLES, BUT NAKA-SAN STILL WOULDN'T TAKE THEM OUT OF ROTATION.
NOPE, HE'D JUST WIPE THEM OFF WITH A DIRTY RAG...
GLUG
GLUG
GLUG
REFILL...
FSHHH!
TWIST
AND RE-SELL!

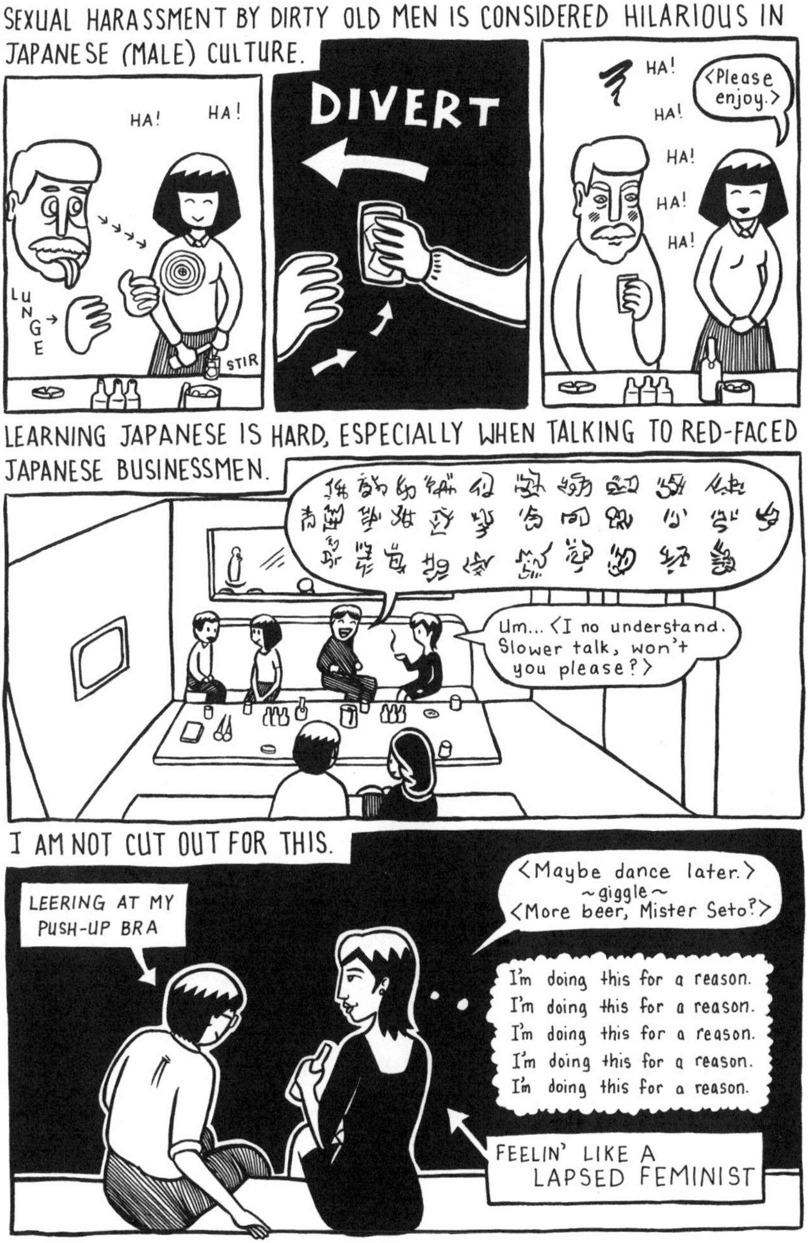
SEXUAL HARASSMENT BY DIRTY OLD MEN IS CONSIDERED HILARIOUS IN JAPANESE (MALE) CULTURE.
HA! HA!
LUNGE
STIR
DIVERT
HA! HA! HA! HA! HA!
<Please enjoy.>
LEARNING JAPANESE IS HARD, ESPECIALLY WHEN TALKING TO RED-FACED JAPANESE BUSINESSMEN.
Um... <I no understand. Slower talk, won't you please?>
I AM NOT CUT OUT FOR THIS.
LEERING AT MY PUSH-UP BRA
<Maybe dance later.> ~giggle~ <More beer, Mister Seto?>
I'm doing this for a reason.
I'm doing this for a reason.
I'm doing this for a reason.
I'm doing this for a reason.
I'm doing this for a reason.
FEELIN' LIKE A LAPSED FEMINIST

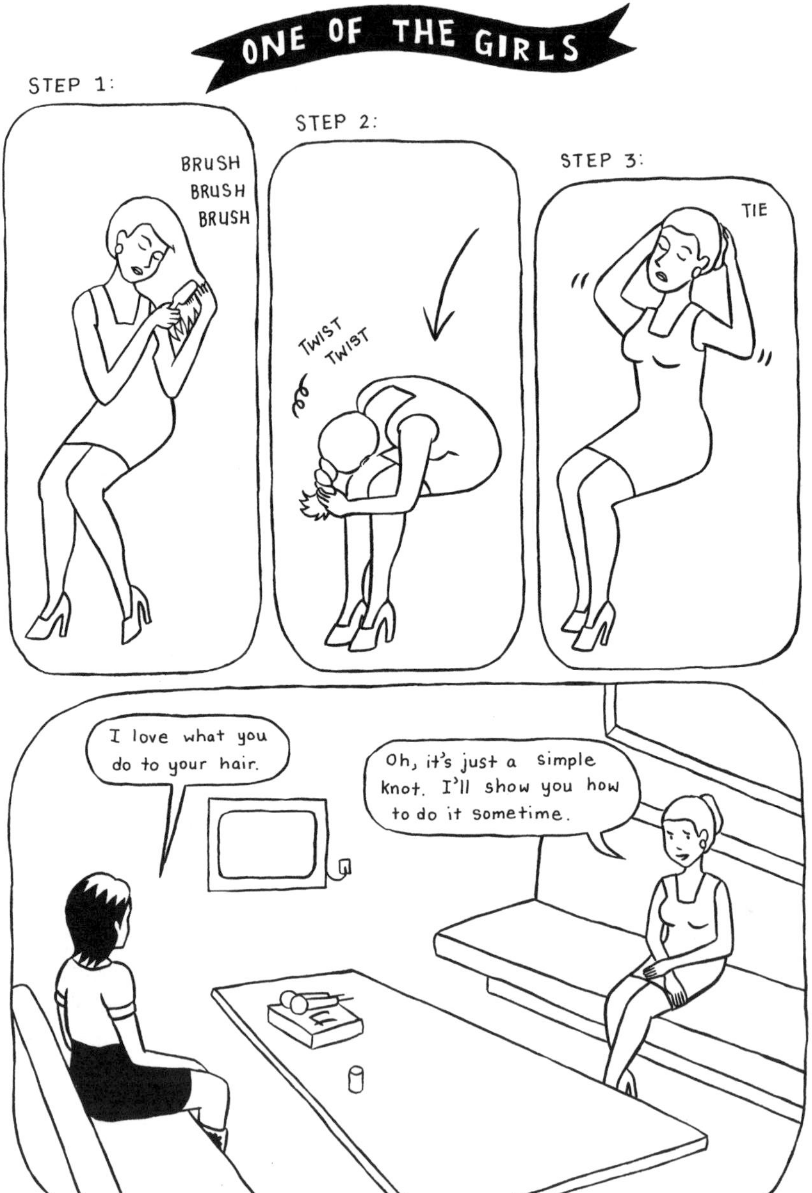
ONE OF THE GIRLS
STEP 1:
BRUSH
BRUSH
BRUSH
STEP 2:
TWIST
TWIST
STEP 3:
TIE
I love what you do to your hair.
Oh, it's just a simple knot. I'll show you how to do it sometime.

IT WASN'T LONG BEFORE I GOT MY OWN REGULAR CUSTOMER.
HIS NAME WAS HITOSHI.

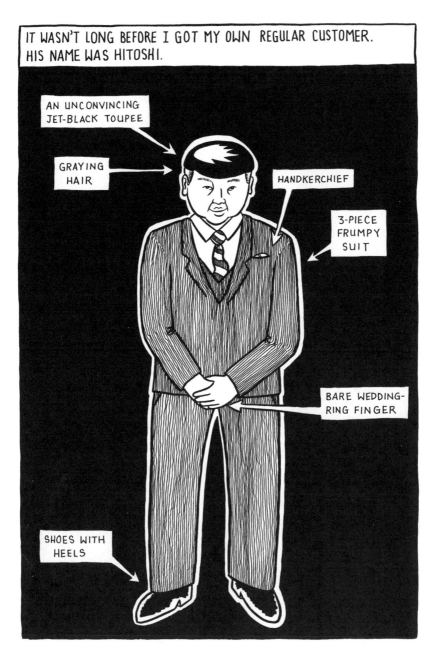

AN UNCONVINCING
JET-BLACK TOUPEE

GRAYING
HAIR

HANDKERCHIEF

3-PIECE
FRUMPY
SUIT

BARE WEDDING-
RING FINGER

SHOES WITH
HEELS

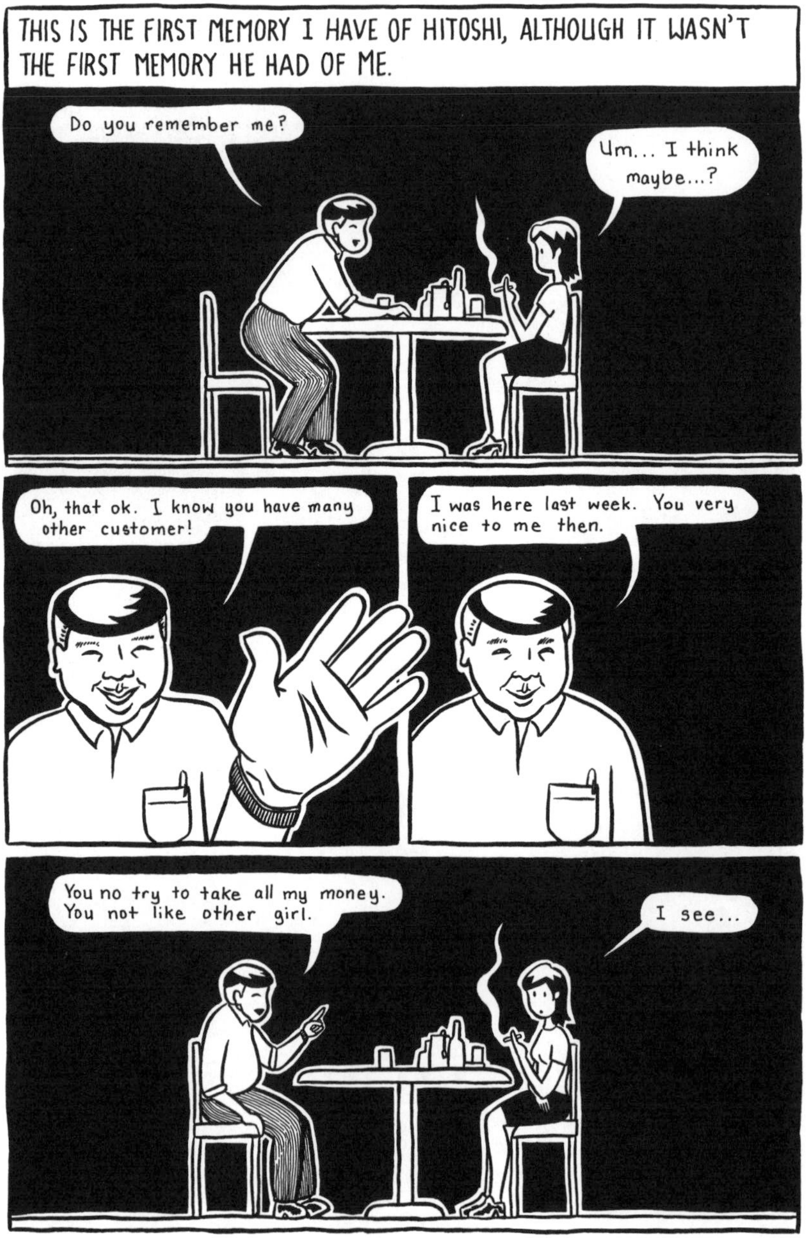
THIS IS THE FIRST MEMORY I HAVE OF HITOSHI, ALTHOUGH IT WASN'T THE FIRST MEMORY HE HAD OF ME.
Do you remember me?
Um... I think maybe...?
Oh, that ok. I know you have many other customer!
I was here last week. You very nice to me then.
You no try to take all my money. You not like other girl.
I see...

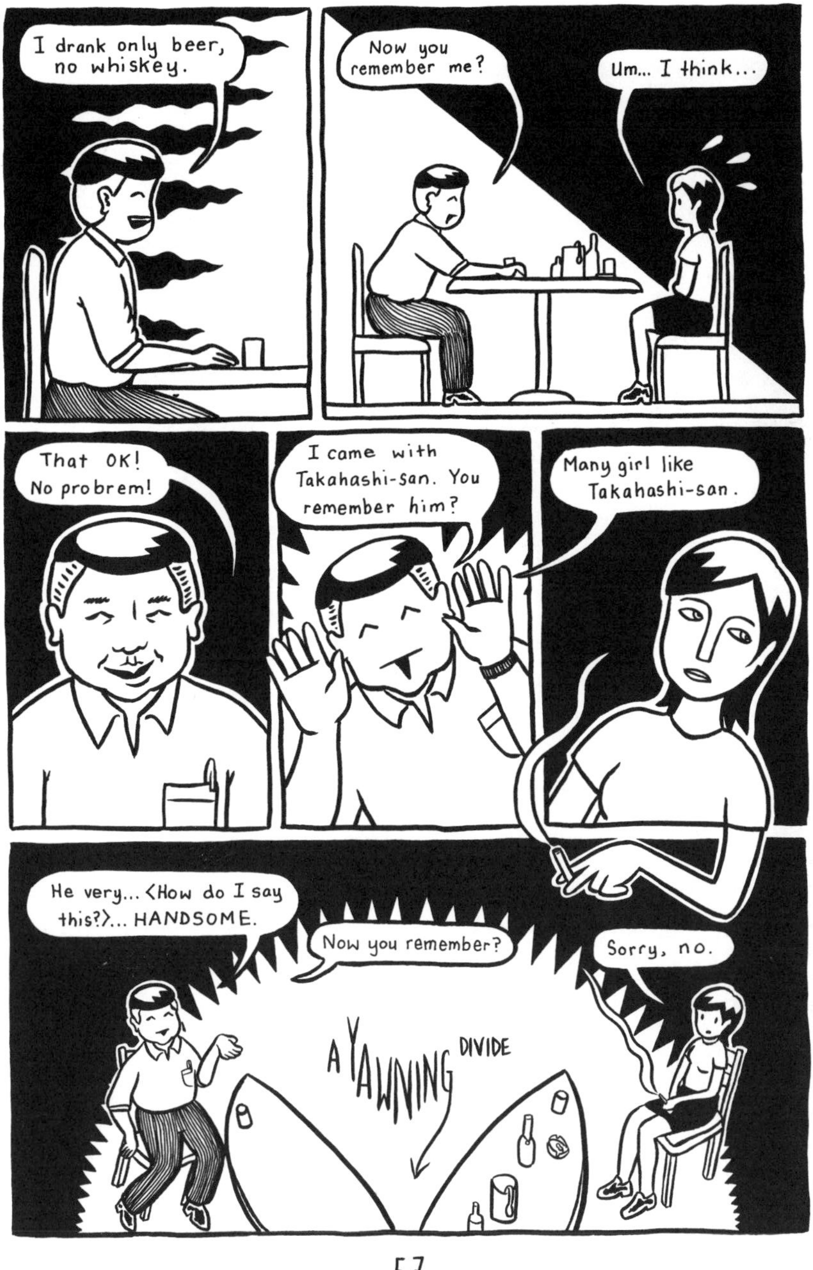
I drank only beer, no whiskey.
Now you remember me?
Um... I think...
That OK! No probrem!
I came with Takahashi-san. You remember him?
Many girl like Takahashi-san.
He very... <How do I say this?>... HANDSOME.
Now you remember?
Sorry, no.
A YAWNING DIVIDE

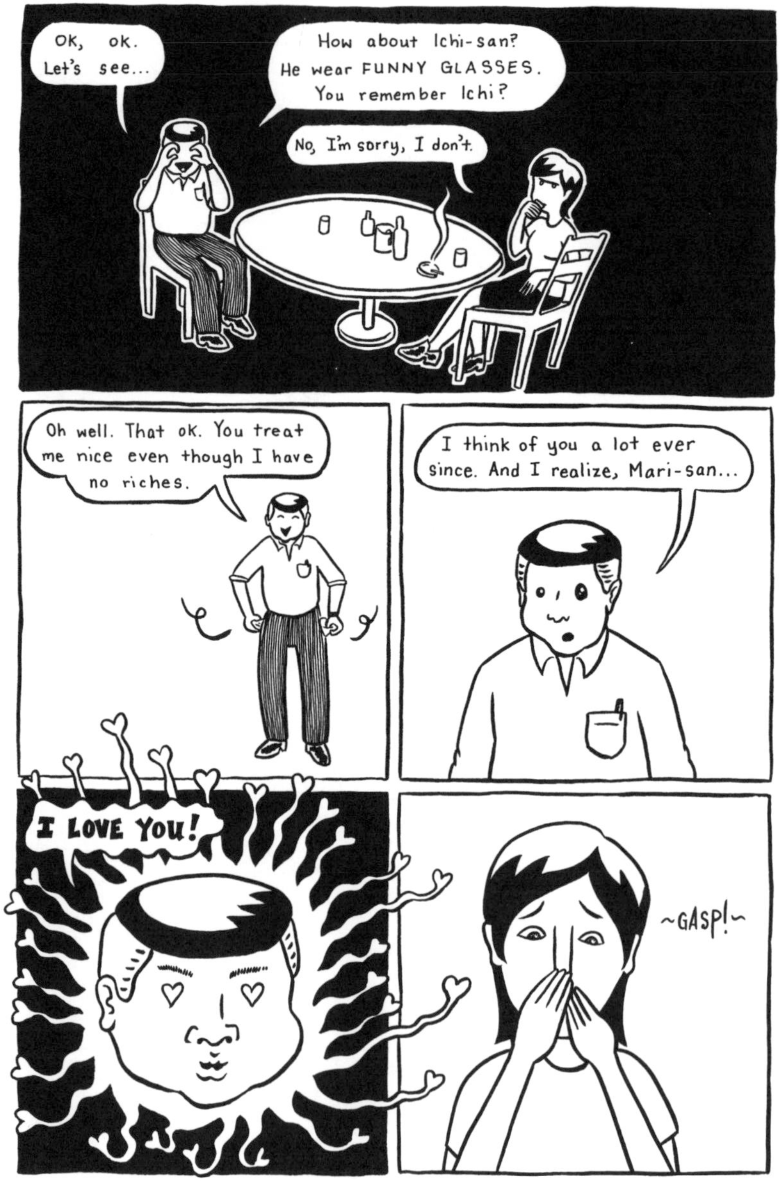
OK, ok. Let's see...
How about Ichi-san? He wear FUNNY GLASSES. You remember Ichi?
No, I'm sorry, I don't.
Oh well. That ok. You treat me nice even though I have no riches.
I think of you a lot ever since. And I realize, Mari-san...
I LOVE YOU!
~GASP!~

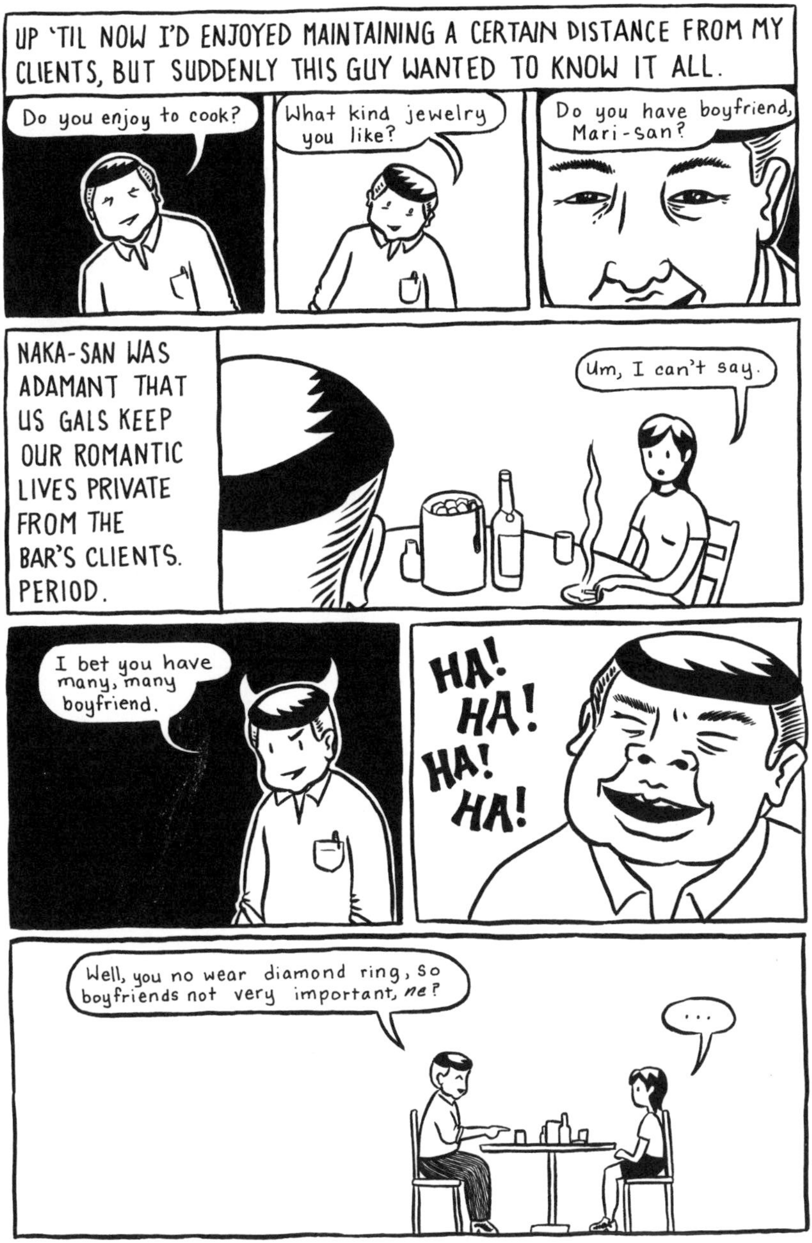
UP 'TIL NOW I'D ENJOYED MAINTAINING A CERTAIN DISTANCE FROM MY CLIENTS, BUT SUDDENLY THIS GUY WANTED TO KNOW IT ALL.
Do you enjoy to cook?
What kind jewelry you like?
Do you have boyfriend, Mari-san?
NAKA-SAN WAS ADAMANT THAT US GALS KEEP OUR ROMANTIC LIVES PRIVATE FROM THE BAR'S CLIENTS. PERIOD.
Um, I can't say.
I bet you have many, many boyfriend.
HA! HA! HA! HA!
Well, you no wear diamond ring, so boyfriends not very important, *ne*?
...

‹Do you speak Japanese?› You speak Japanese?

‹Little bit only.› But I want to learn. That's why I got this job. Well, that and so I can pay rent. Ha ha.

I will teach you, Mari-san! But first, let's play gamble!

Um, I don't think Naka-san allows games...

I RESISTED AT FIRST, BUT HE INSISTED. AND IT SEEMED TO MAKE HIM SO HAPPY.

You very good at this game. ‹Very good job, Mari!›

shuffle

PLUS HE WASN'T MOONING OVER ME QUITE AS MUCH. BUT THEN...

Time for me to go. Here is the money you won. $300.⁰⁰. It will help you with rent, *ne*?

No! I can't take that much money from you!

What kind of businessman am I if I no pay what I owe?

But...

Take. You earned. I insist.

...

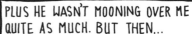

THE MORE HITOSHI CAME IN, AND THE MORE MONEY HE GAVE ME IN TIPS, THE WORSE I FELT.

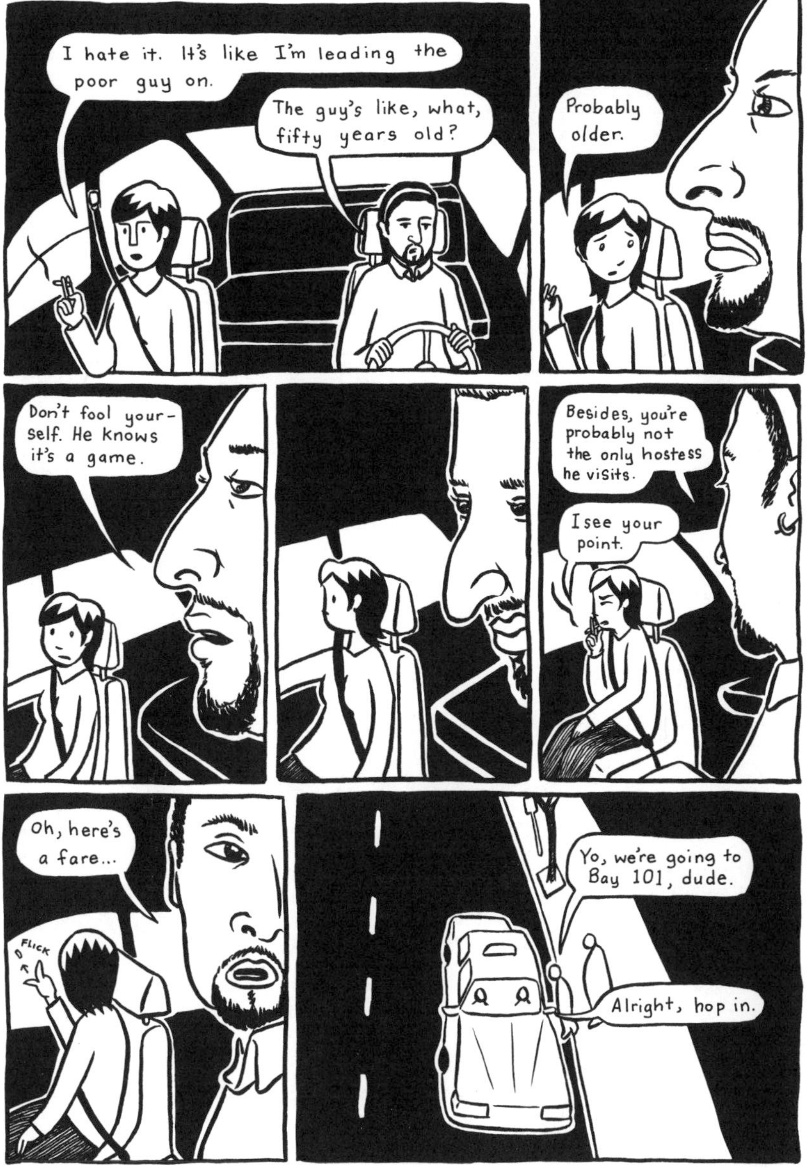
I hate it. It's like I'm leading the poor guy on.
The guy's like, what, fifty years old?
Probably older.
Don't fool yourself. He knows it's a game.
Besides, you're probably not the only hostess he visits.
I see your point.
Oh, here's a fare...
FLICK
Yo, we're going to Bay 101, dude.
Alright, hop in.

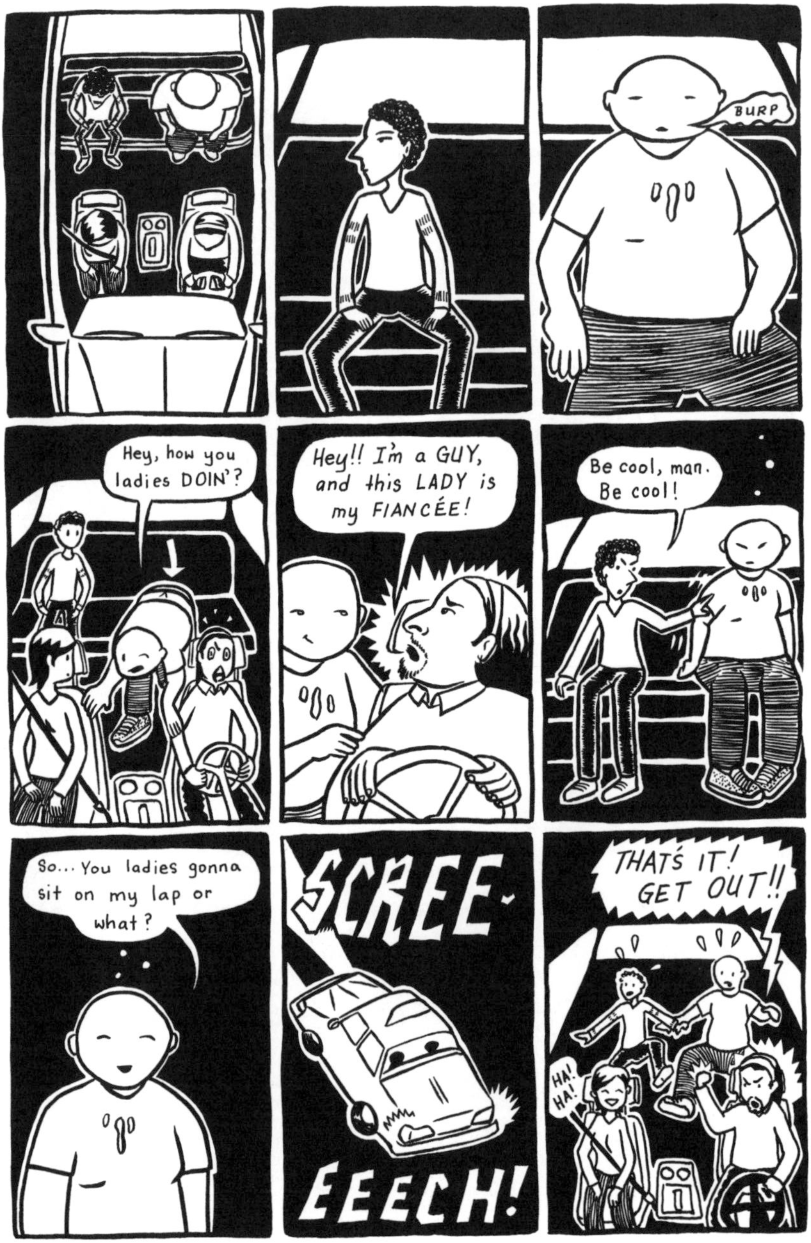
BURP
Hey, how you ladies DOIN'?
Hey!! I'm a GUY, and this LADY is my FIANCÉE!
Be cool, man. Be cool!
So... You ladies gonna sit on my lap or what?
SCREE-
EEECH!
THAT'S IT! GET OUT!!
HA! HA!

WHEN HITOSHI ASKED ME OUT ON A LUNCH DATE, I SAW IT AS A GOOD OPPORTUNITY TO COME CLEAN ABOUT BEING ENGAGED TO GIUSEPPE.

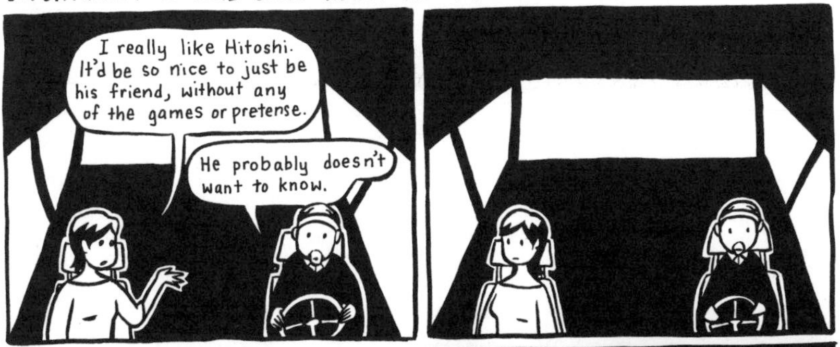
I really like Hitoshi. It'd be so nice to just be his friend, without any of the games or pretense.
He probably doesn't want to know.

BUT WHEN WE WENT TO LUNCH...

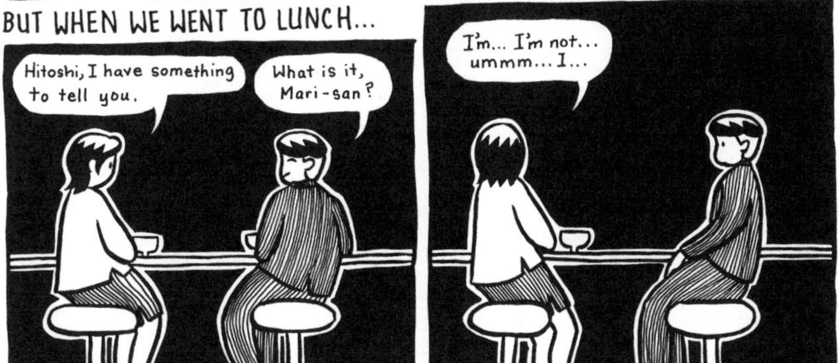
Hitoshi, I have something to tell you.
What is it, Mari-san?
I'm... I'm not... ummm... I...

...I CHICKENED OUT.

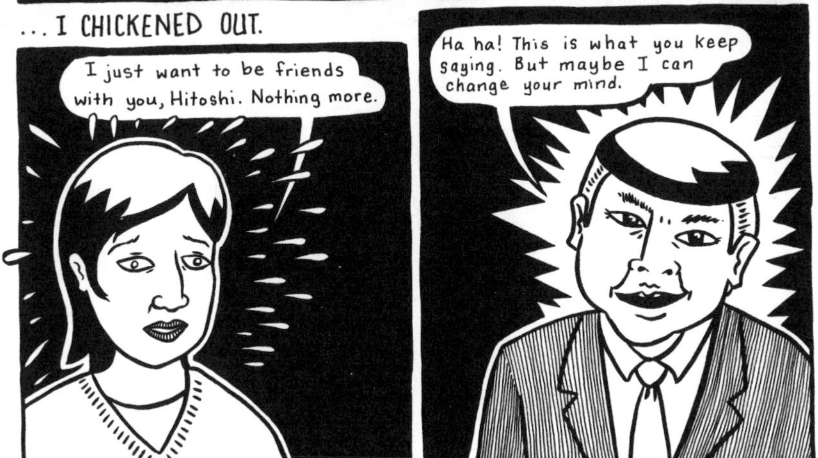
I just want to be friends with you, Hitoshi. Nothing more.
Ha ha! This is what you keep saying. But maybe I can change your mind.

ONE DAY, HITOSHI TOOK ME BY SURPRISE. FROM OUR CONVERSATIONS AT THE BAR, HE KNEW A FEW PERSONAL THINGS ABOUT ME.

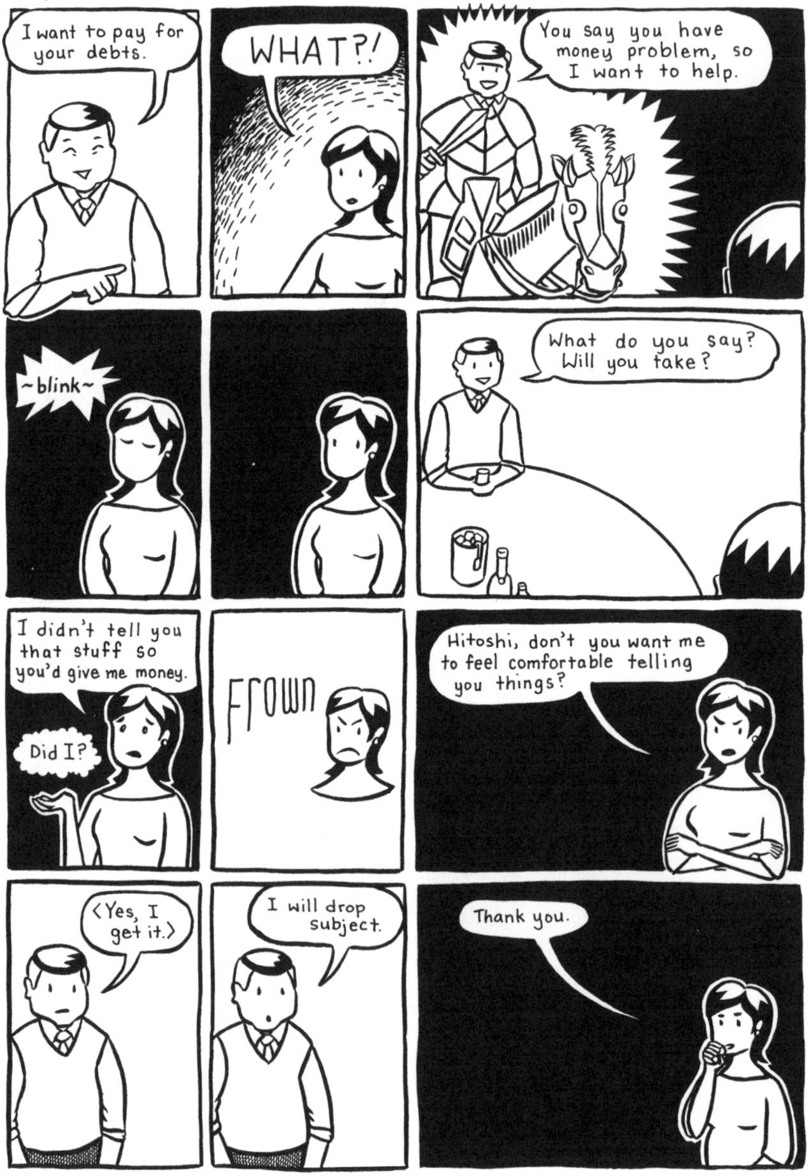
I want to pay for your debts.
WHAT?!
You say you have money problem, so I want to help.
~blink~
What do you say? Will you take?
I didn't tell you that stuff so you'd give me money.
Did I?
Frown
Hitoshi, don't you want me to feel comfortable telling you things?
⟨Yes, I get it.⟩
I will drop subject.
Thank you.

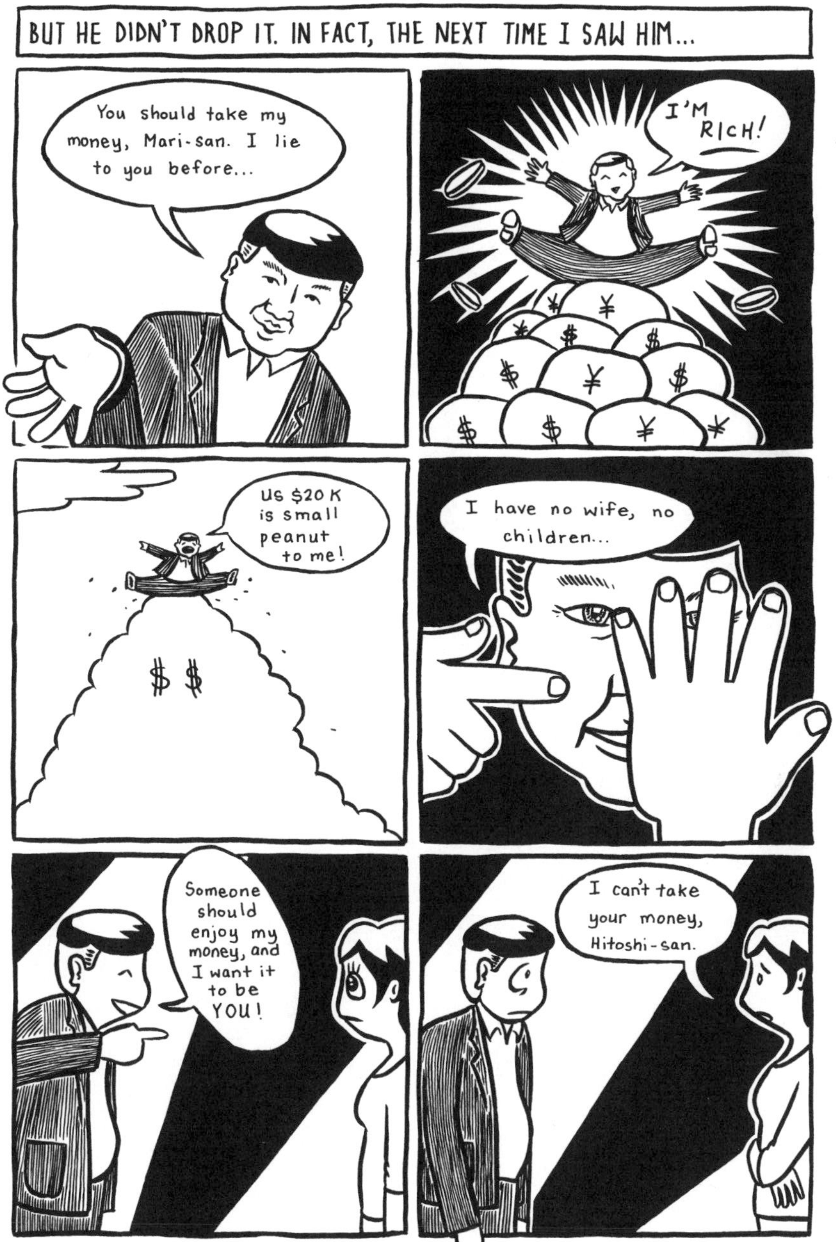
BUT HE DIDN'T DROP IT. IN FACT, THE NEXT TIME I SAW HIM...
You should take my money, Mari-san. I lie to you before...
I'M RICH!
US $20 K is small peanut to me!
I have no wife, no children...
Someone should enjoy my money, and I want it to be YOU!
I can't take your money, Hitoshi-san.

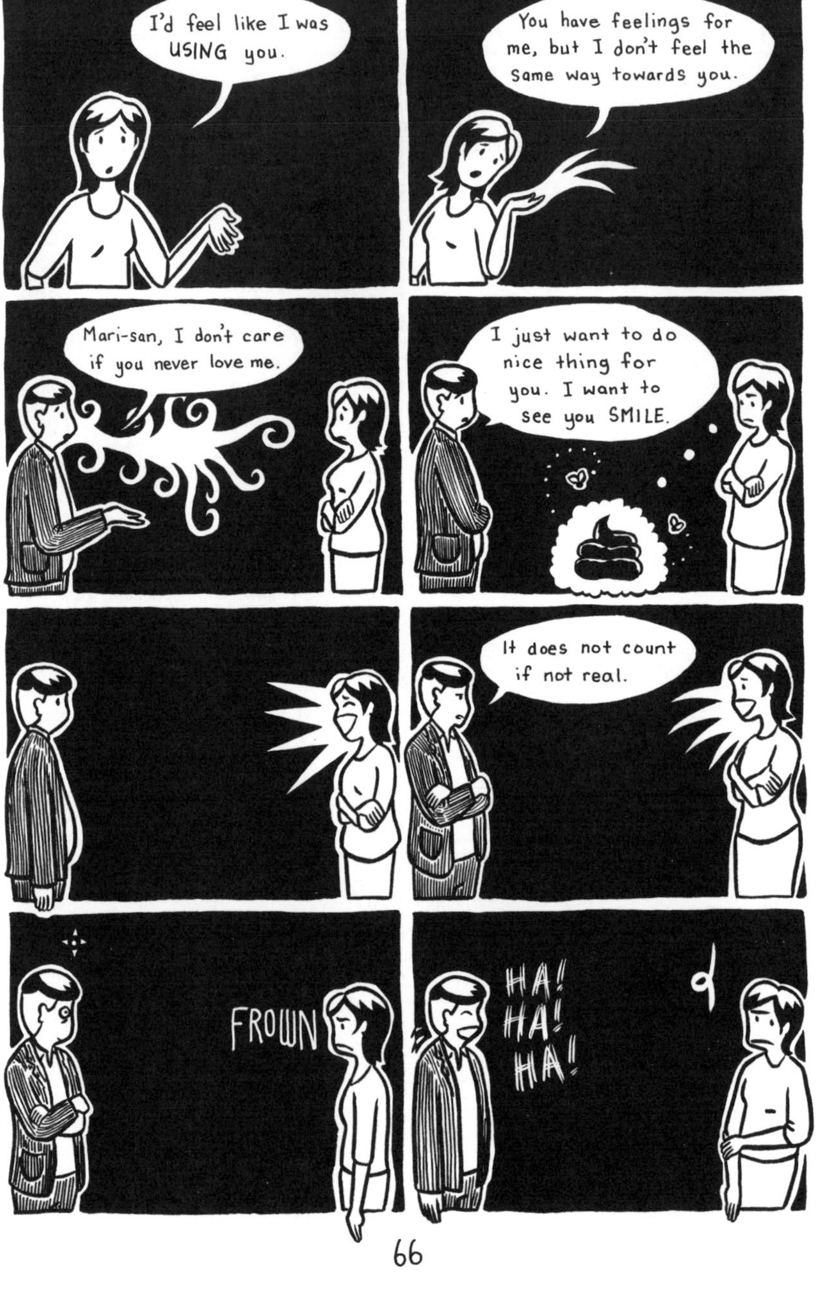
I'd feel like I was USING you.
You have feelings for me, but I don't feel the same way towards you.
Mari-san, I don't care if you never love me.
I just want to do nice thing for you. I want to see you SMILE.
It does not count if not real.
FROWN
HA! HA! HA!

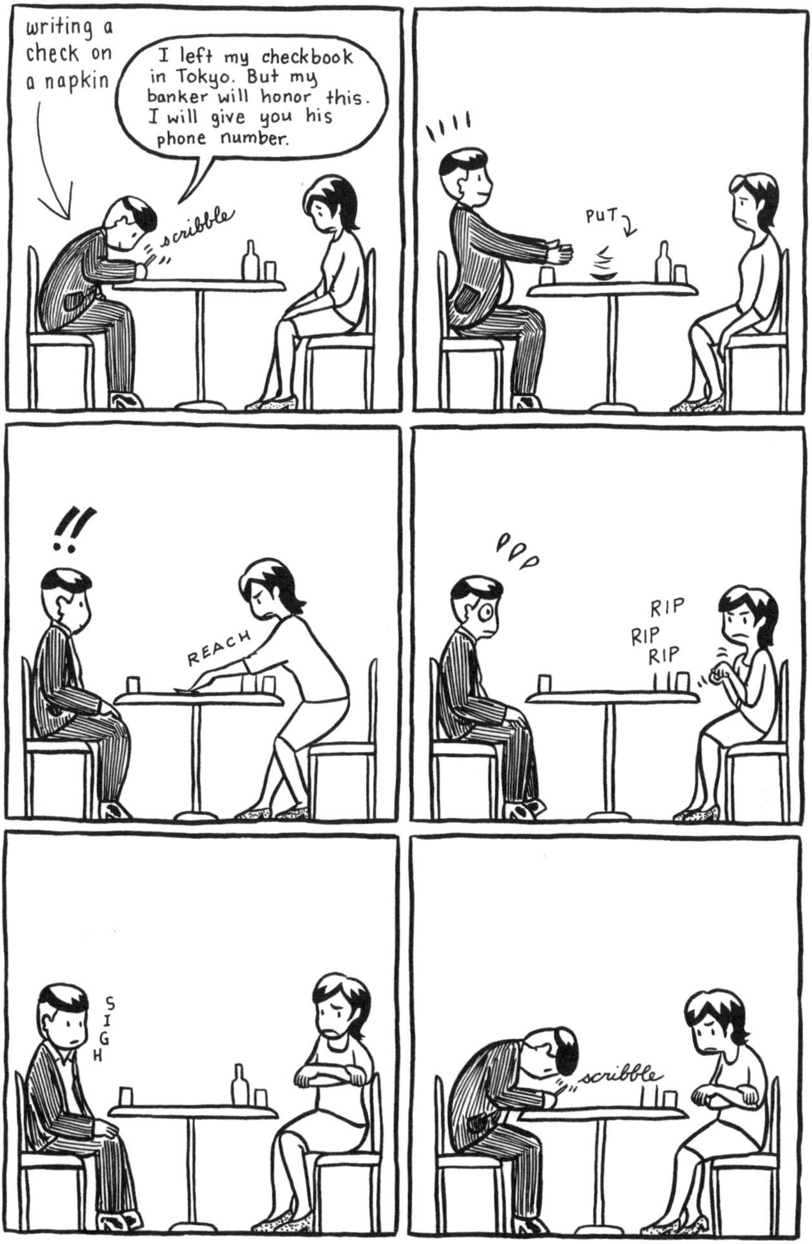
writing a check on a napkin
I left my checkbook in Tokyo. But my banker will honor this. I will give you his phone number.
scribble
PUT
!!
REACH
RIP
RIP
RIP
SIGH
scribble

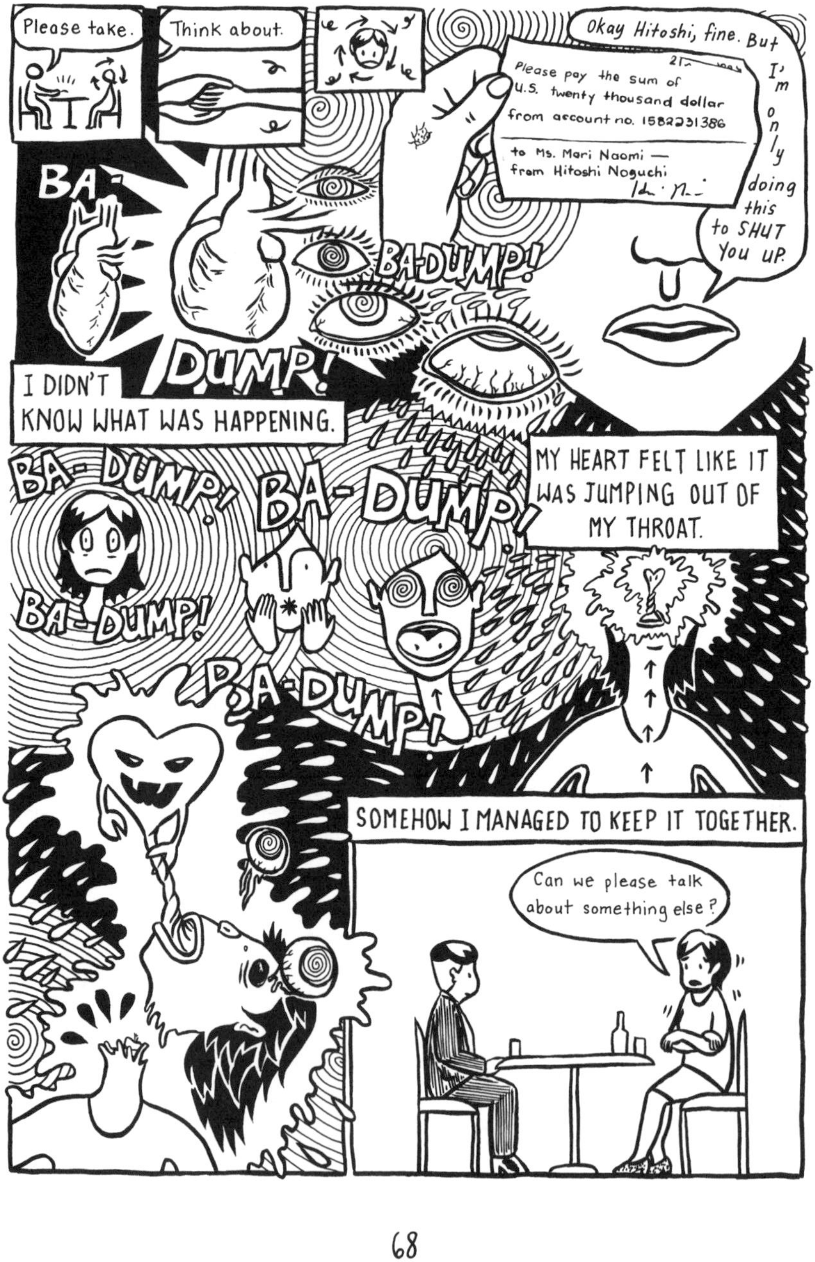

Please take.
Think about.
Okay Hitoshi, fine. But I'm only doing this to SHUT You up.
Please pay the sum of U.S. twenty thousand dollar from account no. 1582231386
to Ms. Mari Naomi — from Hitoshi Noguchi
BA-DUMP!
BADUMP!
I DIDN'T KNOW WHAT WAS HAPPENING.
BA-DUMP!
BA-DUMP!
MY HEART FELT LIKE IT WAS JUMPING OUT OF MY THROAT.
BA-DUMP!
BA-DUMP!
SOMEHOW I MANAGED TO KEEP IT TOGETHER.
Can we please talk about something else?

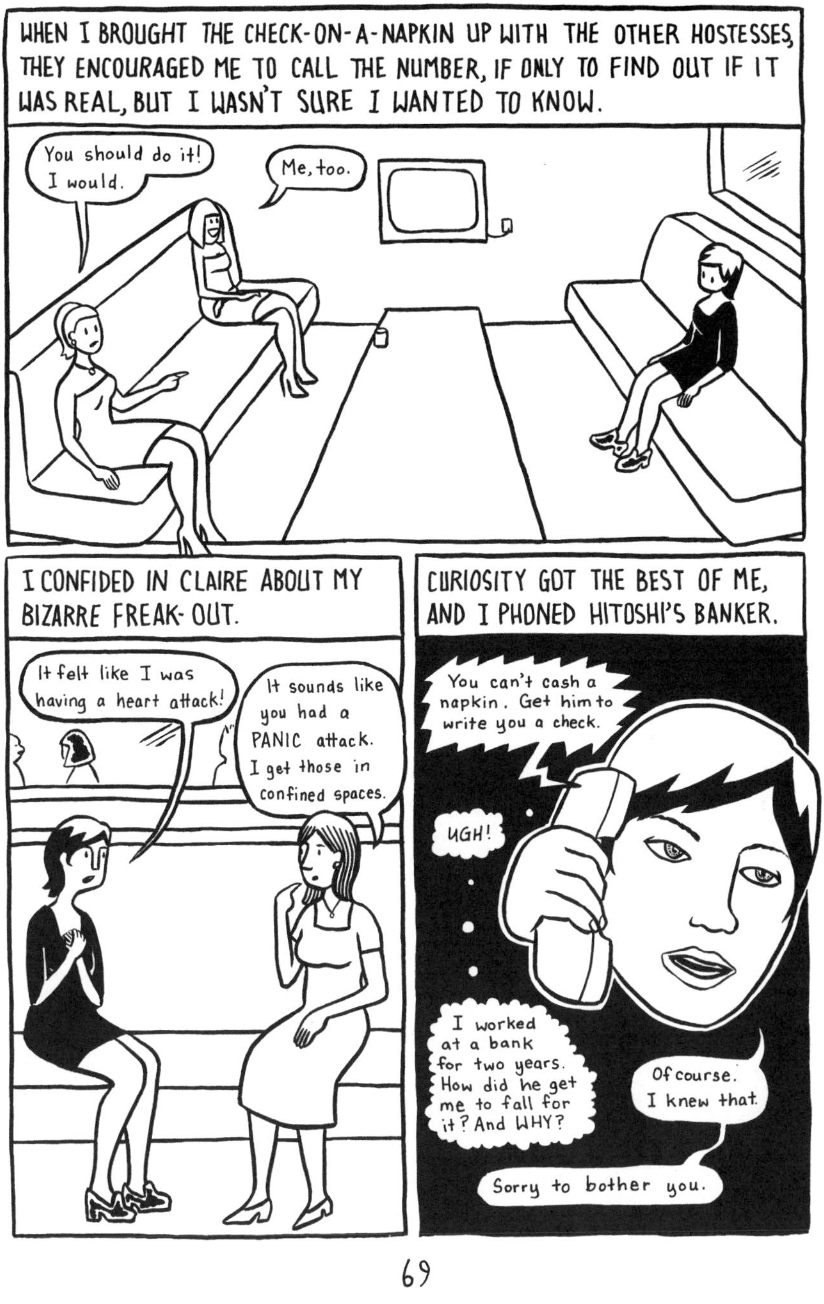
WHEN I BROUGHT THE CHECK-ON-A-NAPKIN UP WITH THE OTHER HOSTESSES, THEY ENCOURAGED ME TO CALL THE NUMBER, IF ONLY TO FIND OUT IF IT WAS REAL, BUT I WASN'T SURE I WANTED TO KNOW.
You should do it! I would.
Me, too.
I CONFIDED IN CLAIRE ABOUT MY BIZARRE FREAK-OUT.
It felt like I was having a heart attack!
It sounds like you had a PANIC attack. I get those in confined spaces.
CURIOSITY GOT THE BEST OF ME, AND I PHONED HITOSHI'S BANKER.
You can't cash a napkin. Get him to write you a check.
UGH!
I worked at a bank for two years. How did he get me to fall for it? And WHY?
Of course. I knew that.
Sorry to bother you.

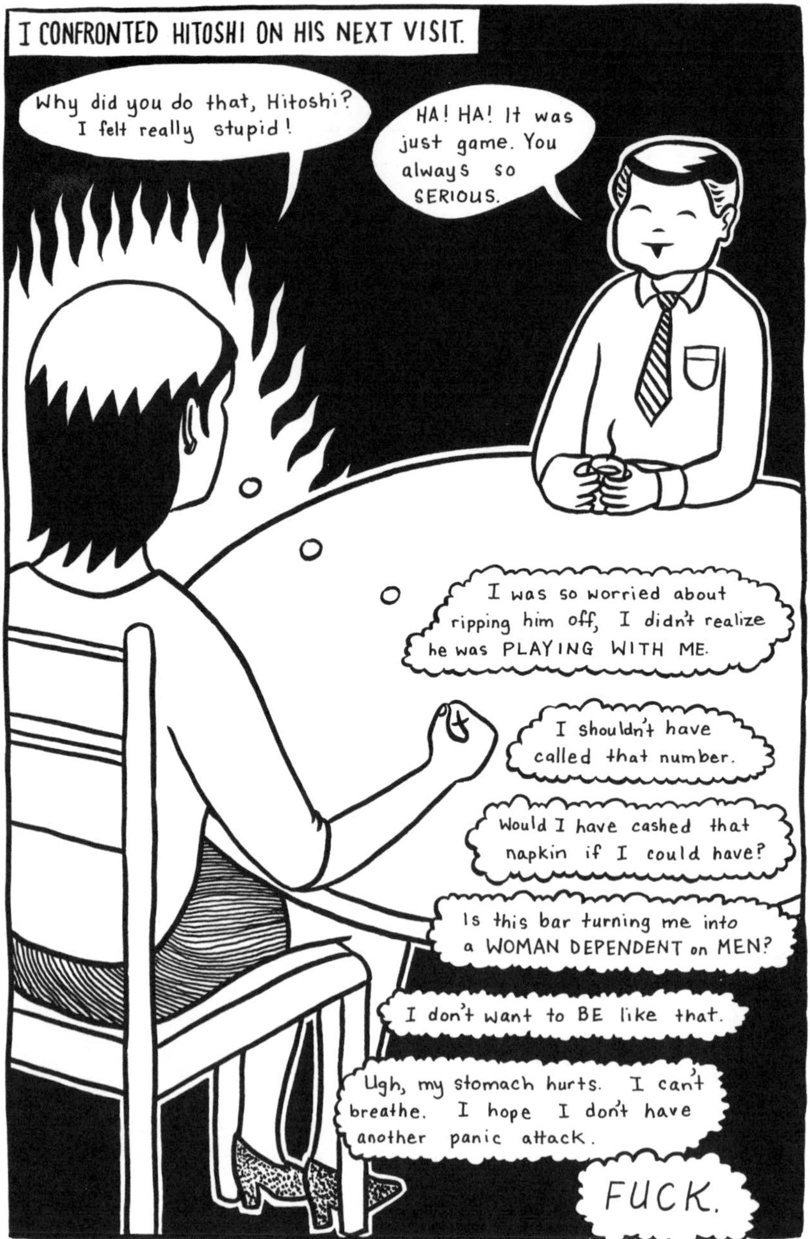
I CONFRONTED HITOSHI ON HIS NEXT VISIT.
Why did you do that, Hitoshi? I felt really stupid!
HA! HA! It was just game. You always so SERIOUS.
I was so worried about ripping him off, I didn't realize he was PLAYING WITH ME.
I shouldn't have called that number.
Would I have cashed that napkin if I could have?
Is this bar turning me into a WOMAN DEPENDENT on MEN?
I don't want to BE like that.
Ugh, my stomach hurts. I can't breathe. I hope I don't have another panic attack.
FUCK.

WORK AT THE BAR WENT DOWNHILL FROM THERE. AND ONE NIGHT, AMIDST A LARGE PARTY OF MEDICAL PROFESSIONALS, I COMPLETELY LOST MY SHIT.

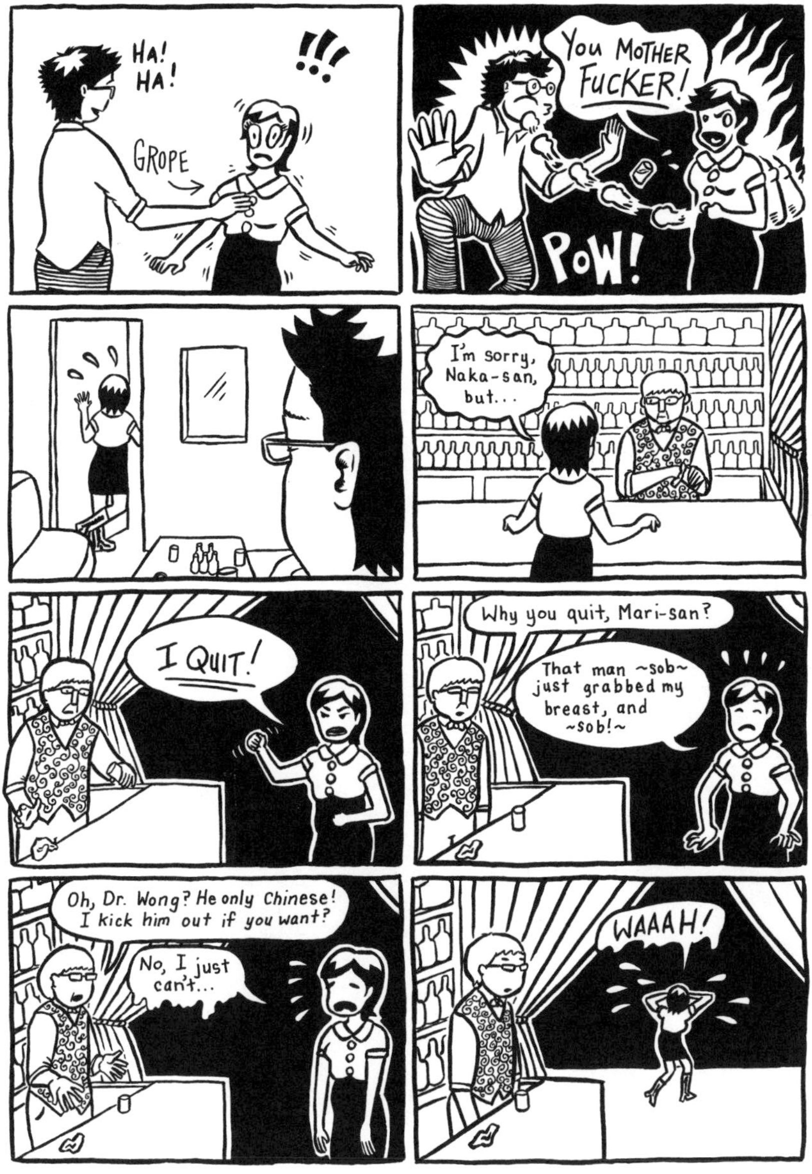

HA! HA!
!!!
GROPE
You MOTHER FUCKER!
POW!
I'm sorry, Naka-san, but...
I QUIT!
Why you quit, Mari-san?
That man ~sob~ just grabbed my breast, and ~sob!~
Oh, Dr. Wong? He only Chinese! I kick him out if you want?
No, I just can't...
WAAAH!

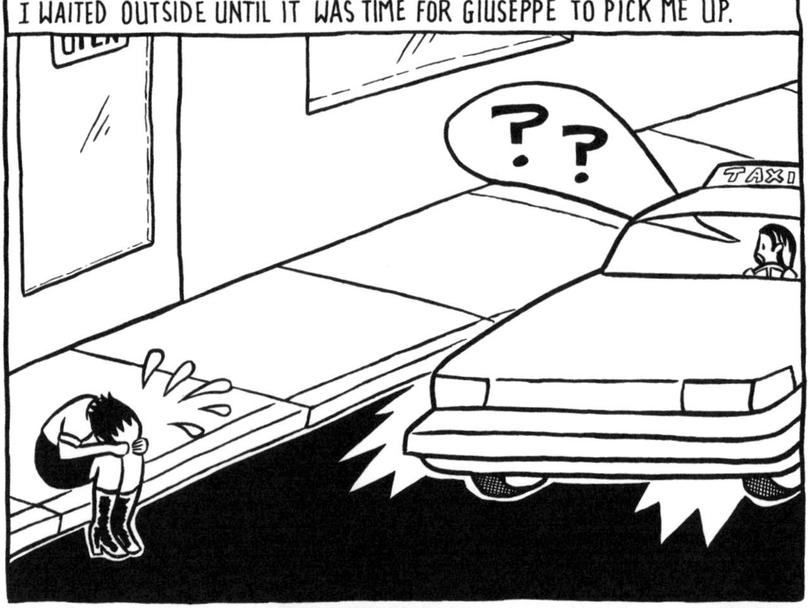
I WAITED OUTSIDE UNTIL IT WAS TIME FOR GIUSEPPE TO PICK ME UP.
??
TAXI

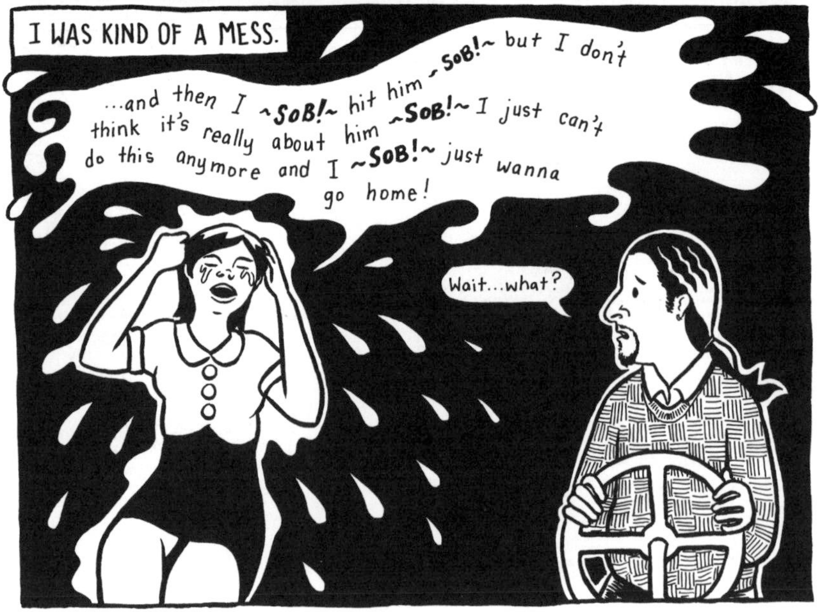
I WAS KIND OF A MESS.
...and then I ~SOB!~ hit him ~SOB!~ but I don't think it's really about him ~SOB!~ I just can't do this anymore and I ~SOB!~ just wanna go home!
Wait...what?

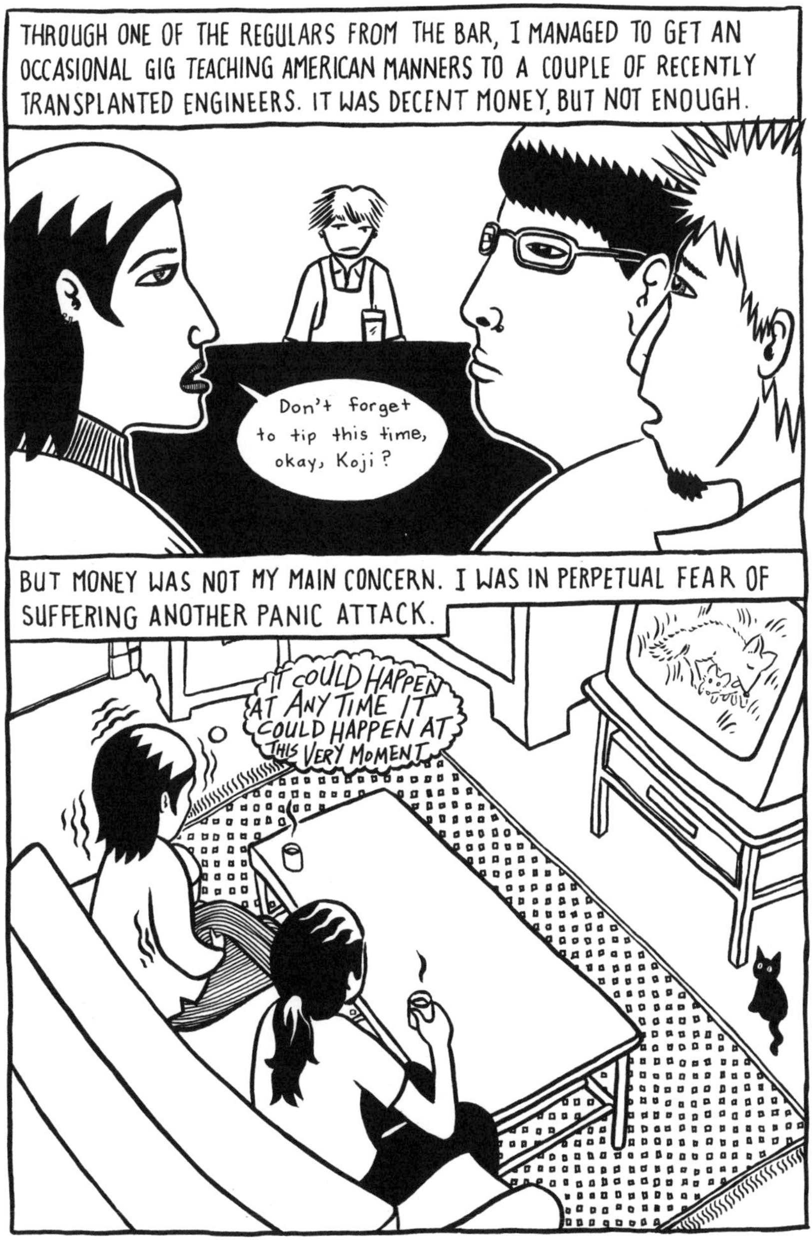
THROUGH ONE OF THE REGULARS FROM THE BAR, I MANAGED TO GET AN OCCASIONAL GIG TEACHING AMERICAN MANNERS TO A COUPLE OF RECENTLY TRANSPLANTED ENGINEERS. IT WAS DECENT MONEY, BUT NOT ENOUGH.
Don't forget to tip this time, okay, Koji?
BUT MONEY WAS NOT MY MAIN CONCERN. I WAS IN PERPETUAL FEAR OF SUFFERING ANOTHER PANIC ATTACK.
IT COULD HAPPEN AT ANY TIME IT COULD HAPPEN AT THIS VERY MOMENT

I KEPT IN TOUCH WITH RYOKO.

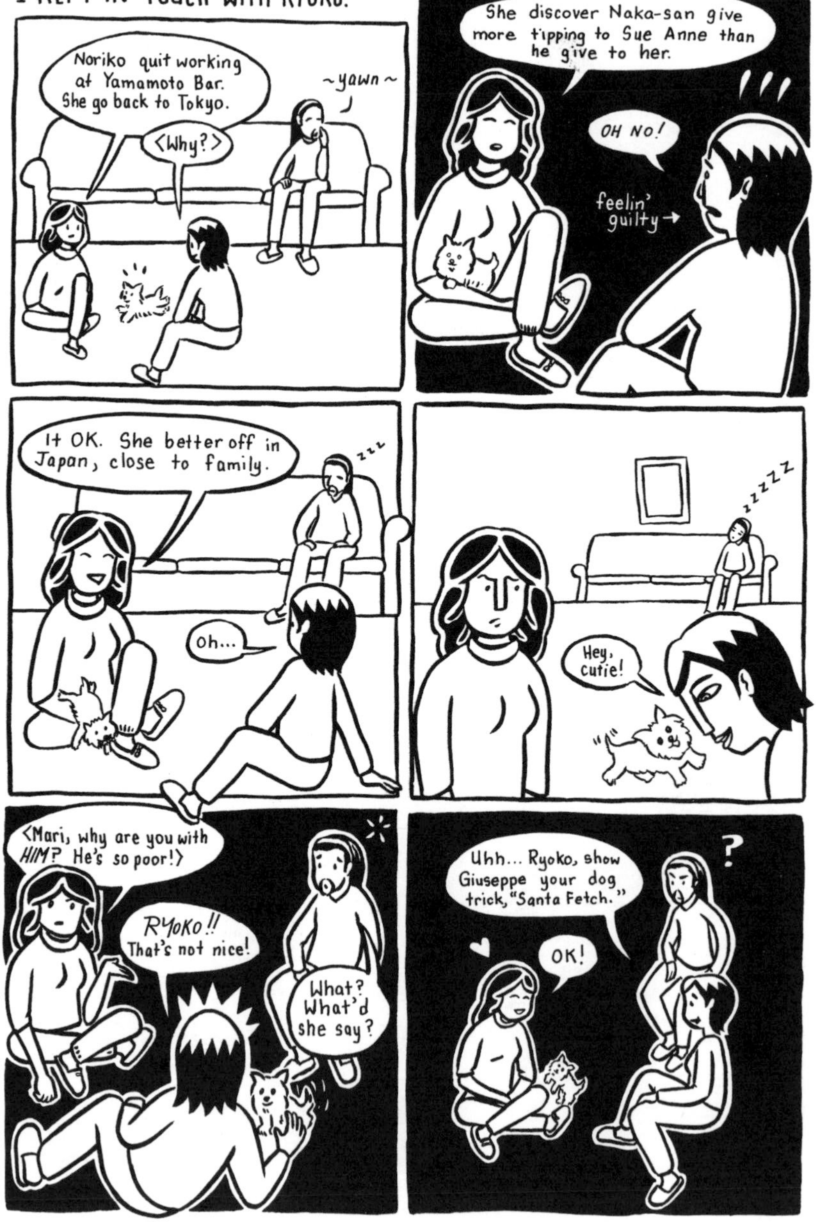
Noriko quit working at Yamamoto Bar. She go back to Tokyo.
~yawn~
<Why?>
She discover Naka-san give more tipping to Sue Anne than he give to her.
OH NO!
feelin' guilty →
It OK. She better off in Japan, close to family.
zzz
Oh...
zzzzz
Hey, cutie!
<Mari, why are you with HIM? He's so poor!>
RYOKO!! That's not nice!
What? What'd she say?
Uhh... Ryoko, show Giuseppe your dog trick, "Santa Fetch."
?
OK!

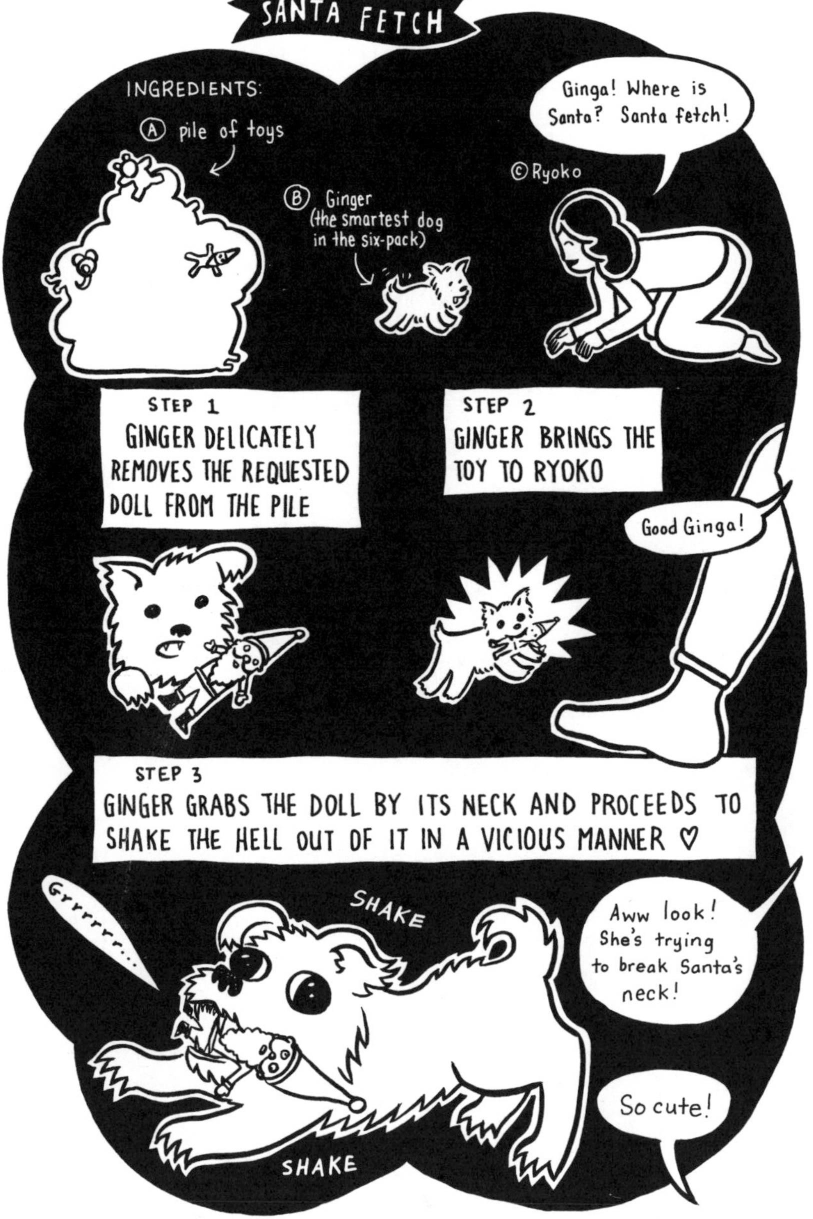
SANTA FETCH
INGREDIENTS:
Ⓐ pile of toys
Ⓑ Ginger (the smartest dog in the six-pack)
Ginga! Where is Santa? Santa fetch!
©Ryoko
STEP 1
GINGER DELICATELY REMOVES THE REQUESTED DOLL FROM THE PILE
STEP 2
GINGER BRINGS THE TOY TO RYOKO
Good Ginga!
STEP 3
GINGER GRABS THE DOLL BY ITS NECK AND PROCEEDS TO SHAKE THE HELL OUT OF IT IN A VICIOUS MANNER ♡
Grrrrrr...
SHAKE
Aww look! She's trying to break Santa's neck!
So cute!
SHAKE

I CONTINUED TO RIDE ALONG WITH GIUSEPPE IN THE CAB, BUT WHAT BEGAN AS A NOVEL, EXCITING ADVENTURE TURNED INTO A DARK AND UNSETTLING CHORE. MOST OF HIS FARES WERE SAD SACKS SHUTTLING TO AND FROM THE VENUES OF THEIR DEMISE.

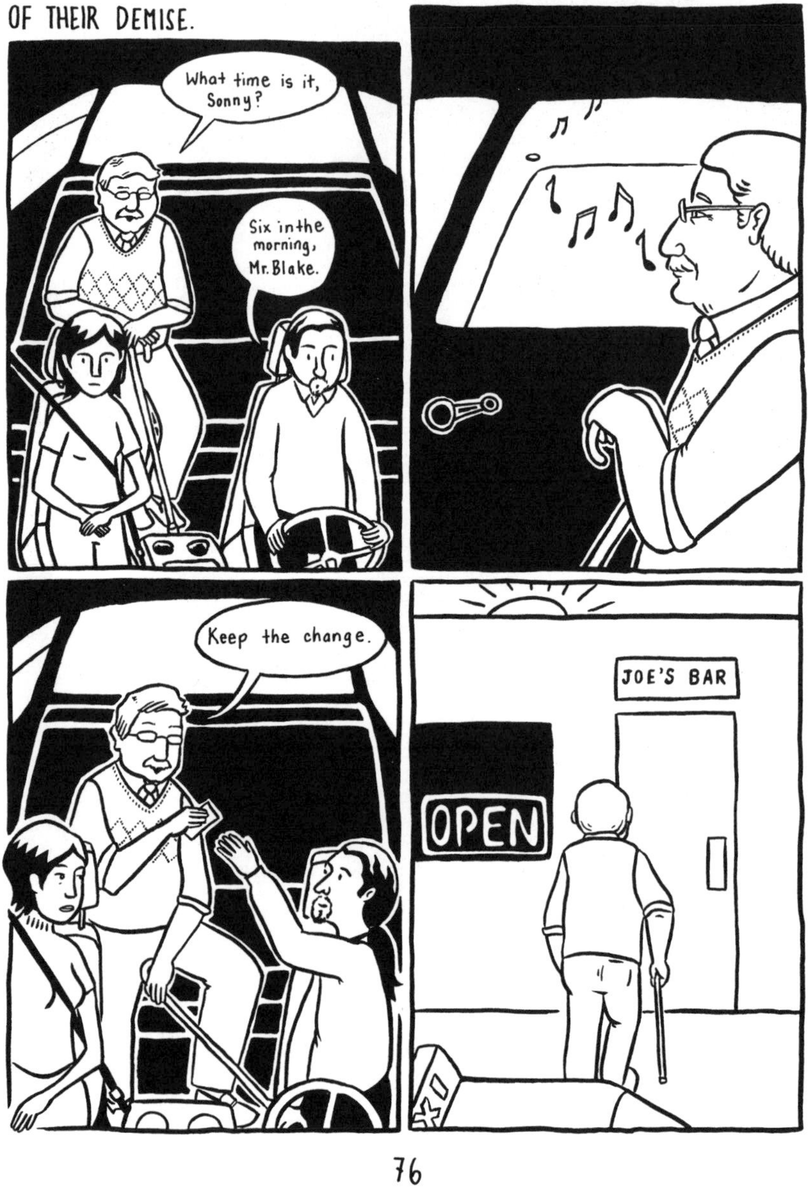
What time is it, Sonny?
Six in the morning, Mr. Blake.
Keep the change.
JOE'S BAR
OPEN

ONE EVENING, THIS HAPPENED.

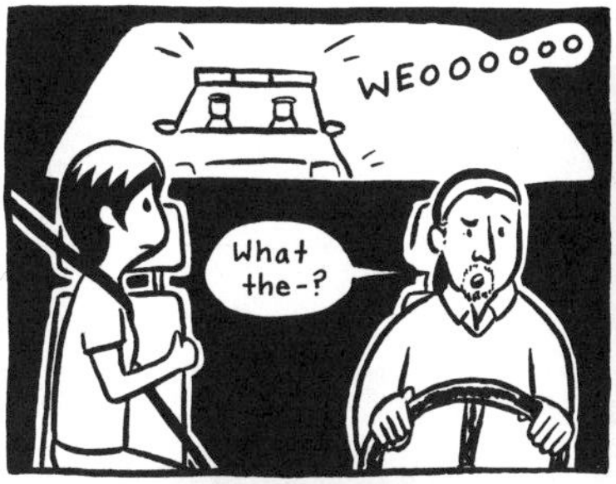
WEOOOOOO
What the-?

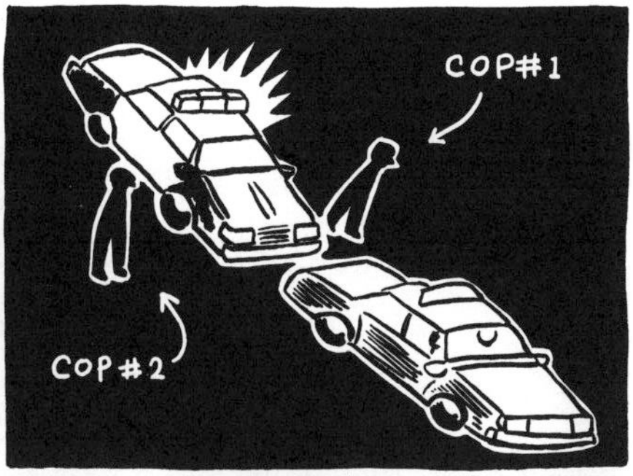
COP#1
COP#2

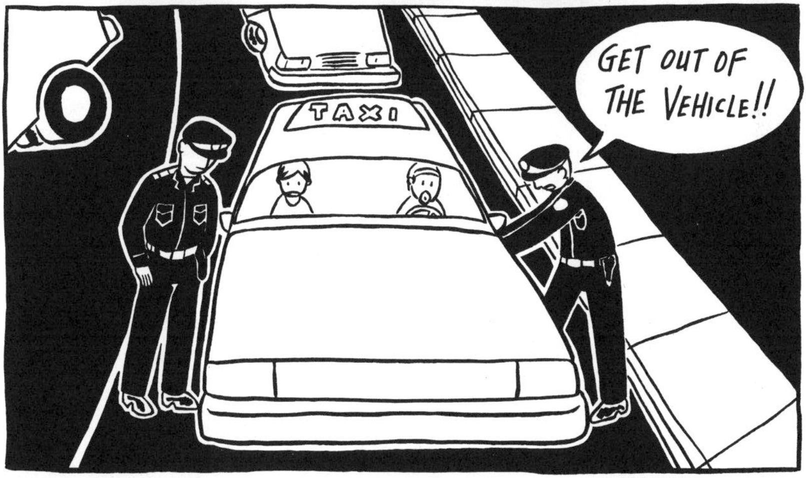
TAXI
GET OUT OF THE VEHICLE!!

COP#1 PINNED GIUSEPPE AGAINST THE CAB.

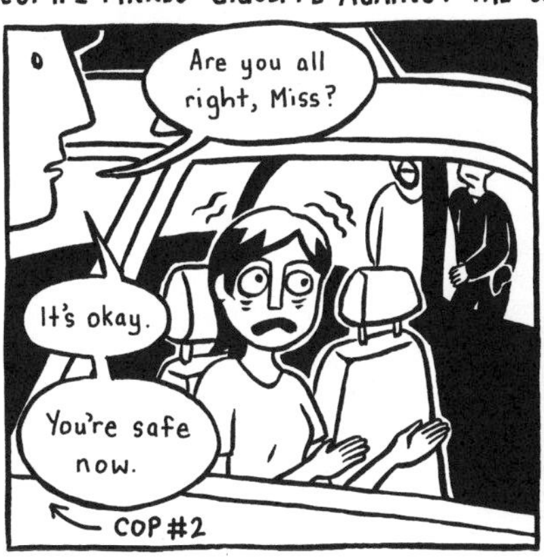
Are you all right, Miss?
It's okay.
You're safe now.
COP#2

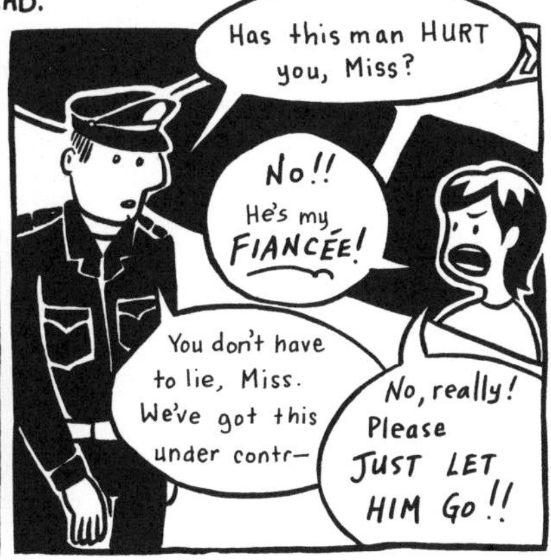
Has this man HURT you, Miss?
No!! He's my FIANCÉE!
You don't have to lie, Miss. We've got this under contr—
No, really! Please JUST LET HIM GO!!

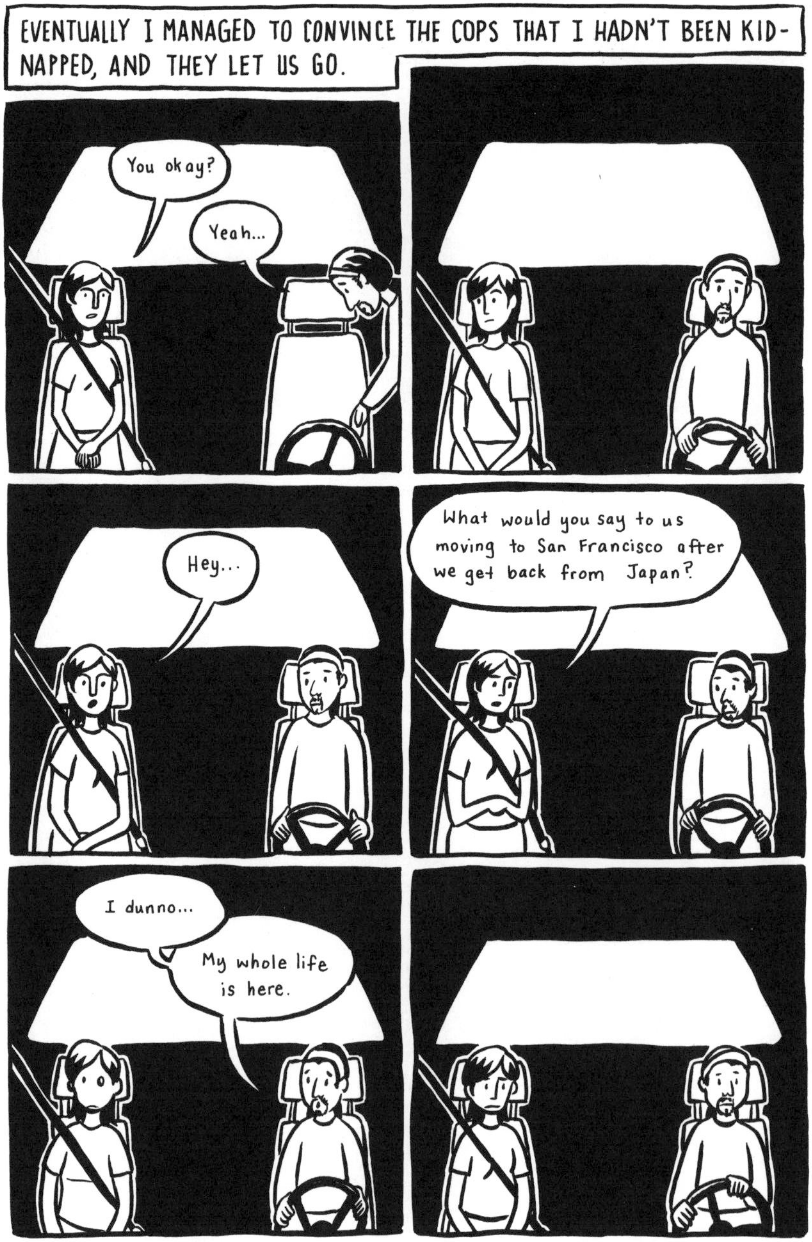
EVENTUALLY I MANAGED TO CONVINCE THE COPS THAT I HADN'T BEEN KIDNAPPED, AND THEY LET US GO.
You okay?
Yeah...
Hey...
What would you say to us moving to San Francisco after we get back from Japan?
I dunno...
My whole life is here.

I STARTED HAVING MORE PANIC ATTACKS, AND THEY FELT DIRECTLY RELATED TO MY NOTORIOUSLY DELICATE STOMACH. THIS WAS THE ROUTINE:

STEP ONE: EATING TIME APPROACHES

STEP TWO: THE FEAR

STEP THREE: FOOD ENTERS THE BODY

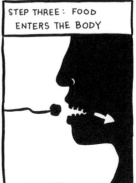

STEP FOUR: RANDOM MORBID THOUGHTS ENTER BRAIN

STEP FIVE: NAUSEA

Are you okay?

STEP SIX: BLINDING STOMACH PAIN

RESULT: FULL-BLOWN PANIC ATTACK

Over time, the results of this process came earlier and earlier in the routine until the attack was almost nonstop.

I STARTED QUESTIONING MY MENTAL HEALTH.

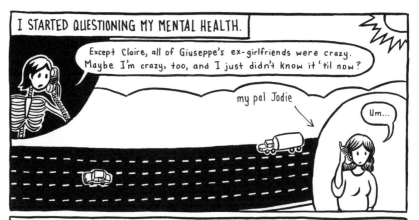

Except Claire, all of Giuseppe's ex-girlfriends were crazy. Maybe I'm crazy, too, and I just didn't know it 'til now?

my pal Jodie

Um...

I STOPPED RIDING ALONG IN THE CAB AND SPENT MY TIME AT HOME, SCARED.

Hey, I got you some take-out.

HASN'T EATEN ALL DAY

I'm not hungry.

Well, I've got to get back to wo—

SOB!

GOD, WHAT IS WRONG WITH MY STOMACH?!!

THE PAIN GOT SO BAD THAT I ENDED UP AT THE ER. BUT THERE WAS A PROBLEM.

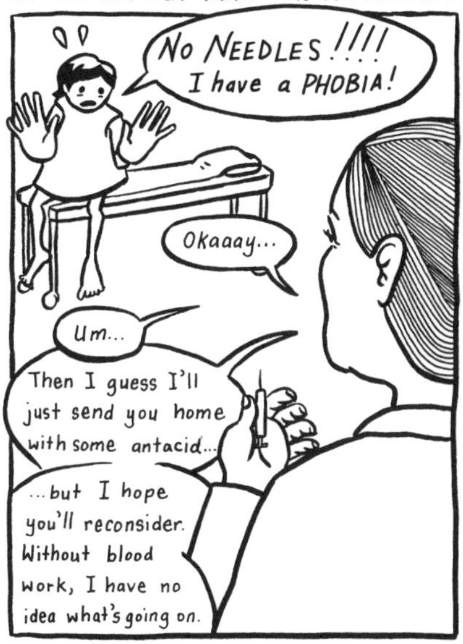
No NEEDLES!!!! I have a PHOBIA!
Okaaay...
Um...
Then I guess I'll just send you home with some antacid...
...but I hope you'll reconsider. Without blood work, I have no idea what's going on.

I GOT SKINNY FROM NOT EATING.

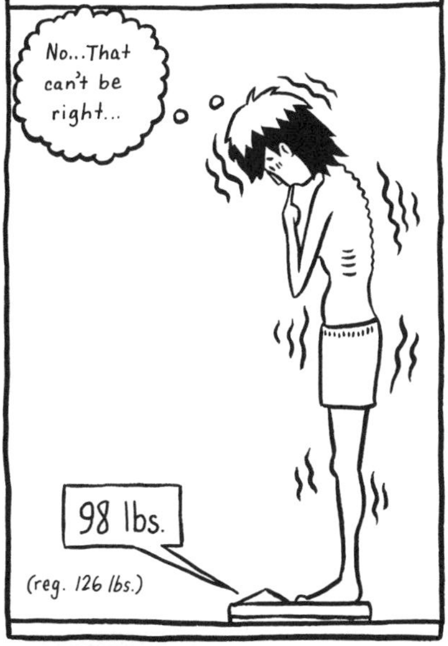
No...That can't be right...
98 lbs.
(reg. 126 lbs.)

I BECAME EXTREMELY ENVIOUS OF RANDOM HAPPY-LOOKING STRANGERS.

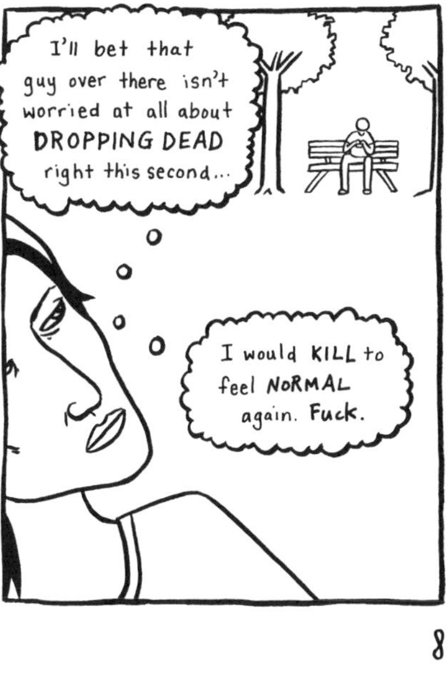
I'll bet that guy over there isn't worried at all about DROPPING DEAD right this second...
I would KILL to feel NORMAL again. Fuck.

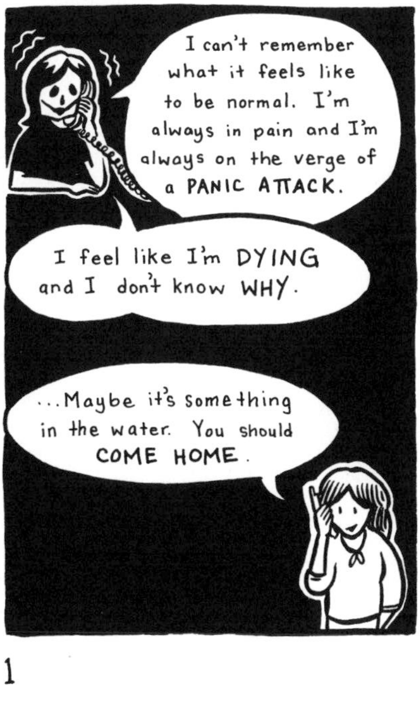
I can't remember what it feels like to be normal. I'm always in pain and I'm always on the verge of a PANIC ATTACK.
I feel like I'm DYING and I don't know WHY.
...Maybe it's something in the water. You should COME HOME.

WHEN MY MOM WAS SWORN IN AS A U.S. CITIZEN, GIUSEPPE AND I DROVE TO SAN FRANCISCO TO ATTEND THE CEREMONY AT THE TOP OF NOB HILL.

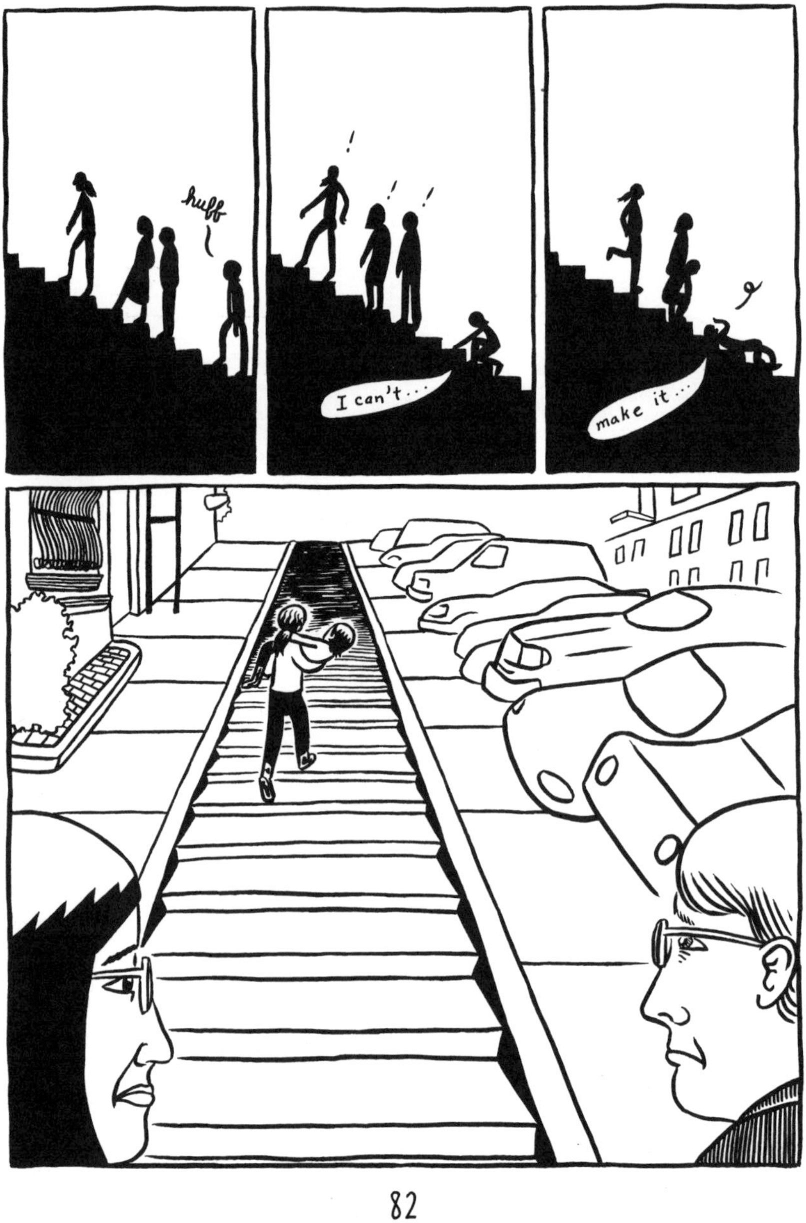
huff
!
! !
I can't...
make it...

I ONLY ATE "SAFE" FOOD, AND I RARELY LEFT THE HOUSE.

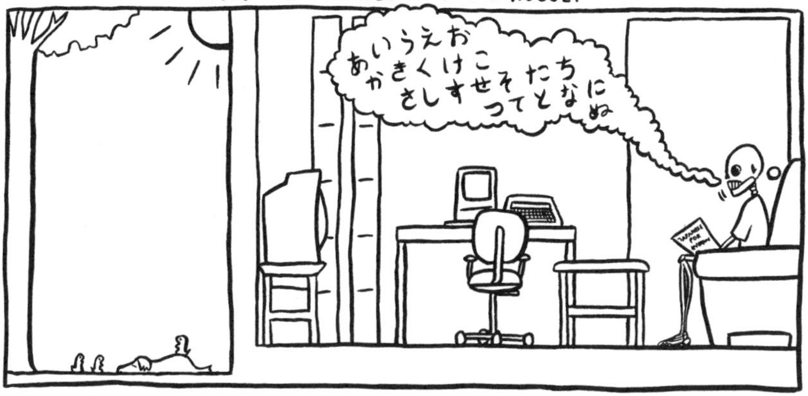
あいうえお かきくけこ さしすせそ たち つてとなに ぬ

AS OUR JAPAN TRIP NEARED, I SLOWLY RECUPERATED TO A SEMBLANCE OF PHYSICAL NORMALCY, THOUGH MY EMOTIONAL SCARS TOOK YEARS TO FADE.

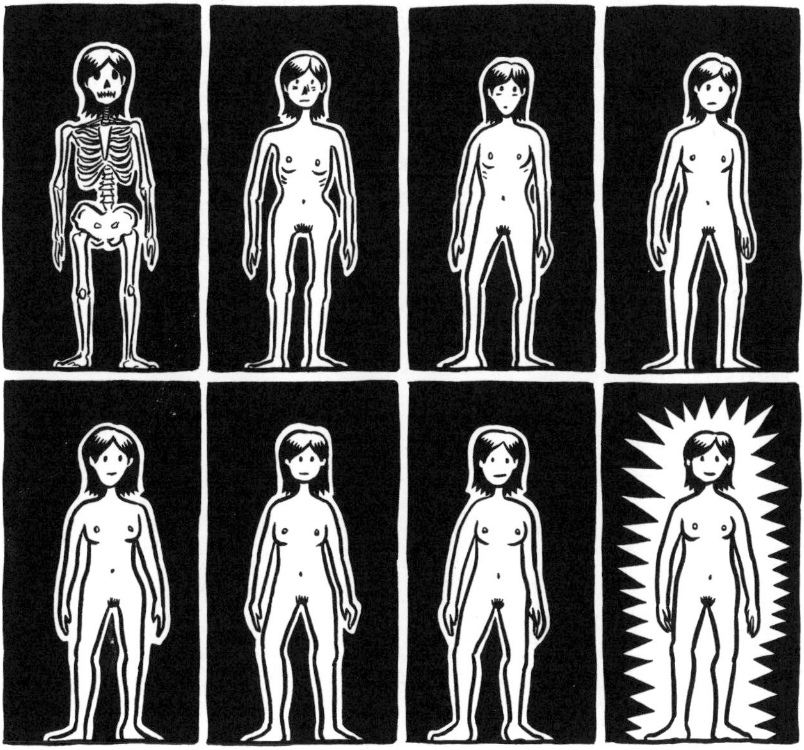

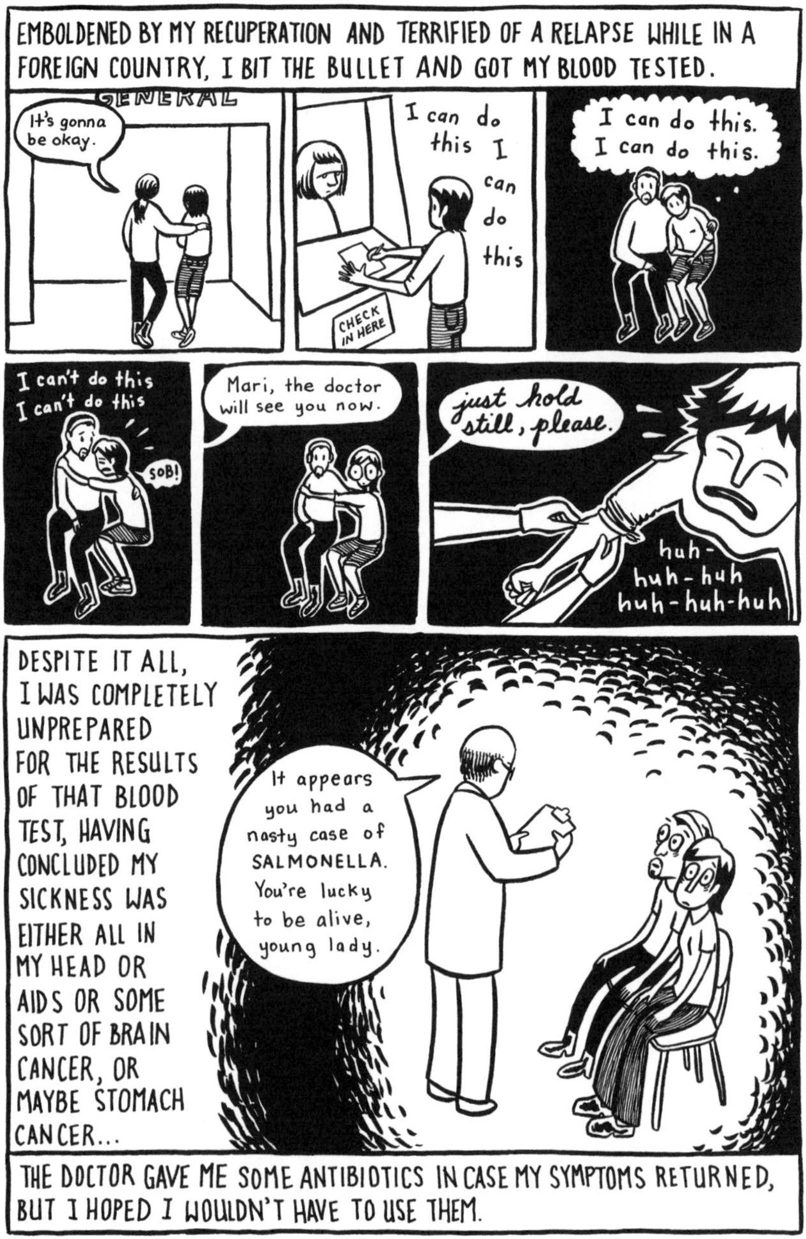
EMBOLDENED BY MY RECUPERATION AND TERRIFIED OF A RELAPSE WHILE IN A FOREIGN COUNTRY, I BIT THE BULLET AND GOT MY BLOOD TESTED.
GENERAL
It's gonna be okay.
I can do this I can do this
CHECK IN HERE
I can do this. I can do this.
I can't do this I can't do this
SOB!
Mari, the doctor will see you now.
just hold still, please.
huh-huh-huh huh-huh-huh
DESPITE IT ALL, I WAS COMPLETELY UNPREPARED FOR THE RESULTS OF THAT BLOOD TEST, HAVING CONCLUDED MY SICKNESS WAS EITHER ALL IN MY HEAD OR AIDS OR SOME SORT OF BRAIN CANCER, OR MAYBE STOMACH CANCER...
It appears you had a nasty case of SALMONELLA. You're lucky to be alive, young lady.
THE DOCTOR GAVE ME SOME ANTIBIOTICS IN CASE MY SYMPTOMS RETURNED, BUT I HOPED I WOULDN'T HAVE TO USE THEM.

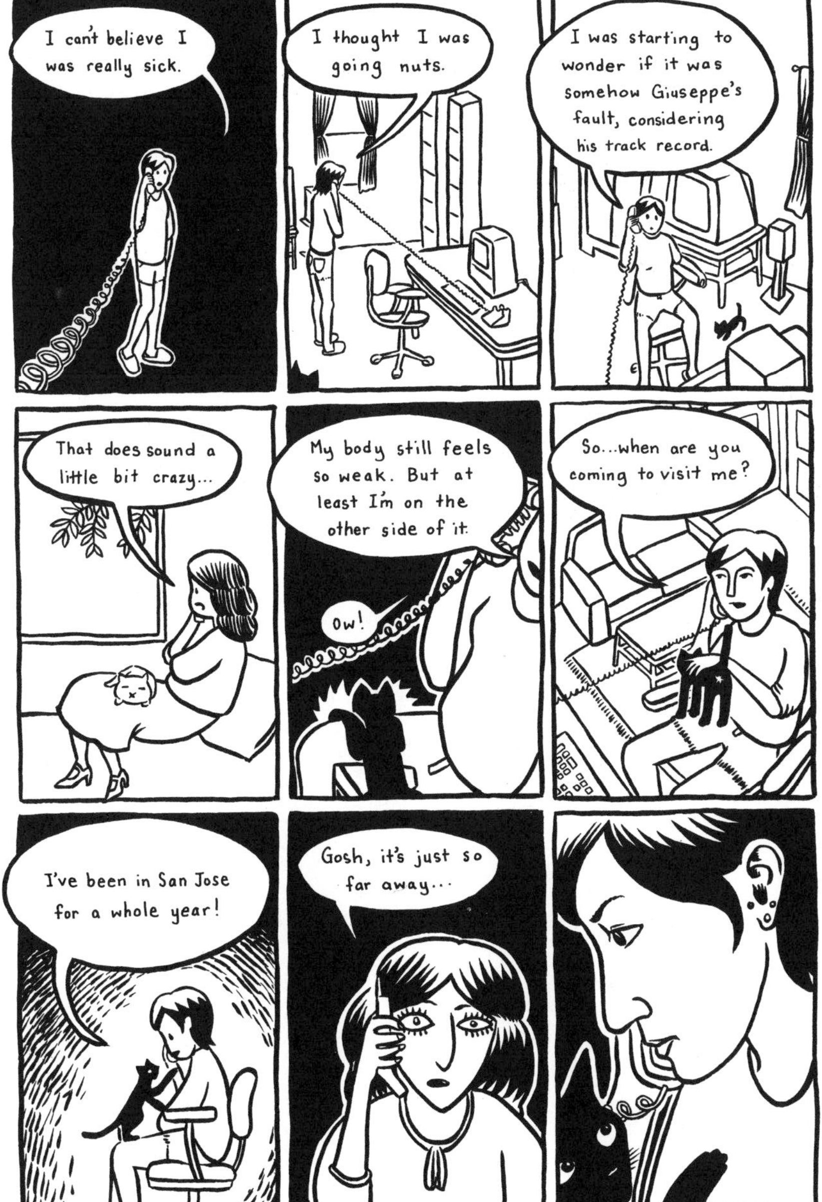
I can't believe I was really sick.
I thought I was going nuts.
I was starting to wonder if it was somehow Giuseppe's fault, considering his track record.
That does sound a little bit crazy...
My body still feels so weak. But at least I'm on the other side of it.
Ow!
So...when are you coming to visit me?
I've been in San Jose for a whole year!
Gosh, it's just so far away...

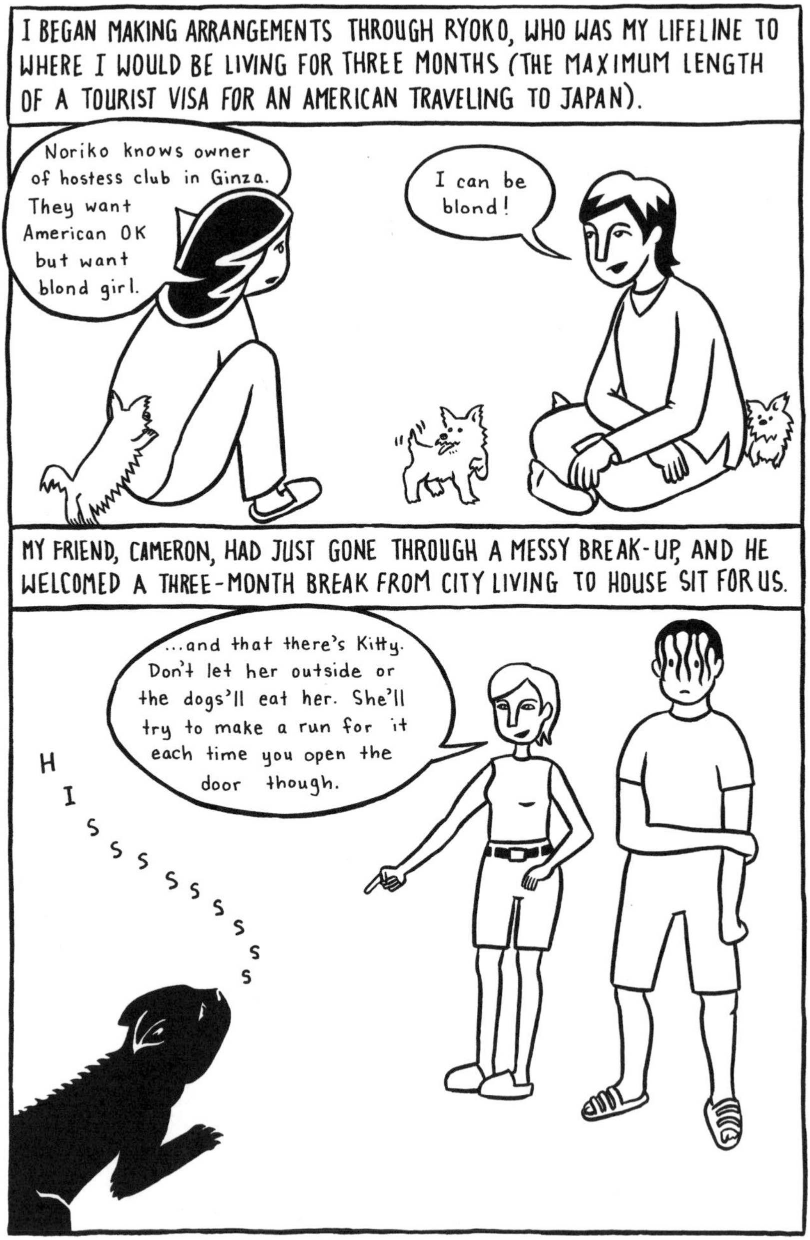
I BEGAN MAKING ARRANGEMENTS THROUGH RYOKO, WHO WAS MY LIFELINE TO WHERE I WOULD BE LIVING FOR THREE MONTHS (THE MAXIMUM LENGTH OF A TOURIST VISA FOR AN AMERICAN TRAVELING TO JAPAN).
Noriko knows owner of hostess club in Ginza. They want American OK but want blond girl.
I can be blond!
MY FRIEND, CAMERON, HAD JUST GONE THROUGH A MESSY BREAK-UP, AND HE WELCOMED A THREE-MONTH BREAK FROM CITY LIVING TO HOUSE SIT FOR US.
...and that there's Kitty. Don't let her outside or the dogs'll eat her. She'll try to make a run for it each time you open the door though.
HISSSSSSSSSS

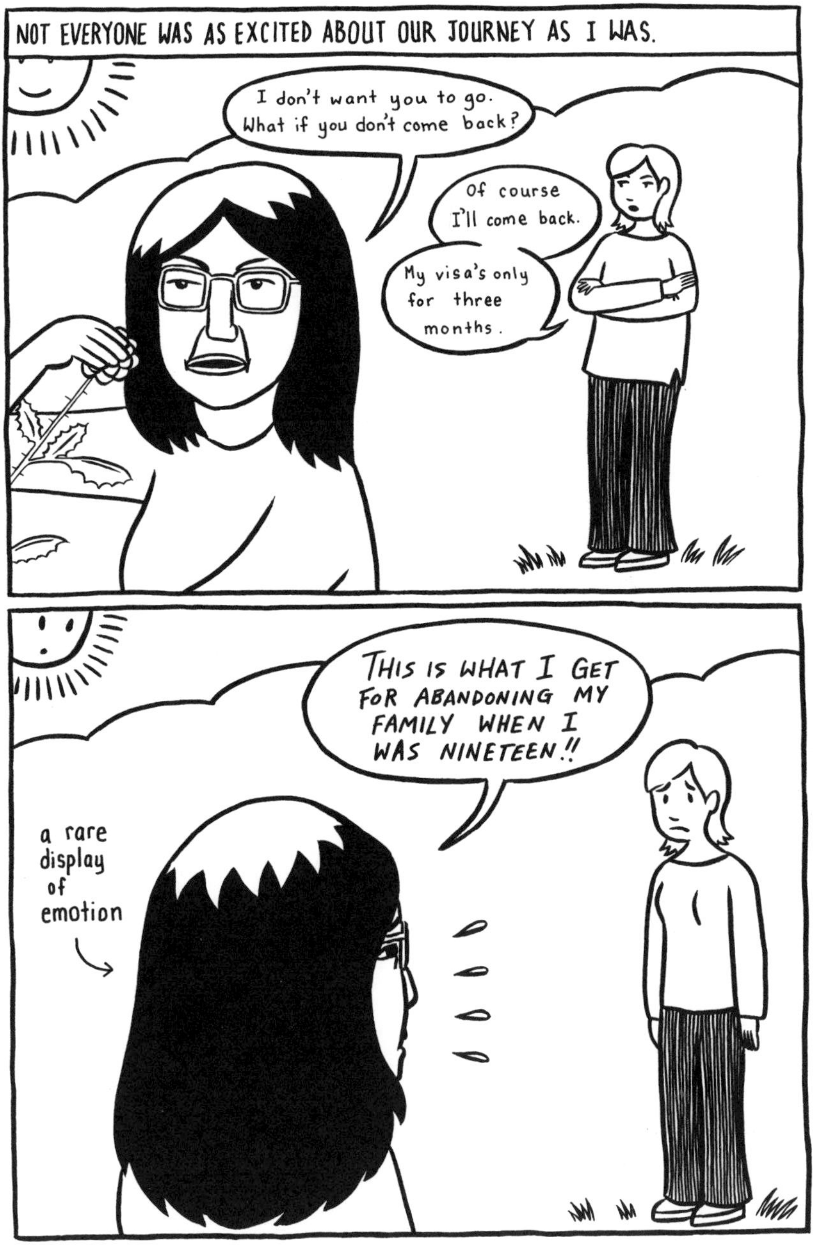
NOT EVERYONE WAS AS EXCITED ABOUT OUR JOURNEY AS I WAS.
I don't want you to go. What if you don't come back?
Of course I'll come back.
My visa's only for three months.
THIS IS WHAT I GET FOR ABANDONING MY FAMILY WHEN I WAS NINETEEN!!
a rare display of emotion

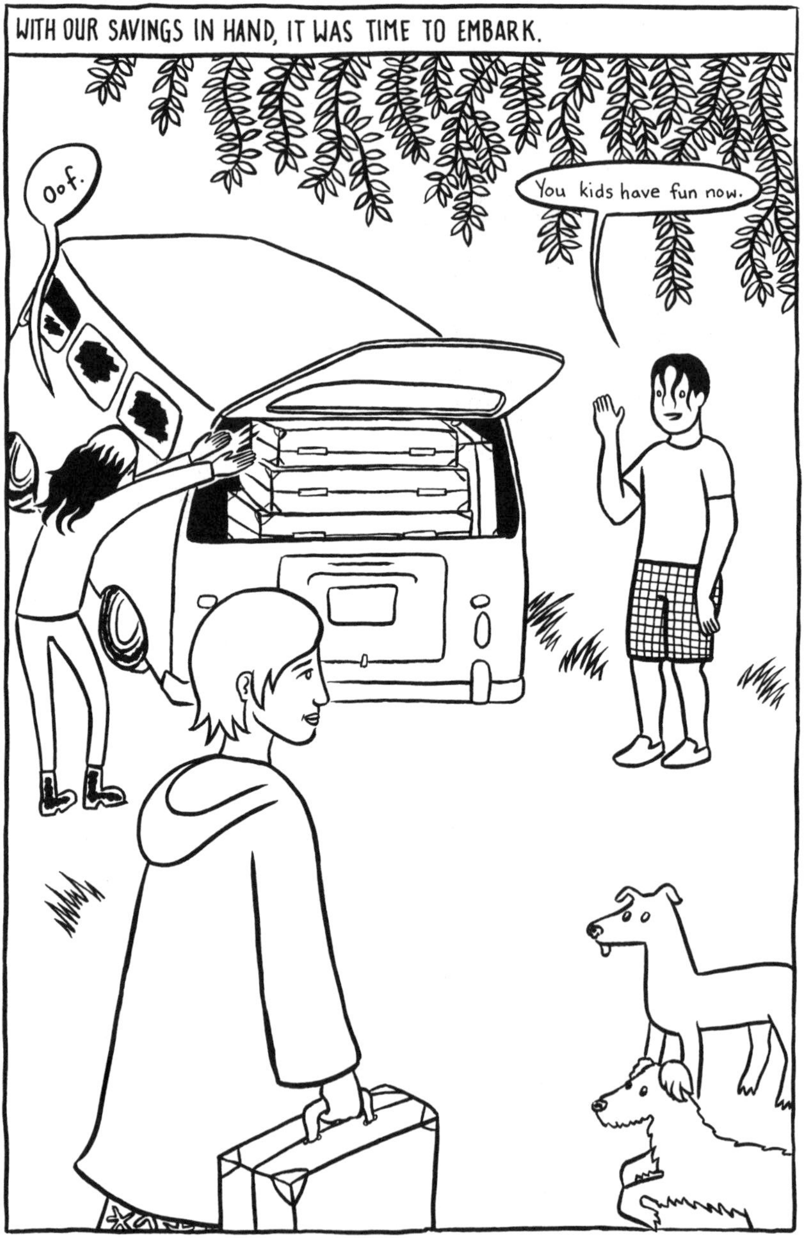
WITH OUR SAVINGS IN HAND, IT WAS TIME TO EMBARK.
Oof.
You kids have fun now.

INTERLUDE

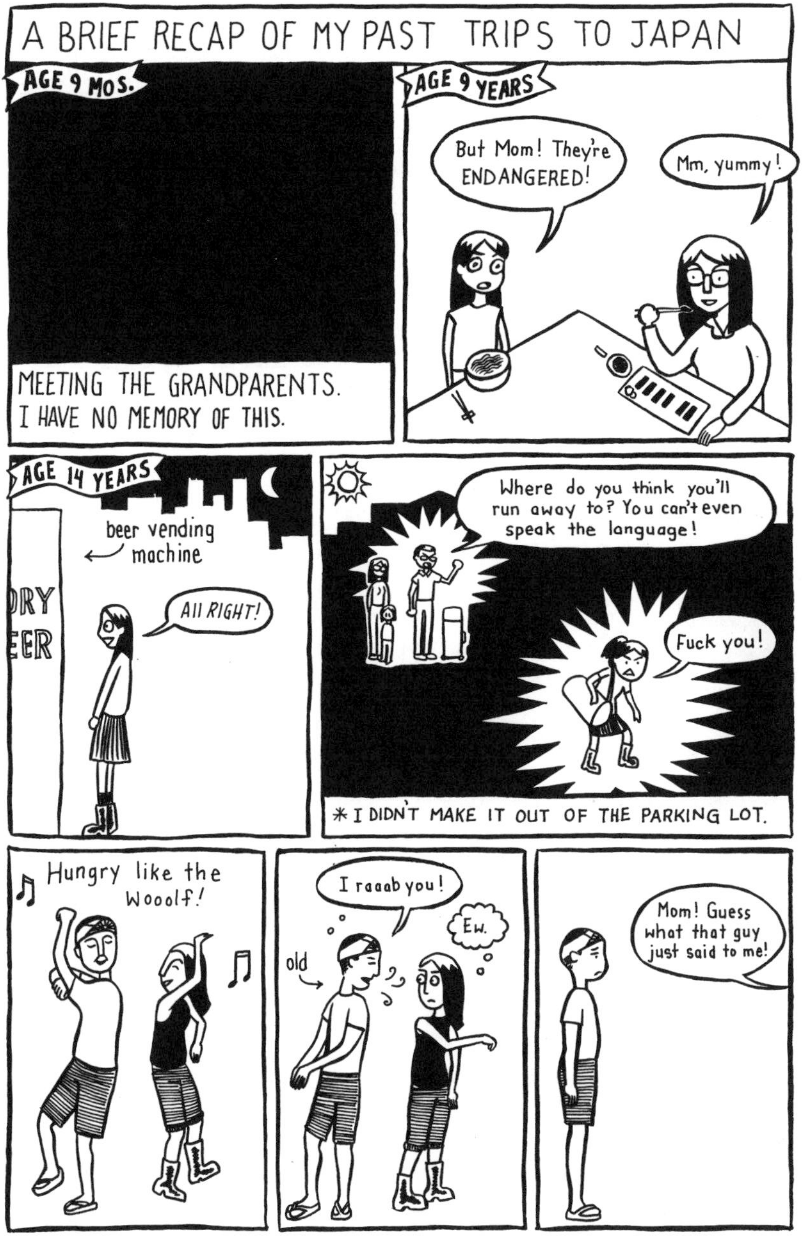
A BRIEF RECAP OF MY PAST TRIPS TO JAPAN
AGE 9 MOS.
MEETING THE GRANDPARENTS.
I HAVE NO MEMORY OF THIS.
AGE 9 YEARS
But Mom! They're ENDANGERED!
Mm, yummy!
AGE 14 YEARS
beer vending machine
ORY
EER
All RIGHT!
Where do you think you'll run away to? You can't even speak the language!
Fuck you!
* I DIDN'T MAKE IT OUT OF THE PARKING LOT.
Hungry like the Wooolf!
I raaab you!
Ew.
old
Mom! Guess what that guy just said to me!

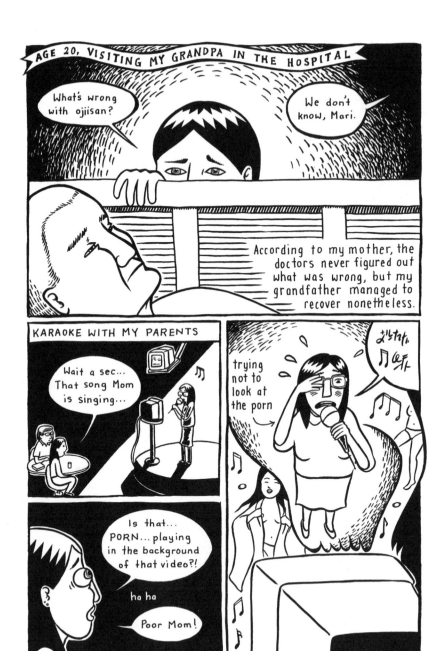

AGE 20, VISITING MY GRANDPA IN THE HOSPITAL

What's wrong with ojiisan?

We don't know, Mari.

According to my mother, the doctors never figured out what was wrong, but my grandfather managed to recover nonetheless.

KARAOKE WITH MY PARENTS

Wait a sec... That song Mom is singing...

trying not to look at the porn

Is that... PORN... playing in the background of that video?!

ha ha

Poor Mom!

92

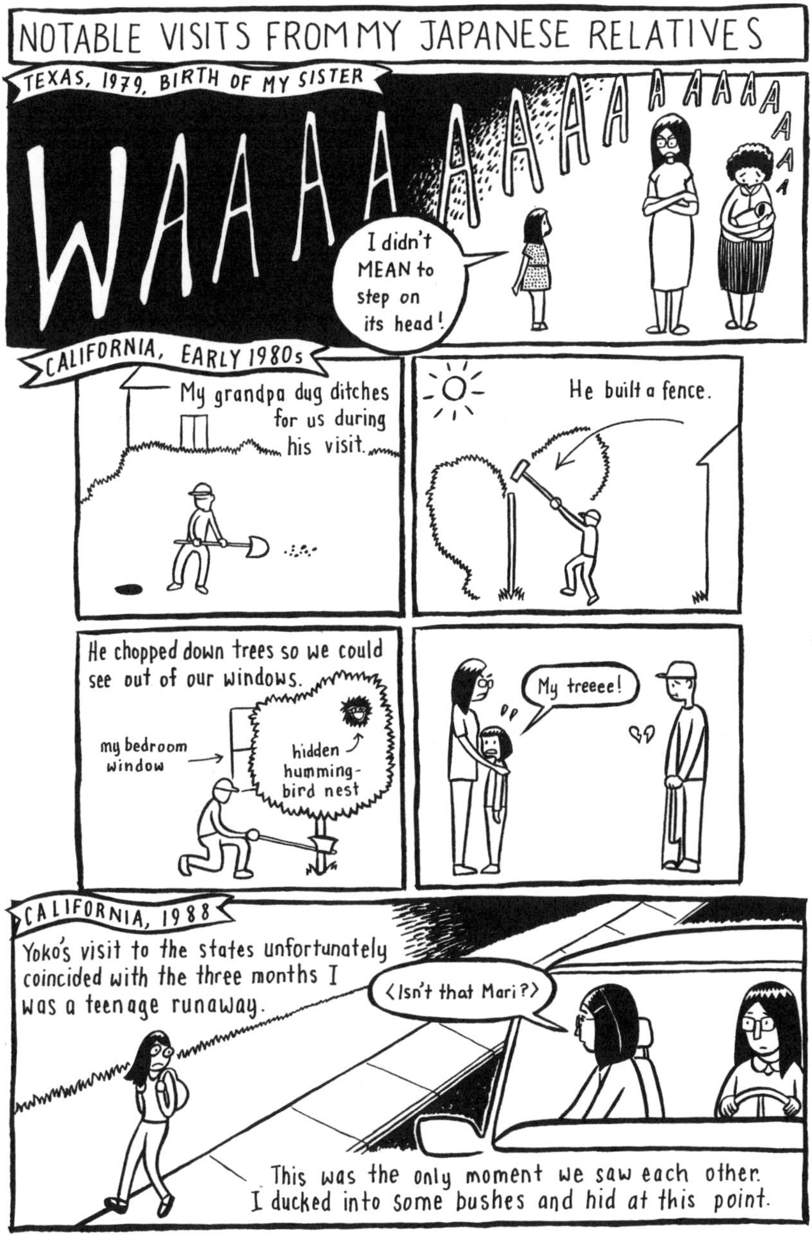
NOTABLE VISITS FROM MY JAPANESE RELATIVES
TEXAS, 1979, BIRTH OF MY SISTER
WAAAAAAAAAAAAAAAAA
I didn't MEAN to step on its head!
CALIFORNIA, EARLY 1980s
My grandpa dug ditches for us during his visit.
He built a fence.
He chopped down trees so we could see out of our windows.
my bedroom window
hidden humming-bird nest
My treeee!
CALIFORNIA, 1988
Yoko's visit to the states unfortunately coincided with the three months I was a teenage runaway.
<Isn't that Mari?>
This was the only moment we saw each other. I ducked into some bushes and hid at this point.

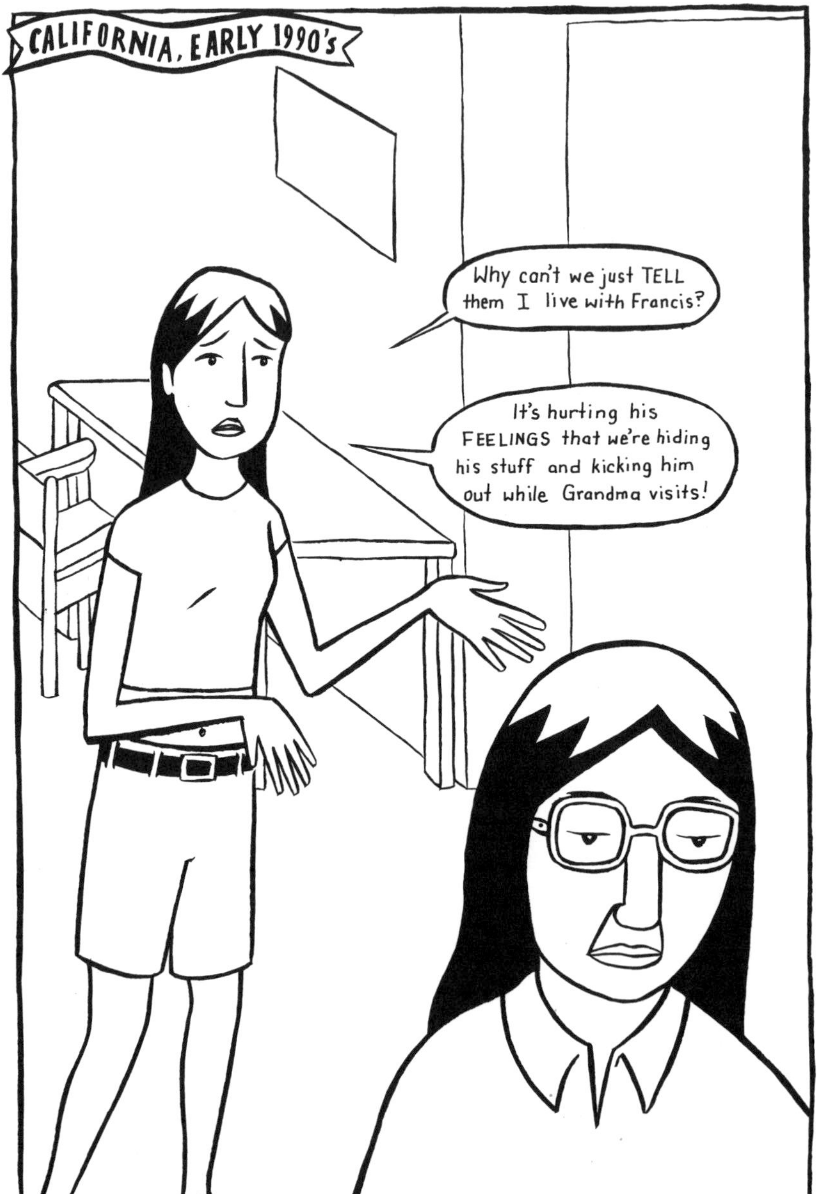
CALIFORNIA, EARLY 1990's
Why can't we just TELL them I live with Francis?
It's hurting his FEELINGS that we're hiding his stuff and kicking him out while Grandma visits!

BOOK TWO

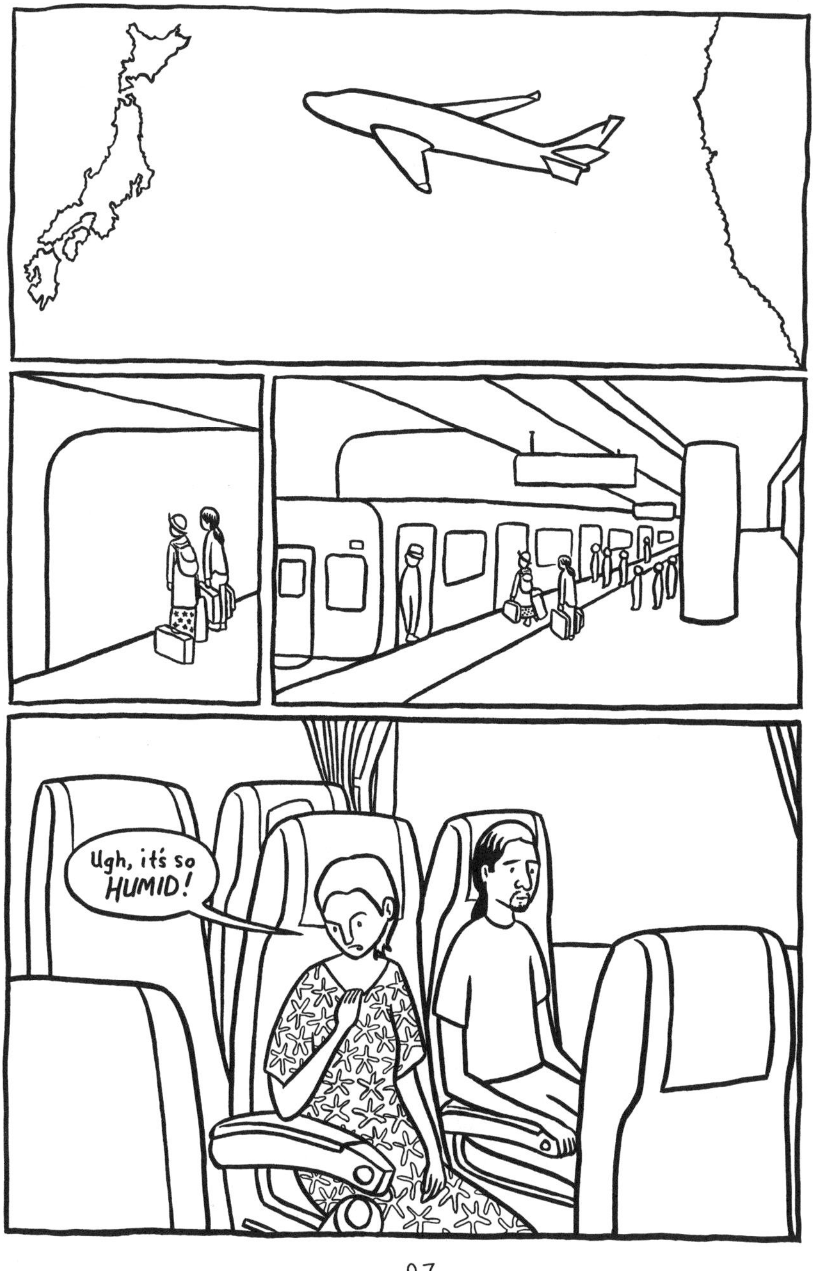
Ugh, it's so HUMID!

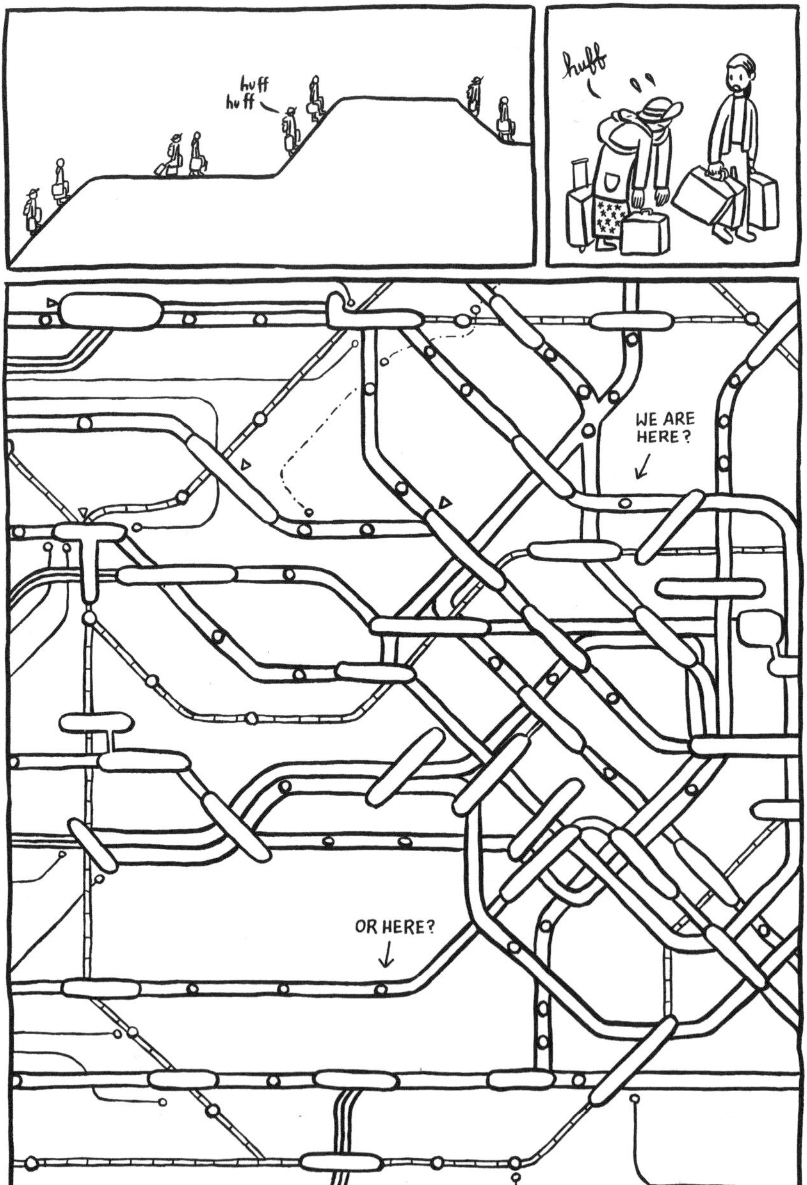
huff
huff
huff
WE ARE HERE?
OR HERE?

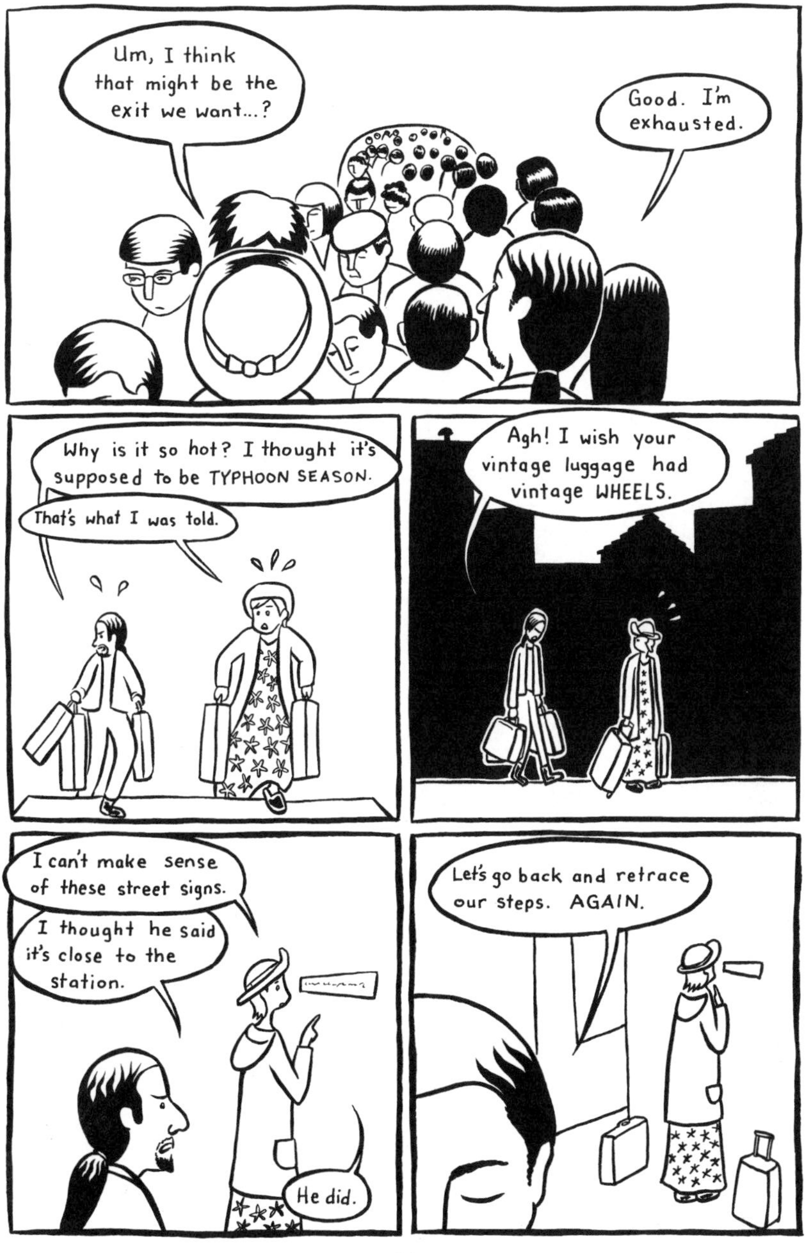
Um, I think that might be the exit we want...?
Good. I'm exhausted.
Why is it so hot? I thought it's supposed to be TYPHOON SEASON.
That's what I was told.
Agh! I wish your vintage luggage had vintage WHEELS.
I can't make sense of these street signs.
I thought he said it's close to the station.
He did.
Let's go back and retrace our steps. AGAIN.

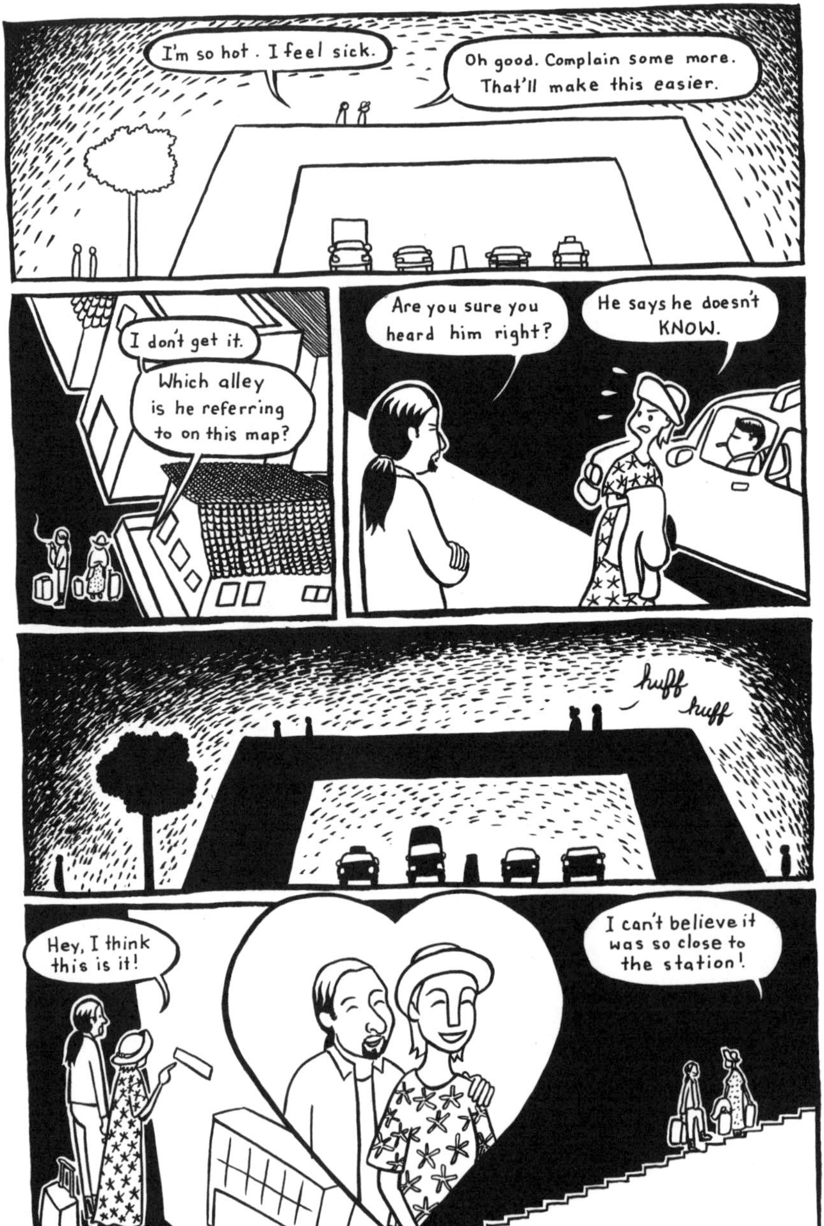
I'm so hot. I feel sick.
Oh good. Complain some more. That'll make this easier.
I don't get it.
Which alley is he referring to on this map?
Are you sure you heard him right?
He says he doesn't KNOW.
huff huff
Hey, I think this is it!
I can't believe it was so close to the station!

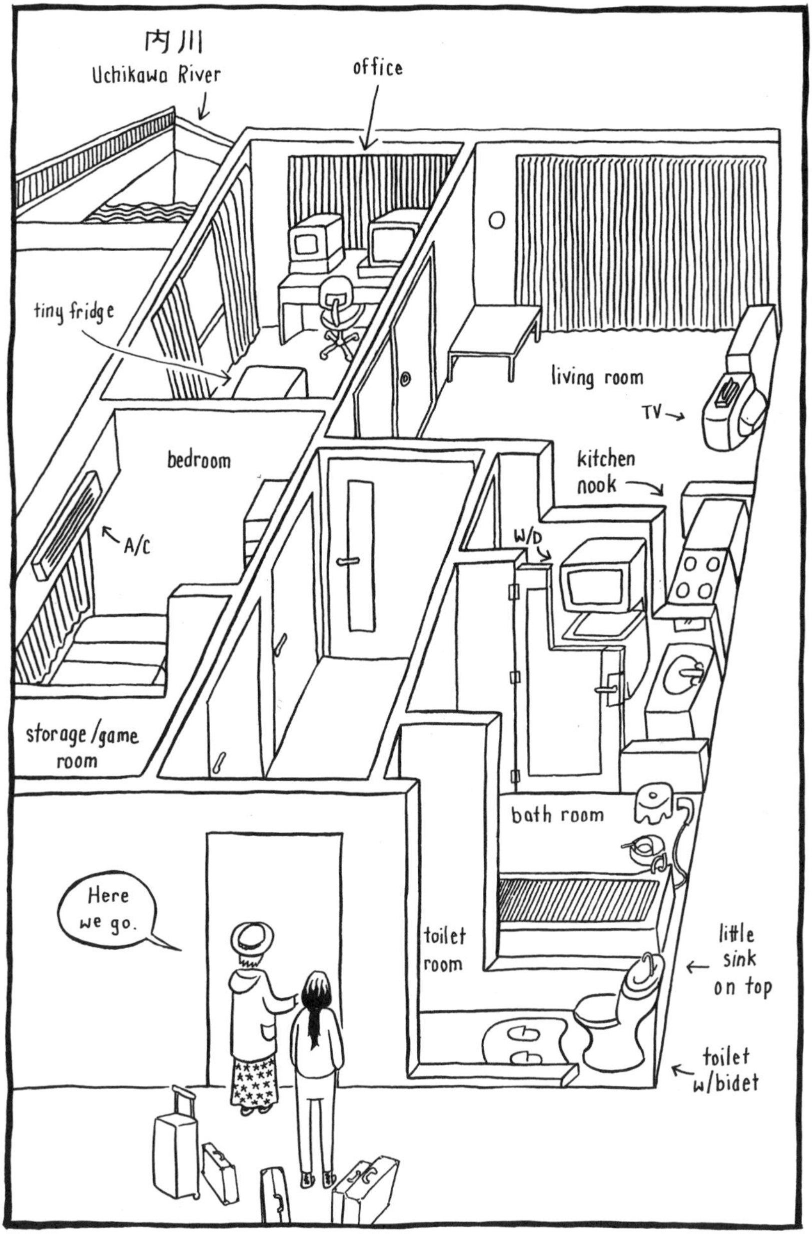
内川
Uchikawa River
office
tiny fridge
living room
TV
bedroom
kitchen nook
A/C
W/D
storage/game room
bath room
Here we go.
toilet room
little sink on top
toilet w/bidet

AFTER A LONG SLEEP, WE WOKE UP EXCITED AND READY FOR ADVENTURE. THERE WAS A LOT TO EXPLORE IN OUR LITTLE TOKYO SUBURB.

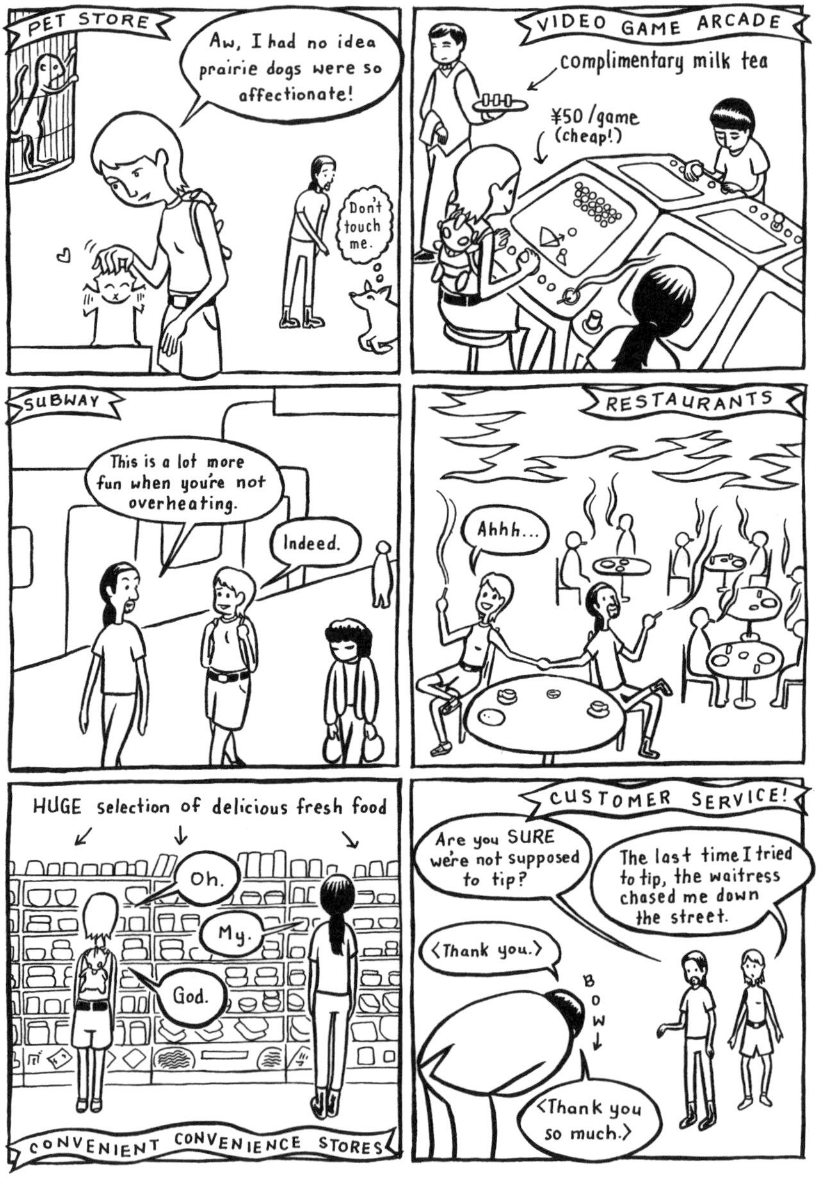

PET STORE
Aw, I had no idea prairie dogs were so affectionate!
Don't touch me.
VIDEO GAME ARCADE
complimentary milk tea
¥50 /game (cheap!)
SUBWAY
This is a lot more fun when you're not overheating.
Indeed.
RESTAURANTS
Ahhh...
HUGE selection of delicious fresh food
Oh.
My.
God.
CONVENIENT CONVENIENCE STORES
CUSTOMER SERVICE!
Are you SURE we're not supposed to tip?
The last time I tried to tip, the waitress chased me down the street.
⟨Thank you.⟩
BOW
⟨Thank you so much.⟩

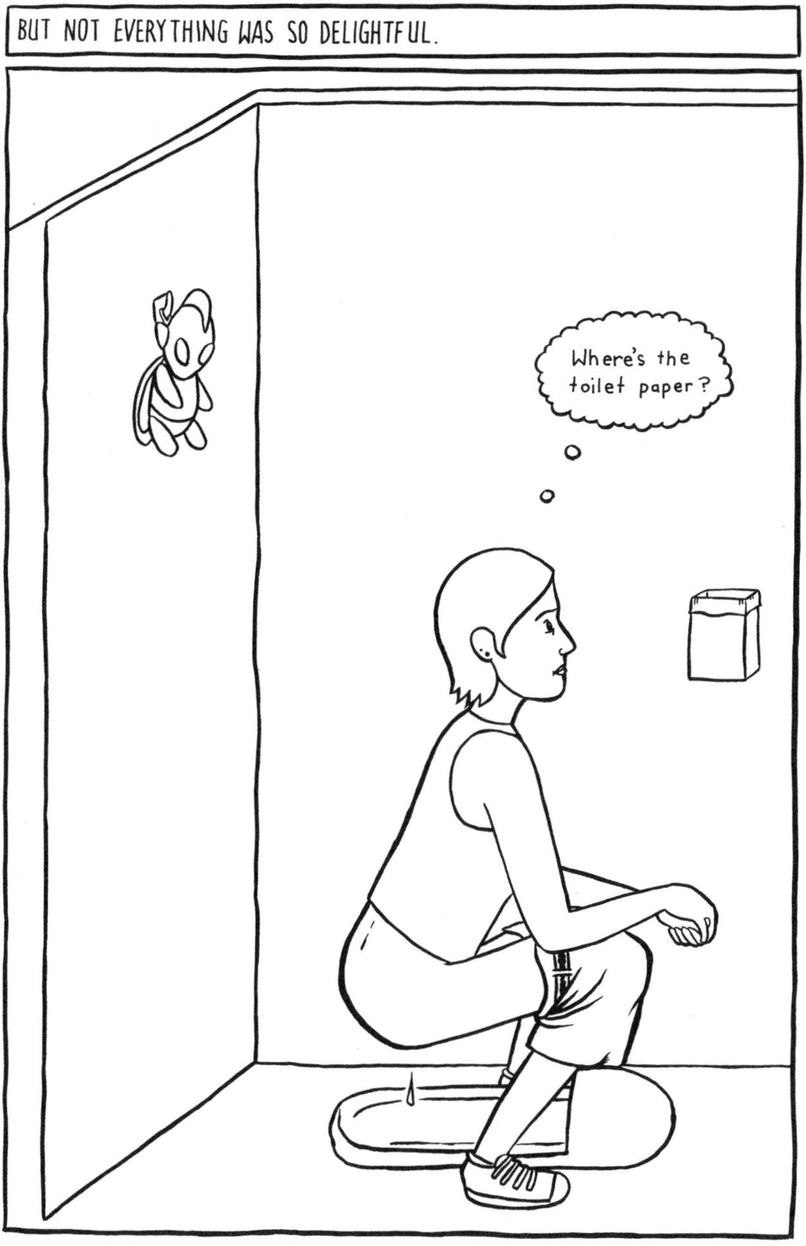
BUT NOT EVERYTHING WAS SO DELIGHTFUL.
Where's the toilet paper?

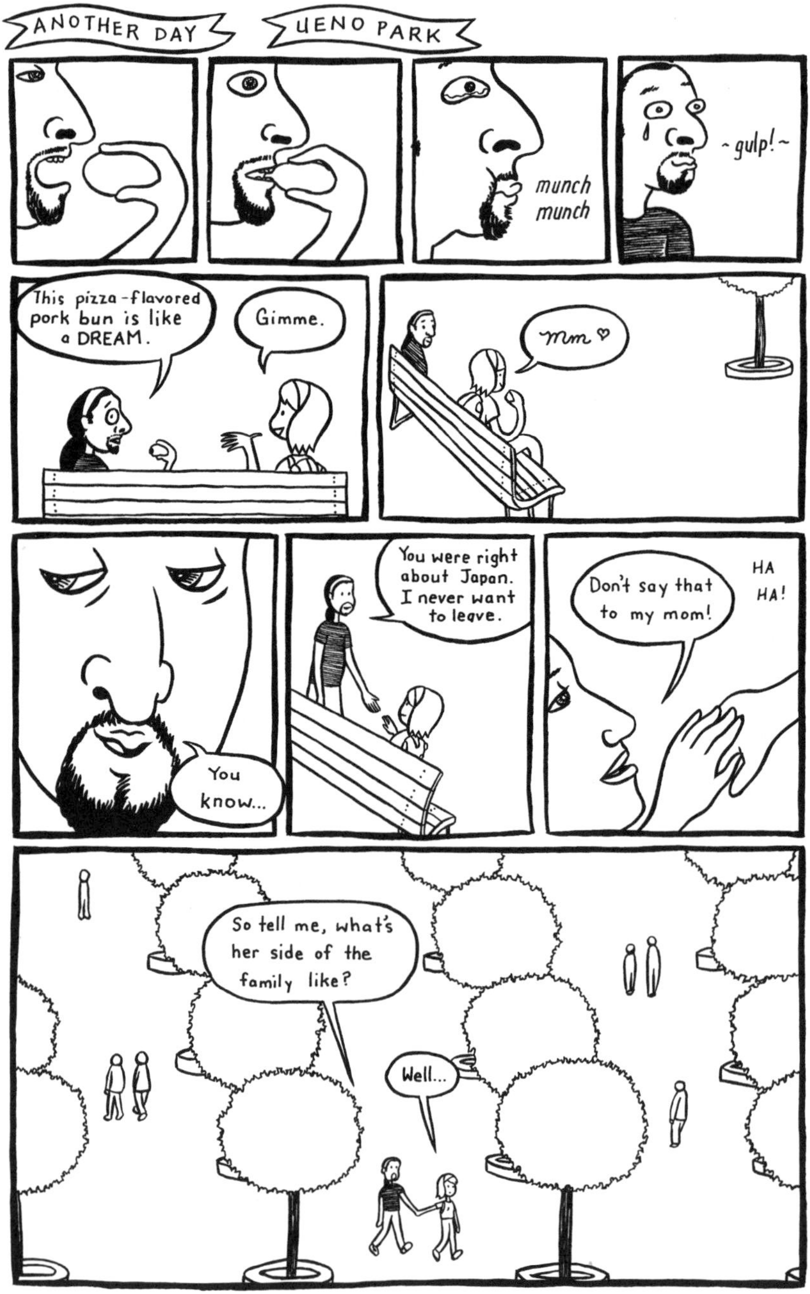
ANOTHER DAY
UENO PARK
munch munch
~gulp!~
This pizza-flavored pork bun is like a DREAM.
Gimme.
Mm ♡
You know...
You were right about Japan. I never want to leave.
Don't say that to my mom!
HA HA!
So tell me, what's her side of the family like?
Well...

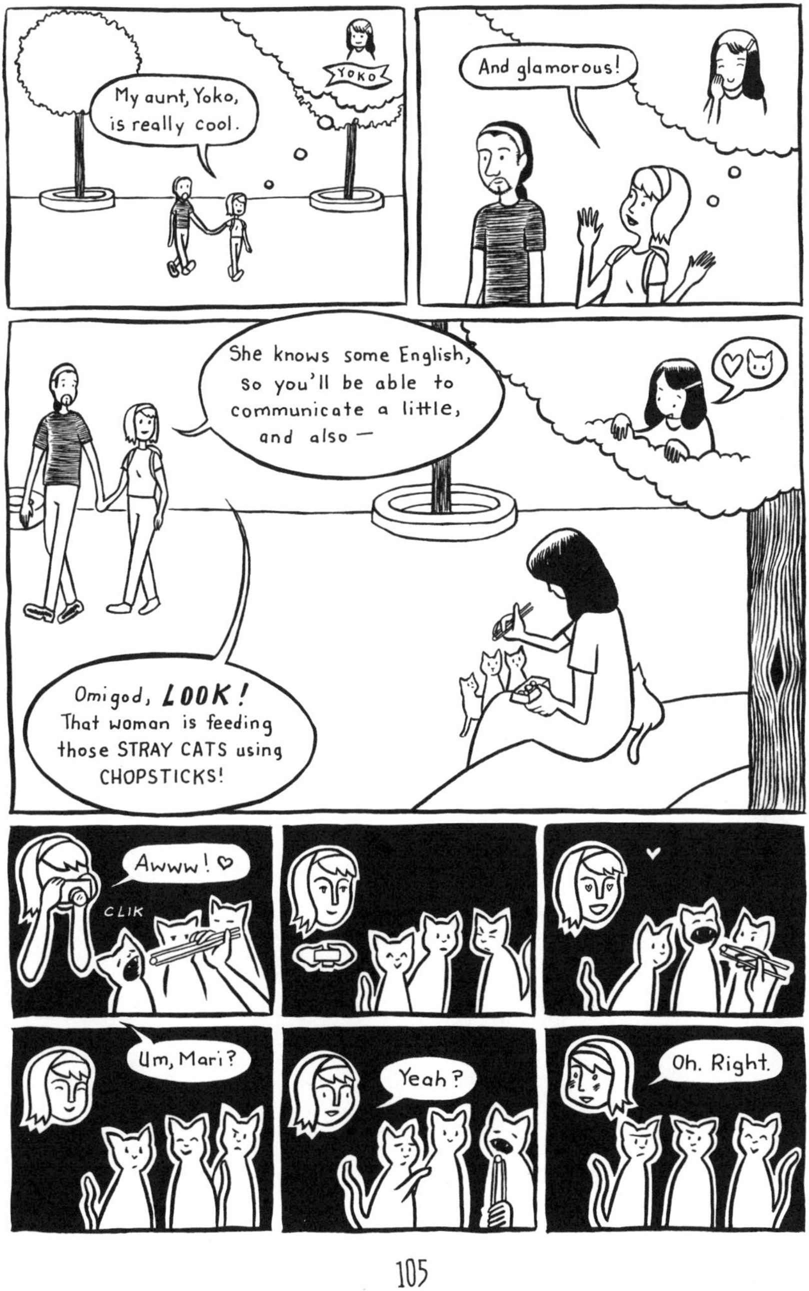
YOKO
My aunt, Yoko, is really cool.
And glamorous!
She knows some English, so you'll be able to communicate a little, and also —
Omigod, LOOK! That woman is feeding those STRAY CATS using CHOPSTICKS!
Awww! ♡
CLIK
Um, Mari?
Yeah?
Oh. Right.

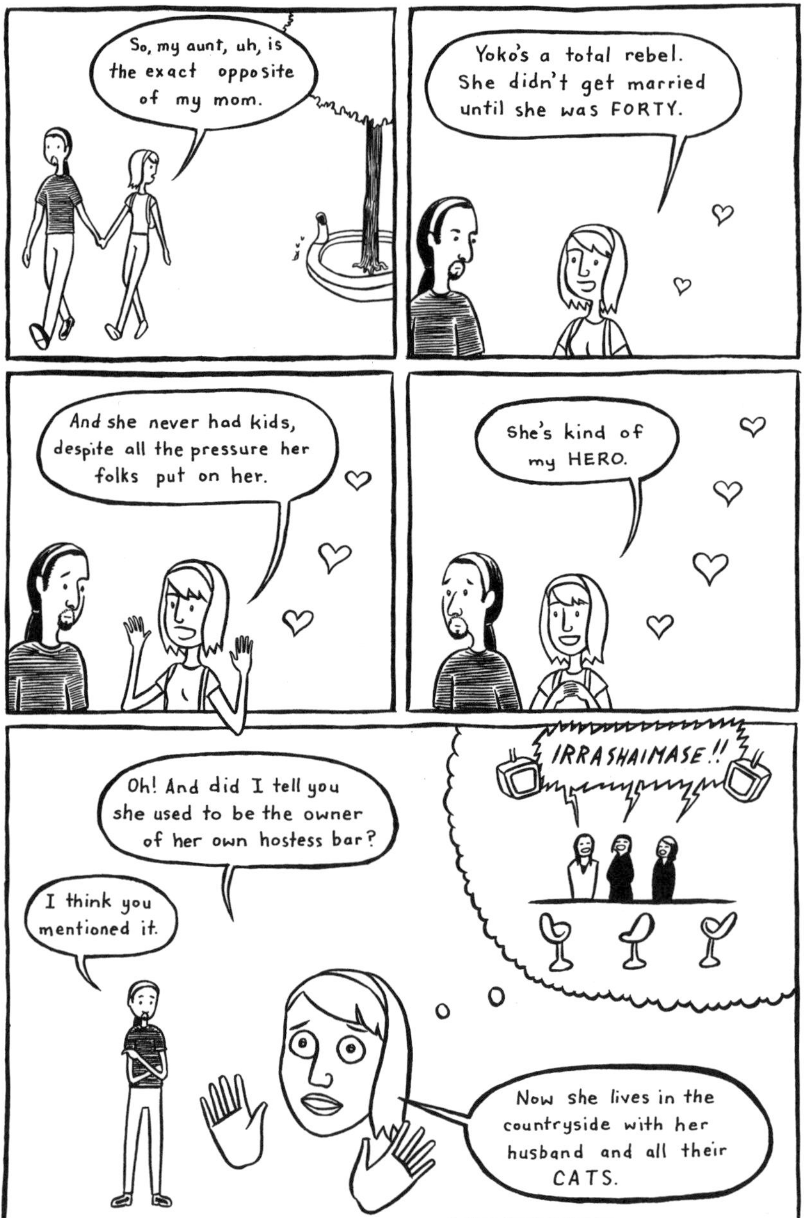
So, my aunt, uh, is the exact opposite of my mom.
Yoko's a total rebel. She didn't get married until she was FORTY.
And she never had kids, despite all the pressure her folks put on her.
She's kind of my HERO.
Oh! And did I tell you she used to be the owner of her own hostess bar?
IRRASHAIMASE!!
I think you mentioned it.
Now she lives in the countryside with her husband and all their CATS.

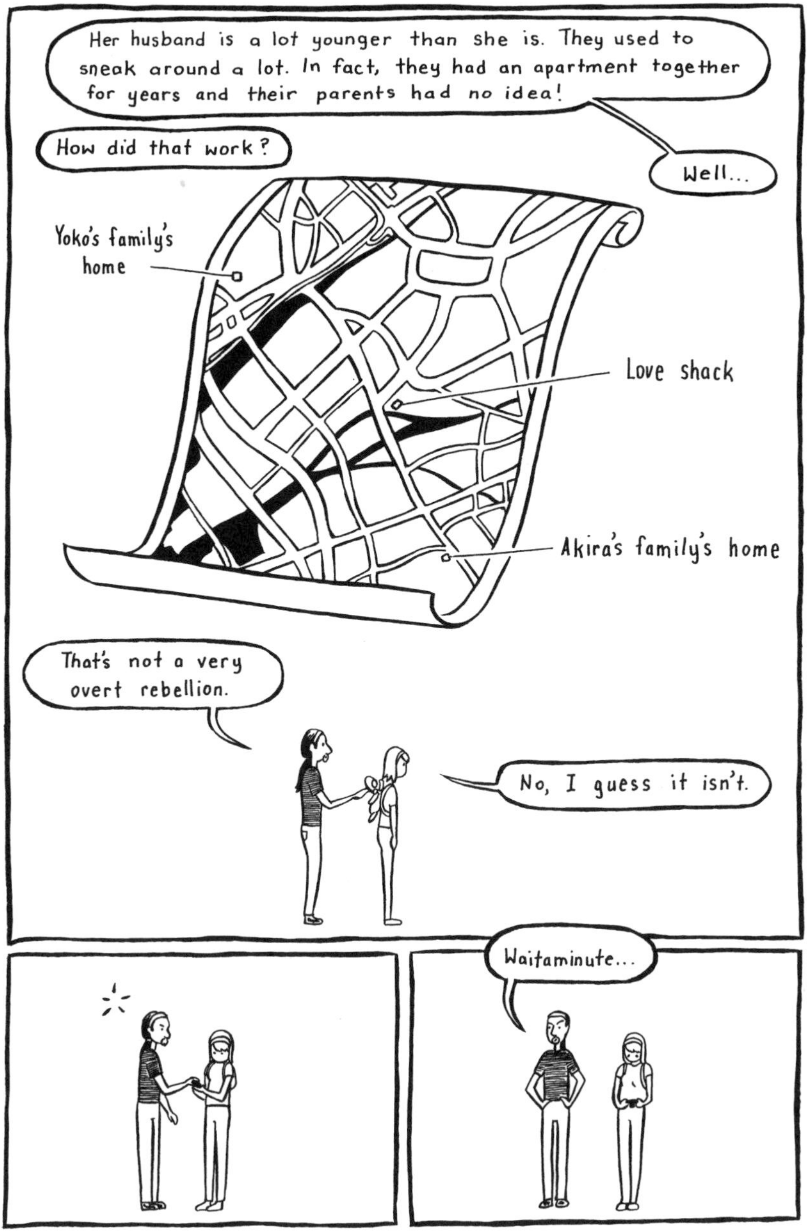
Her husband is a lot younger than she is. They used to sneak around a lot. In fact, they had an apartment together for years and their parents had no idea!
How did that work?
Well...
Yoko's family's home
Love shack
Akira's family's home
That's not a very overt rebellion.
No, I guess it isn't.
Waitaminute...

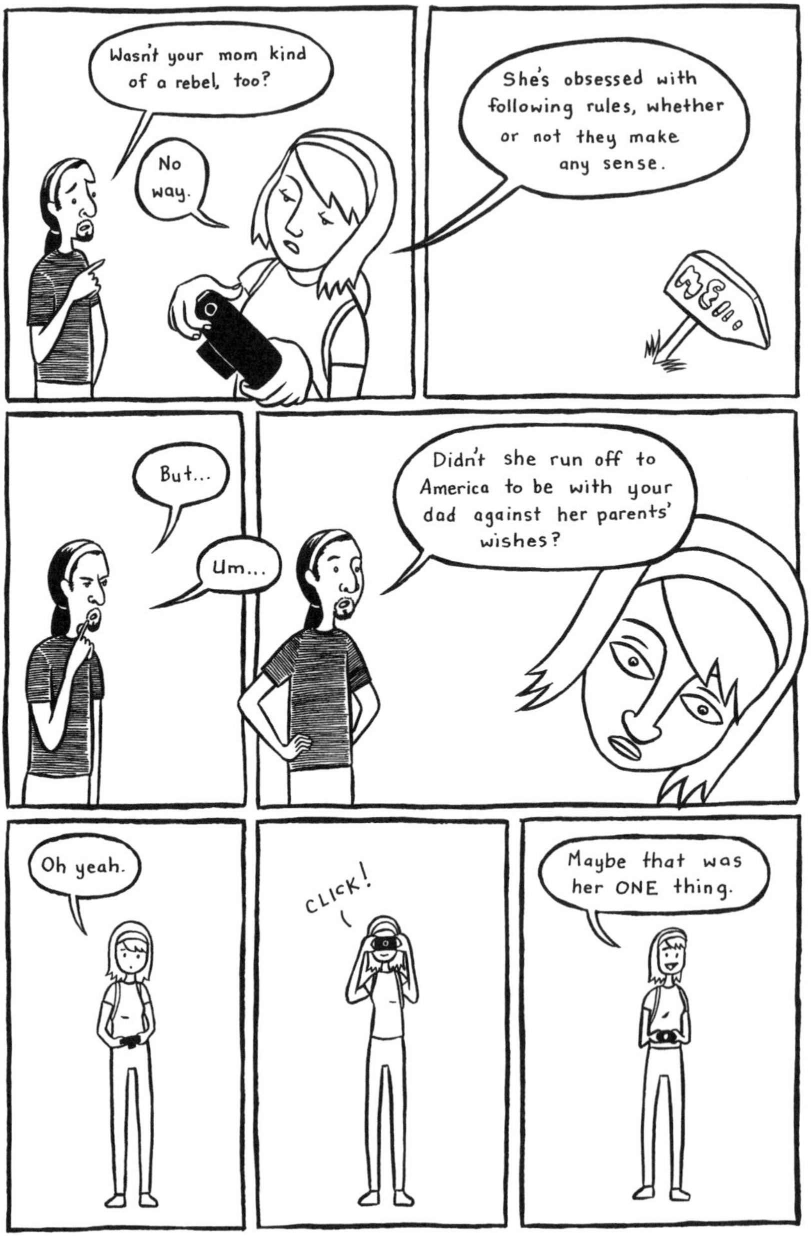
Wasn't your mom kind of a rebel, too?
No way.
She's obsessed with following rules, whether or not they make any sense.
But...
Um...
Didn't she run off to America to be with your dad against her parents' wishes?
Oh yeah.
CLICK!
Maybe that was her ONE thing.

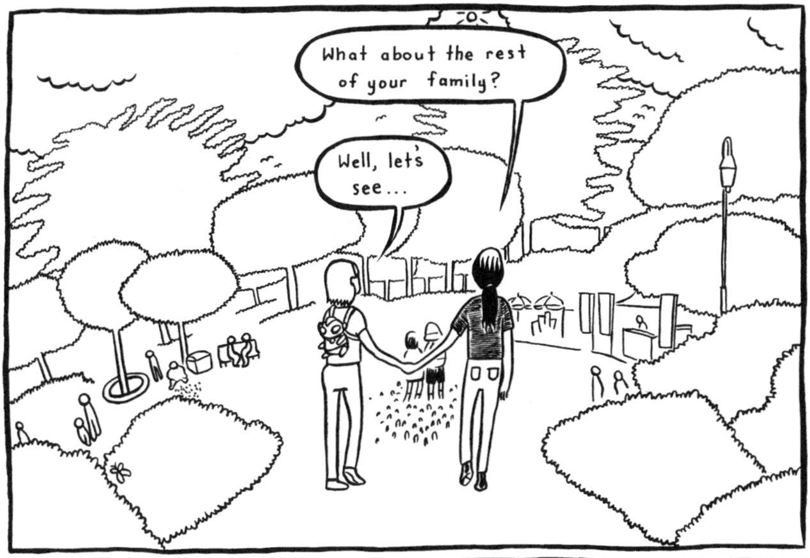
What about the rest of your family?
Well, let's see...

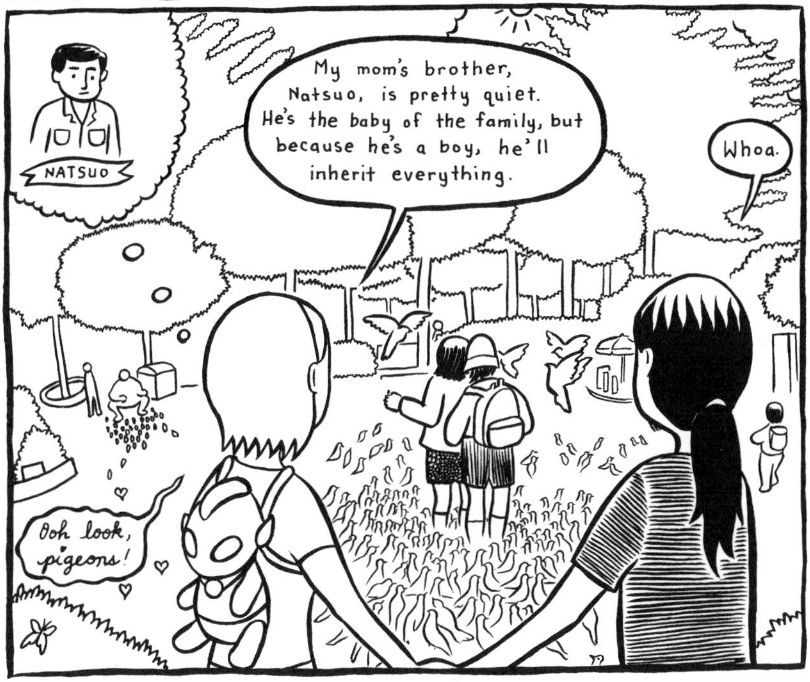
NATSUO
My mom's brother, Natsuo, is pretty quiet. He's the baby of the family, but because he's a boy, he'll inherit everything.
Whoa.
Ooh look, pigeons!

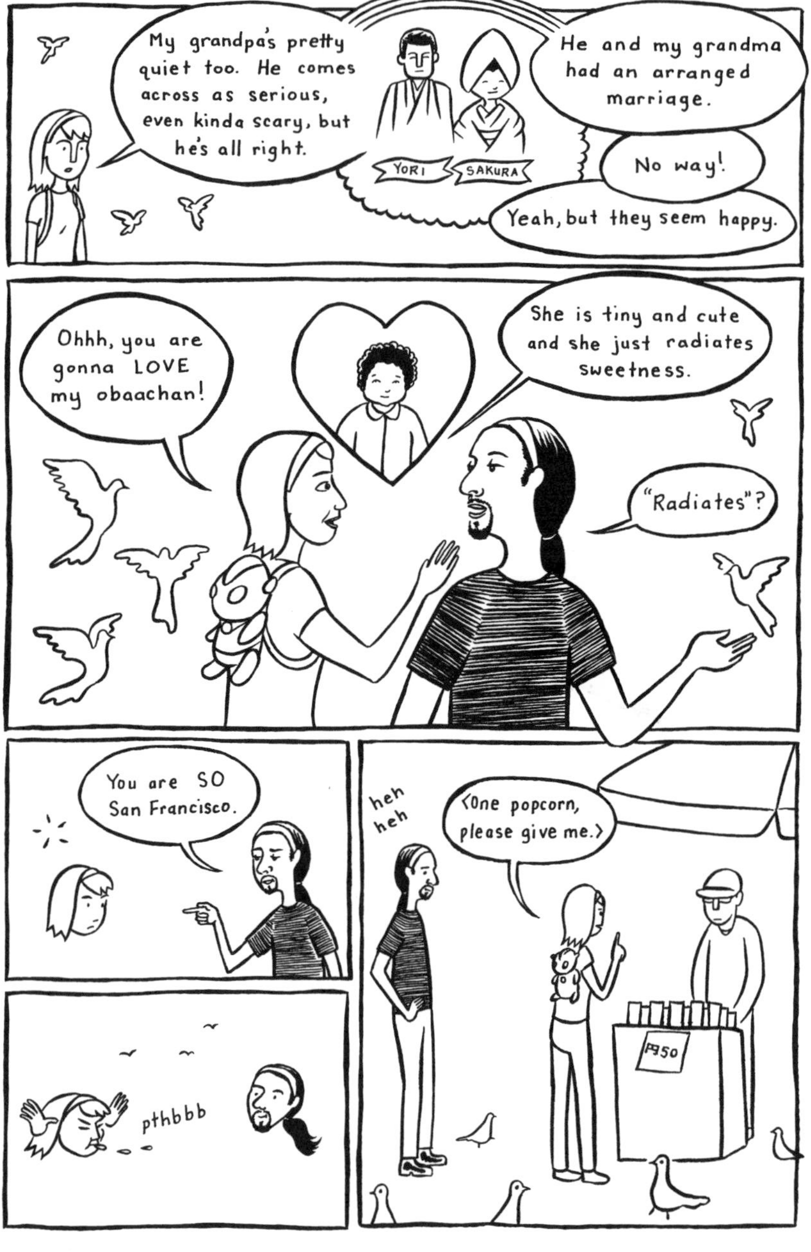

My grandpa's pretty quiet too. He comes across as serious, even kinda scary, but he's all right.
YORI
SAKURA
He and my grandma had an arranged marriage.
No way!
Yeah, but they seem happy.
Ohhh, you are gonna LOVE my obaachan!
She is tiny and cute and she just radiates sweetness.
"Radiates"?
You are SO San Francisco.
pthbbb
heh heh
<One popcorn, please give me.>
₱50

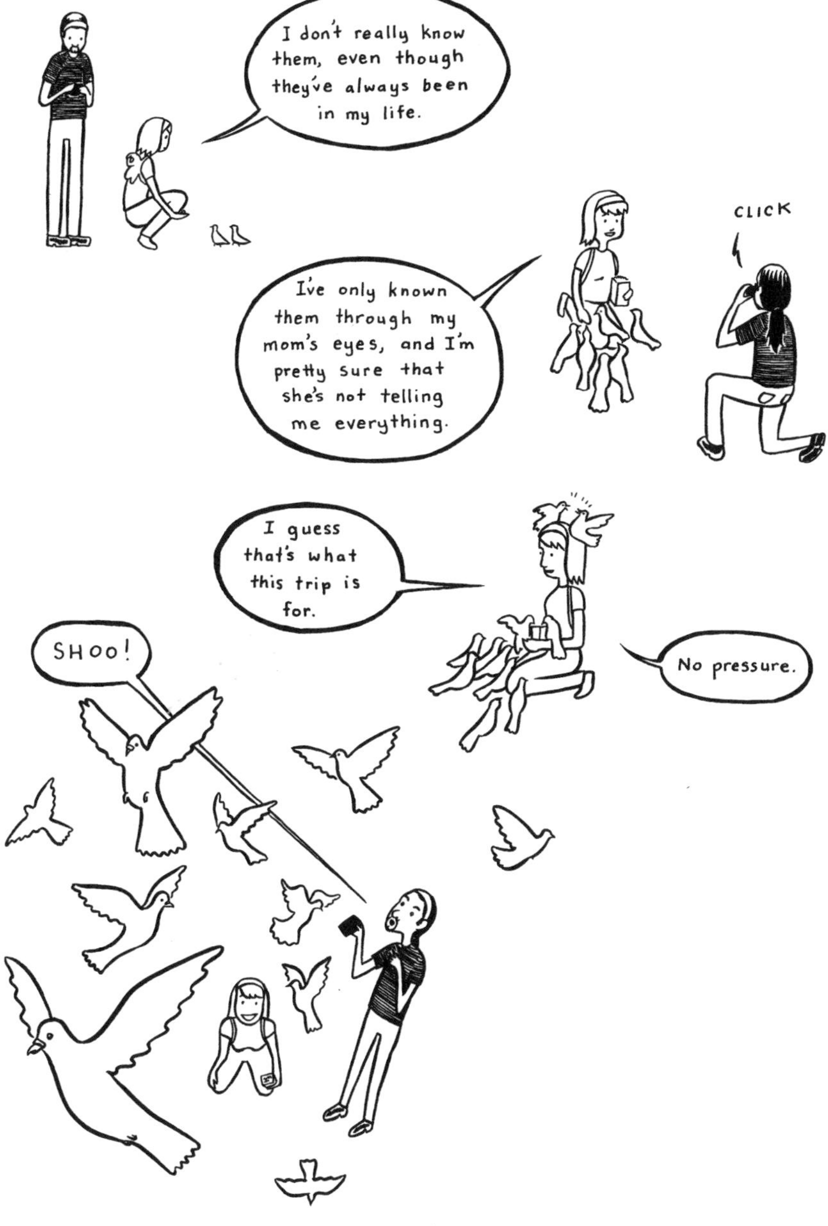
I don't really know them, even though they've always been in my life.
I've only known them through my mom's eyes, and I'm pretty sure that she's not telling me everything.
CLICK
I guess that's what this trip is for.
No pressure.
SHOO!

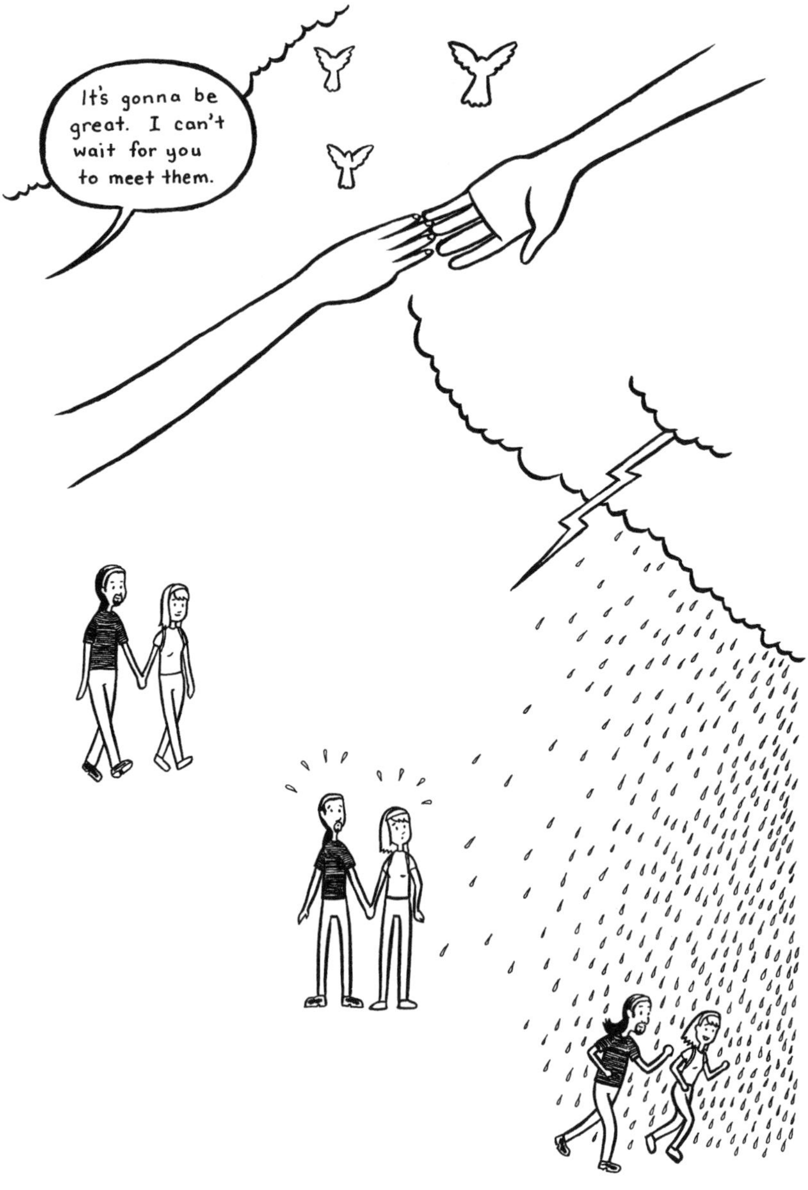
It's gonna be great. I can't wait for you to meet them.

WE ARRANGED TO MEET NORIKO AT HER APARTMENT IN ROPPONGI.

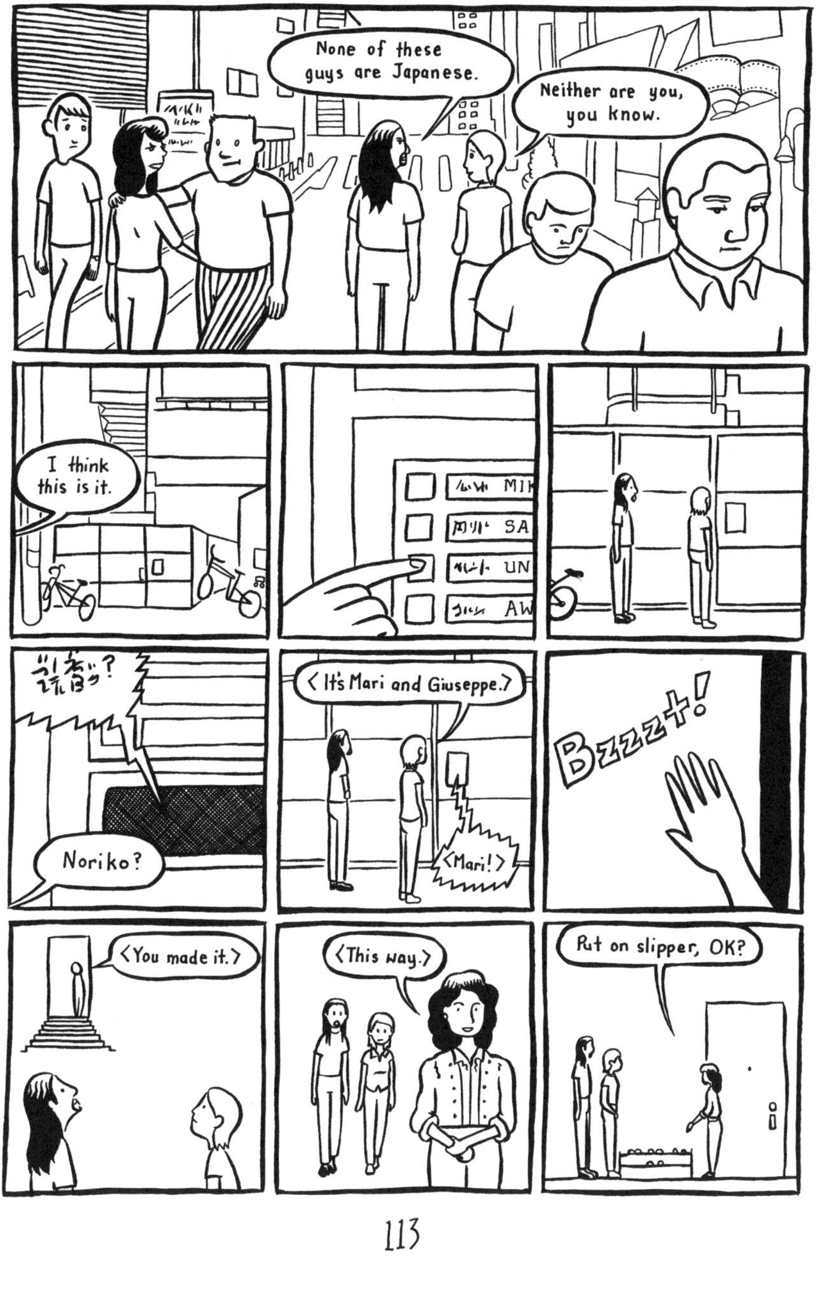

None of these guys are Japanese.
Neither are you, you know.
I think this is it.
Noriko?
<It's Mari and Giuseppe.>
<Mari!>
Bzzzt!
<You made it.>
<This way.>
Put on slipper, OK?

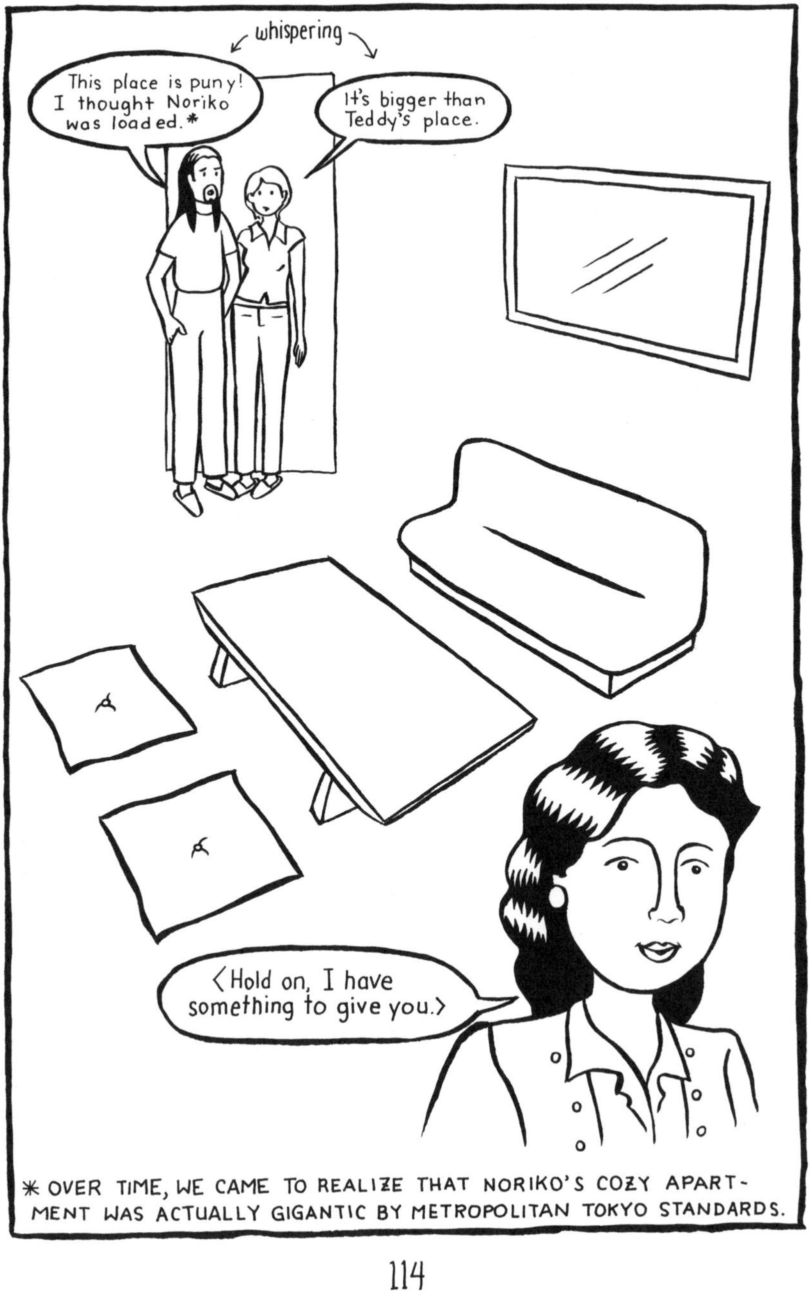
whispering
This place is puny! I thought Noriko was loaded.*
It's bigger than Teddy's place.
〈Hold on, I have something to give you.〉
* OVER TIME, WE CAME TO REALIZE THAT NORIKO'S COZY APARTMENT WAS ACTUALLY GIGANTIC BY METROPOLITAN TOKYO STANDARDS.

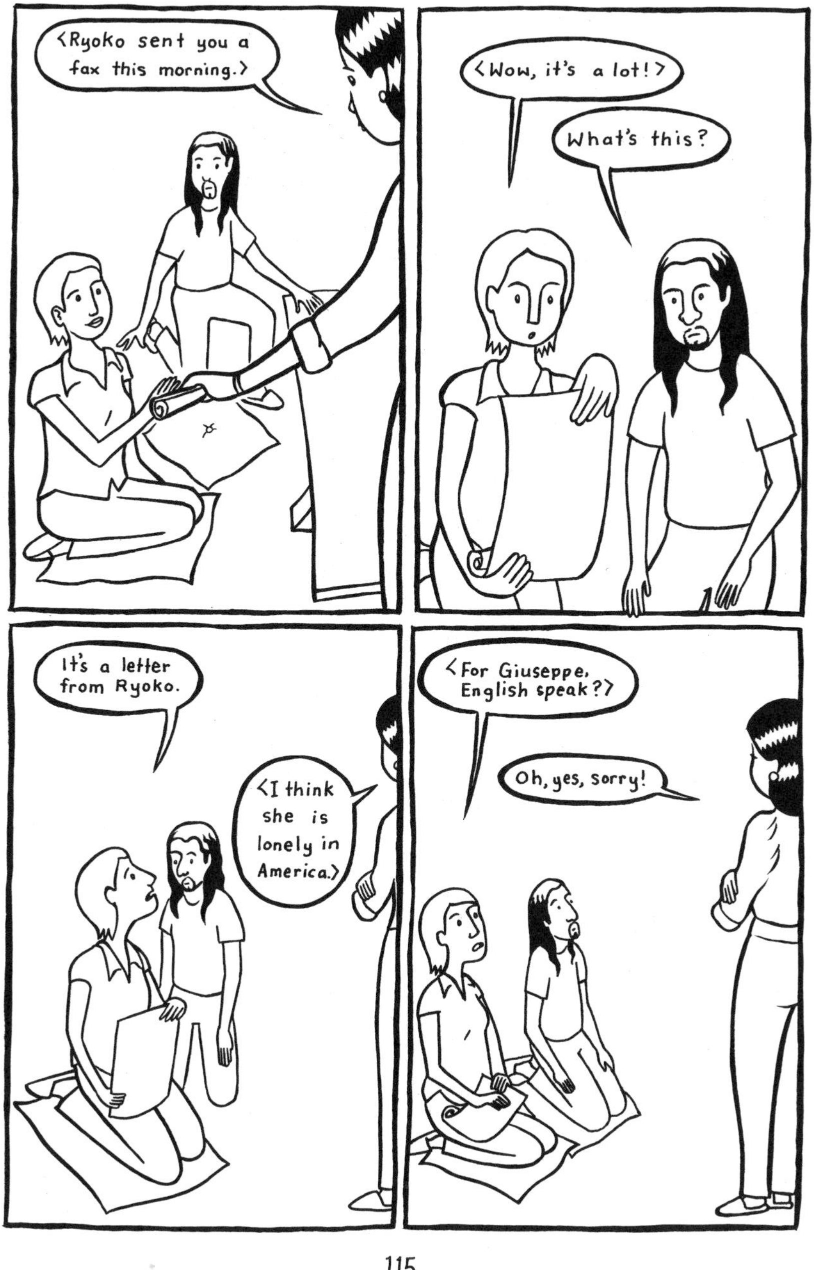

<Ryoko sent you a fax this morning.>
<Wow, it's a lot!>
What's this?
It's a letter from Ryoko.
<I think she is lonely in America.>
<For Giuseppe, English speak?>
Oh, yes, sorry!

NORIKO TOOK US TO HER FRIEND'S BAR IN THE FANCY GINZA DISTRICT.

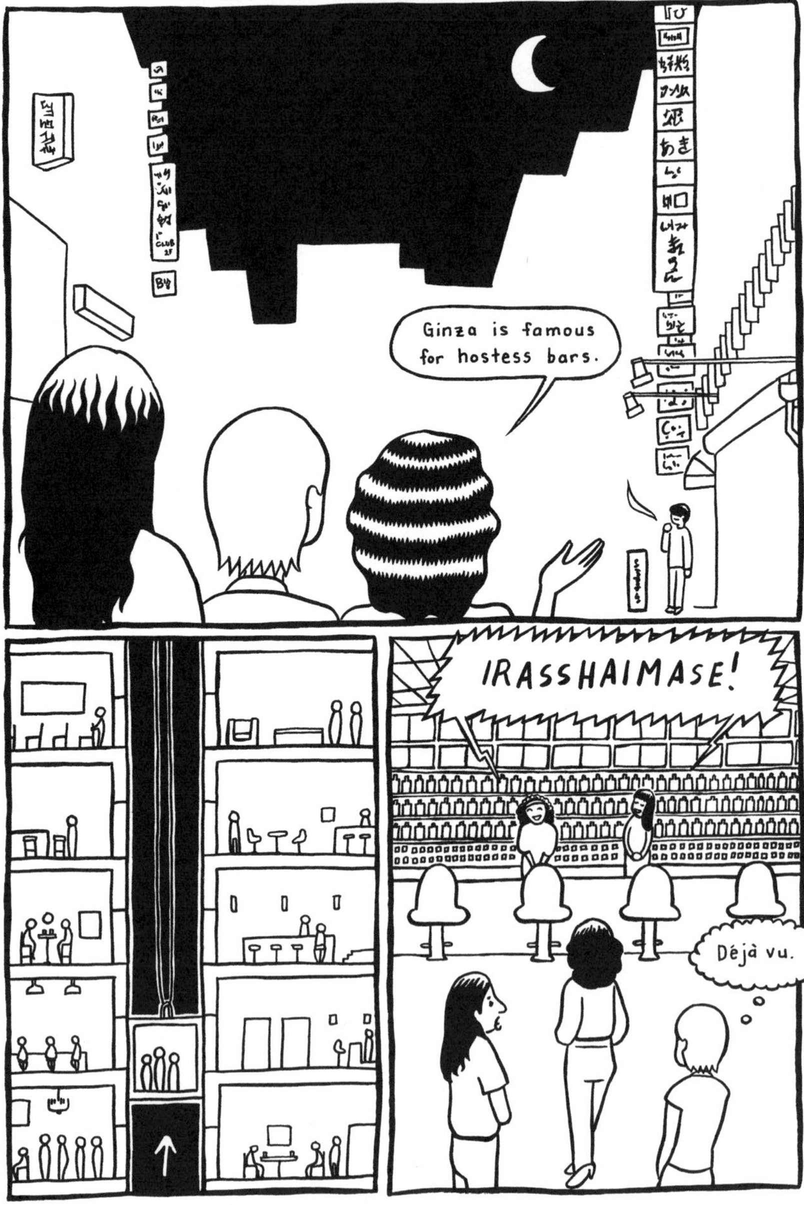
Ginza is famous for hostess bars.
IRASSHAIMASE!
Déjà vu.

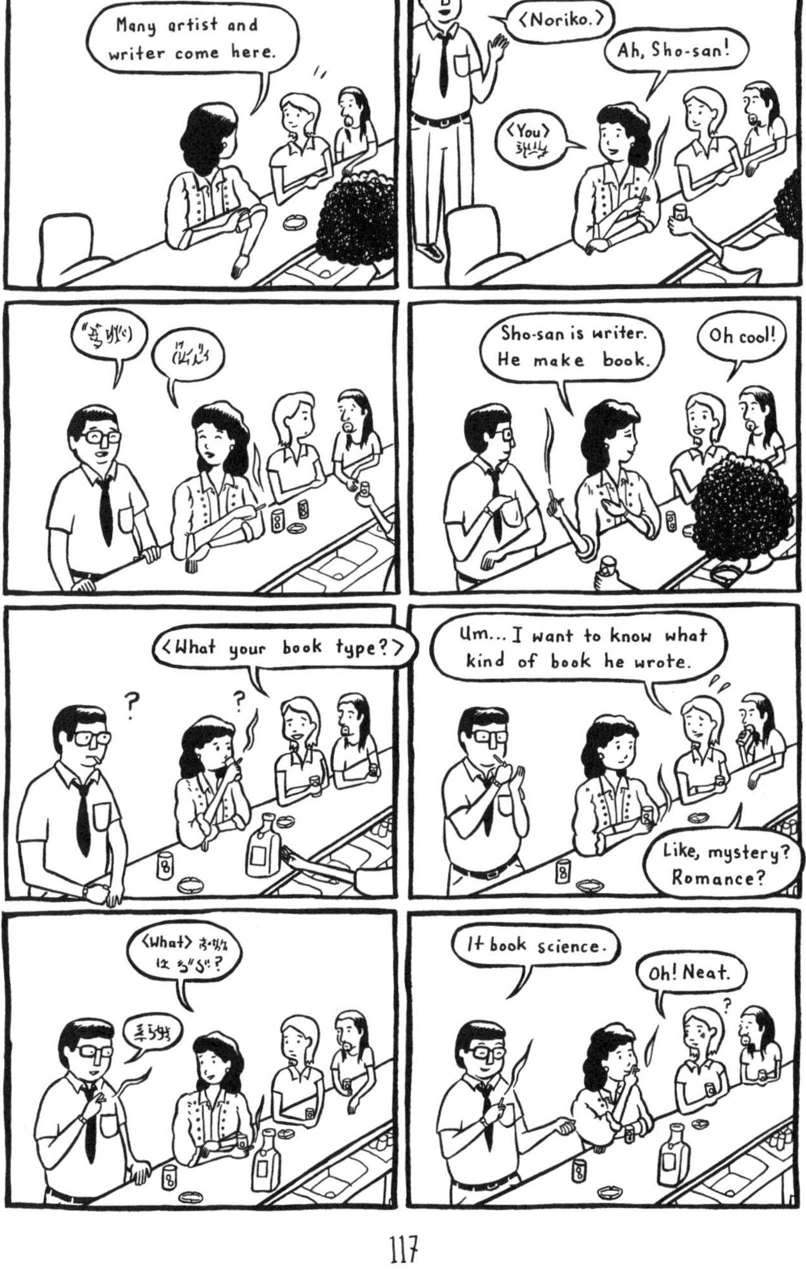

Many artist and writer come here.
<Noriko.>
Ah, Sho-san!
<You>
Sho-san is writer. He make book.
Oh cool!
<What your book type?>
Um... I want to know what kind of book he wrote.
Like, mystery? Romance?
<What>
It book science.
Oh! Neat.

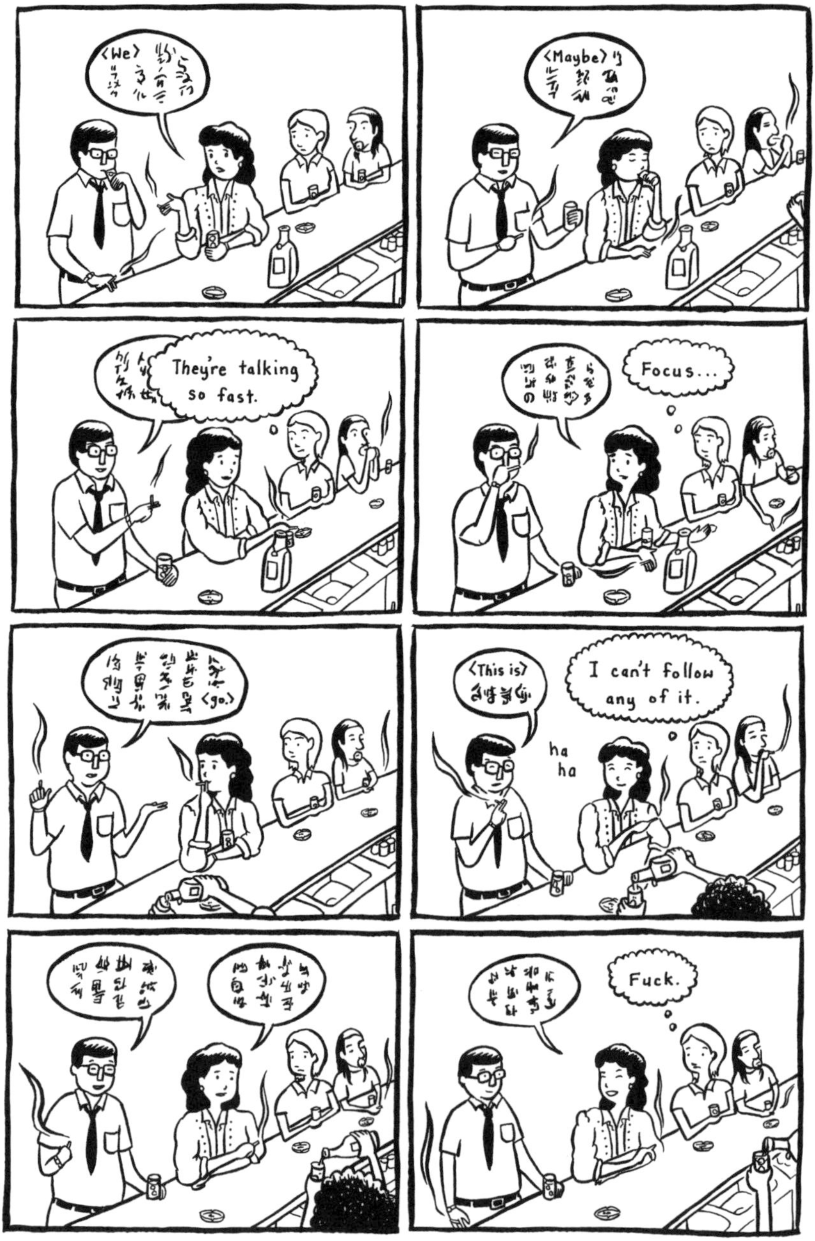
<We>
<Maybe>
They're talking so fast.
Focus...
<go.>
<This is>
I can't follow any of it.
ha ha
Fuck.

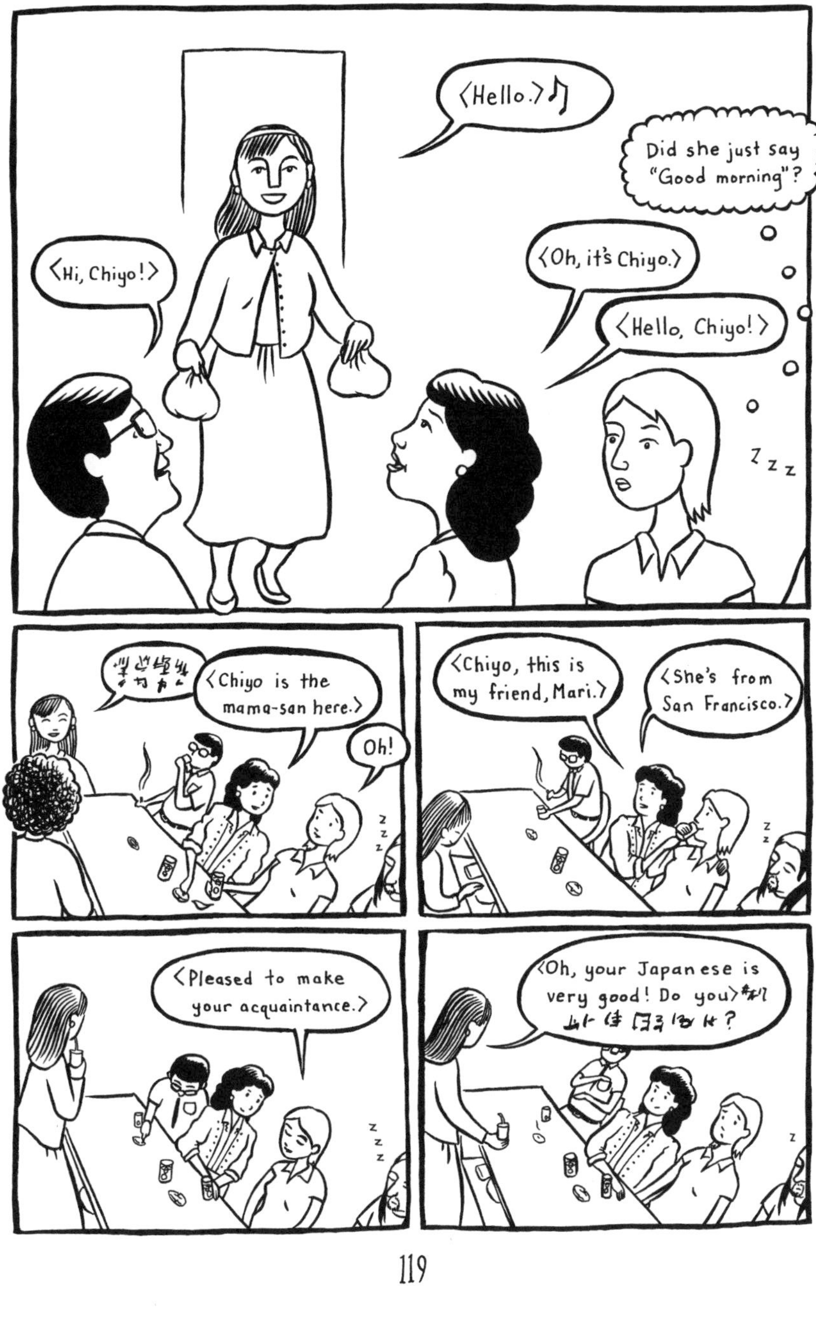
<Hello.>♫
Did she just say "Good morning"?
<Hi, Chiyo!>
<Oh, it's Chiyo.>
<Hello, Chiyo!>
Z z z
<Chiyo is the mama-san here.>
Oh!
<Chiyo, this is my friend, Mari.>
<She's from San Francisco.>
<Pleased to make your acquaintance.>
<Oh, your Japanese is very good! Do you>

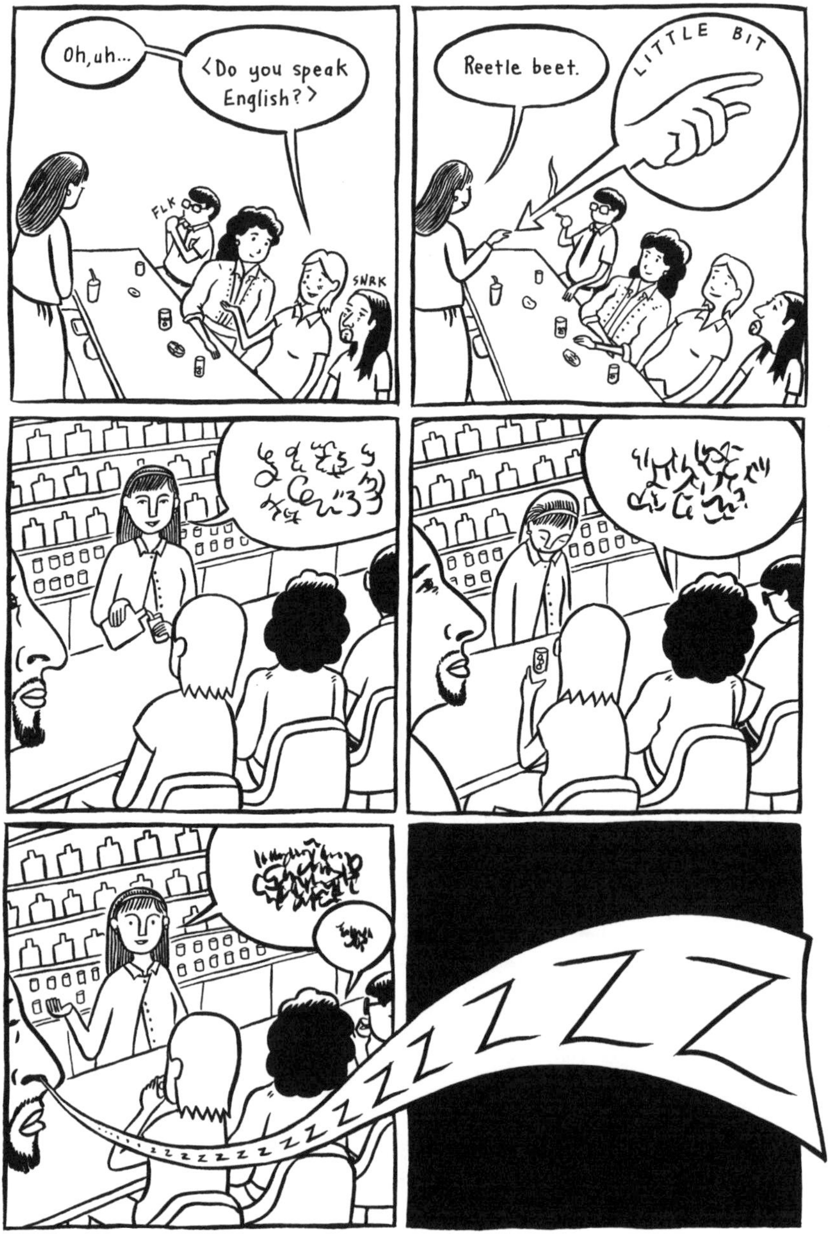
Oh, uh...
<Do you speak English?>
FLK
SNRK
Reetle beet.
LITTLE BIT

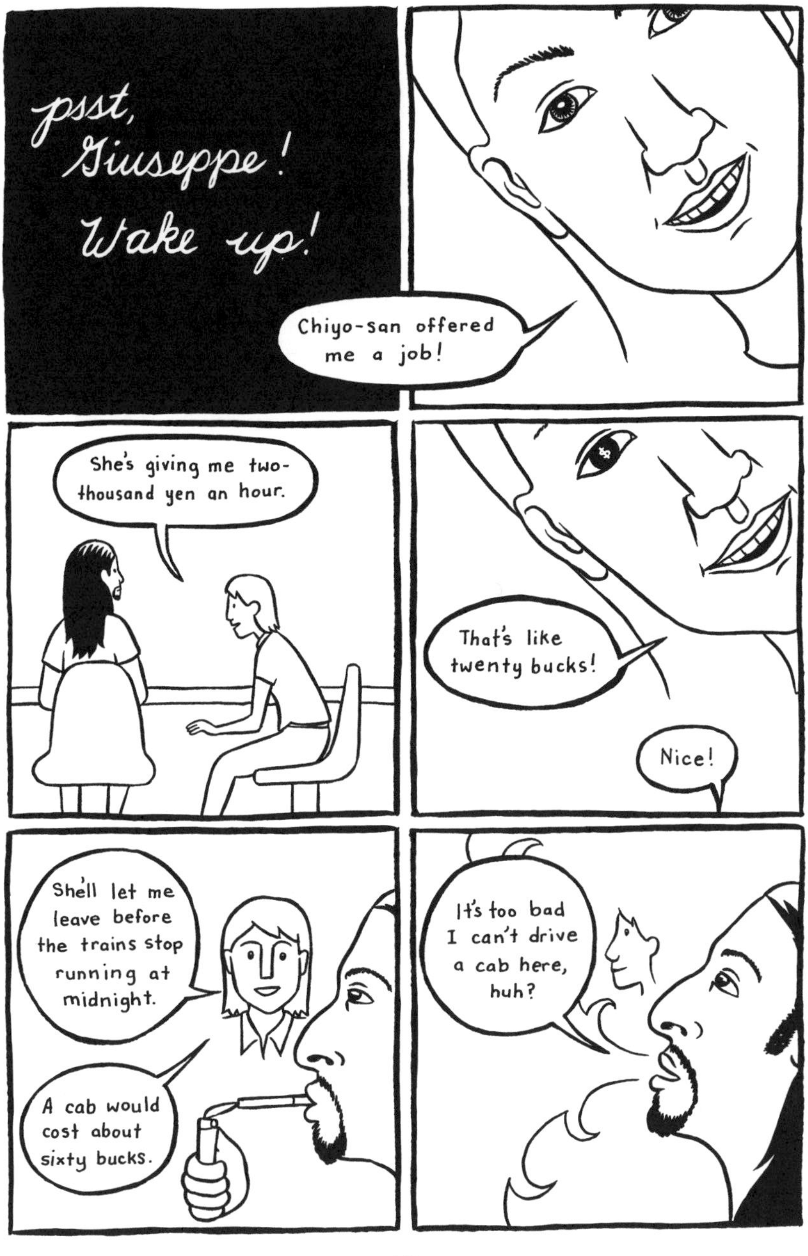
psst, Giuseppe! Wake up!
Chiyo-san offered me a job!
She's giving me two-thousand yen an hour.
That's like twenty bucks!
Nice!
She'll let me leave before the trains stop running at midnight.
A cab would cost about sixty bucks.
It's too bad I can't drive a cab here, huh?

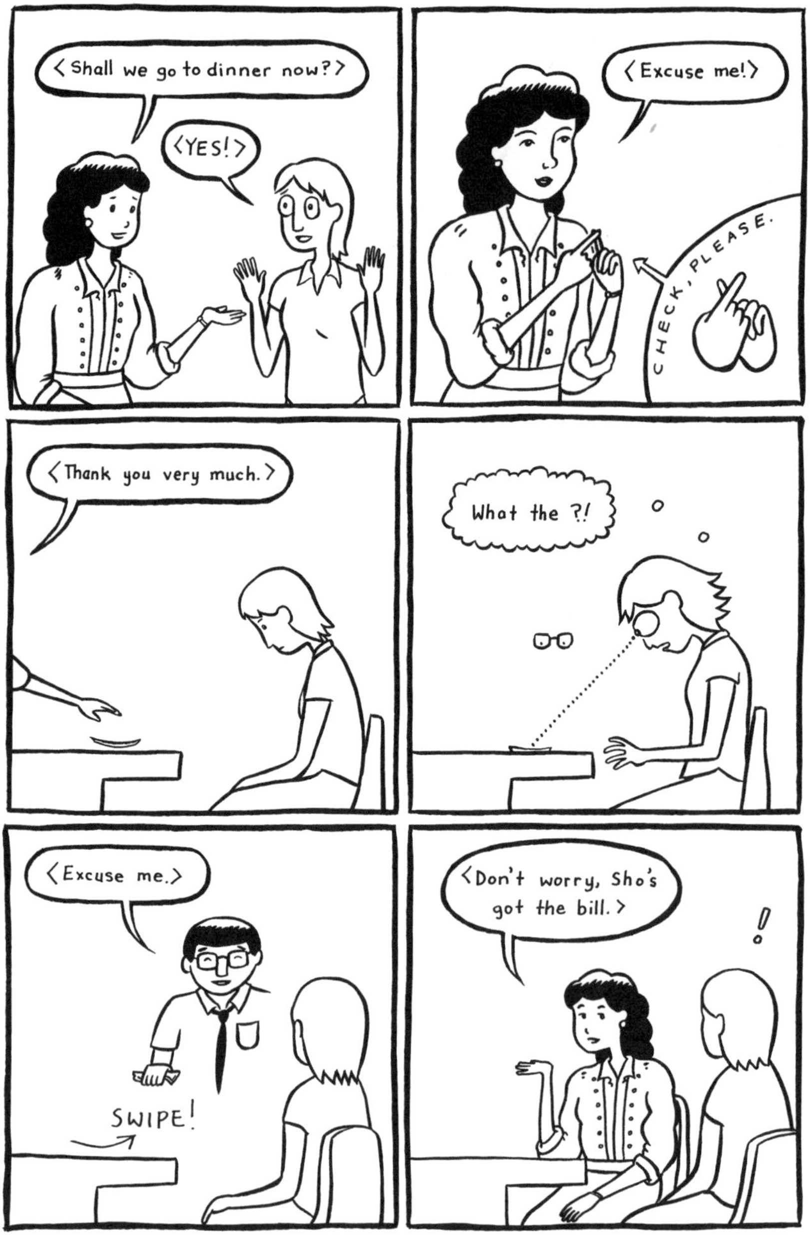
<Shall we go to dinner now?>
<YES!>
<Excuse me!>
CHECK, PLEASE.
<Thank you very much.>
What the ?!
<Excuse me.>
SWIPE!
<Don't worry, Sho's got the bill.>
!

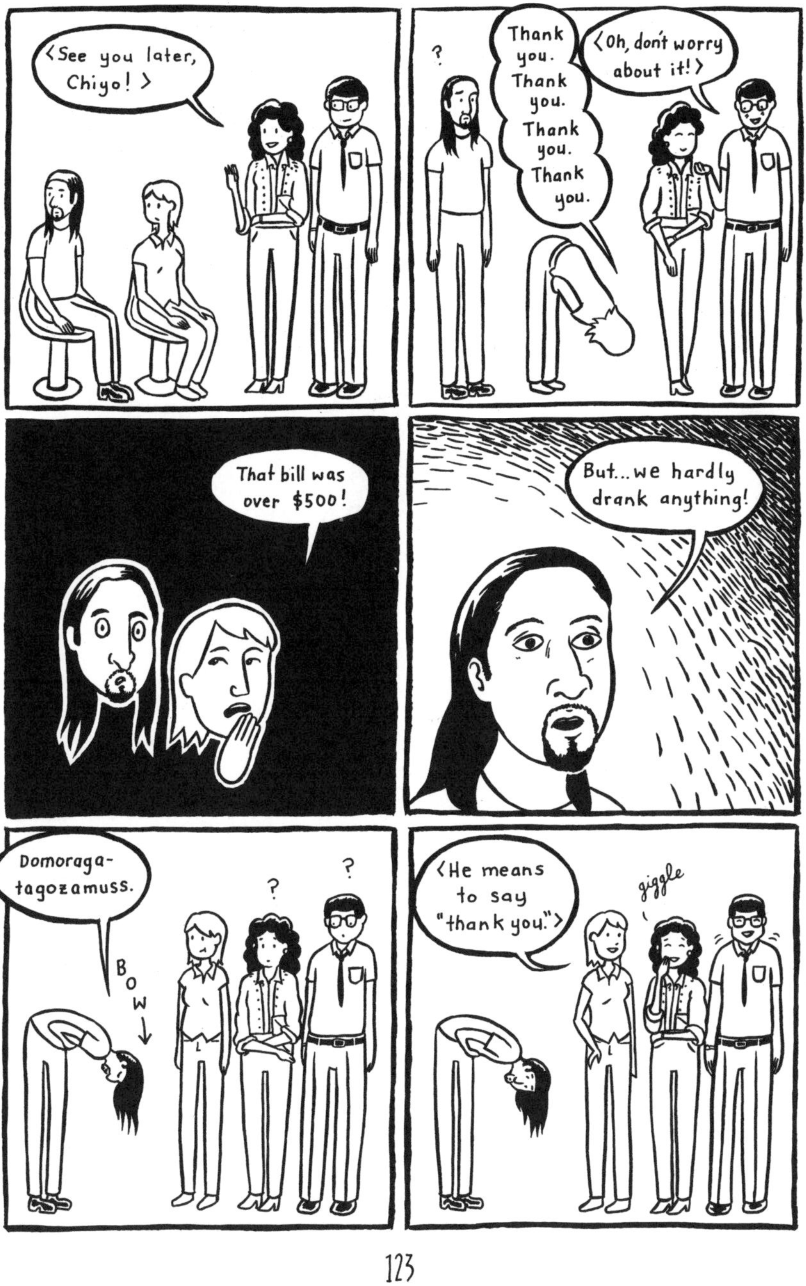

<See you later, Chiyo! >
?
Thank you. Thank you. Thank you. Thank you.
<Oh, don't worry about it!>
That bill was over $500!
But...we hardly drank anything!
Domoraga-tagozamuss.
BOW
?
?
<He means to say "thank you.">
giggle

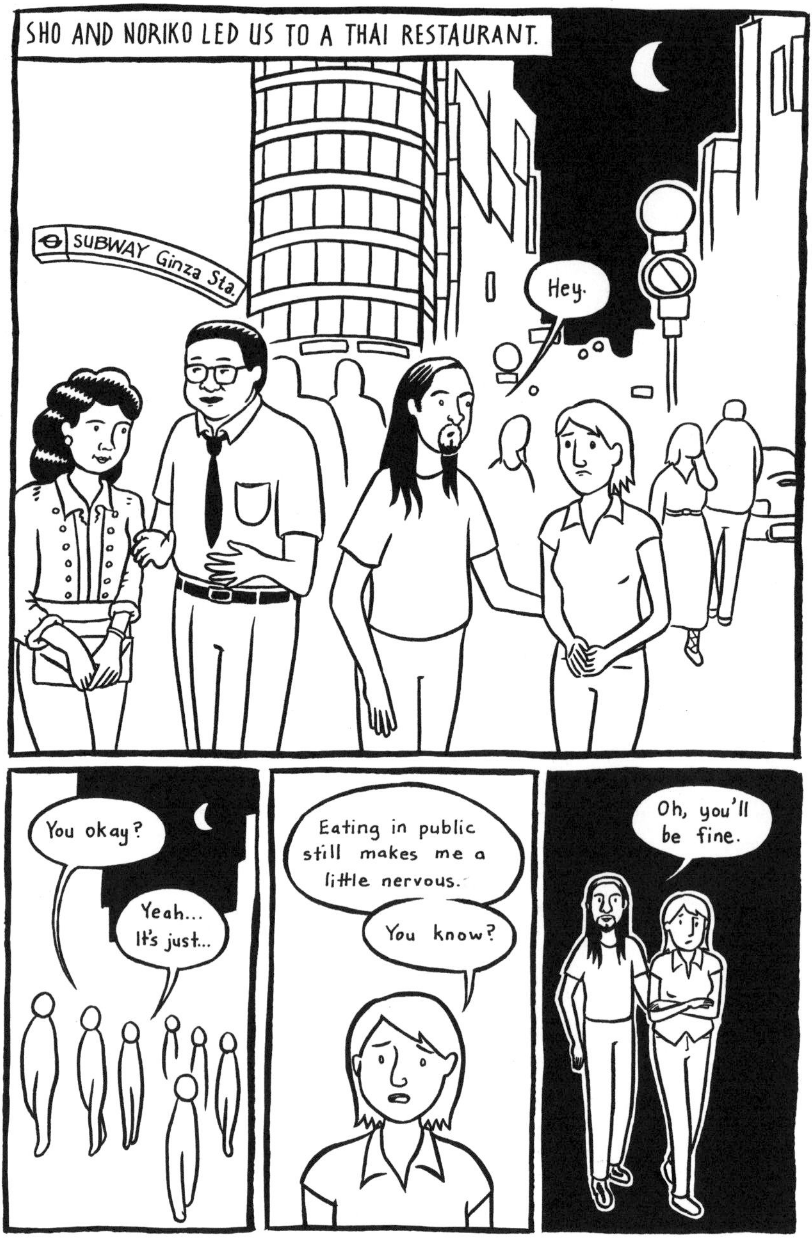
SHO AND NORIKO LED US TO A THAI RESTAURANT.
SUBWAY Ginza Sta.
Hey.
You okay?
Yeah... It's just...
Eating in public still makes me a little nervous.
You know?
Oh, you'll be fine.

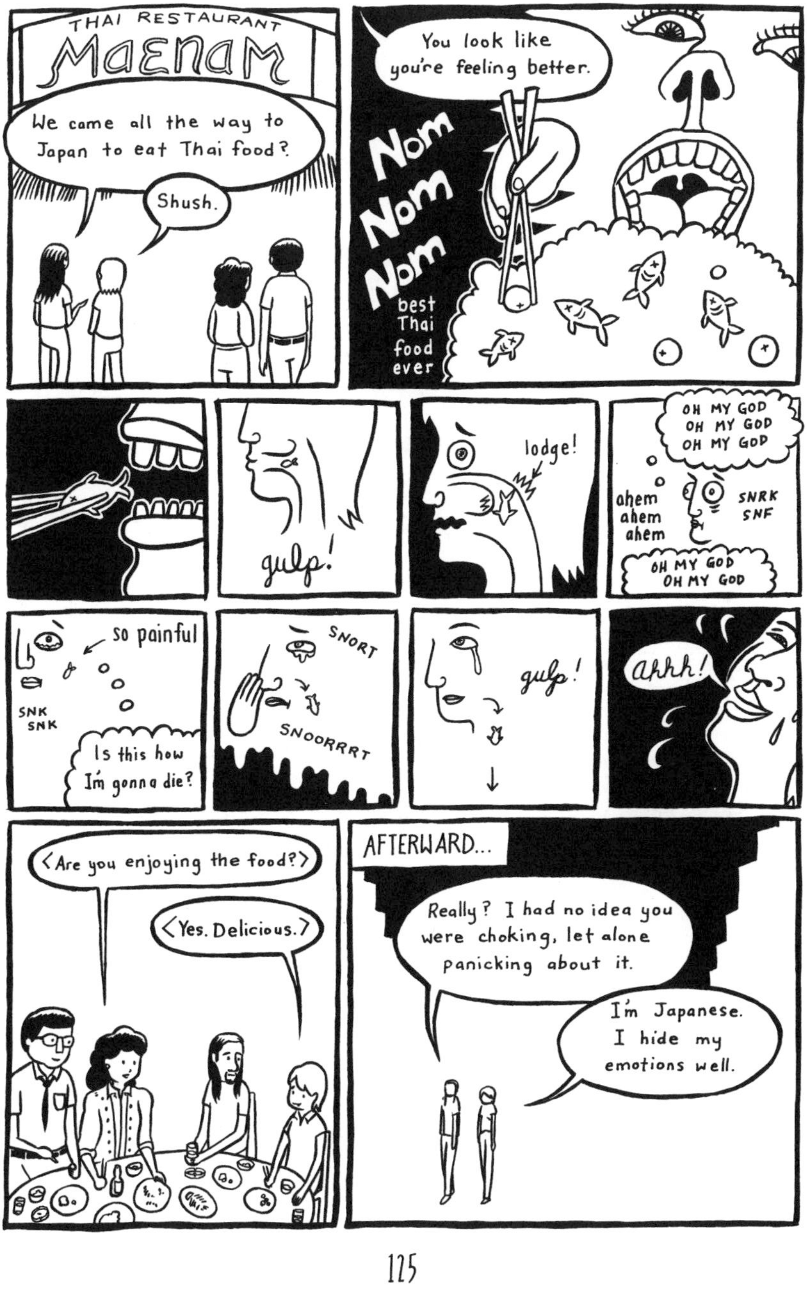
THAI RESTAURANT
MAENAM
We came all the way to Japan to eat Thai food?
Shush.
You look like you're feeling better.
Nom Nom Nom
best Thai food ever
gulp!
lodge!
OH MY GOD OH MY GOD OH MY GOD
ahem ahem ahem
SNRK SNF
OH MY GOD OH MY GOD
so painful
SNK SNK
Is this how I'm gonna die?
SNORT
SNOORRRT
gulp!
Ahhh!
<Are you enjoying the food?>
<Yes. Delicious.>
AFTERWARD...
Really? I had no idea you were choking, let alone panicking about it.
I'm Japanese. I hide my emotions well.

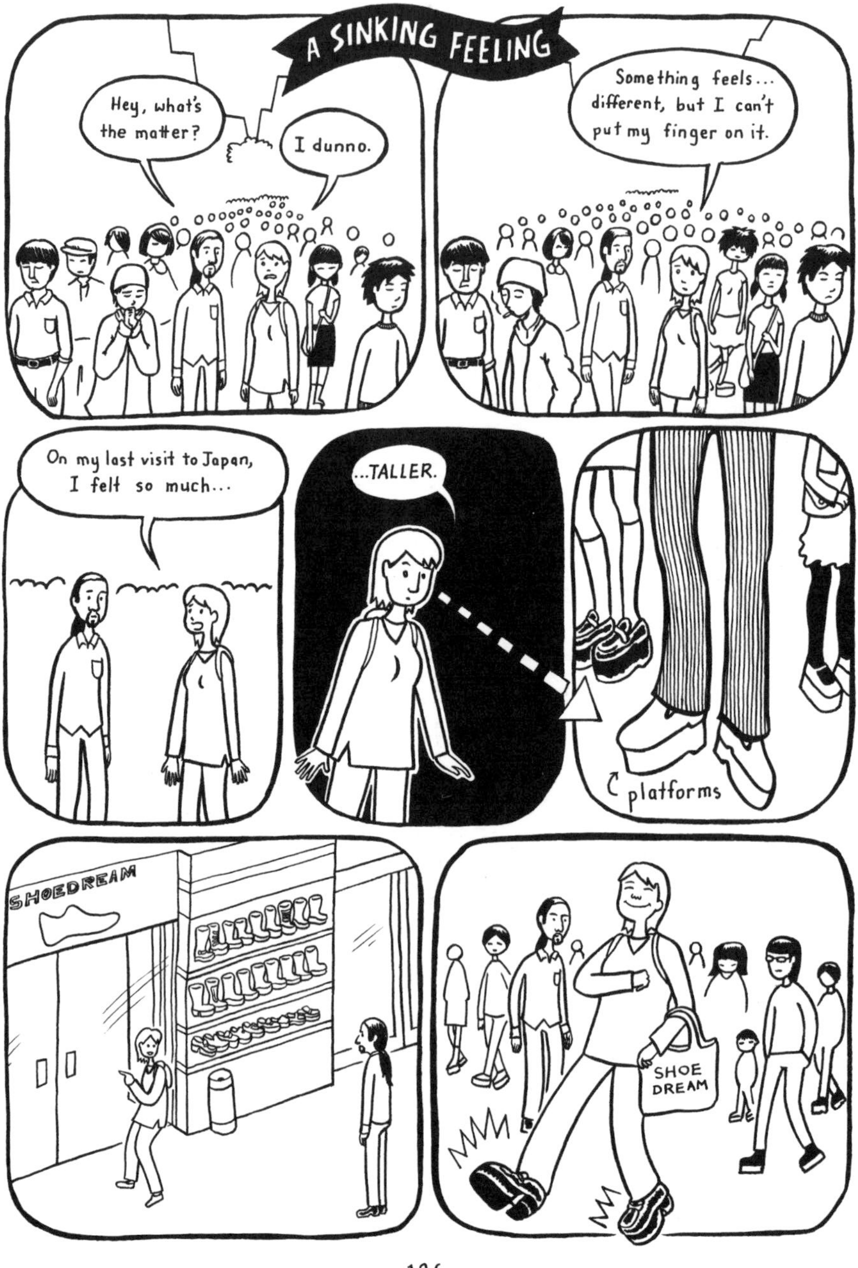
A SINKING FEELING
Hey, what's the matter?
I dunno.
Something feels... different, but I can't put my finger on it.
On my last visit to Japan, I felt so much...
...TALLER.
platforms
SHOEDREAM
SHOE DREAM

ONE EVENING, NORIKO TOOK US TO HER FRIEND'S BAR IN ROPPONGI.

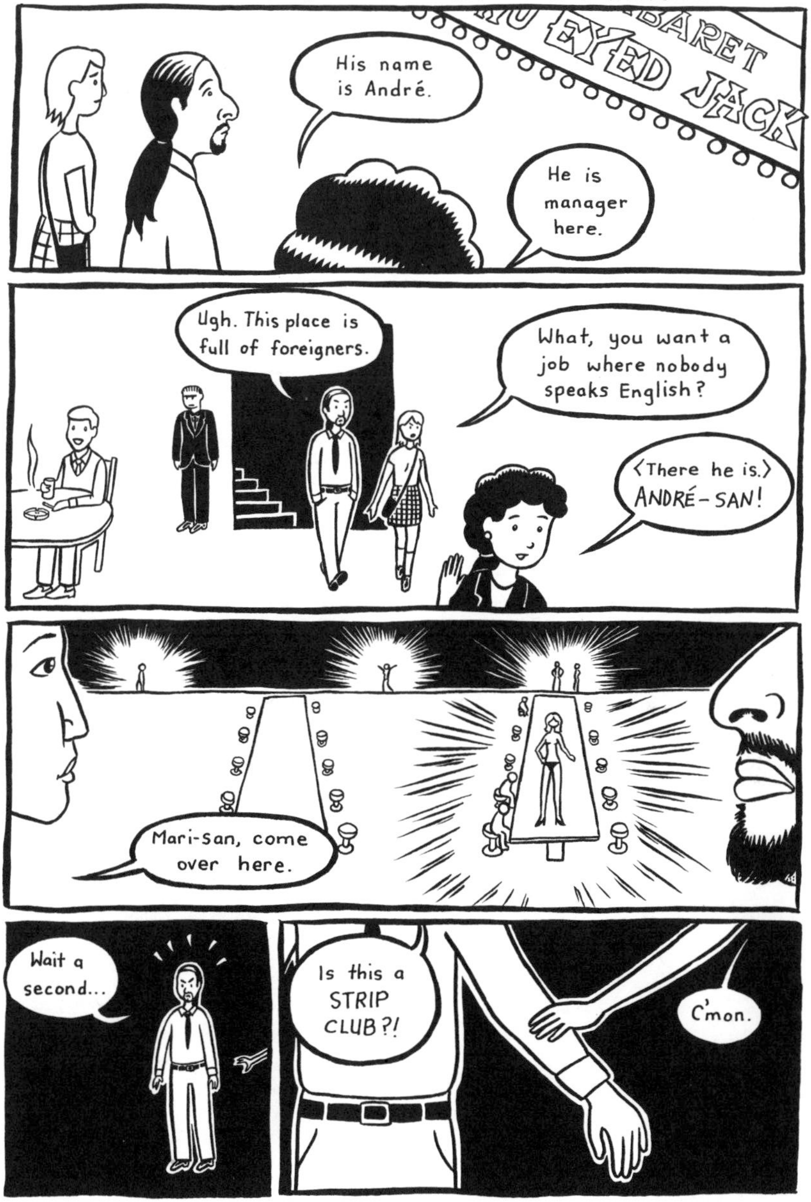
BARET
EYED JACK
His name is André.
He is manager here.
Ugh. This place is full of foreigners.
What, you want a job where nobody speaks English?
⟨There he is.⟩ ANDRÉ-SAN!
Mari-san, come over here.
Wait a second...
Is this a STRIP CLUB?!
C'mon.

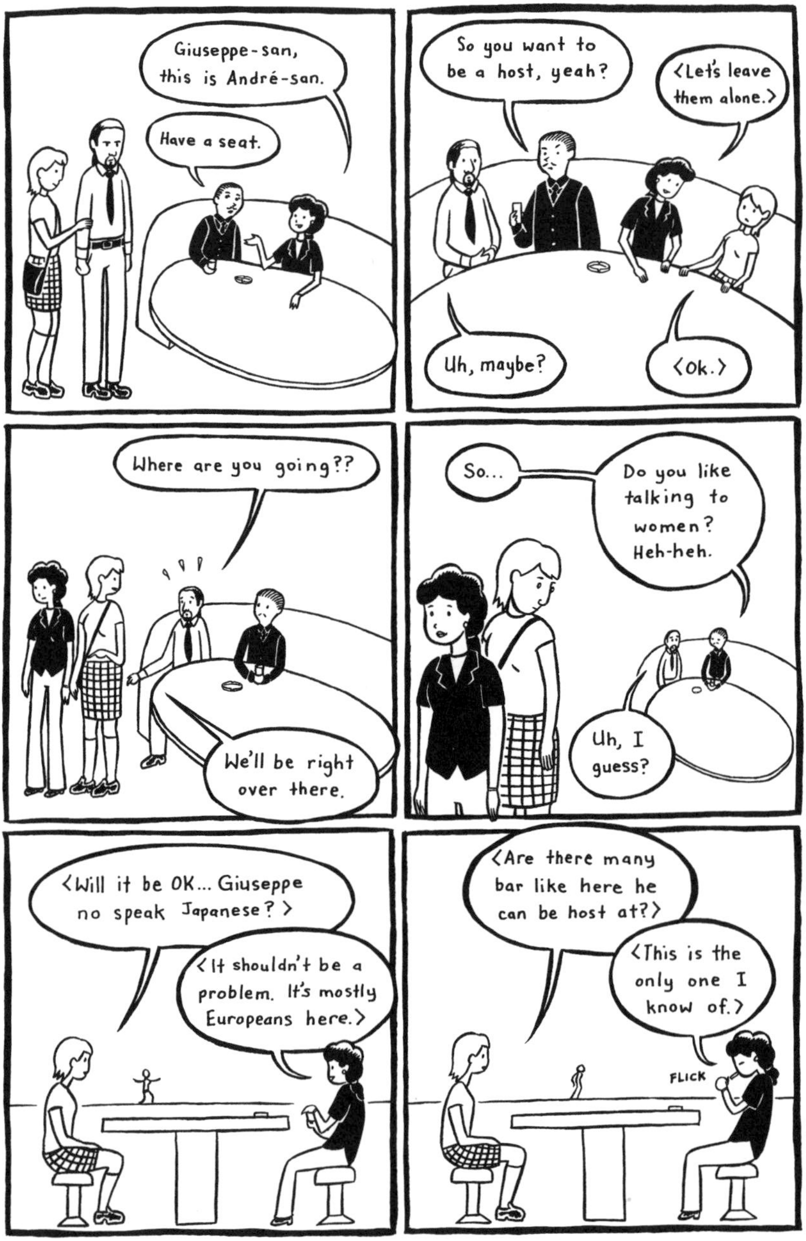
Giuseppe-san, this is André-san.
Have a seat.
So you want to be a host, yeah?
Uh, maybe?
<Let's leave them alone.>
<Ok.>
Where are you going??
We'll be right over there.
So...
Do you like talking to women? Heh-heh.
Uh, I guess?
<Will it be OK... Giuseppe no speak Japanese?>
<It shouldn't be a problem. It's mostly Europeans here.>
<Are there many bar like here he can be host at?>
<This is the only one I know of.>
FLICK

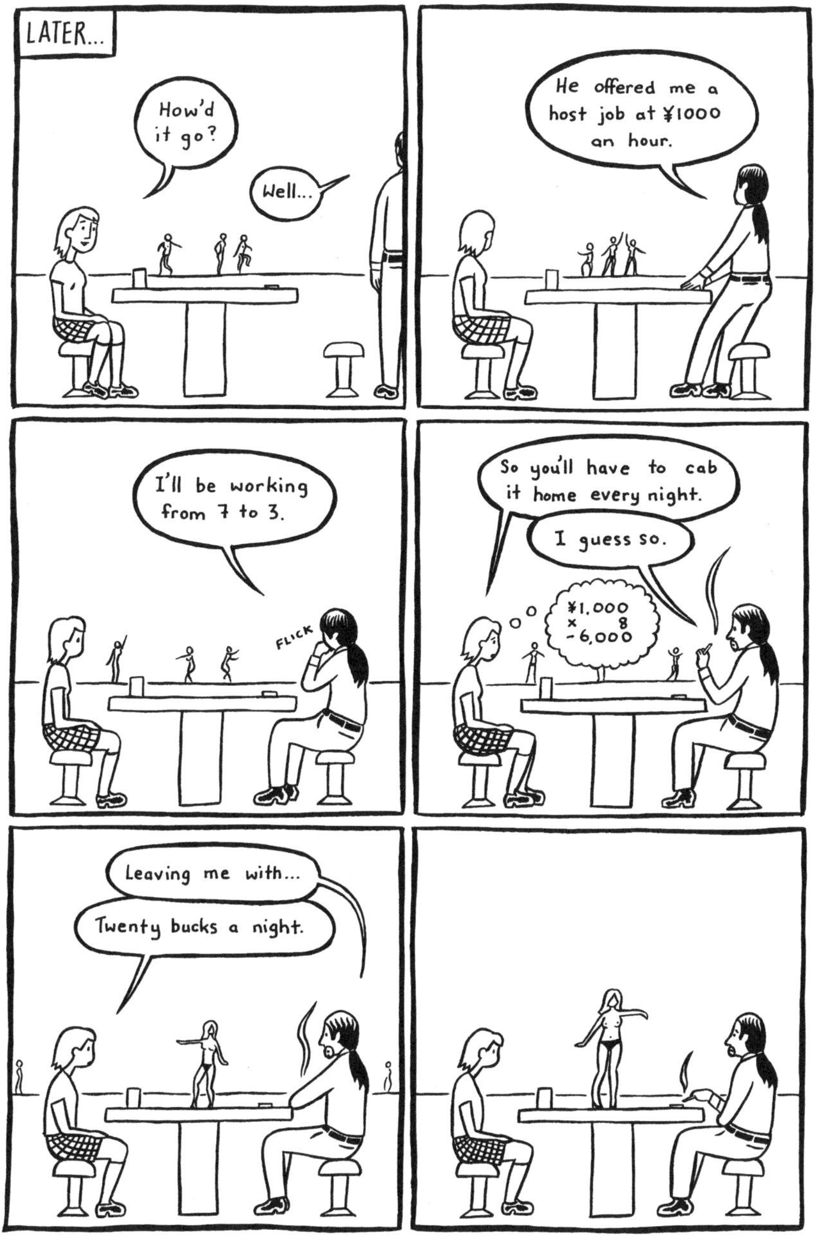
LATER...
How'd it go?
Well...
He offered me a host job at ¥1000 an hour.
I'll be working from 7 to 3.
FLICK
So you'll have to cab it home every night.
I guess so.
¥1,000
× 8
-6,000
Leaving me with...
Twenty bucks a night.

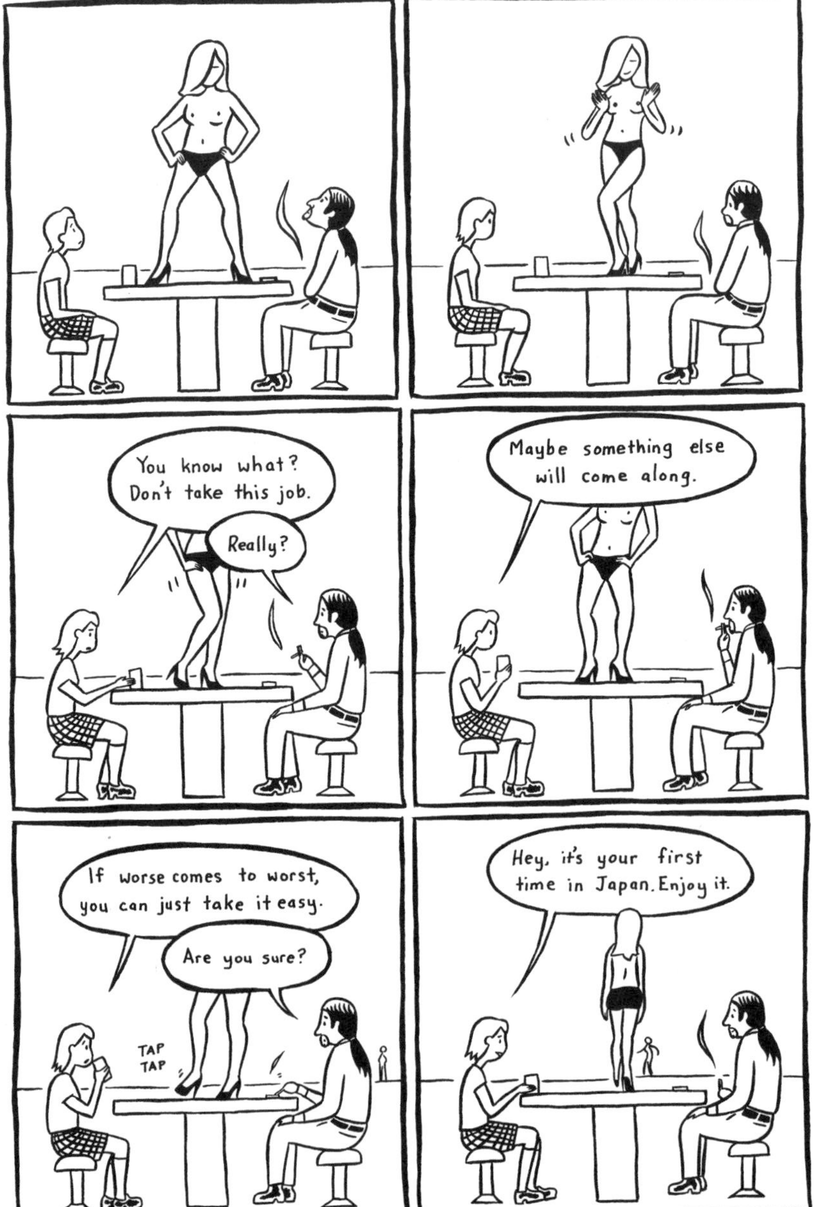
You know what? Don't take this job.
Really?
Maybe something else will come along.
If worse comes to worst, you can just take it easy.
Are you sure?
TAP TAP
Hey, it's your first time in Japan. Enjoy it.

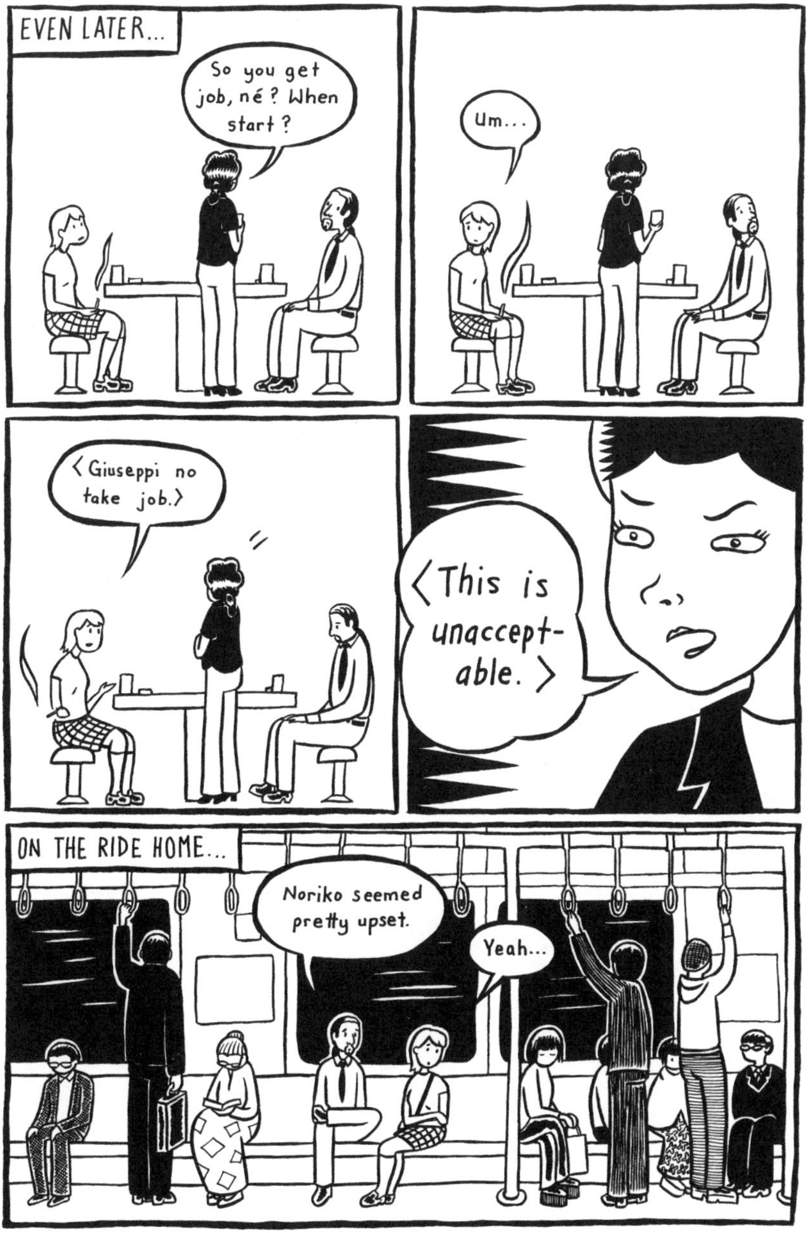
EVEN LATER...
So you get job, né? When start?
Um...
〈Giuseppi no take job.〉
〈This is unacceptable.〉
ON THE RIDE HOME...
Noriko seemed pretty upset.
Yeah...

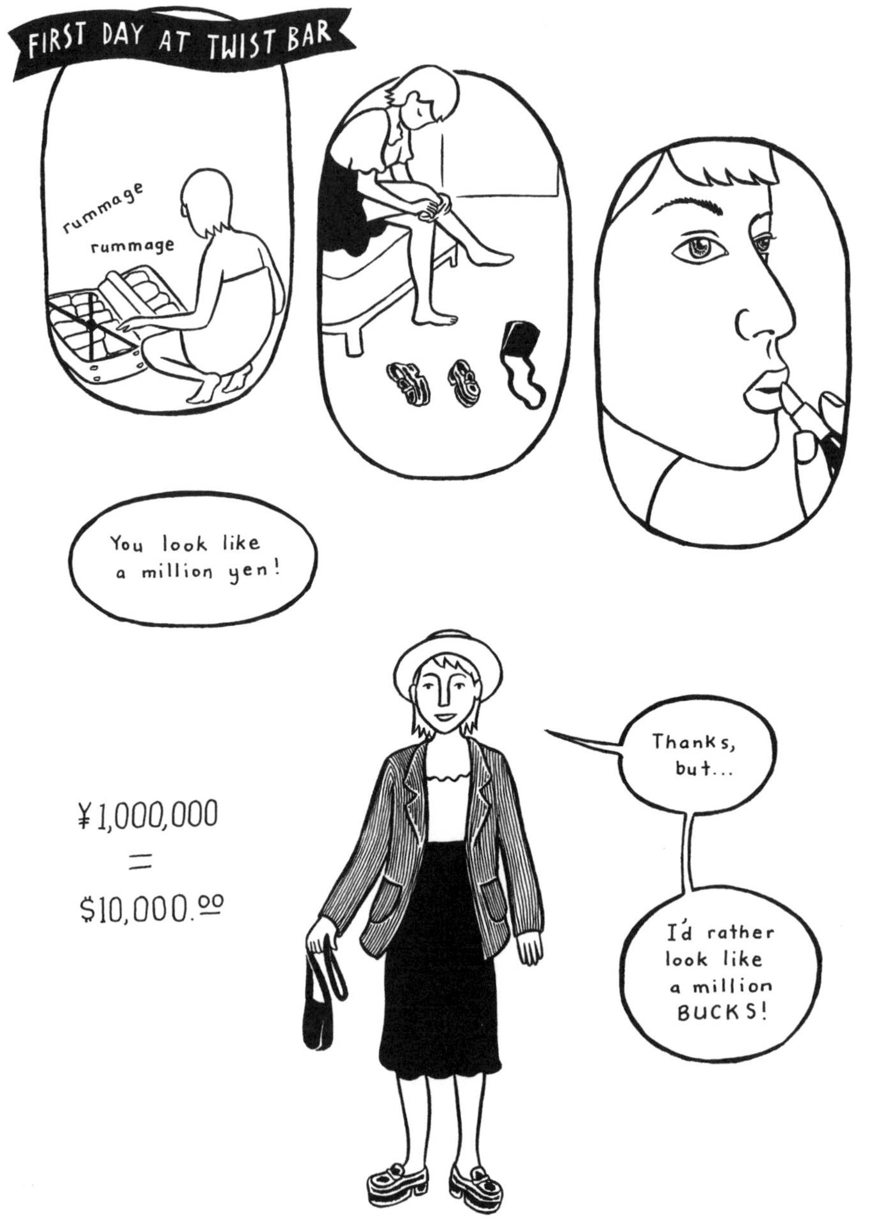
FIRST DAY AT TWIST BAR
rummage
rummage
You look like a million yen!
Thanks, but...
I'd rather look like a million BUCKS!
¥1,000,000 = $10,000.00

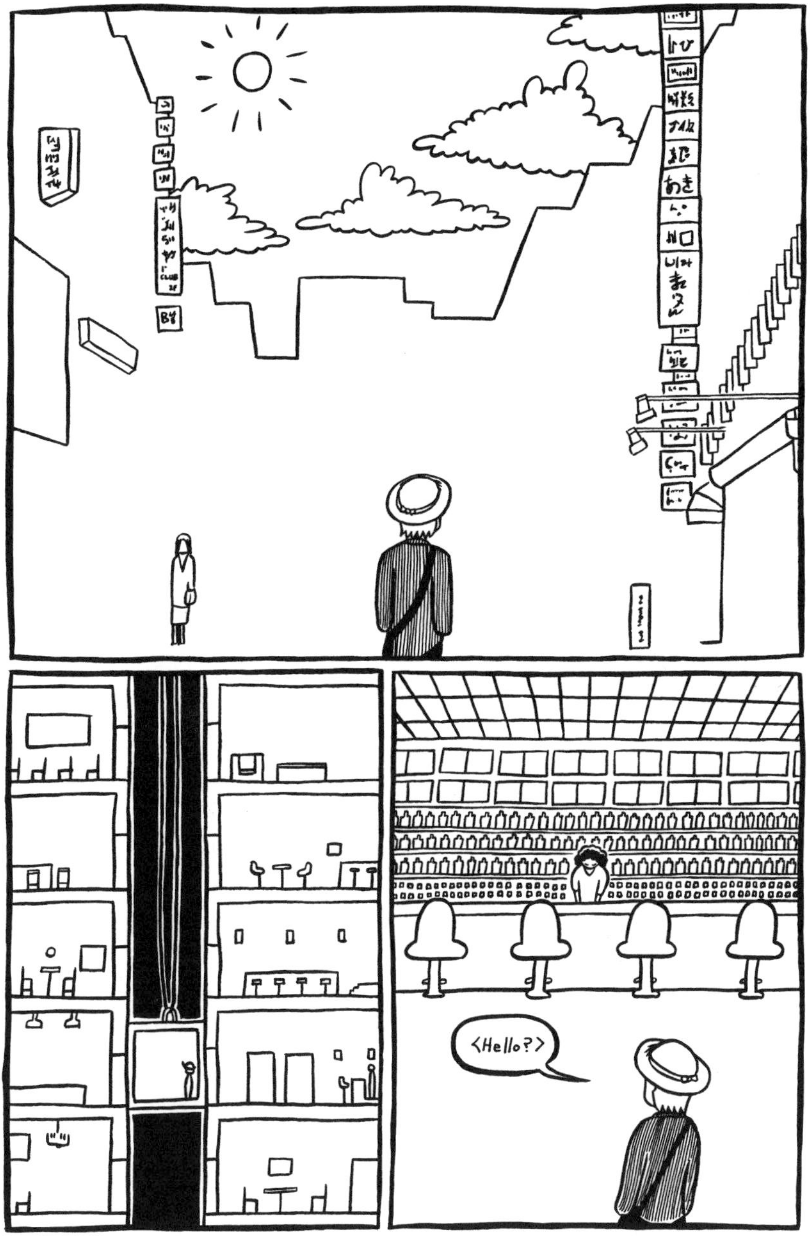
<Hello?>

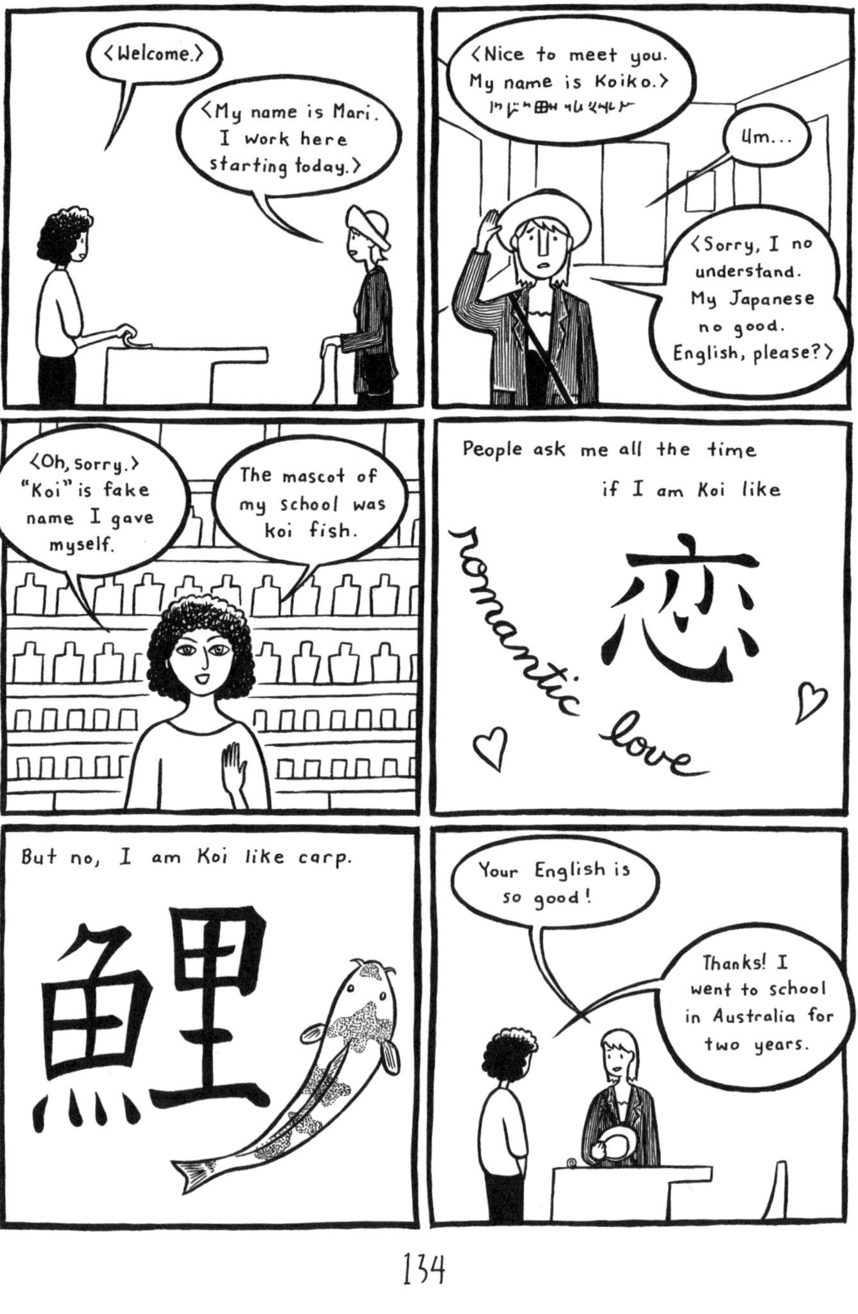

<Welcome.>
<My name is Mari. I work here starting today.>
<Nice to meet you. My name is Koiko.>
Um...
<Sorry, I no understand. My Japanese no good. English, please?>
<Oh, sorry.> "Koi" is fake name I gave myself.
The mascot of my school was koi fish.
People ask me all the time if I am Koi like
恋
romantic love
But no, I am Koi like carp.
鯉
Your English is so good!
Thanks! I went to school in Australia for two years.

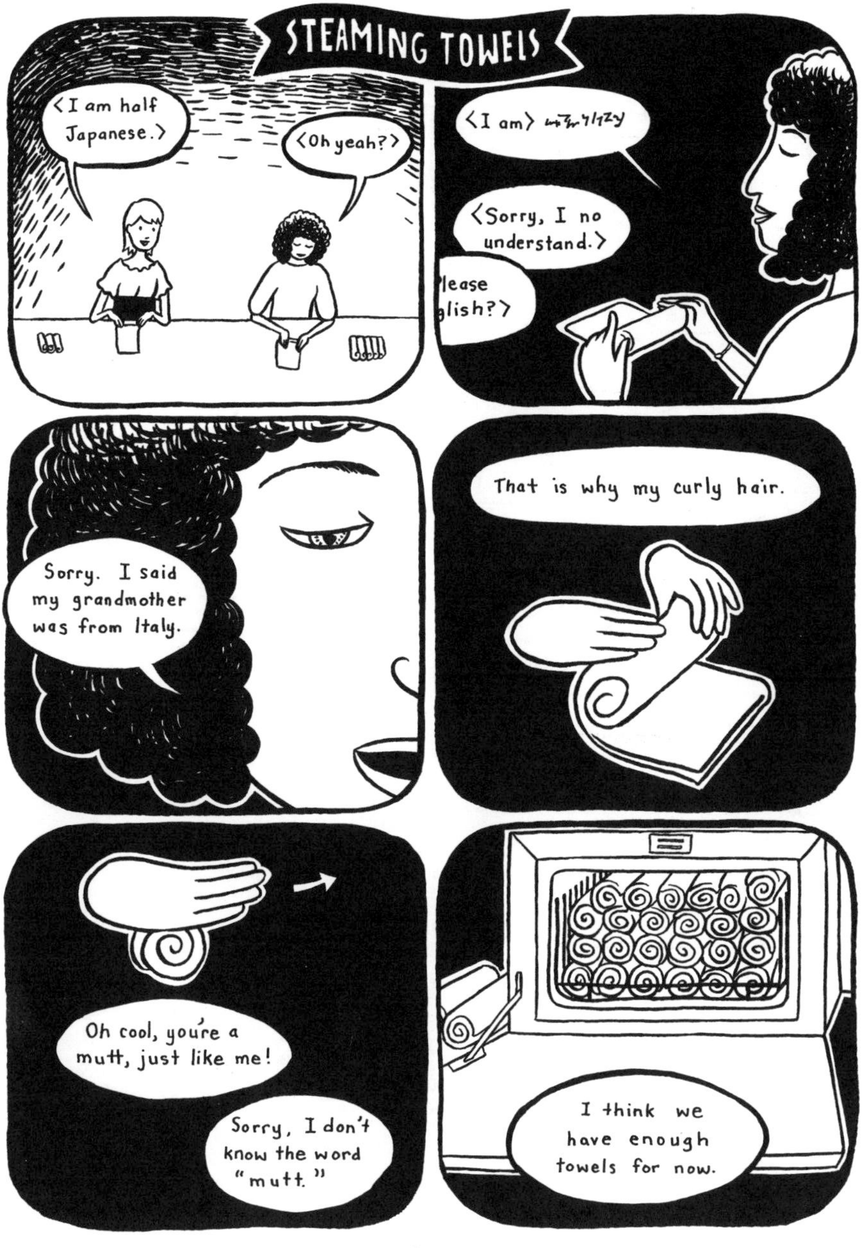
STEAMING TOWELS
<I am half Japanese.>
<Oh yeah?>
<I am>
<Sorry, I no understand.>
lease
lish?>
Sorry. I said my grandmother was from Italy.
That is why my curly hair.
Oh cool, you're a mutt, just like me!
Sorry, I don't know the word "mutt."
I think we have enough towels for now.

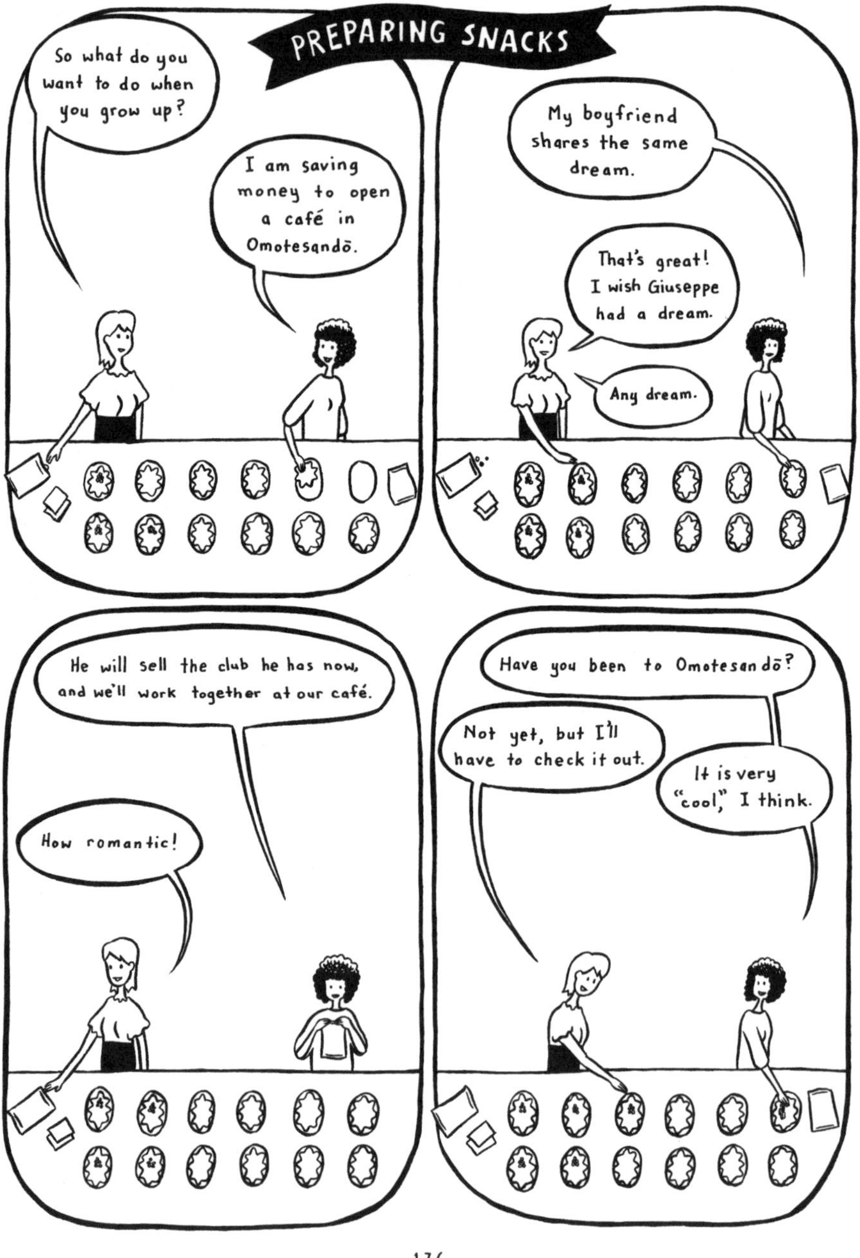
PREPARING SNACKS
So what do you want to do when you grow up?
I am saving money to open a café in Omotesandō.
My boyfriend shares the same dream.
That's great! I wish Giuseppe had a dream.
Any dream.
He will sell the club he has now, and we'll work together at our café.
How romantic!
Have you been to Omotesandō?
Not yet, but I'll have to check it out.
It is very "cool," I think.

SAMPLE WET SNACK DISHES

Chiyo's home-made kimpira

sautéed burdock root
carrots
sesame seeds

Chiyo's home-made potato salad

potatoes
cucumbers
carrots
apples
mayonnaise

SAMPLE DRY SNACK BASKETS

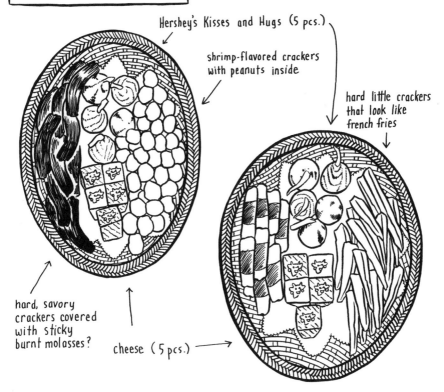

Hershey's Kisses and Hugs (5 pcs.)

shrimp-flavored crackers
with peanuts inside

hard little crackers
that look like
french fries

hard, savory
crackers covered
with sticky
burnt molasses?

cheese (5 pcs.)

137

THERE WERE SOME SIMILARITIES BETWEEN TWIST AND YAMAMOTO.

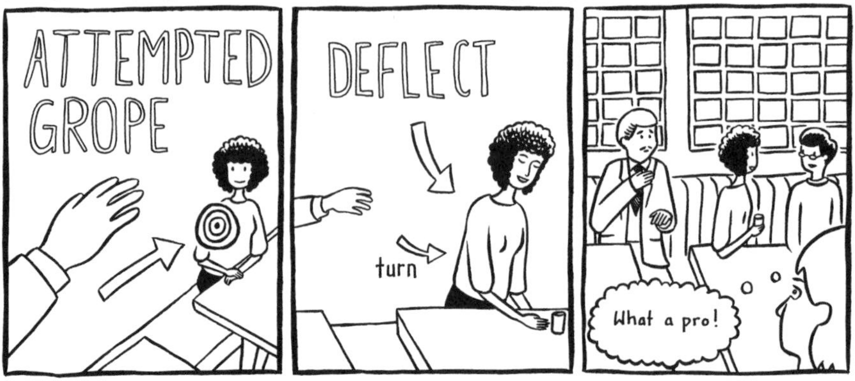
ATTEMPTED GROPE
DEFLECT
turn
What a pro!

TWIST'S CLIENTELE WAS GENERALLY MORE WELL-MANNERED, HOWEVER, AND I OFTEN FOUND MYSELF SURROUNDED BY AN ARTY, LITERATE CROWD ENGAGED IN RELEVANT, INTELLECTUAL BANTER. I THINK.

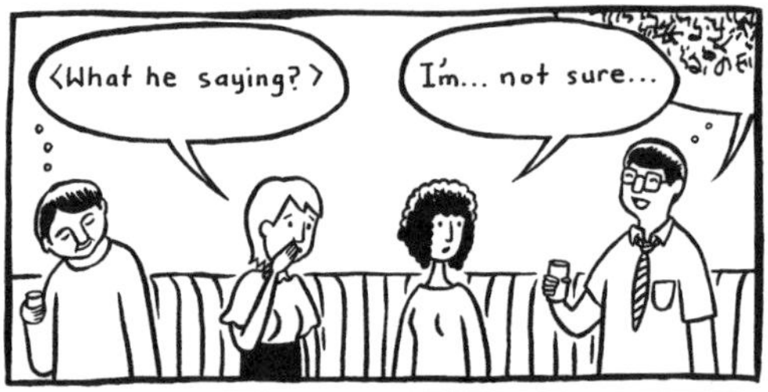
<What he saying?>
I'm... not sure...

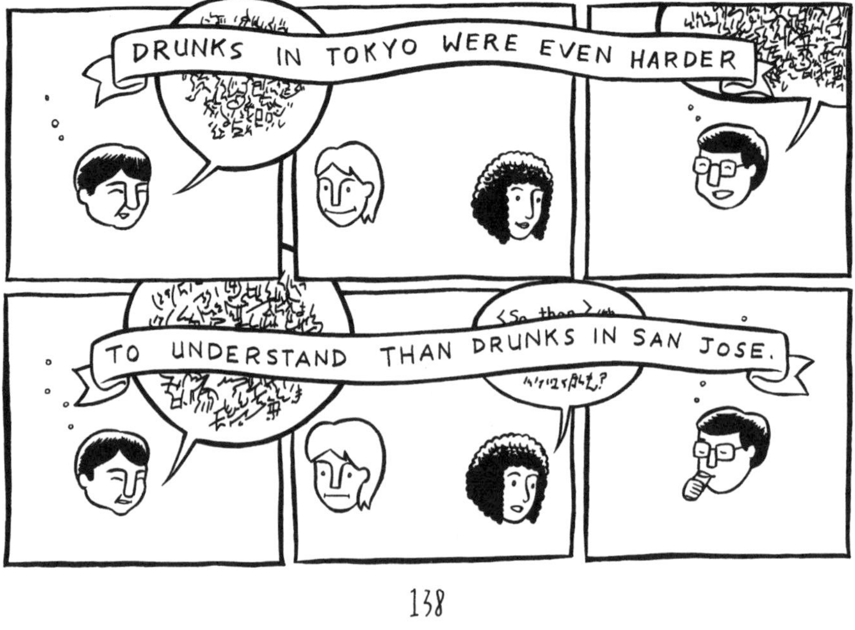
DRUNKS IN TOKYO WERE EVEN HARDER
TO UNDERSTAND THAN DRUNKS IN SAN JOSE.

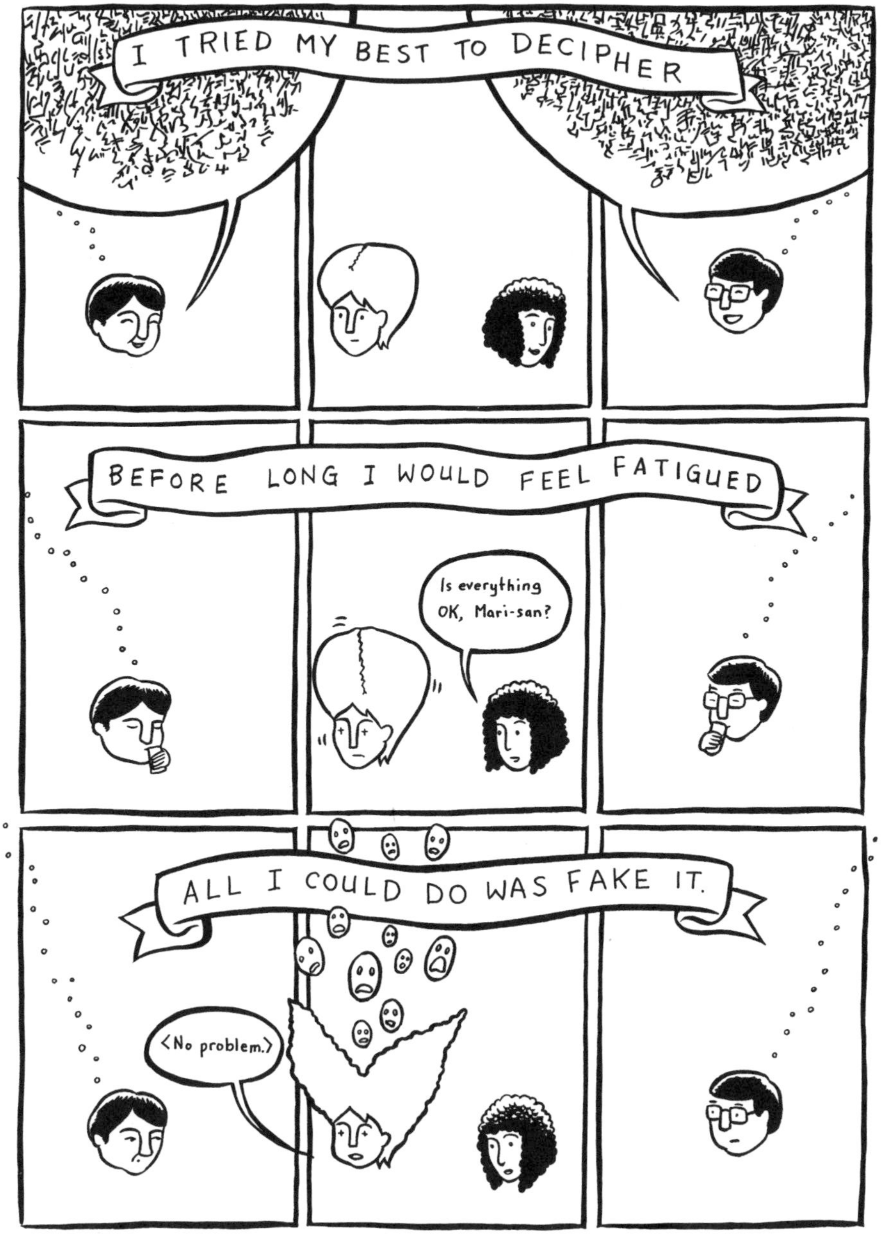
I TRIED MY BEST TO DECIPHER
BEFORE LONG I WOULD FEEL FATIGUED
Is everything OK, Mari-san?
ALL I COULD DO WAS FAKE IT.
<No problem.>

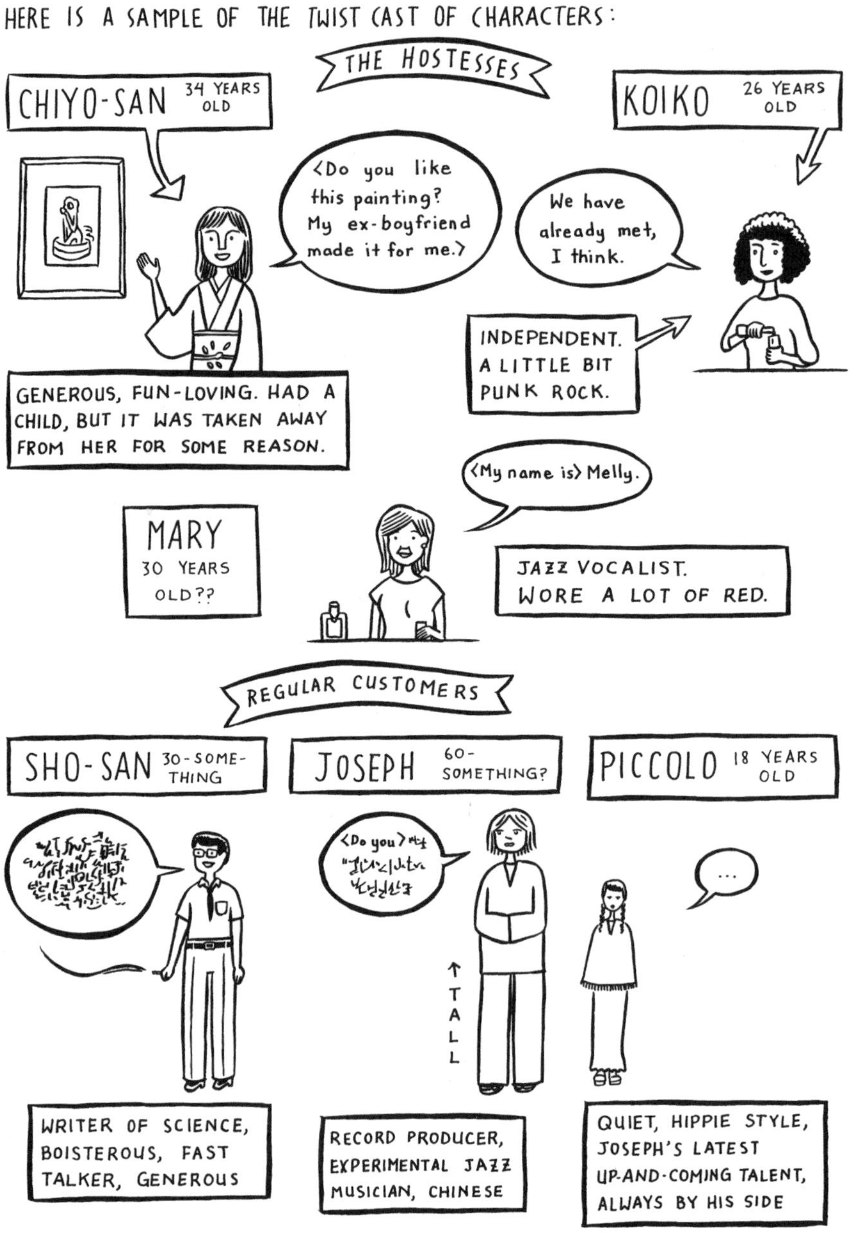
HERE IS A SAMPLE OF THE TWIST CAST OF CHARACTERS:
THE HOSTESSES
CHIYO-SAN 34 YEARS OLD
<Do you like this painting? My ex-boyfriend made it for me.>
GENEROUS, FUN-LOVING. HAD A CHILD, BUT IT WAS TAKEN AWAY FROM HER FOR SOME REASON.
KOIKO 26 YEARS OLD
We have already met, I think.
INDEPENDENT. A LITTLE BIT PUNK ROCK.
MARY 30 YEARS OLD??
<My name is> Melly.
JAZZ VOCALIST. WORE A LOT OF RED.
REGULAR CUSTOMERS
SHO-SAN 30-SOMETHING
WRITER OF SCIENCE, BOISTEROUS, FAST TALKER, GENEROUS
JOSEPH 60-SOMETHING?
<Do you>
TALL
RECORD PRODUCER, EXPERIMENTAL JAZZ MUSICIAN, CHINESE
PICCOLO 18 YEARS OLD
...
QUIET, HIPPIE STYLE, JOSEPH'S LATEST UP-AND-COMING TALENT, ALWAYS BY HIS SIDE

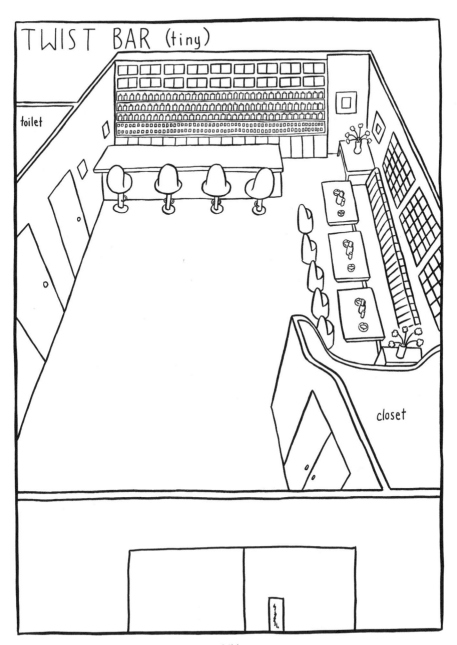

TWIST BAR (tiny)

toilet

closet

To Mari,

Hi, how's goin? I write down what you should do.

1. Vacuum the floor.
2. Set the tables and chair.
you'll see the papers and toothsticks behind the picture of Chiyo.
3. Make hot water and put it into the jar.

4. Make some snack baskets.

5. Put the bottle back there are some you can't, just leave them That'll be fine

6. Oh, & don't forget to turn the lights on.

~~B Itou san~~
Anyway you'll be fine.

7. Bring the green basket in.
Make 24 folded towls and put them into the steamer.

OK

Dear Mari,

I'm coming around 9-o'clock tonight. (with some customer)

Mary will help you (I hope she'll come anyhow.)

If you have time, can you make the House Bottle full with Nikka or Royal bottles?! customers' ones
Thanx (of course ☺)
See you later Koiko

142

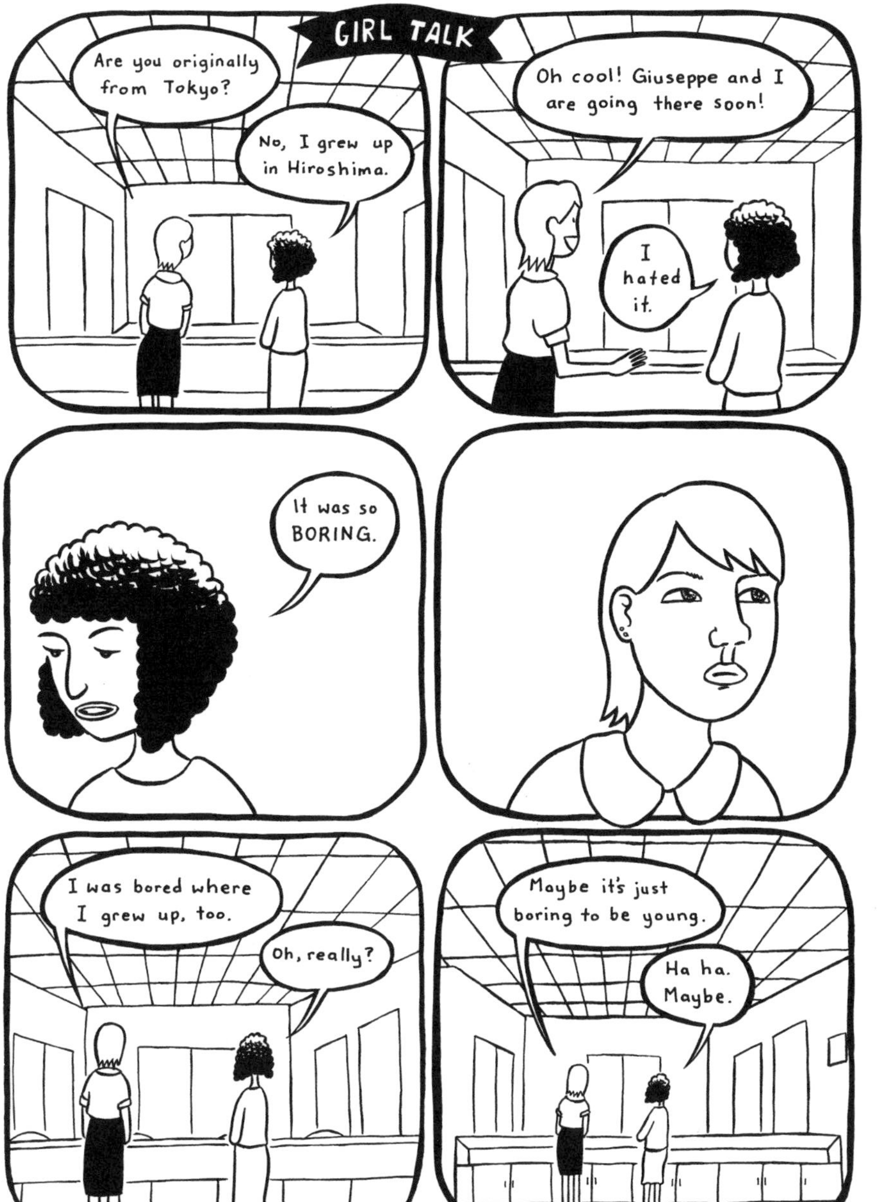
GIRL TALK
Are you originally from Tokyo?
No, I grew up in Hiroshima.
Oh cool! Giuseppe and I are going there soon!
I hated it.
It was so BORING.
I was bored where I grew up, too.
Oh, really?
Maybe it's just boring to be young.
Ha ha. Maybe.

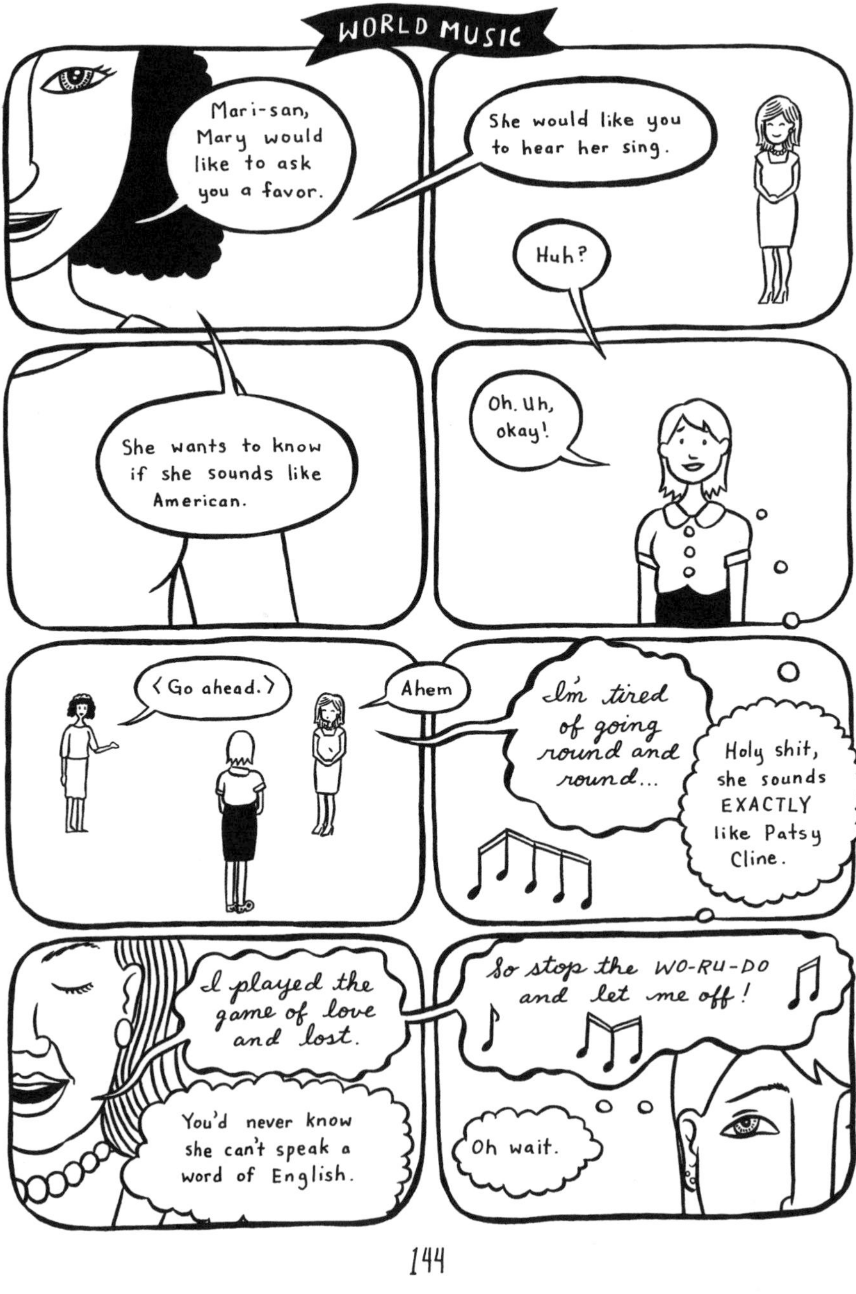
WORLD MUSIC
Mari-san, Mary would like to ask you a favor.
She would like you to hear her sing.
Huh?
She wants to know if she sounds like American.
Oh. Uh, okay!
〈Go ahead.〉
Ahem
I'm tired of going round and round...
Holy shit, she sounds EXACTLY like Patsy Cline.
I played the game of love and lost.
You'd never know she can't speak a word of English.
So stop the WO-RU-DO and let me off!
Oh wait.

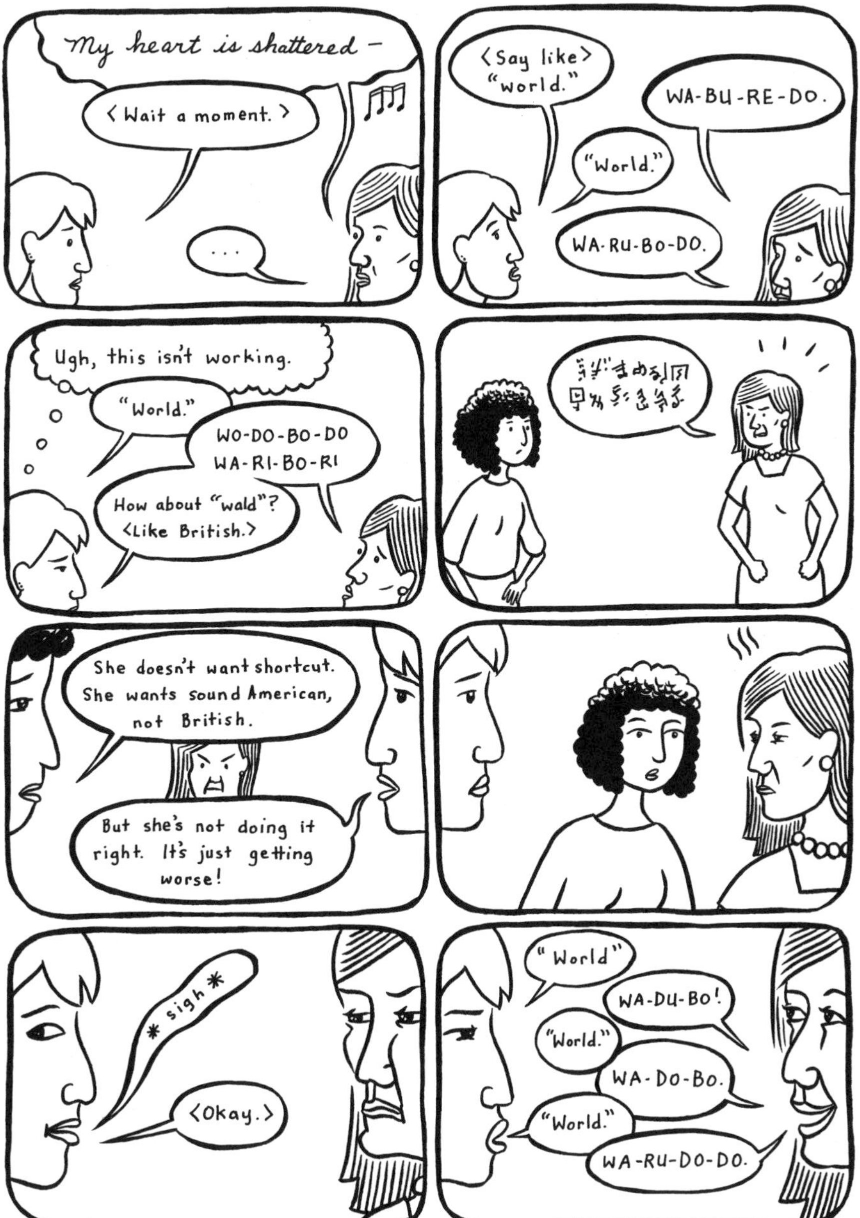
My heart is shattered -
〈 Wait a moment. 〉
. . .
〈 Say like 〉 "world."
WA-BU-RE-DO.
"World."
WA-RU-BO-DO.
Ugh, this isn't working.
"World."
WO-DO-BO-DO
WA-RI-BO-RI
How about "wald"? 〈Like British.〉
She doesn't want shortcut. She wants sound American, not British.
But she's not doing it right. It's just getting worse!
* sigh *
〈Okay.〉
"World"
WA-DU-BO!
"World."
WA-DO-BO.
"World."
WA-RU-DO-DO.

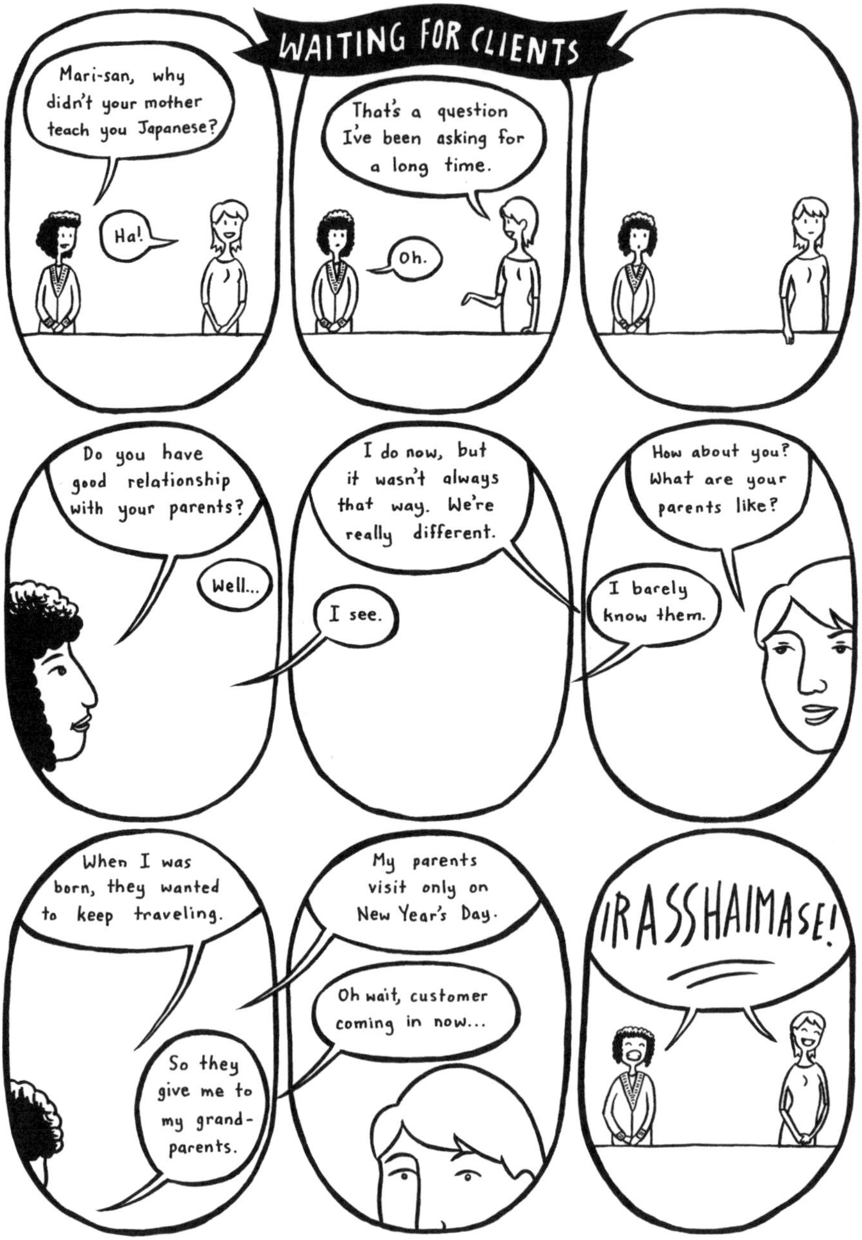
WAITING FOR CLIENTS
Mari-san, why didn't your mother teach you Japanese?
Ha!
That's a question I've been asking for a long time.
Oh.
Do you have good relationship with your parents?
Well...
I do now, but it wasn't always that way. We're really different.
I see.
How about you? What are your parents like?
I barely know them.
When I was born, they wanted to keep traveling.
So they give me to my grand-parents.
My parents visit only on New Year's Day.
Oh wait, customer coming in now...
IRASSHAIMASE!

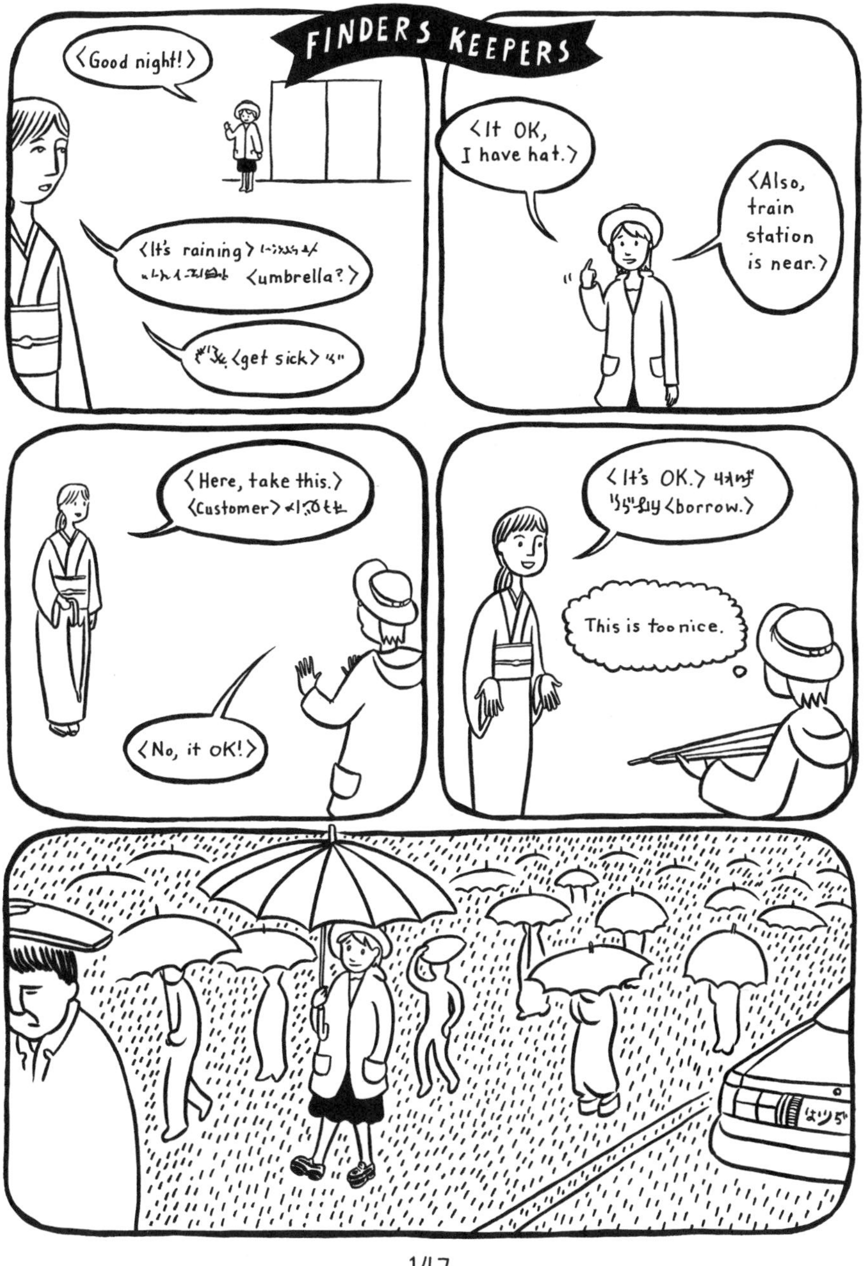
FINDERS KEEPERS
〈Good night!〉
〈It's raining〉 〈umbrella?〉
〈get sick〉
〈It OK, I have hat.〉
〈Also, train station is near.〉
〈Here, take this.〉 〈Customer〉
〈No, it OK!〉
〈It's OK.〉 〈borrow.〉
This is too nice.

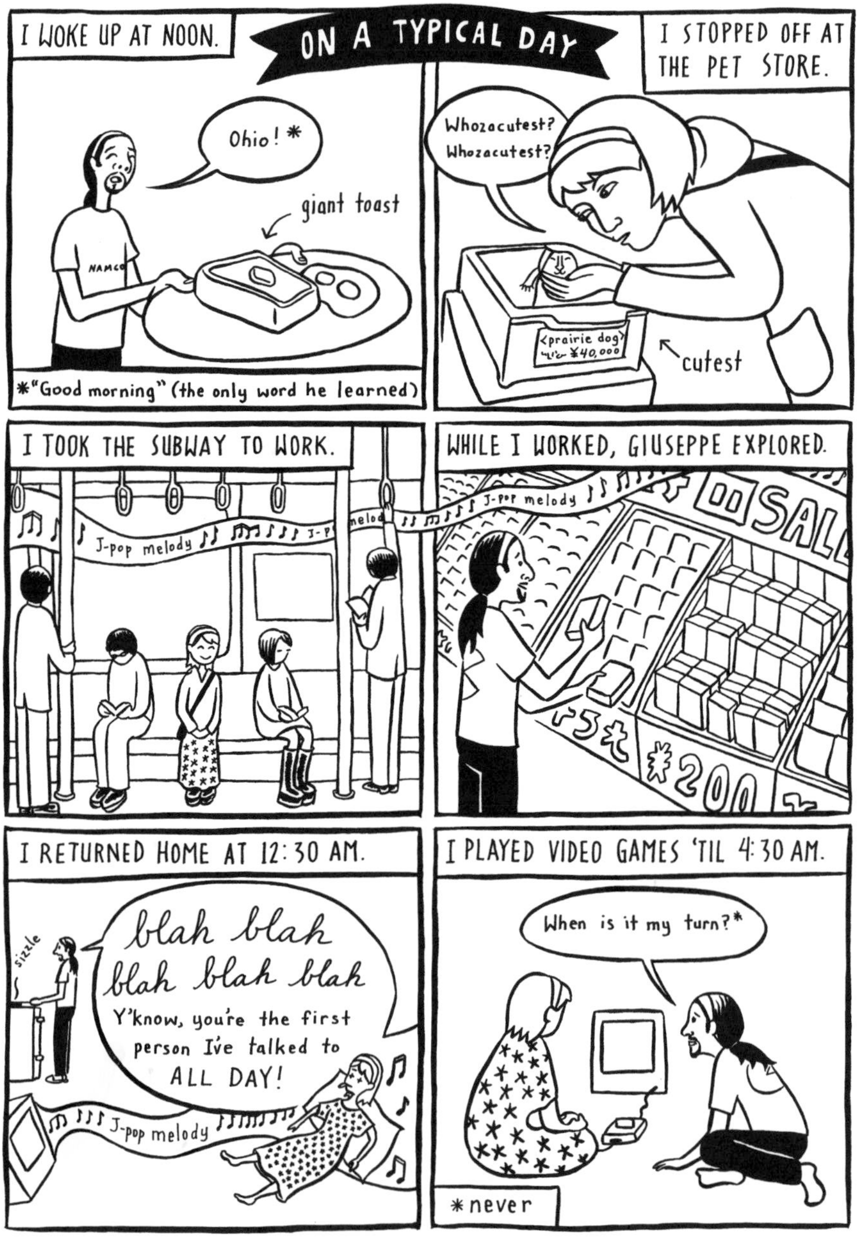

I WOKE UP AT NOON.
ON A TYPICAL DAY
Ohio! *
giant toast
NAMCO
*"Good morning" (the only word he learned)
I STOPPED OFF AT THE PET STORE.
Whozacutest? Whozacutest?
<prairie dog> ¥40,000
cutest
I TOOK THE SUBWAY TO WORK.
J-pop melody
WHILE I WORKED, GIUSEPPE EXPLORED.
J-pop melody
SAL
¥200
I RETURNED HOME AT 12:30 AM.
sizzle
blah blah blah blah blah
Y'know, you're the first person I've talked to ALL DAY!
J-pop melody
I PLAYED VIDEO GAMES 'TIL 4:30 AM.
When is it my turn?*
*never

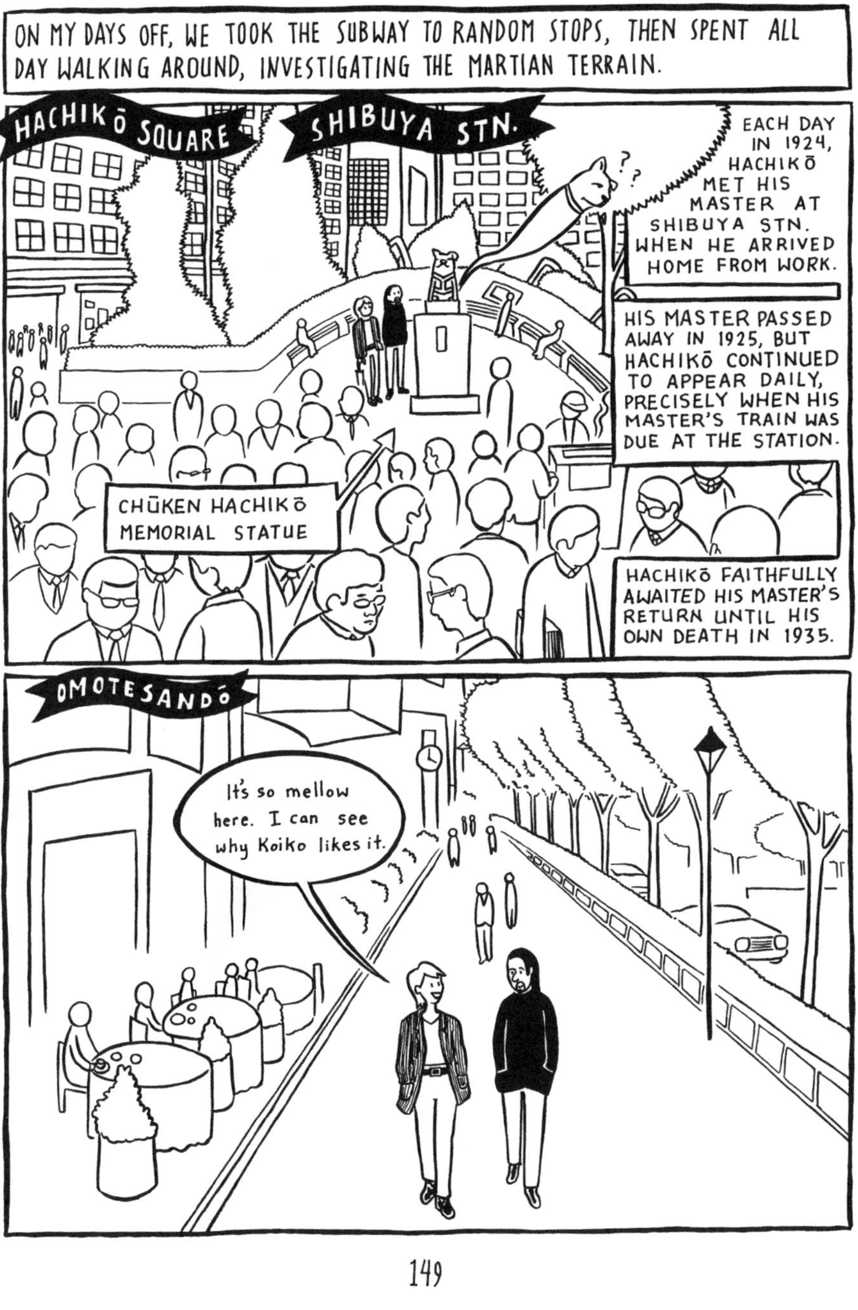
ON MY DAYS OFF, WE TOOK THE SUBWAY TO RANDOM STOPS, THEN SPENT ALL DAY WALKING AROUND, INVESTIGATING THE MARTIAN TERRAIN.
HACHIKŌ SQUARE
SHIBUYA STN.
EACH DAY IN 1924, HACHIKŌ MET HIS MASTER AT SHIBUYA STN. WHEN HE ARRIVED HOME FROM WORK.
? ?
HIS MASTER PASSED AWAY IN 1925, BUT HACHIKŌ CONTINUED TO APPEAR DAILY, PRECISELY WHEN HIS MASTER'S TRAIN WAS DUE AT THE STATION.
CHŪKEN HACHIKŌ MEMORIAL STATUE
HACHIKŌ FAITHFULLY AWAITED HIS MASTER'S RETURN UNTIL HIS OWN DEATH IN 1935.
OMOTESANDŌ
It's so mellow here. I can see why Koiko likes it.

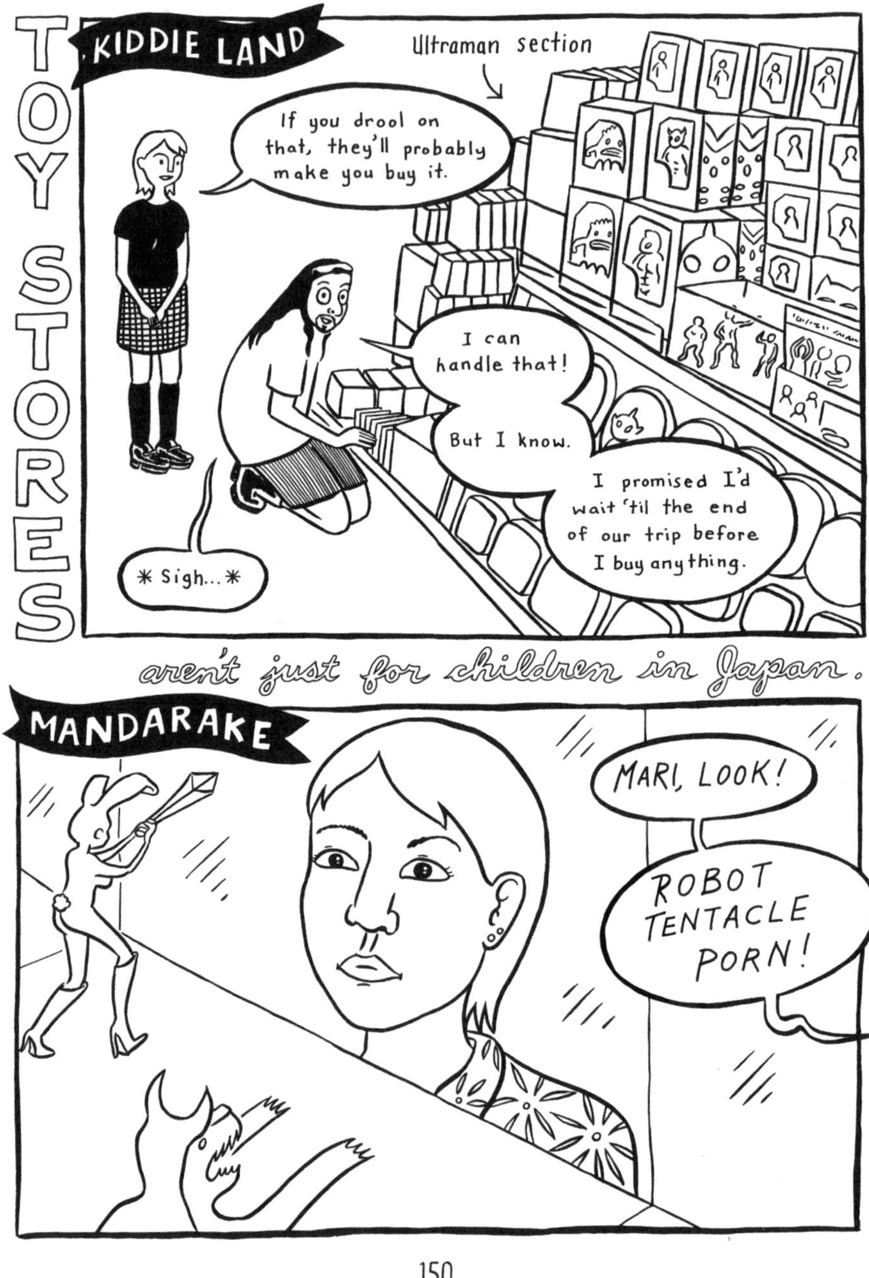
TOY STORES
KIDDIE LAND
Ultraman section
If you drool on that, they'll probably make you buy it.
I can handle that!
But I know.
I promised I'd wait 'til the end of our trip before I buy anything.
* Sigh... *
aren't just for children in Japan.
MANDARAKE
MARI, LOOK!
ROBOT TENTACLE PORN!

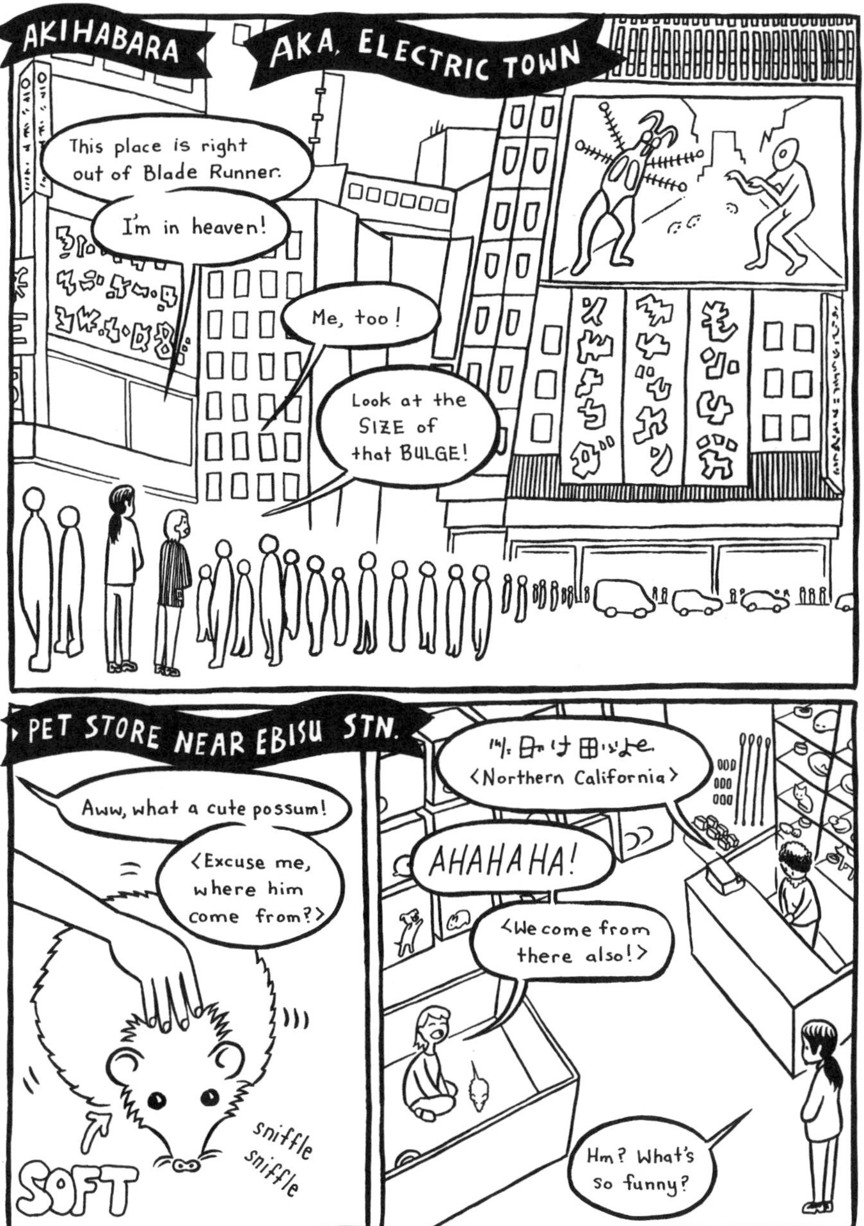
AKIHABARA
AKA, ELECTRIC TOWN
This place is right out of Blade Runner.
I'm in heaven!
Me, too!
Look at the SIZE of that BULGE!
PET STORE NEAR EBISU STN.
Aww, what a cute possum!
<Excuse me, where him come from?>
SOFT
sniffle sniffle
<Northern California>
AHAHAHA!
<We come from there also!>
Hm? What's so funny?

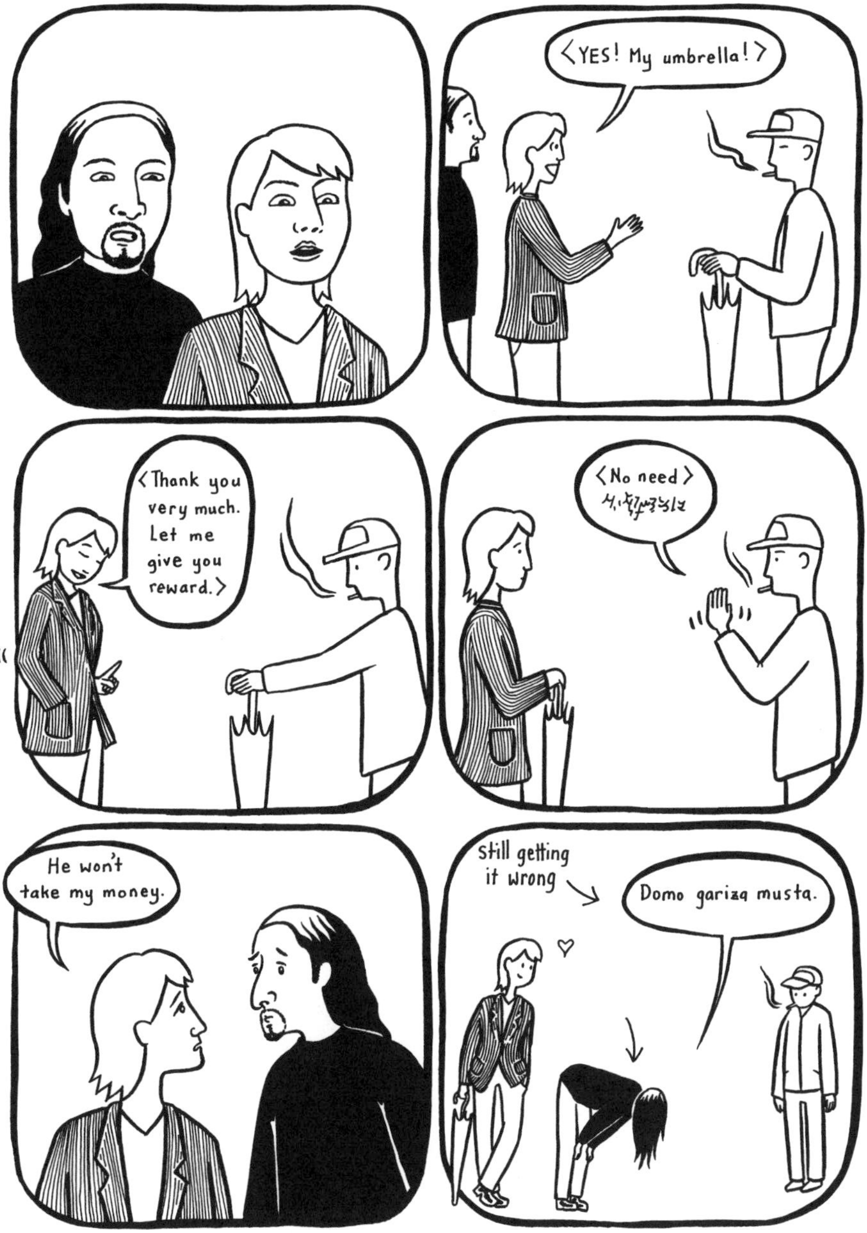

<YES! My umbrella!>
<Thank you very much. Let me give you reward.>
<No need>
He won't take my money.
Still getting it wrong
Domo gariza musta.

TEDDY HAD BUSINESS IN TOKYO, SO HE JOINED US AT THE APARTMENT FOR A WEEK.

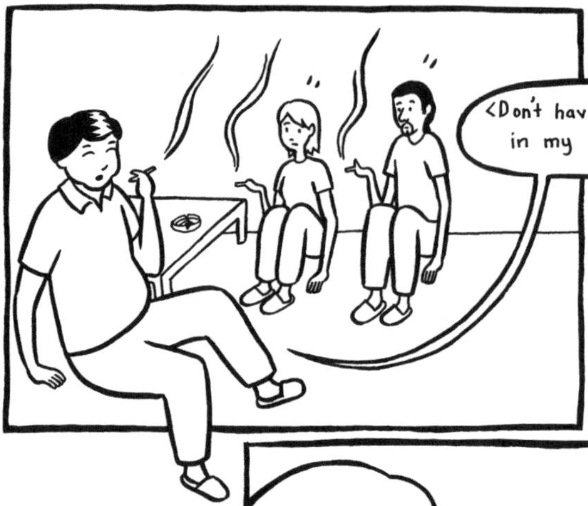
<Don't have sexual intercourse in my apartment, OK?>

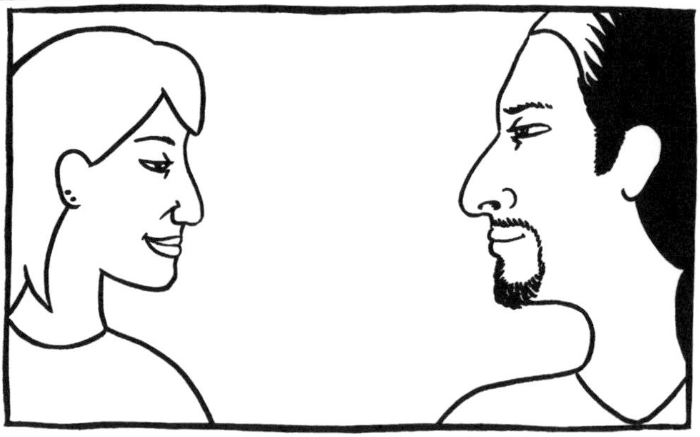

UP 'TIL THIS POINT WE'D BEEN TOO JET-LAGGED TO HAVE SEX, BUT TEDDY'S UNREASON-ABLE DEMAND BROUGHT OUT THE ANTI-AUTHORITARIAN IN BOTH OF US.

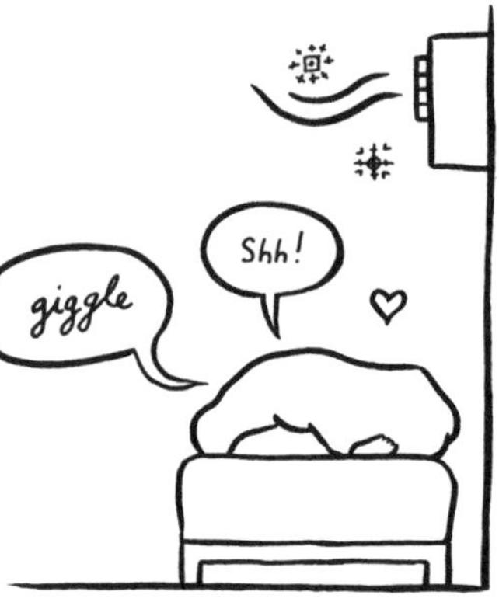
giggle
Shh!

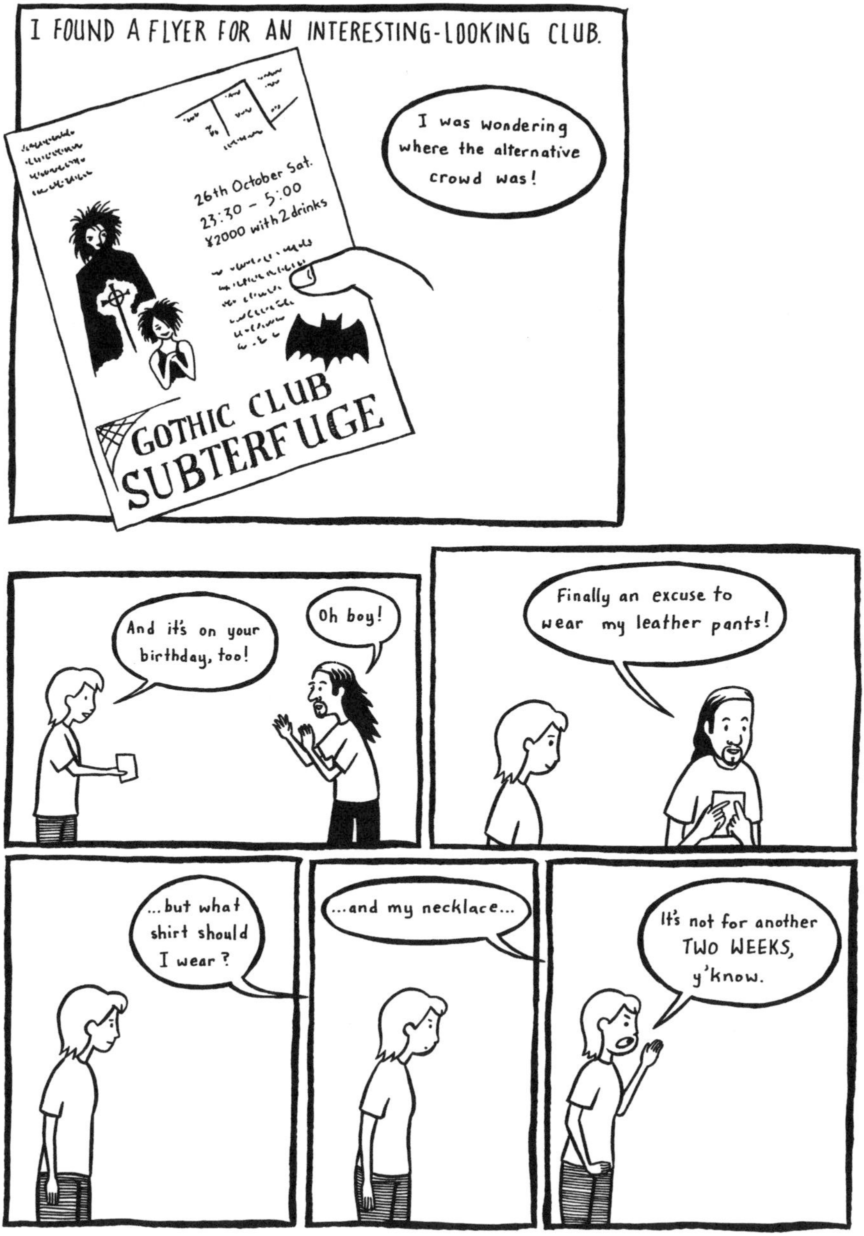
I FOUND A FLYER FOR AN INTERESTING-LOOKING CLUB.
26th October Sat.
23:30 - 5:00
¥2000 with 2 drinks
GOTHIC CLUB
SUBTERFUGE
I was wondering where the alternative crowd was!
And it's on your birthday, too!
Oh boy!
Finally an excuse to wear my leather pants!
...but what shirt should I wear?
...and my necklace...
It's not for another TWO WEEKS, y'know.

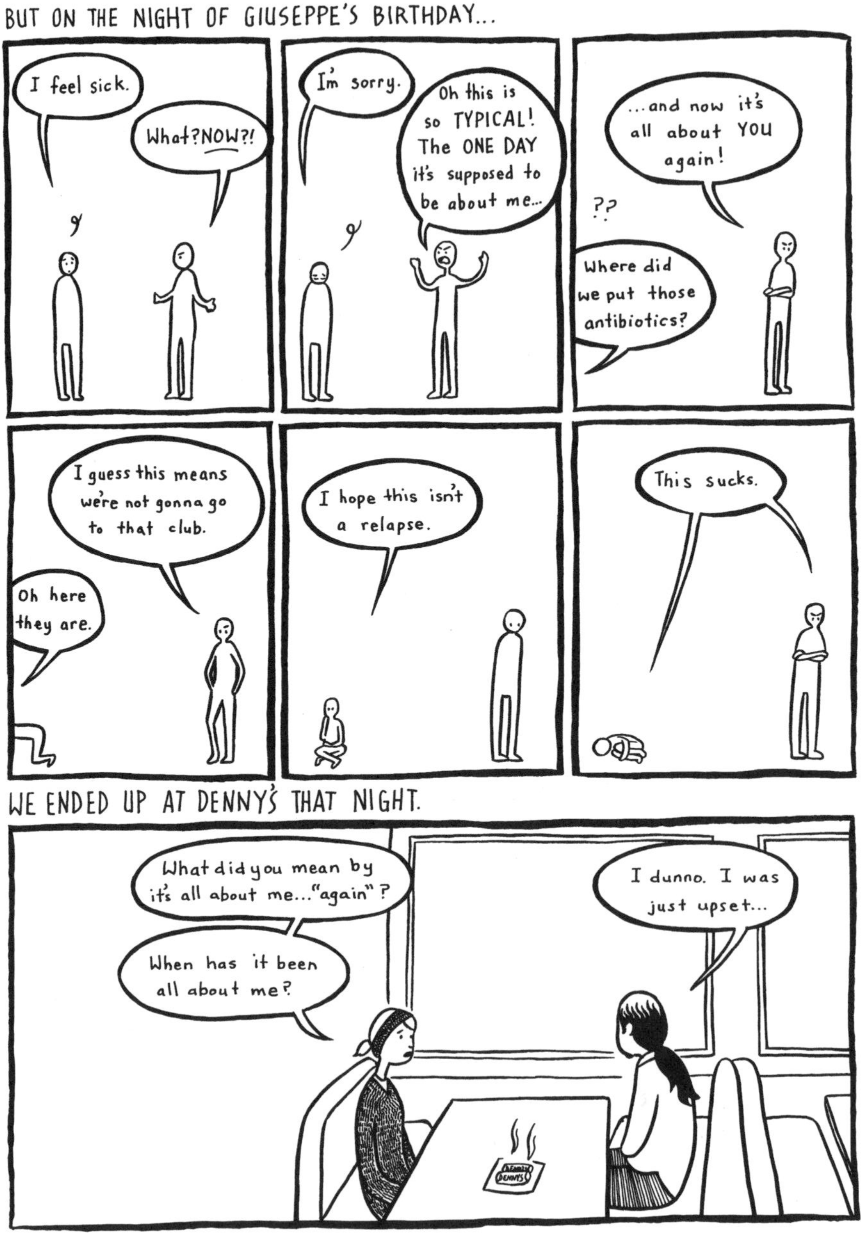
BUT ON THE NIGHT OF GIUSEPPE'S BIRTHDAY...
I feel sick.
What? NOW?!
I'm sorry.
Oh this is so TYPICAL! The ONE DAY it's supposed to be about me...
...and now it's all about YOU again!
??
Where did we put those antibiotics?
I guess this means we're not gonna go to that club.
Oh here they are.
I hope this isn't a relapse.
This sucks.
WE ENDED UP AT DENNY'S THAT NIGHT.
What did you mean by it's all about me..."again"?
When has it been all about me?
I dunno. I was just upset...

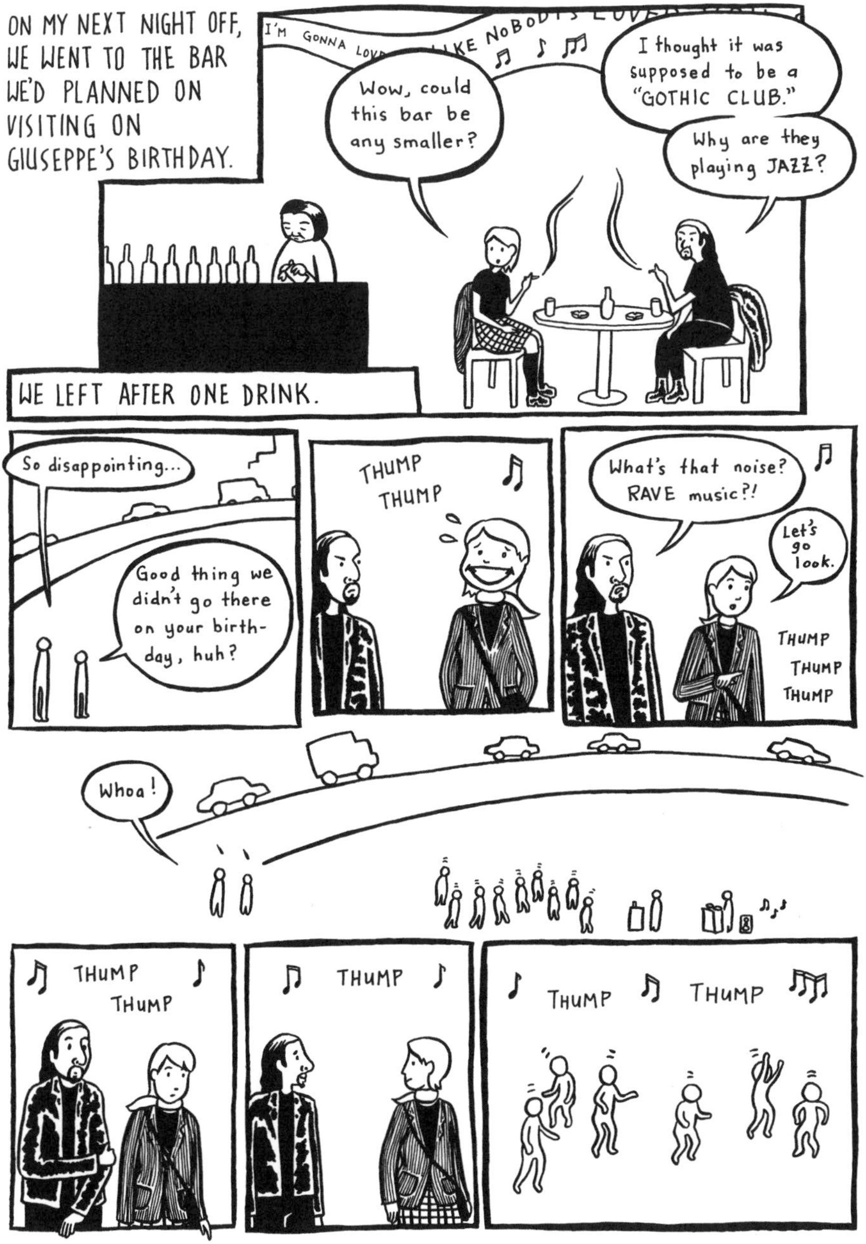
ON MY NEXT NIGHT OFF, WE WENT TO THE BAR WE'D PLANNED ON VISITING ON GIUSEPPE'S BIRTHDAY.
I'M GONNA
LIKE
Wow, could this bar be any smaller?
I thought it was supposed to be a "GOTHIC CLUB."
Why are they playing JAZZ?
WE LEFT AFTER ONE DRINK.
So disappointing...
Good thing we didn't go there on your birthday, huh?
THUMP THUMP
What's that noise? RAVE music?!
Let's go look.
THUMP THUMP THUMP
Whoa!
THUMP THUMP
THUMP
THUMP THUMP

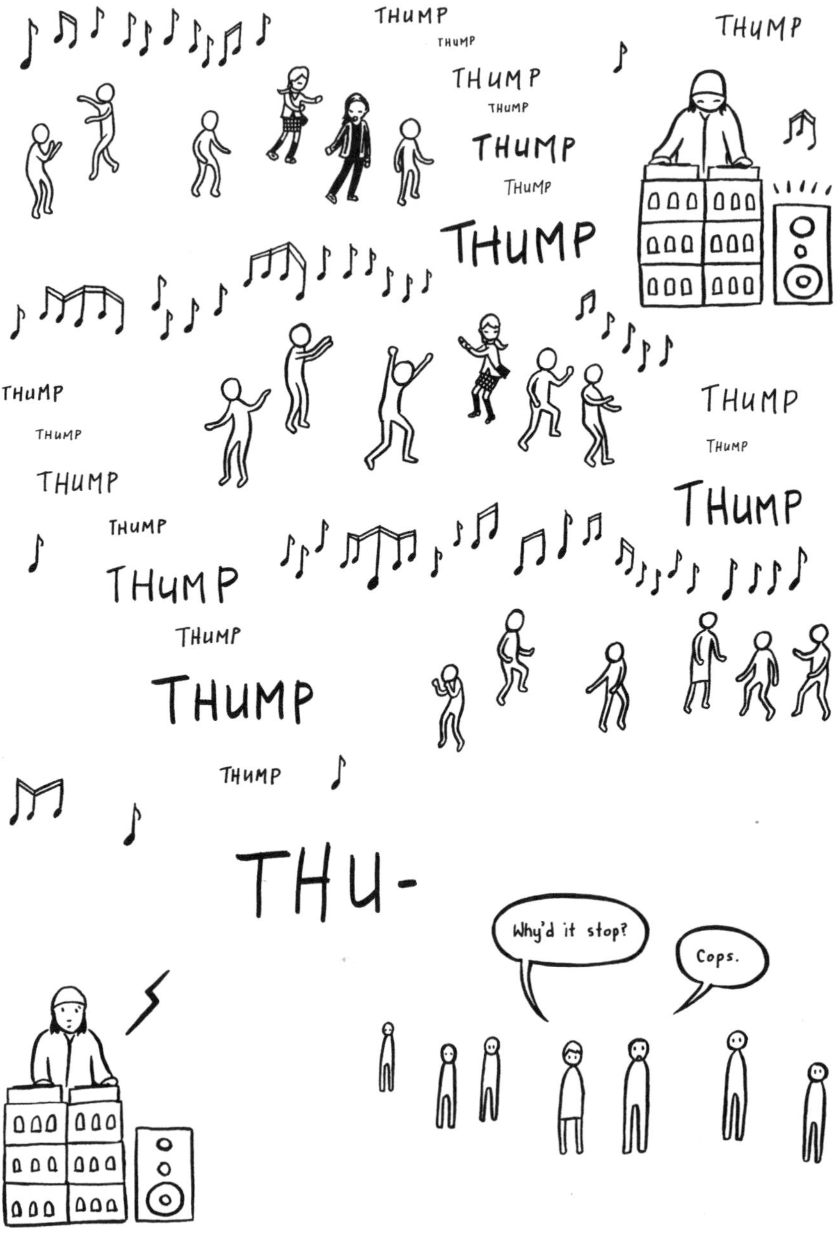
THUMP
THUMP
THUMP
THUMP
THUMP
THUMP
THUMP
THUMP
THUMP
THUMP
THUMP
THUMP
THUMP
THUMP
THUMP
THUMP
THUMP
THUMP
THU-
Why'd it stop?
Cops.

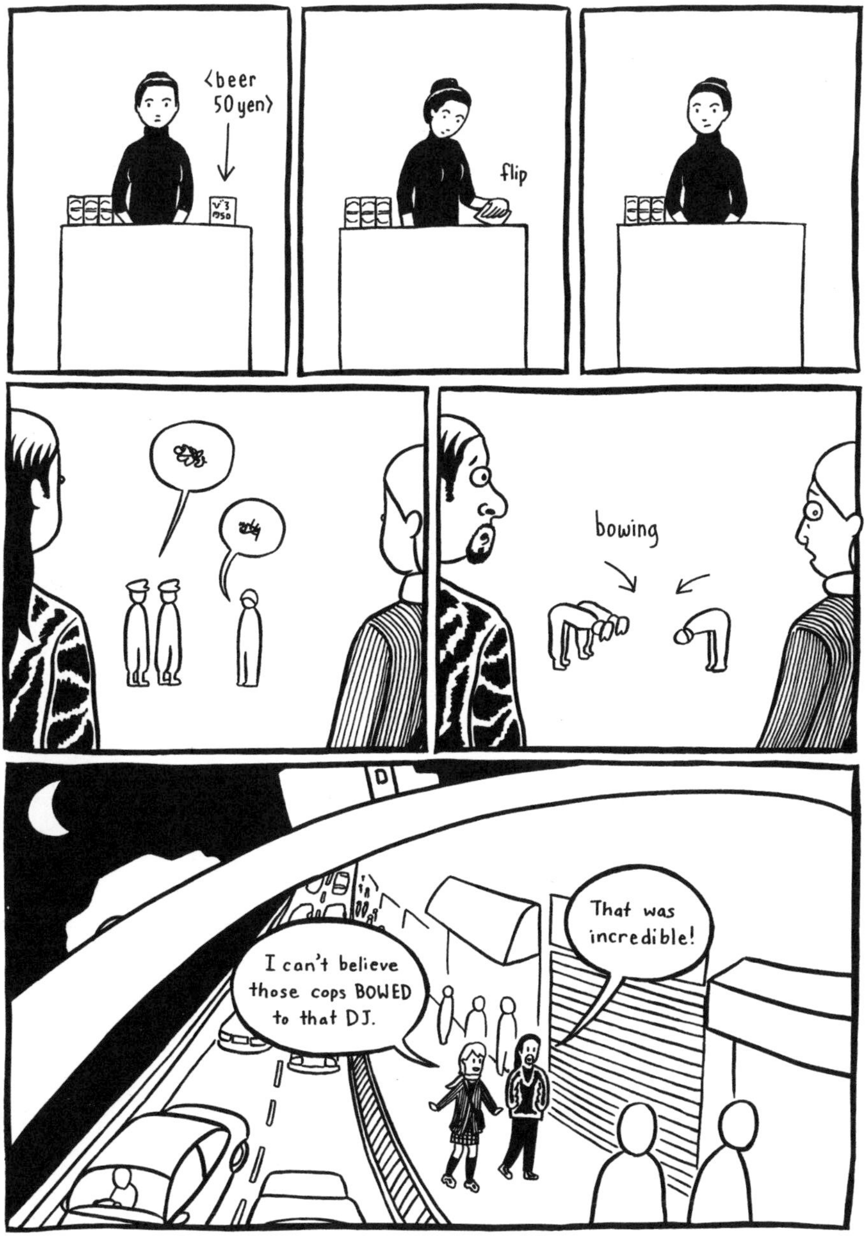
<beer
50 yen>
flip
bowing
I can't believe those cops BOWED to that DJ.
That was incredible!

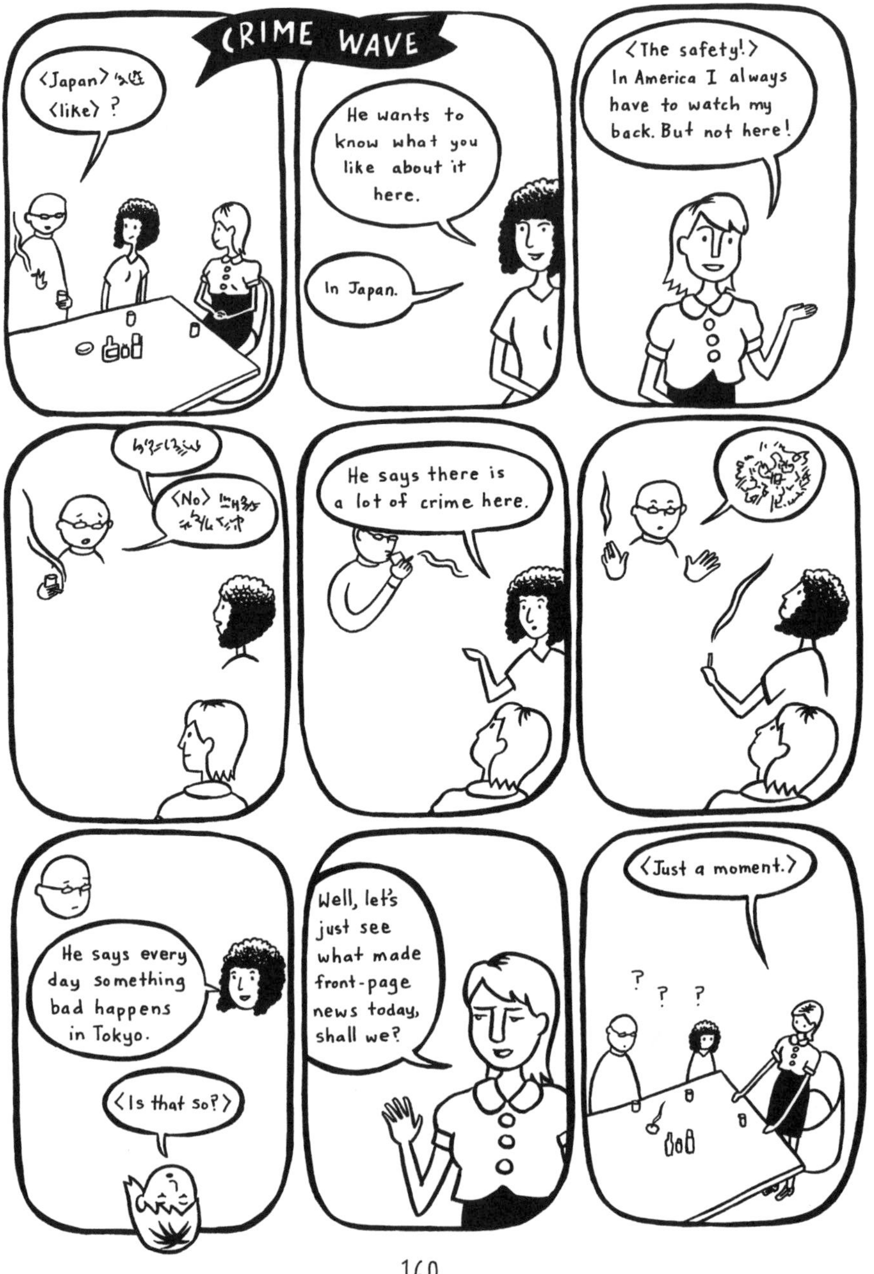
CRIME WAVE
<Japan>
<like> ?
He wants to know what you like about it here.
In Japan.
<The safety!> In America I always have to watch my back. But not here!
<No>
He says there is a lot of crime here.
He says every day something bad happens in Tokyo.
<Is that so?>
Well, let's just see what made front-page news today, shall we?
<Just a moment.>
? ? ?

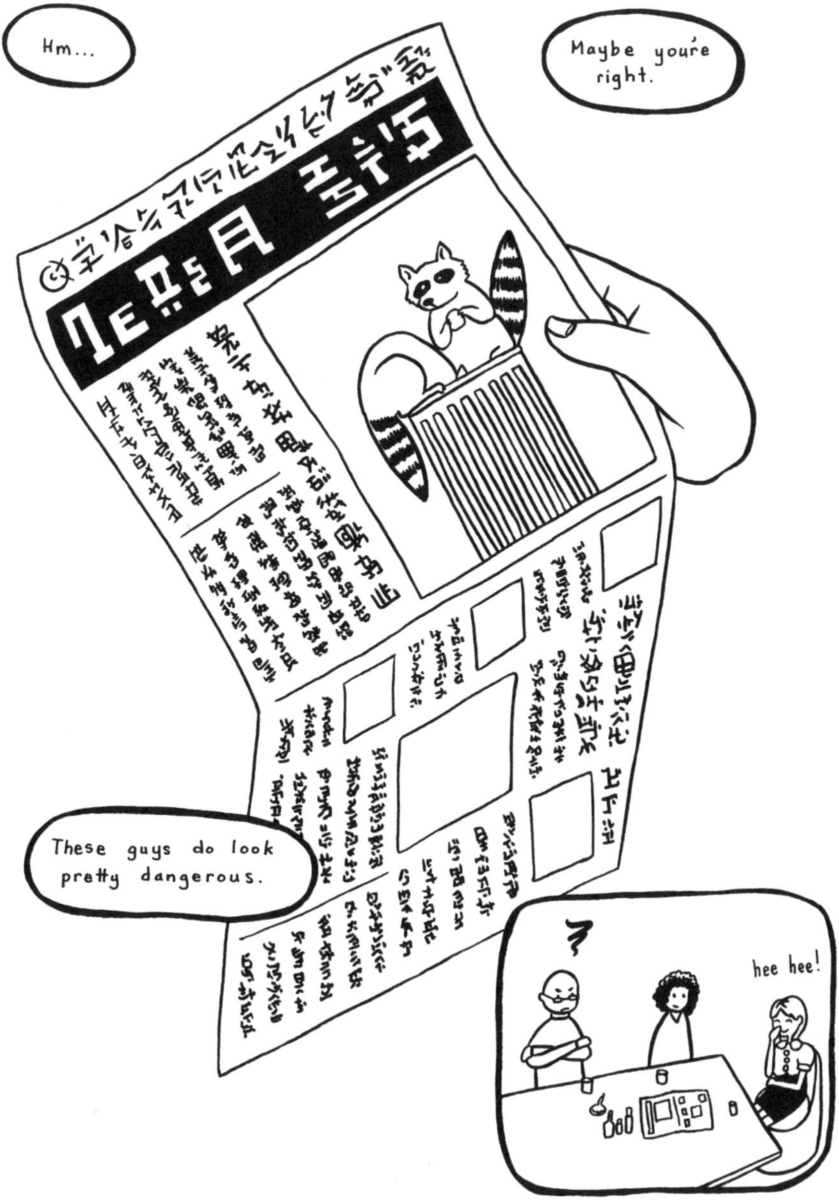
Hm...
Maybe you're right.
These guys do look pretty dangerous.
hee hee!

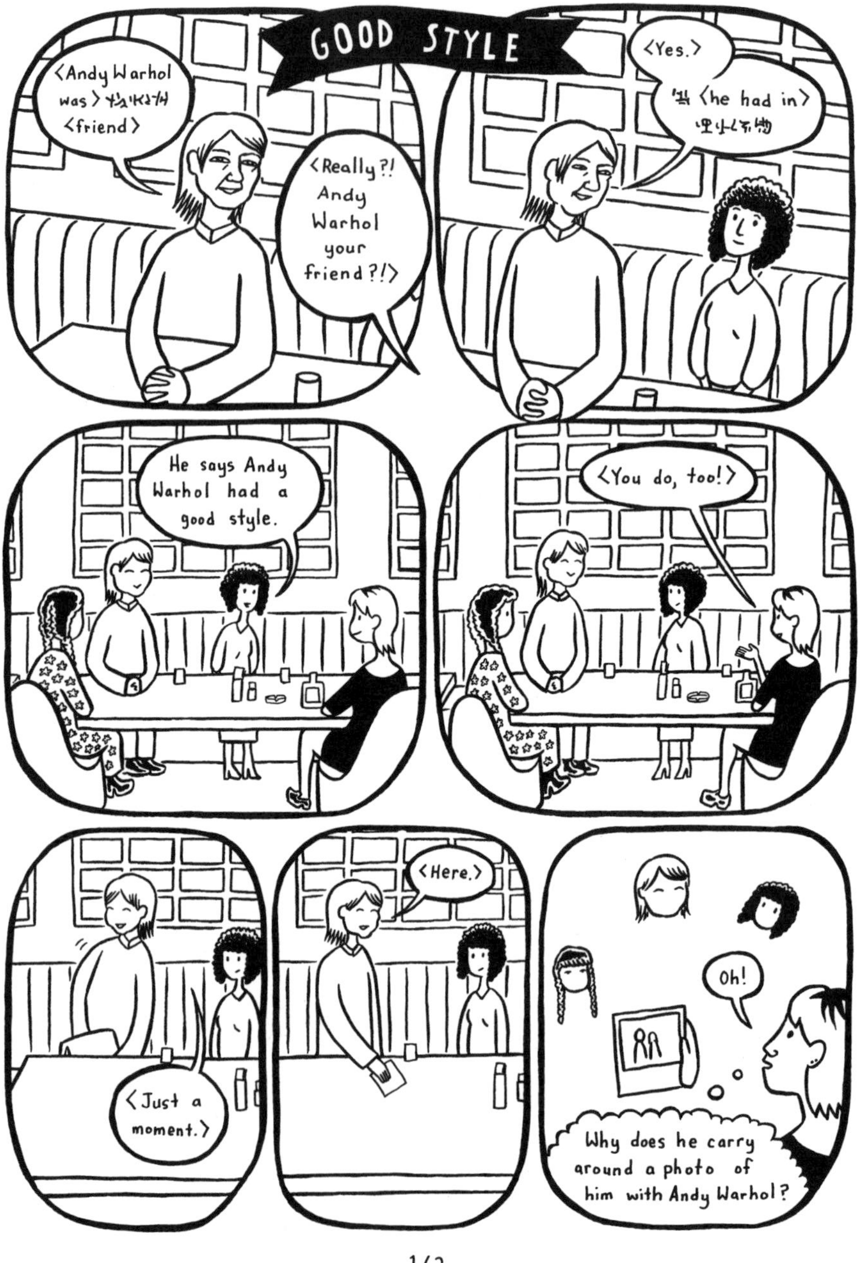
GOOD STYLE
<Andy Warhol was>
<friend>
<Really?! Andy Warhol your friend?!>
<Yes.>
<he had in>
He says Andy Warhol had a good style.
<You do, too!>
<Just a moment.>
<Here.>
Oh!
Why does he carry around a photo of him with Andy Warhol?

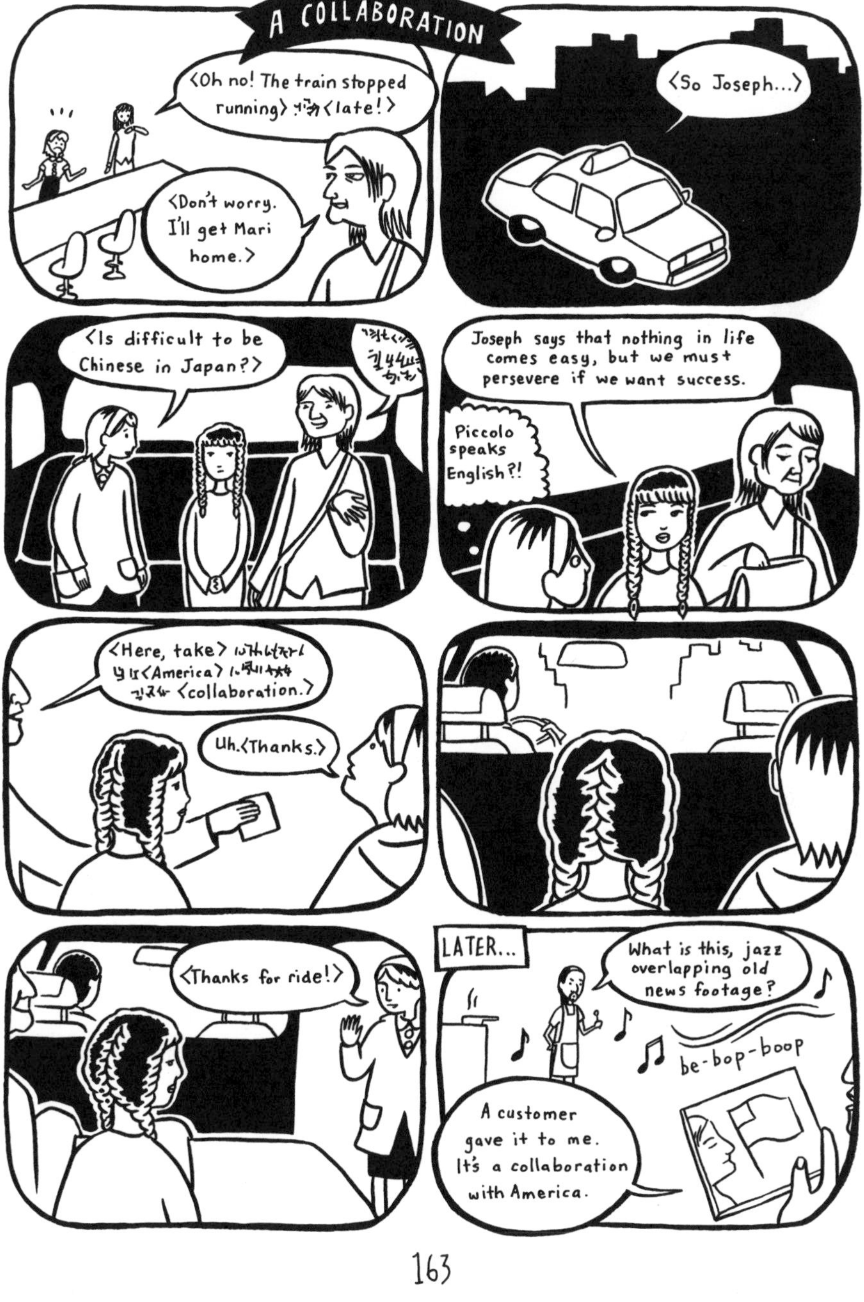
A COLLABORATION
<Oh no! The train stopped running> <late!>
<Don't worry. I'll get Mari home.>
<So Joseph...>
<Is difficult to be Chinese in Japan?>
Joseph says that nothing in life comes easy, but we must persevere if we want success.
Piccolo speaks English?!
<Here, take> <America> <collaboration.>
Uh.<Thanks.>
<Thanks for ride!>
LATER...
What is this, jazz overlapping old news footage?
be-bop-boop
A customer gave it to me. It's a collaboration with America.

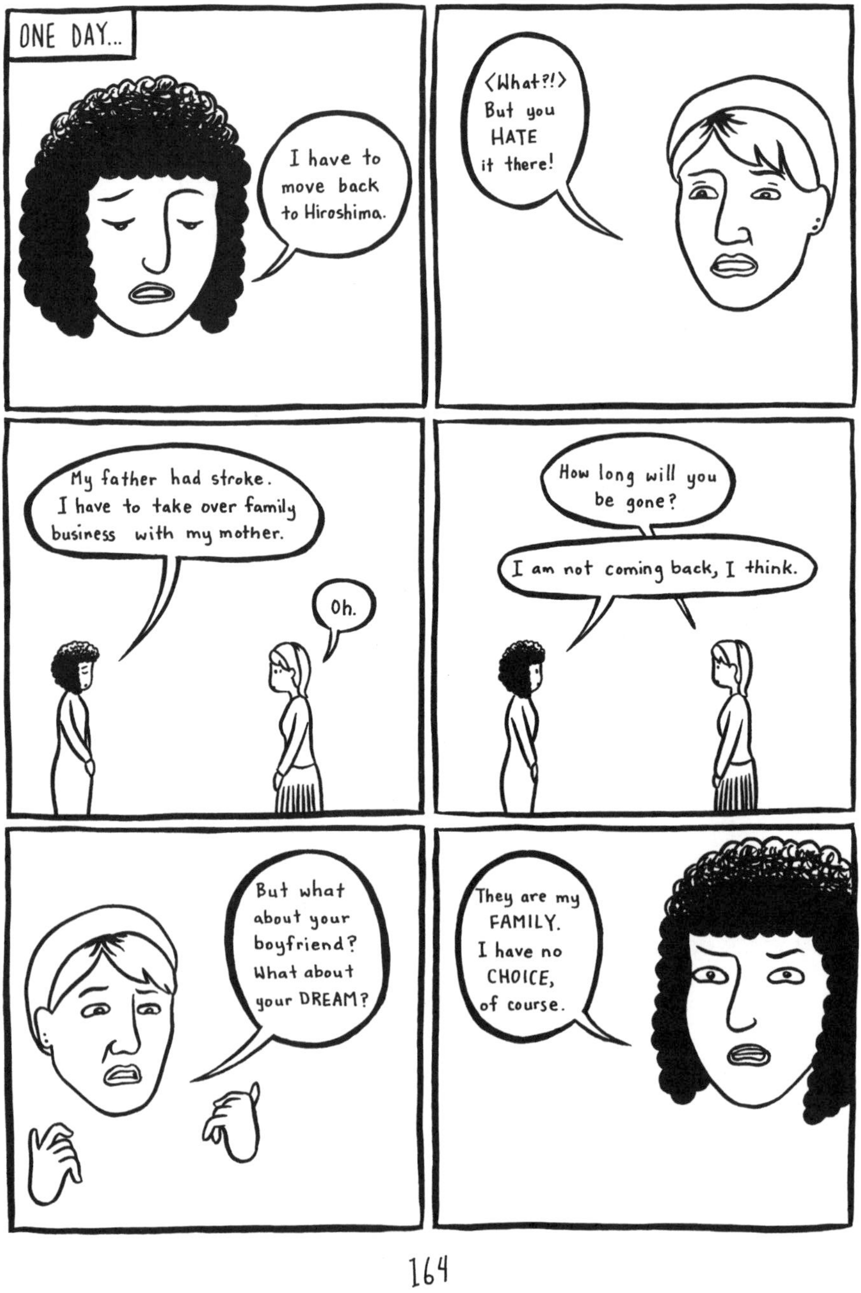
ONE DAY...
I have to move back to Hiroshima.
<What?!> But you HATE it there!
My father had stroke. I have to take over family business with my mother.
Oh.
How long will you be gone?
I am not coming back, I think.
But what about your boyfriend? What about your DREAM?
They are my FAMILY. I have no CHOICE, of course.

THE CULTURAL DIVIDE WAS MUCH DEEPER THAN I'D THOUGHT POSSIBLE.

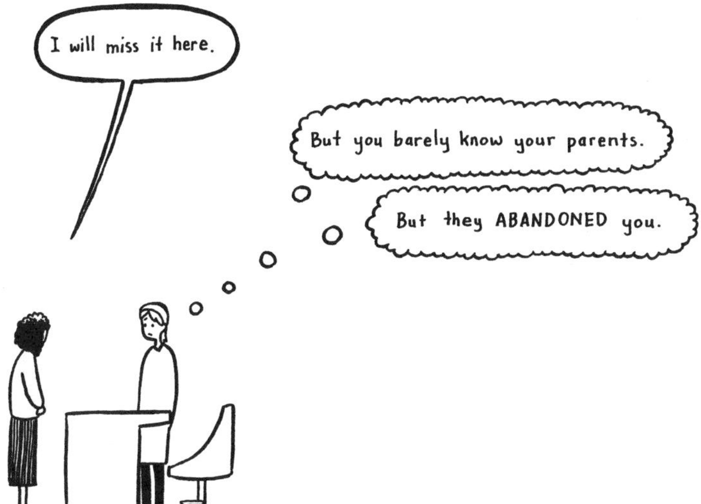
I will miss it here.
But you barely know your parents.
But they ABANDONED you.

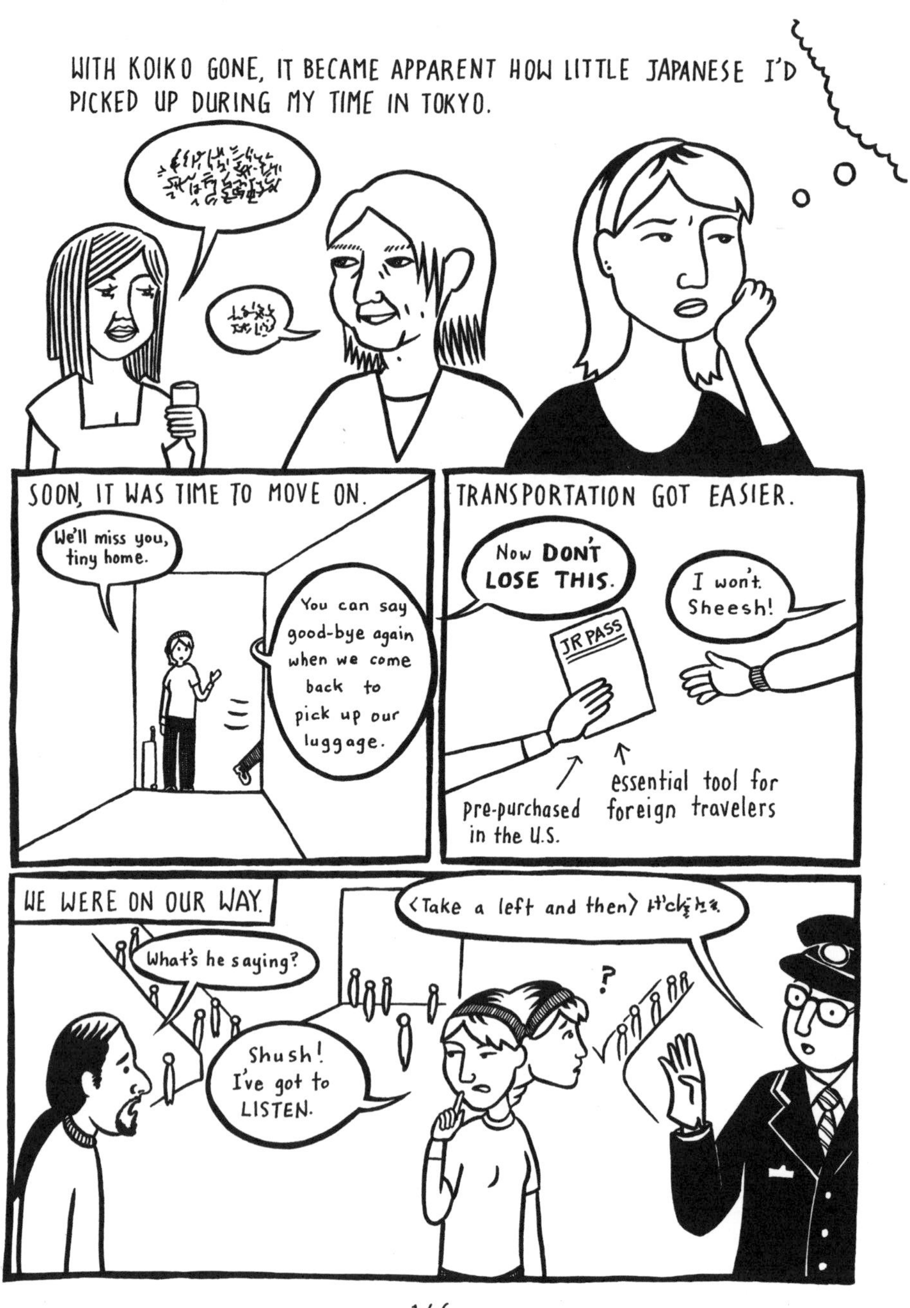
WITH KOIKO GONE, IT BECAME APPARENT HOW LITTLE JAPANESE I'D PICKED UP DURING MY TIME IN TOKYO.
SOON, IT WAS TIME TO MOVE ON.
We'll miss you, tiny home.
You can say good-bye again when we come back to pick up our luggage.
TRANSPORTATION GOT EASIER.
Now DON'T LOSE THIS.
I won't. Sheesh!
JR PASS
pre-purchased in the U.S.
essential tool for foreign travelers
WE WERE ON OUR WAY.
What's he saying?
<Take a left and then>
Shush! I've got to LISTEN.
?

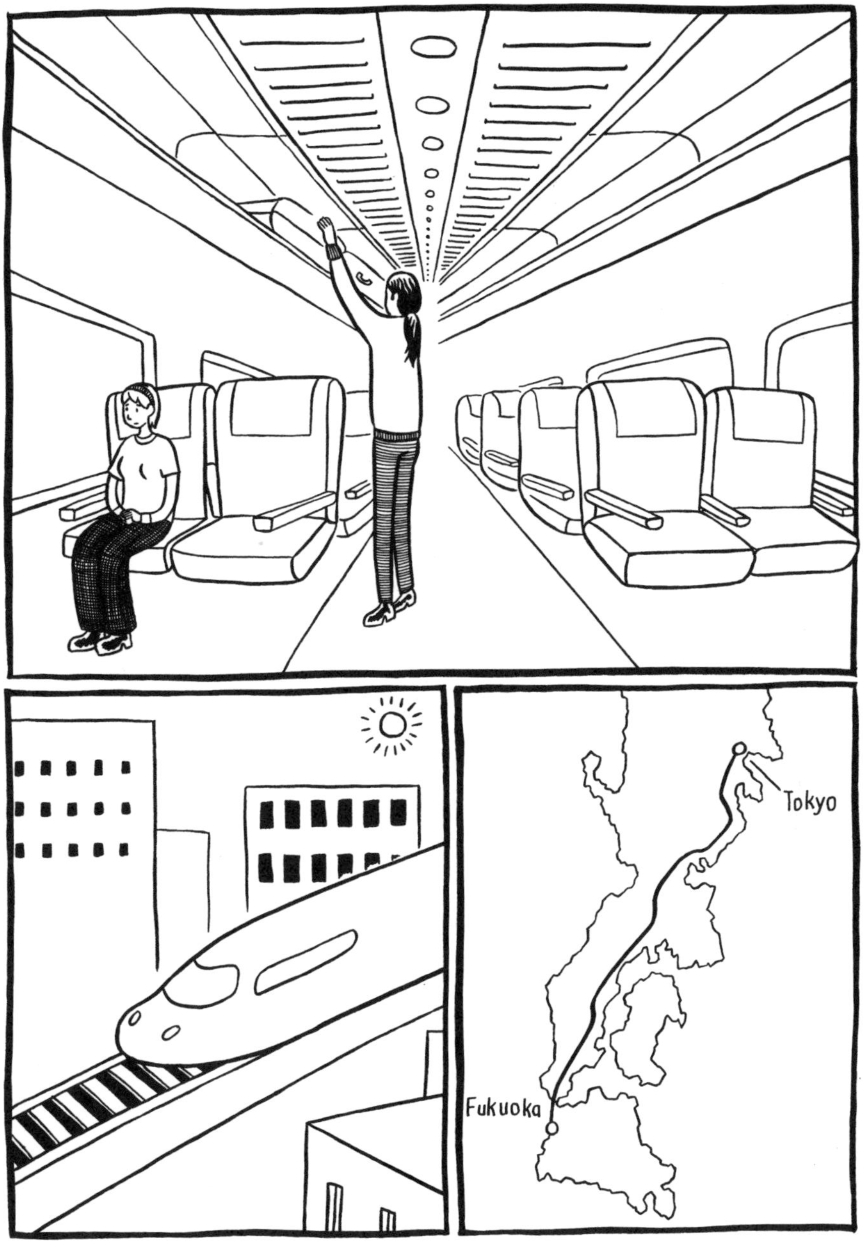
Tokyo
Fukuoka

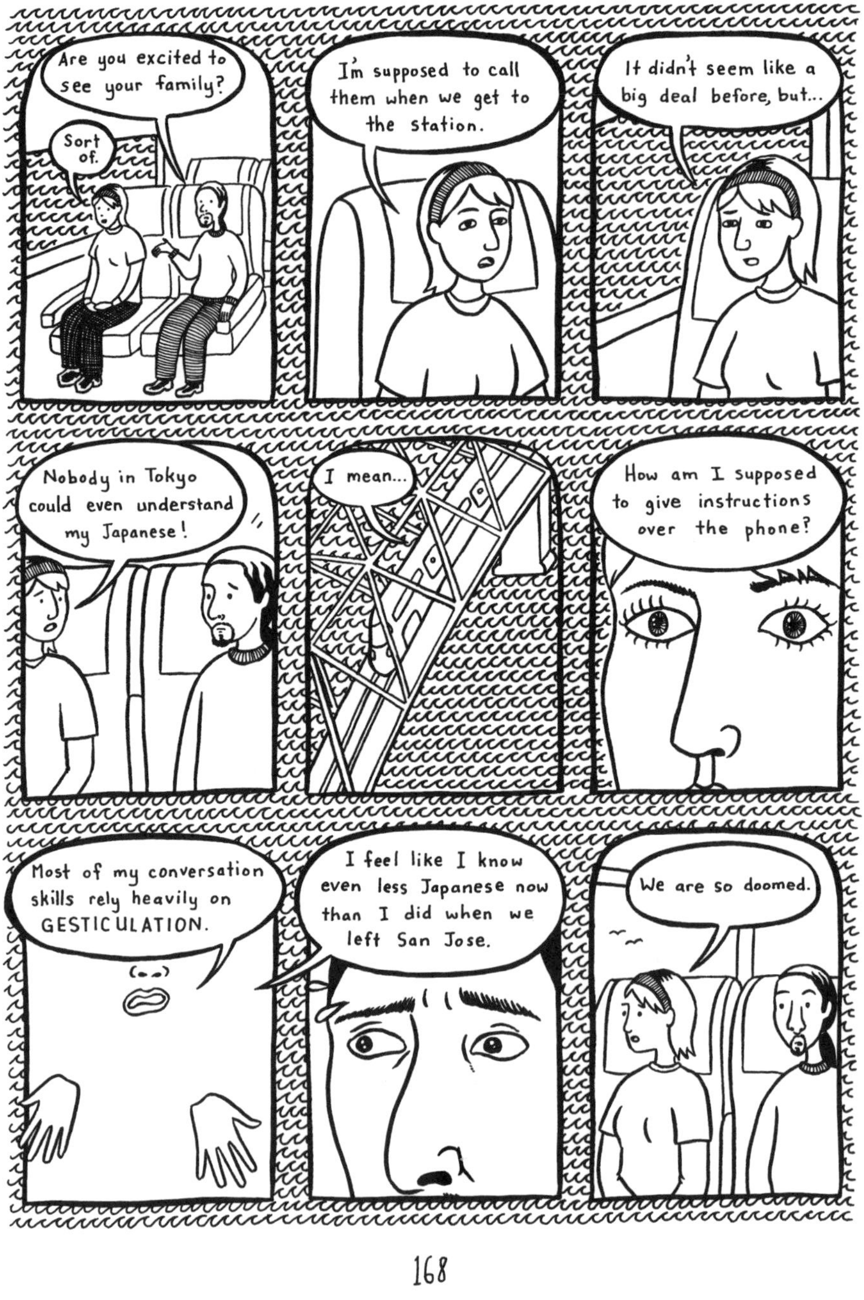
Are you excited to see your family?
Sort of.
I'm supposed to call them when we get to the station.
It didn't seem like a big deal before, but...
Nobody in Tokyo could even understand my Japanese!
I mean...
How am I supposed to give instructions over the phone?
Most of my conversation skills rely heavily on GESTICULATION.
I feel like I know even less Japanese now than I did when we left San Jose.
We are so doomed.

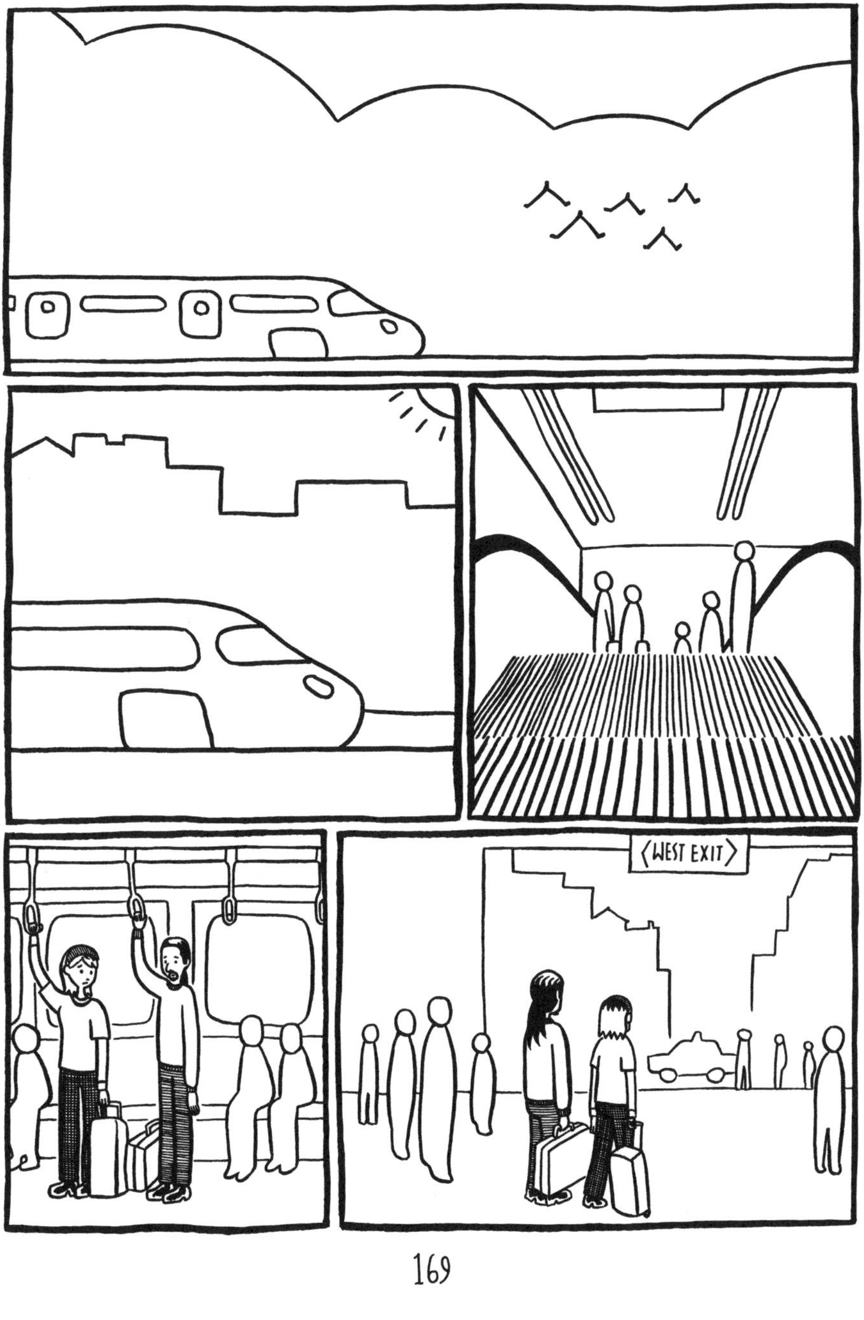
WEST EXIT

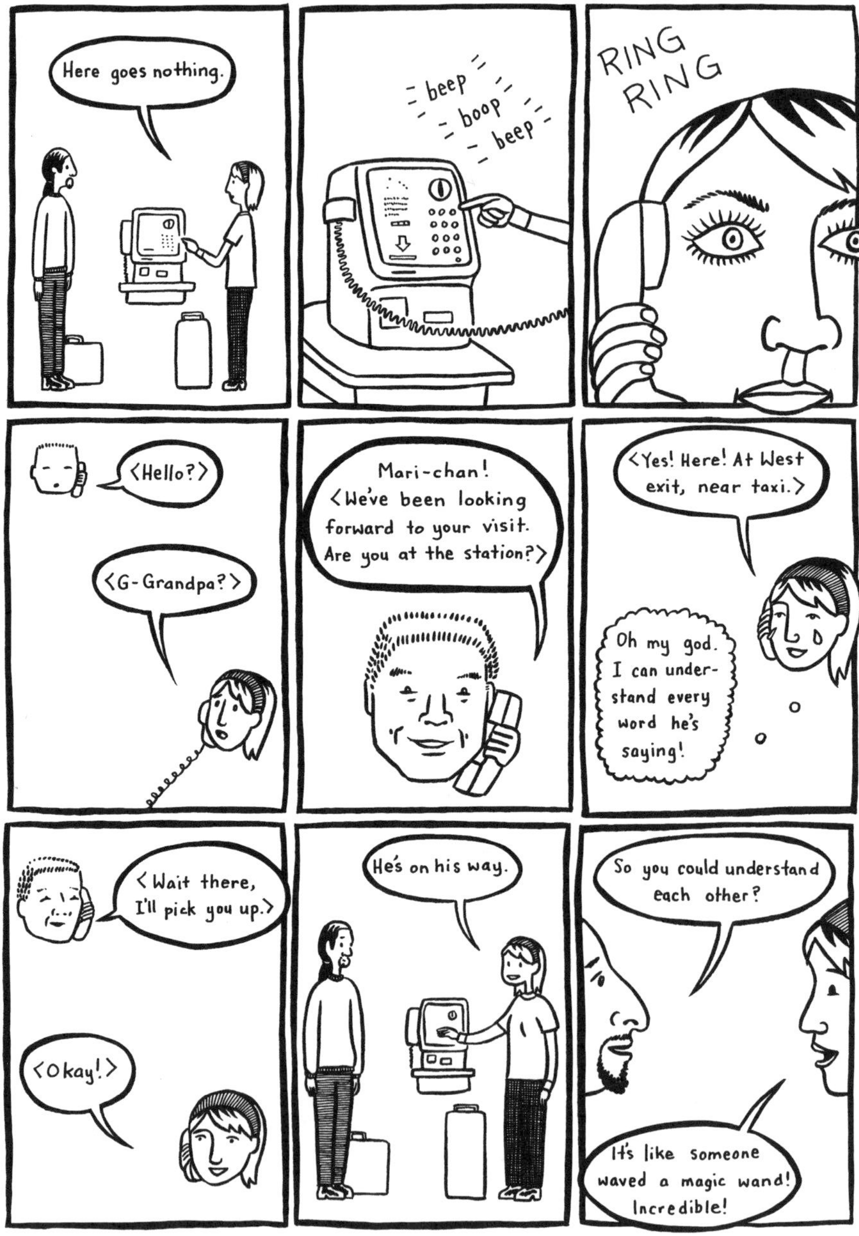
Here goes nothing.
beep boop beep
RING RING
<Hello?>
<G-Grandpa?>
Mari-chan! <We've been looking forward to your visit. Are you at the station?>
<Yes! Here! At West exit, near taxi.>
Oh my god. I can understand every word he's saying!
<Wait there, I'll pick you up.>
<Okay!>
He's on his way.
So you could understand each other?
It's like someone waved a magic wand! Incredible!

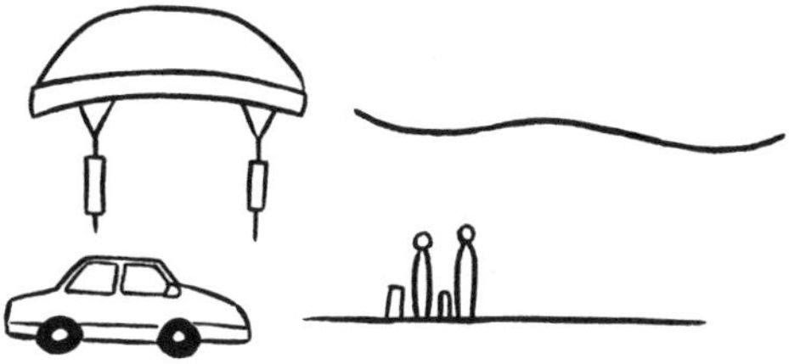

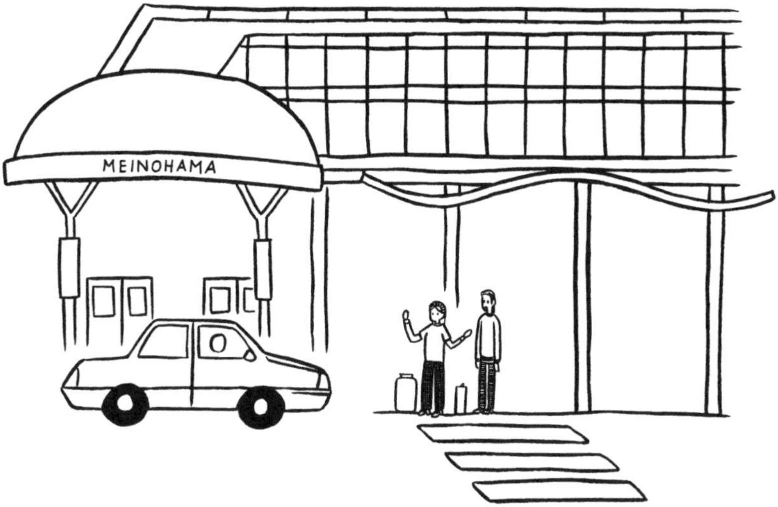
MEINOHAMA

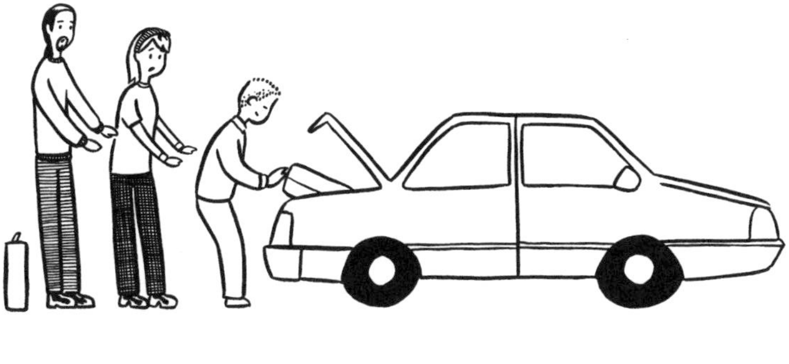

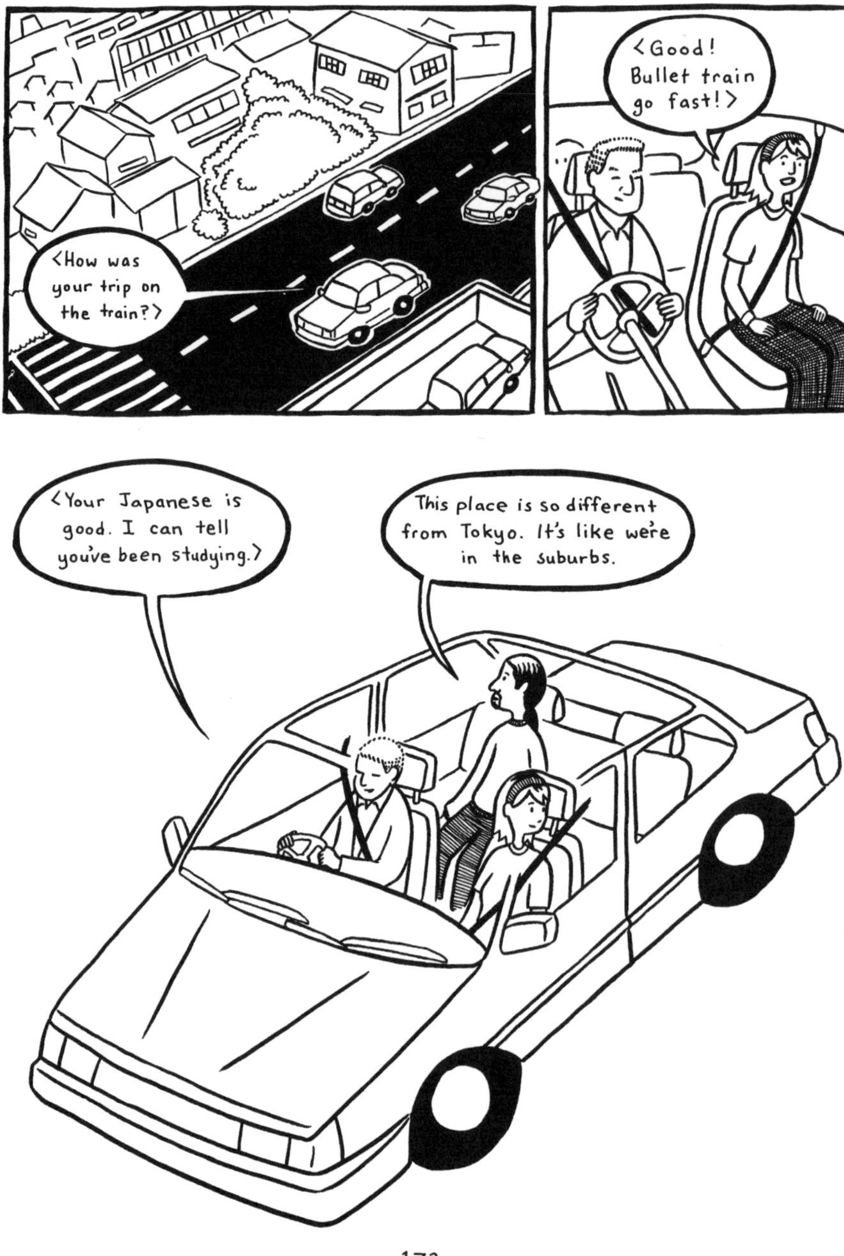
<How was your trip on the train?>
<Good! Bullet train go fast!>
<Your Japanese is good. I can tell you've been studying.>
This place is so different from Tokyo. It's like we're in the suburbs.

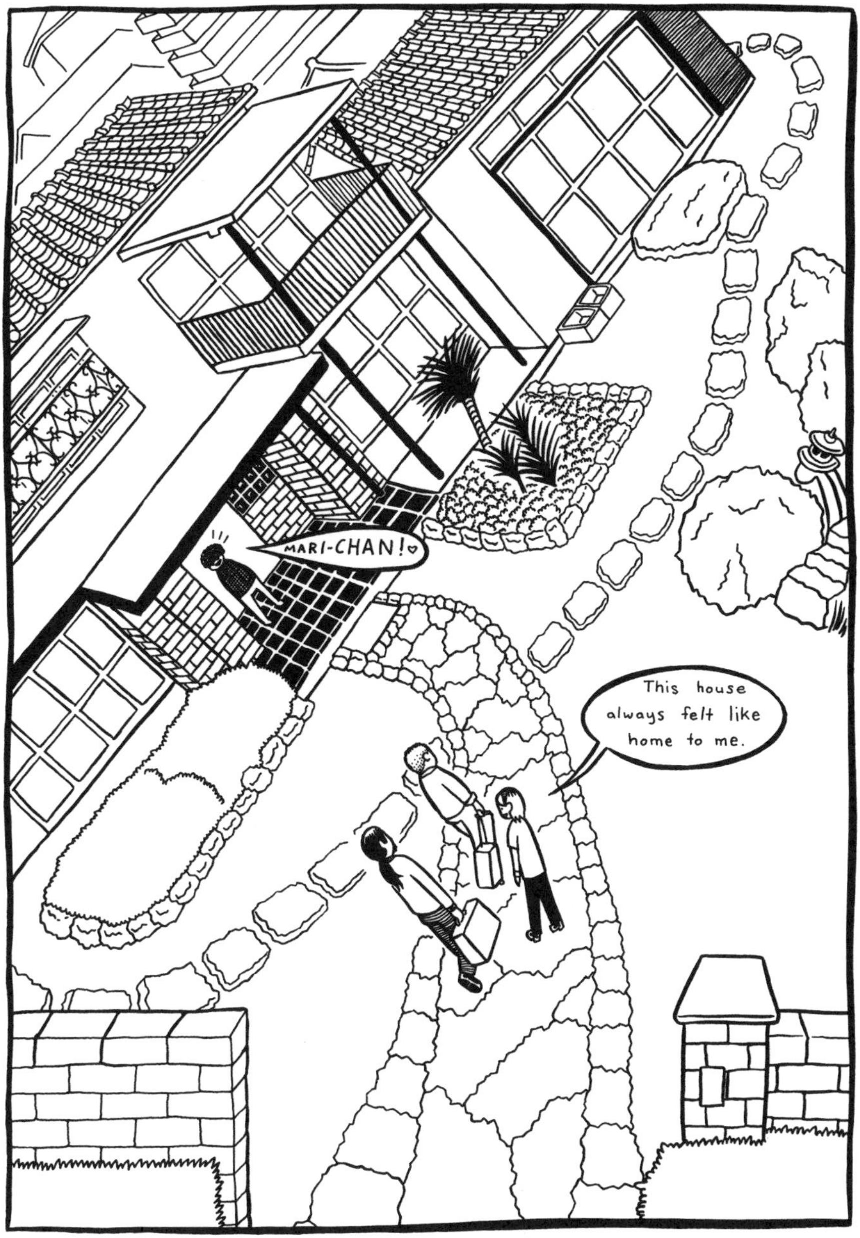
MARI-CHAN!♡
This house always felt like home to me.

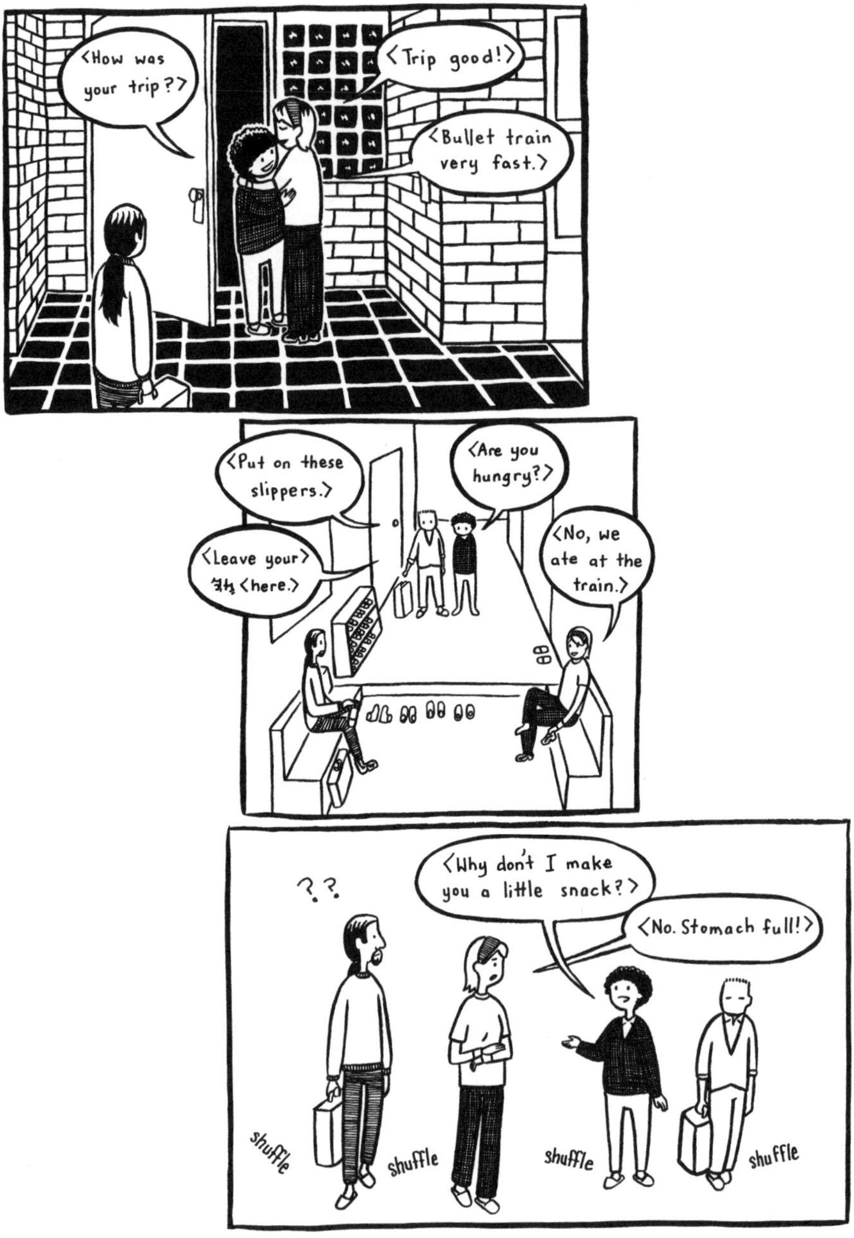

<How was your trip?>
<Trip good!>
<Bullet train very fast.>
<Put on these slippers.>
<Are you hungry?>
<Leave your> <here.>
<No, we ate at the train.>
??
<Why don't I make you a little snack?>
<No. Stomach full!>
shuffle
shuffle
shuffle
shuffle

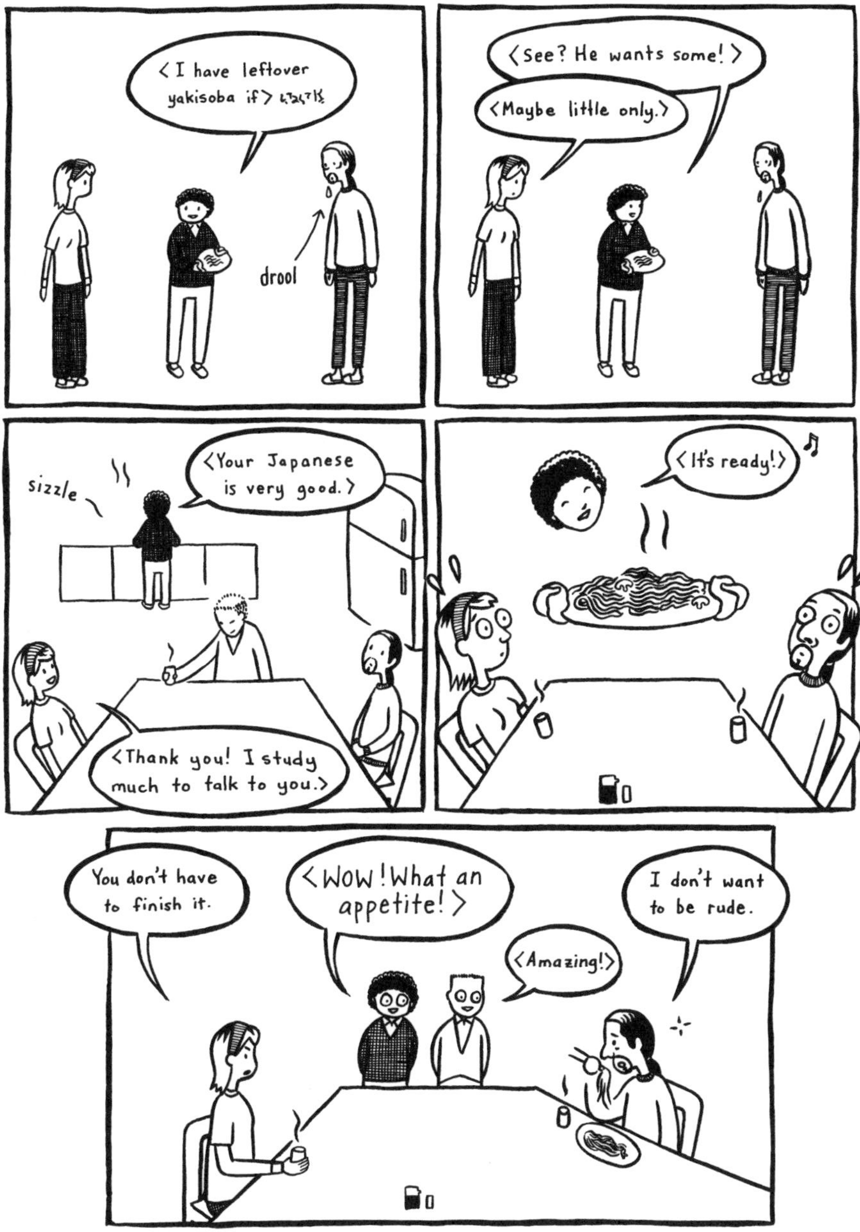
< I have leftover yakisoba if >
drool
< See? He wants some! >
<Maybe little only.>
sizzle
<Your Japanese is very good.>
<Thank you! I study much to talk to you.>
<It's ready!>
You don't have to finish it.
<WOW! What an appetite!>
<Amazing!>
I don't want to be rude.

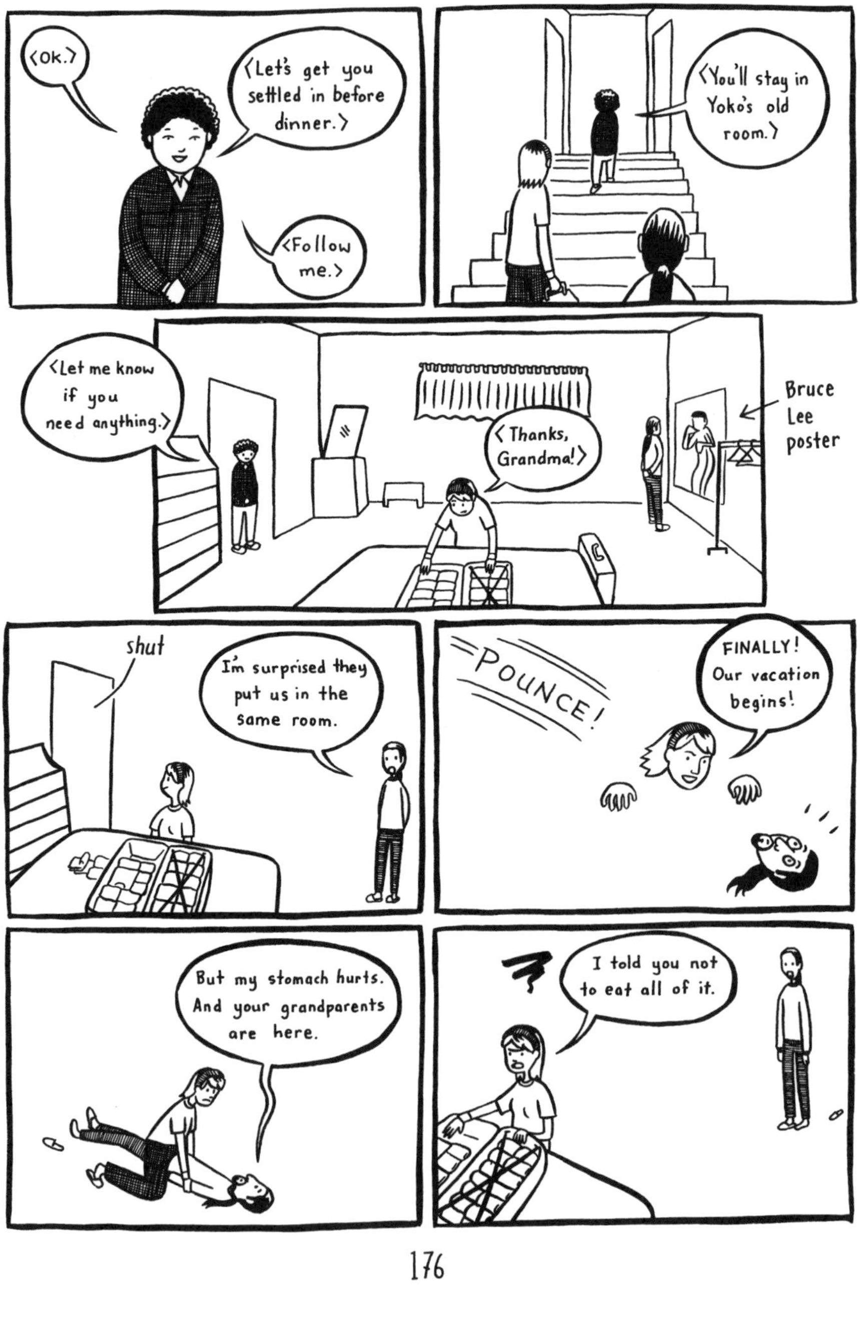

〈Ok.〉
〈Let's get you settled in before dinner.〉
〈Follow me.〉
〈You'll stay in Yoko's old room.〉
〈Let me know if you need anything.〉
〈Thanks, Grandma!〉
Bruce Lee poster
shut
I'm surprised they put us in the same room.
POUNCE!
FINALLY! Our vacation begins!
But my stomach hurts. And your grandparents are here.
I told you not to eat all of it.

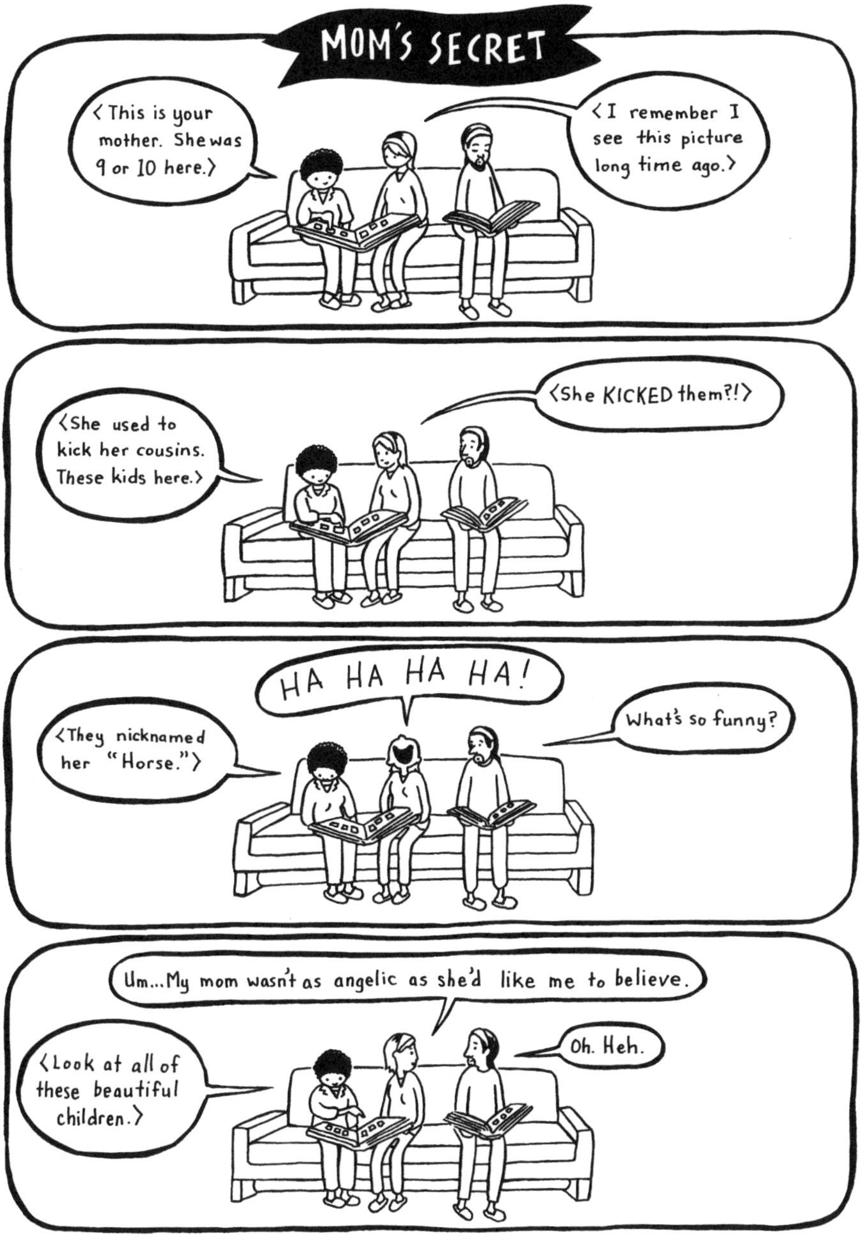
MOM'S SECRET
<This is your mother. She was 9 or 10 here.>
<I remember I see this picture long time ago.>
<She used to kick her cousins. These kids here.>
<She KICKED them?!>
<They nicknamed her "Horse.">
HA HA HA HA!
What's so funny?
<Look at all of these beautiful children.>
Um...My mom wasn't as angelic as she'd like me to believe.
Oh. Heh.

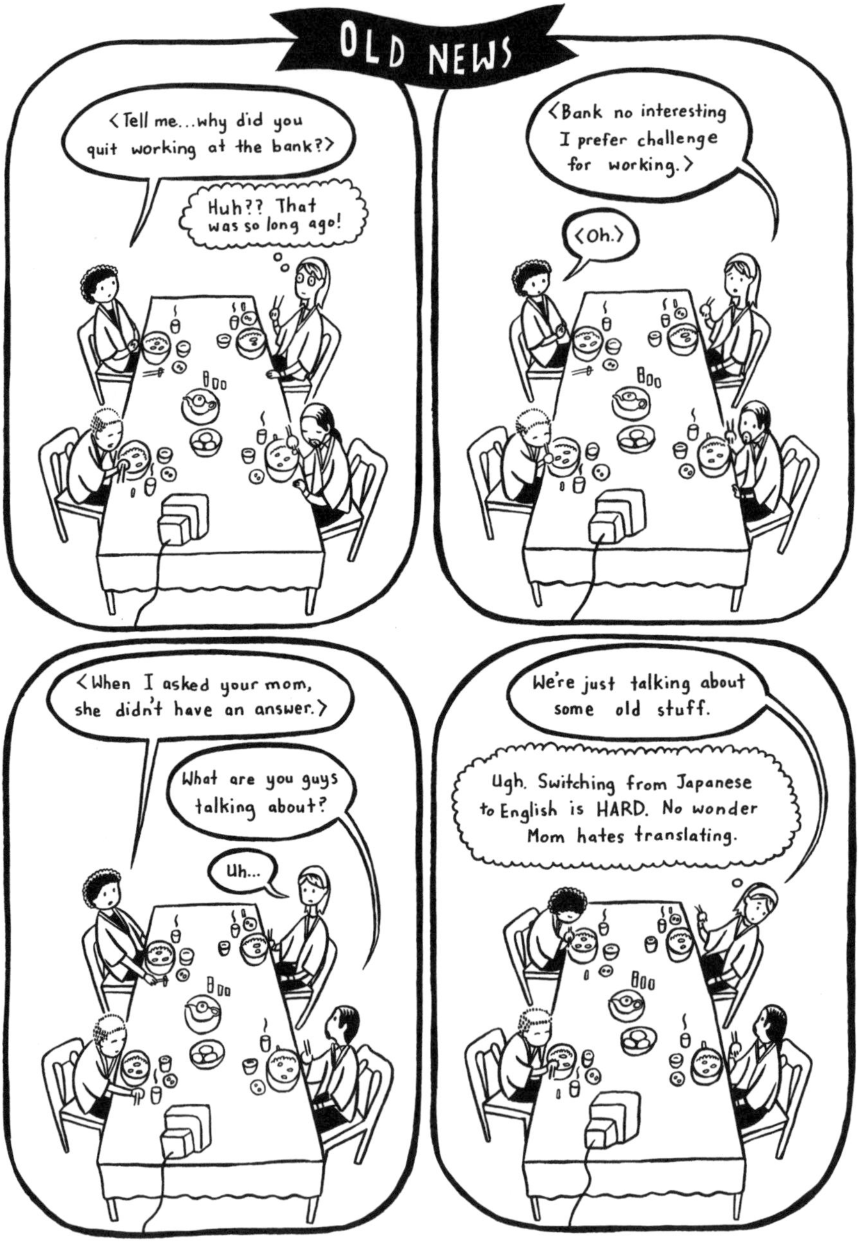
OLD NEWS
<Tell me...why did you quit working at the bank?>
Huh?? That was so long ago!
<Bank no interesting I prefer challenge for working.>
<Oh.>
<When I asked your mom, she didn't have an answer.>
What are you guys talking about?
Uh...
We're just talking about some old stuff.
Ugh. Switching from Japanese to English is HARD. No wonder Mom hates translating.

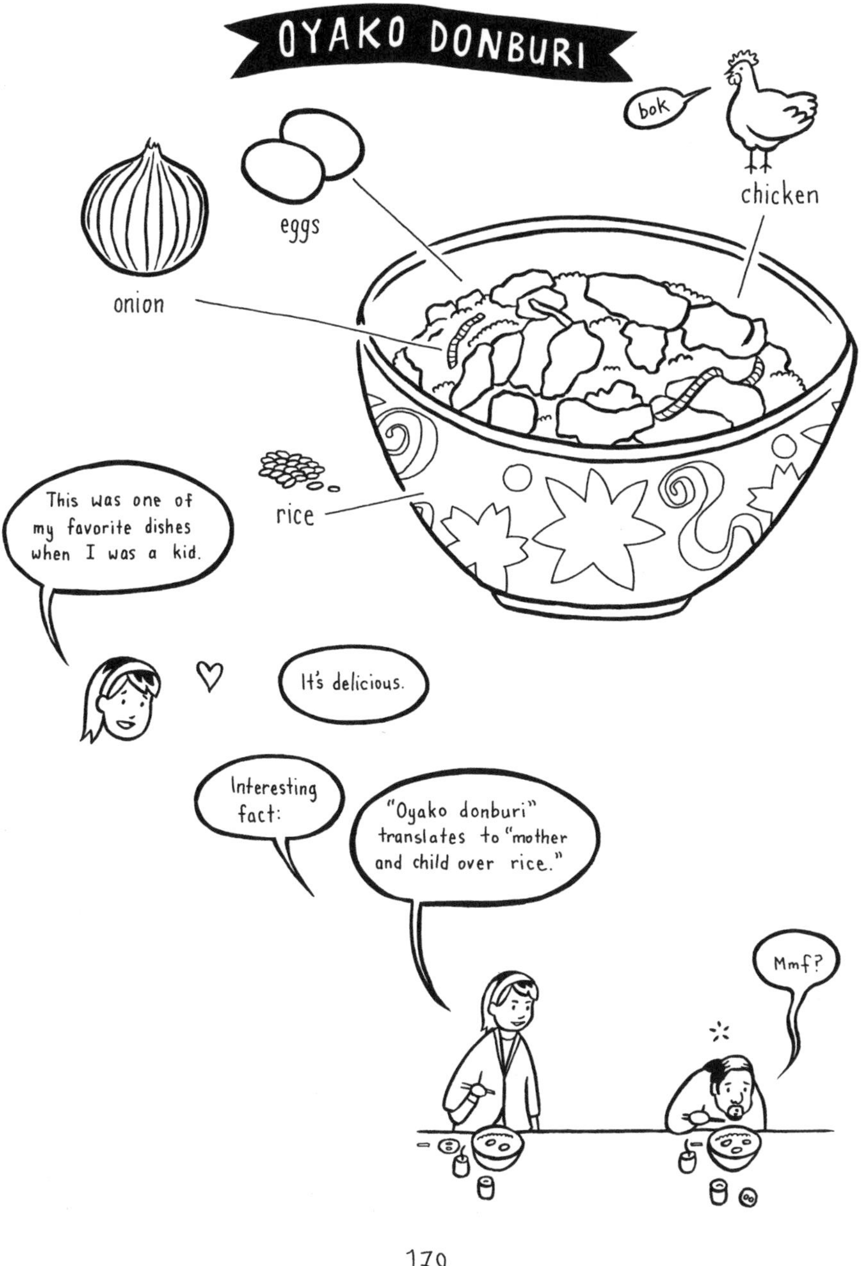
OYAKO DONBURI
bok
chicken
eggs
onion
rice
This was one of my favorite dishes when I was a kid.
It's delicious.
Interesting fact:
"Oyako donburi" translates to "mother and child over rice."
Mmf?

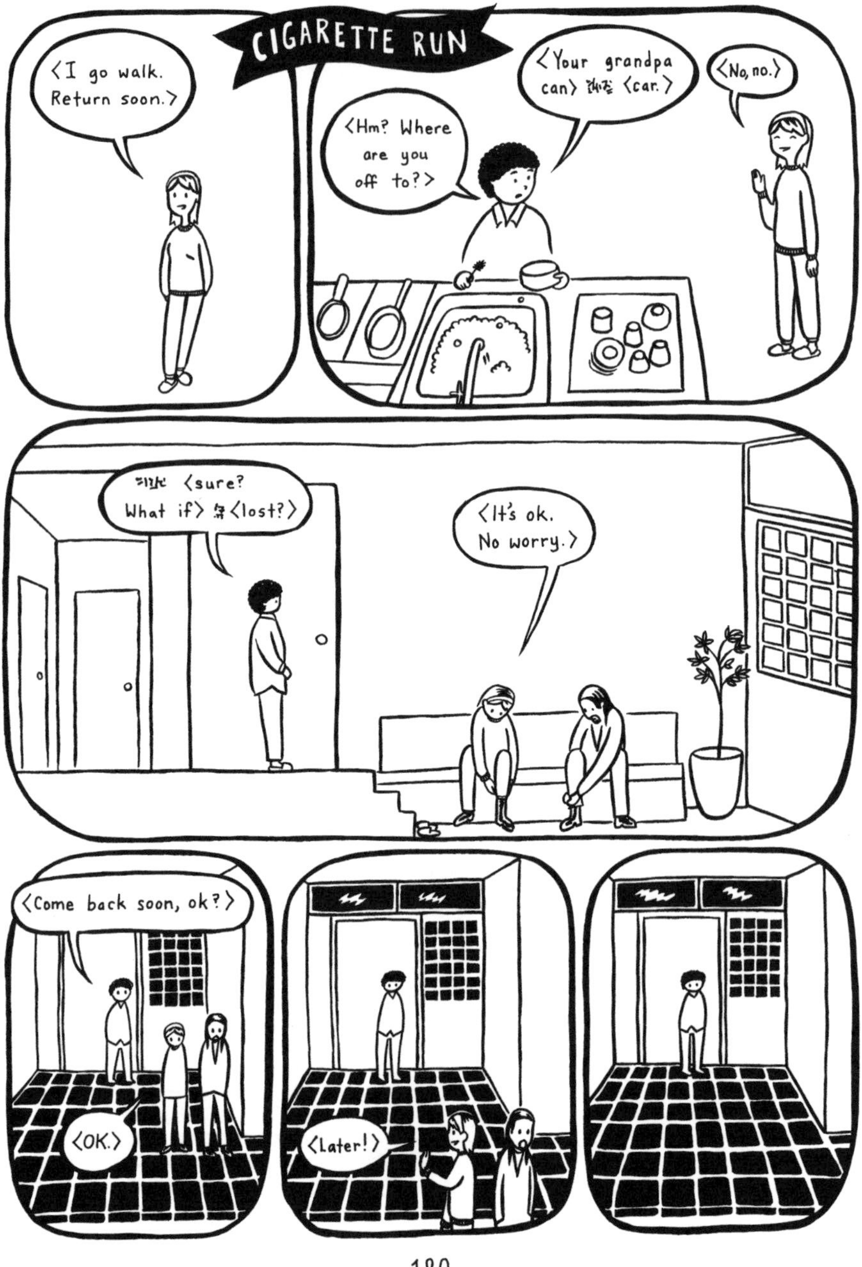
CIGARETTE RUN
⟨I go walk. Return soon.⟩
⟨Hm? Where are you off to?⟩
⟨Your grandpa can⟩ ⟨car.⟩
⟨No, no.⟩
⟨sure? What if⟩ ⟨lost?⟩
⟨It's ok. No worry.⟩
⟨Come back soon, ok?⟩
⟨OK.⟩
⟨Later!⟩

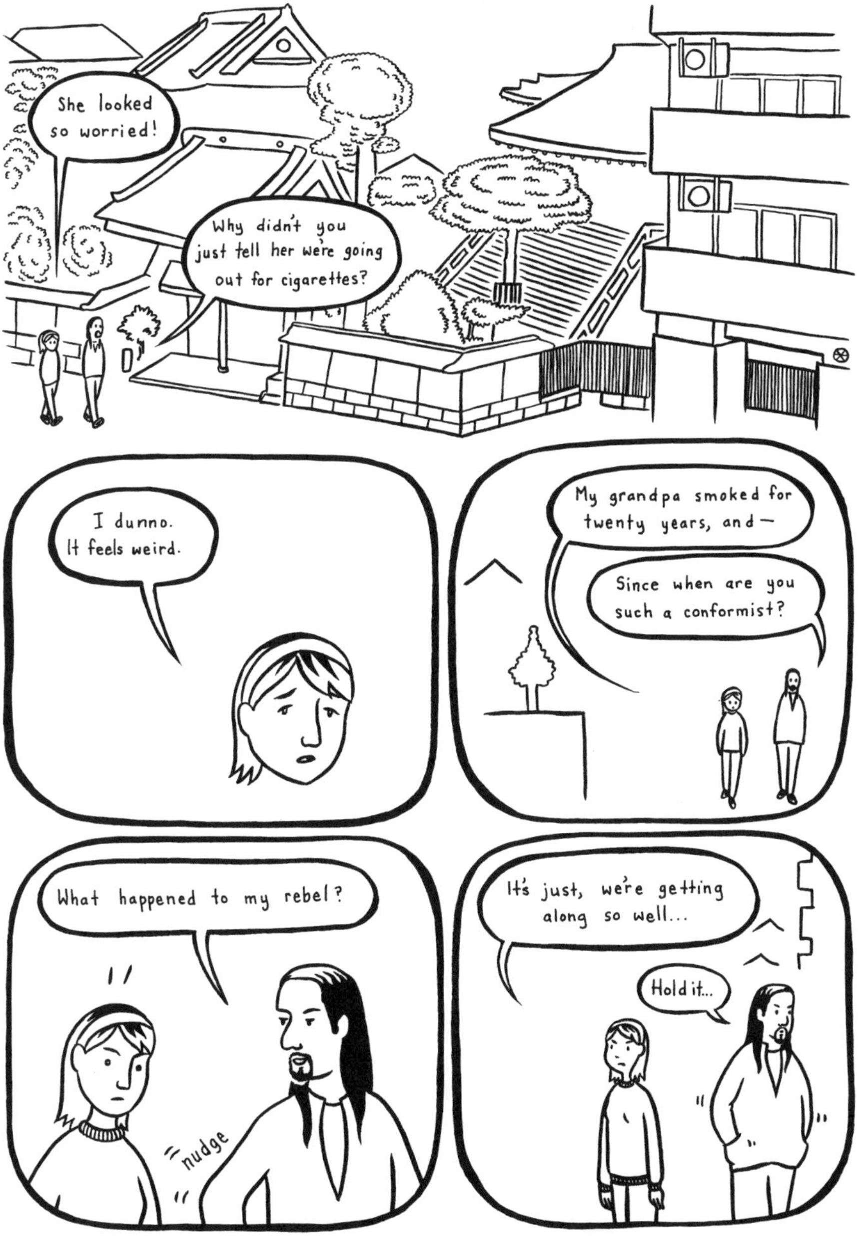
She looked so worried!
Why didn't you just tell her we're going out for cigarettes?
I dunno. It feels weird.
My grandpa smoked for twenty years, and—
Since when are you such a conformist?
What happened to my rebel?
nudge
It's just, we're getting along so well...
Hold it...

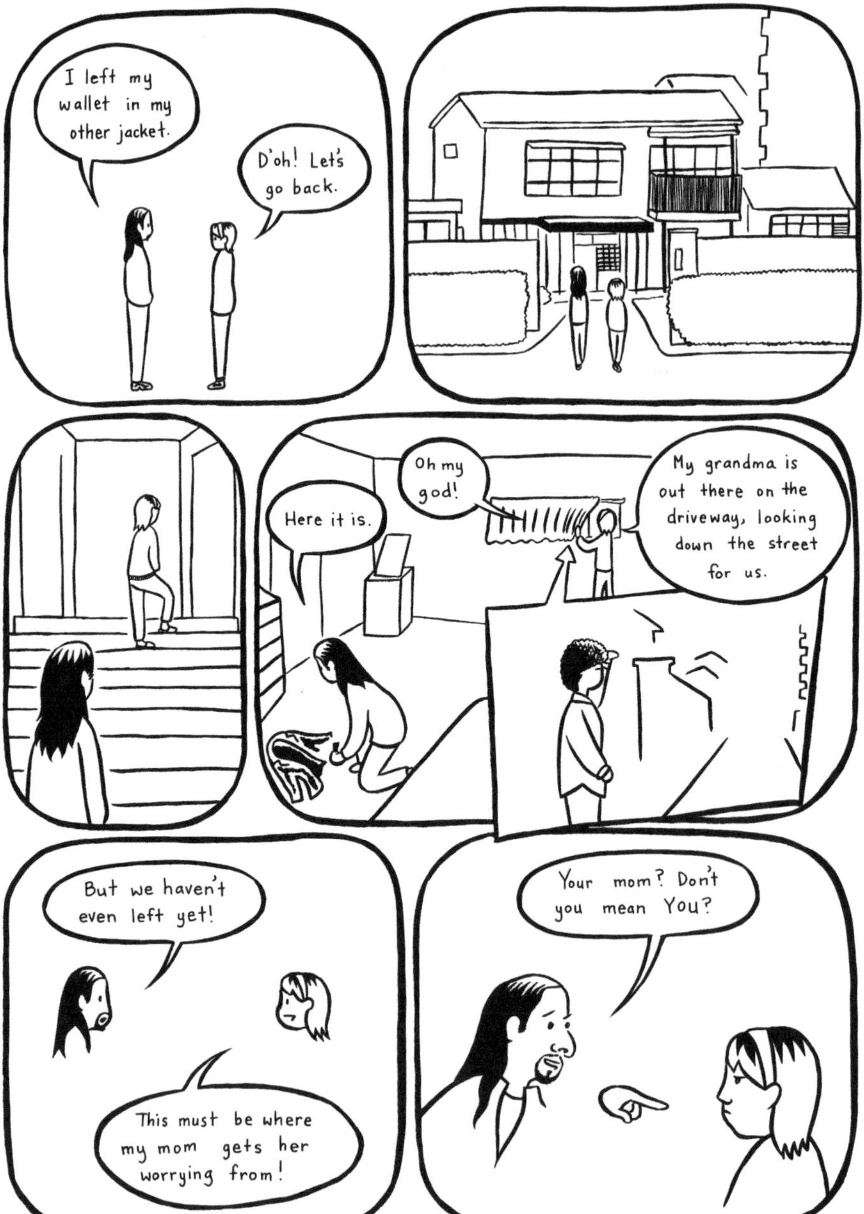
I left my wallet in my other jacket.
D'oh! Let's go back.
Here it is.
Oh my god!
My grandma is out there on the driveway, looking down the street for us.
But we haven't even left yet!
This must be where my mom gets her worrying from!
Your mom? Don't you mean YOU?

PRAYER

‹This is where we pray to›츠카 ‹family. Let's pray together now.›

Oh! Um, well, actually... I guess, ‹OK.›

devout Atheist

Since when are you such a CONFORMIST?

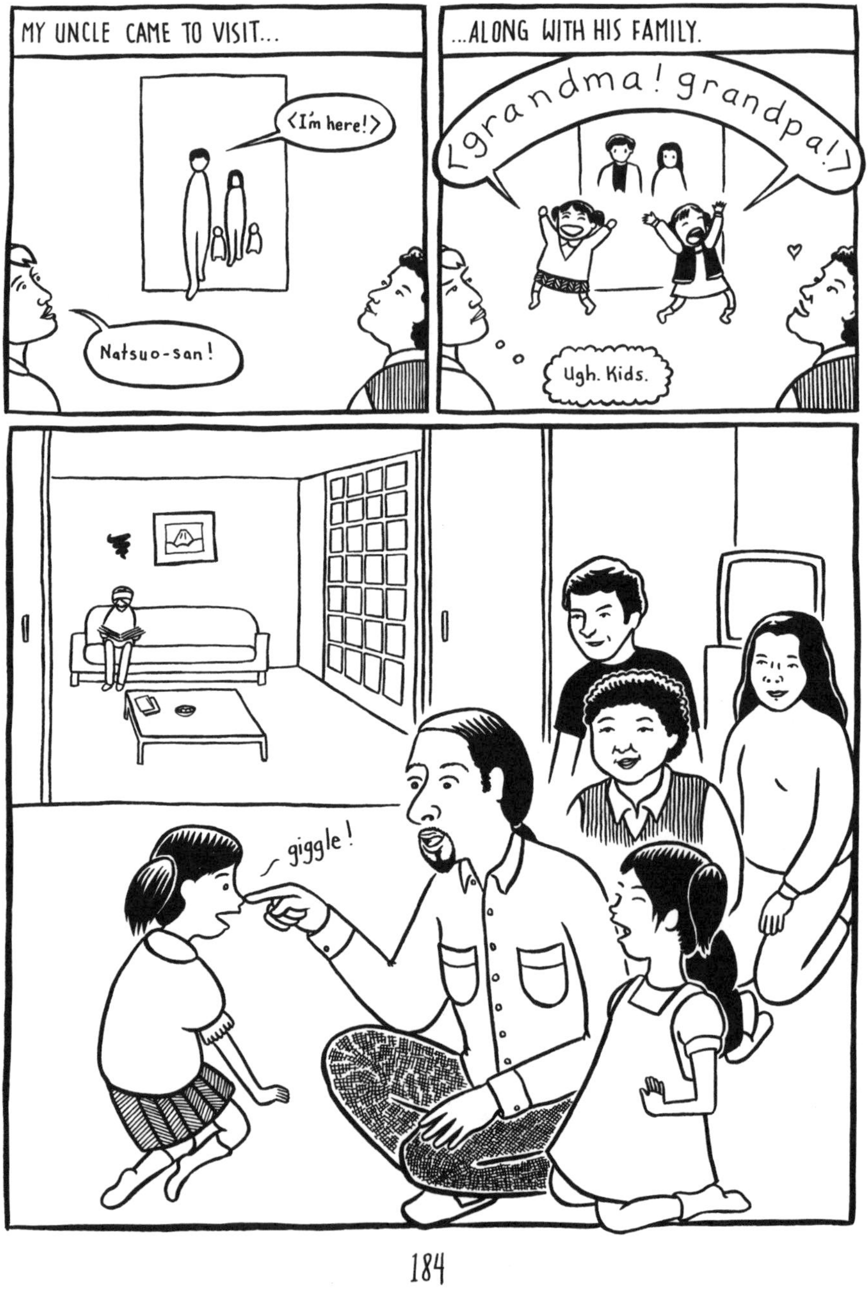
MY UNCLE CAME TO VISIT...
<I'm here!>
Natsuo-san!
...ALONG WITH HIS FAMILY.
<grandma! grandpa!>
Ugh. Kids.
giggle!

WE WENT TO A YAKITORI RESTAURANT I'D BEEN TO MANY TIMES OVER THE YEARS.

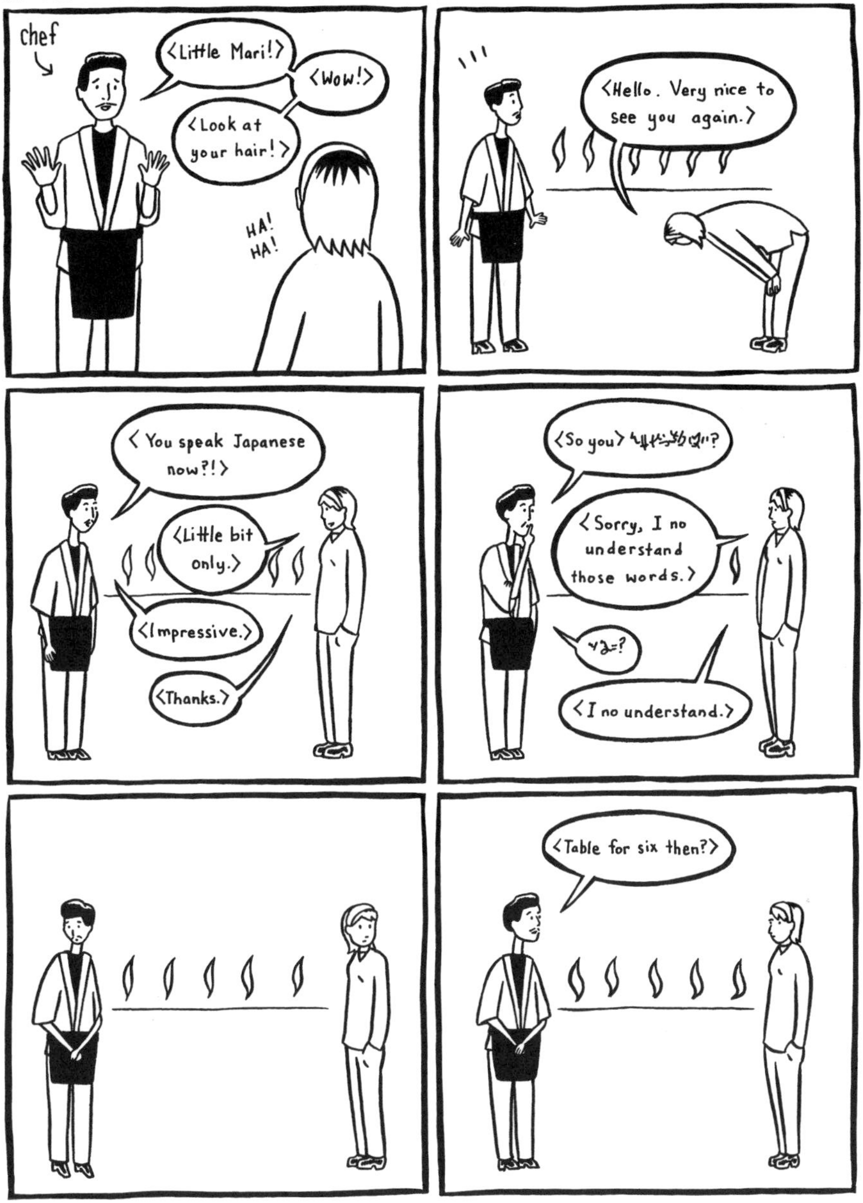
chef
<Little Mari!>
<Wow!>
<Look at your hair!>
HA! HA!
<Hello. Very nice to see you again.>
<You speak Japanese now?!>
<Little bit only.>
<Impressive.>
<Thanks.>
<So you>
<Sorry, I no understand those words.>
<I no understand.>
<Table for six then?>

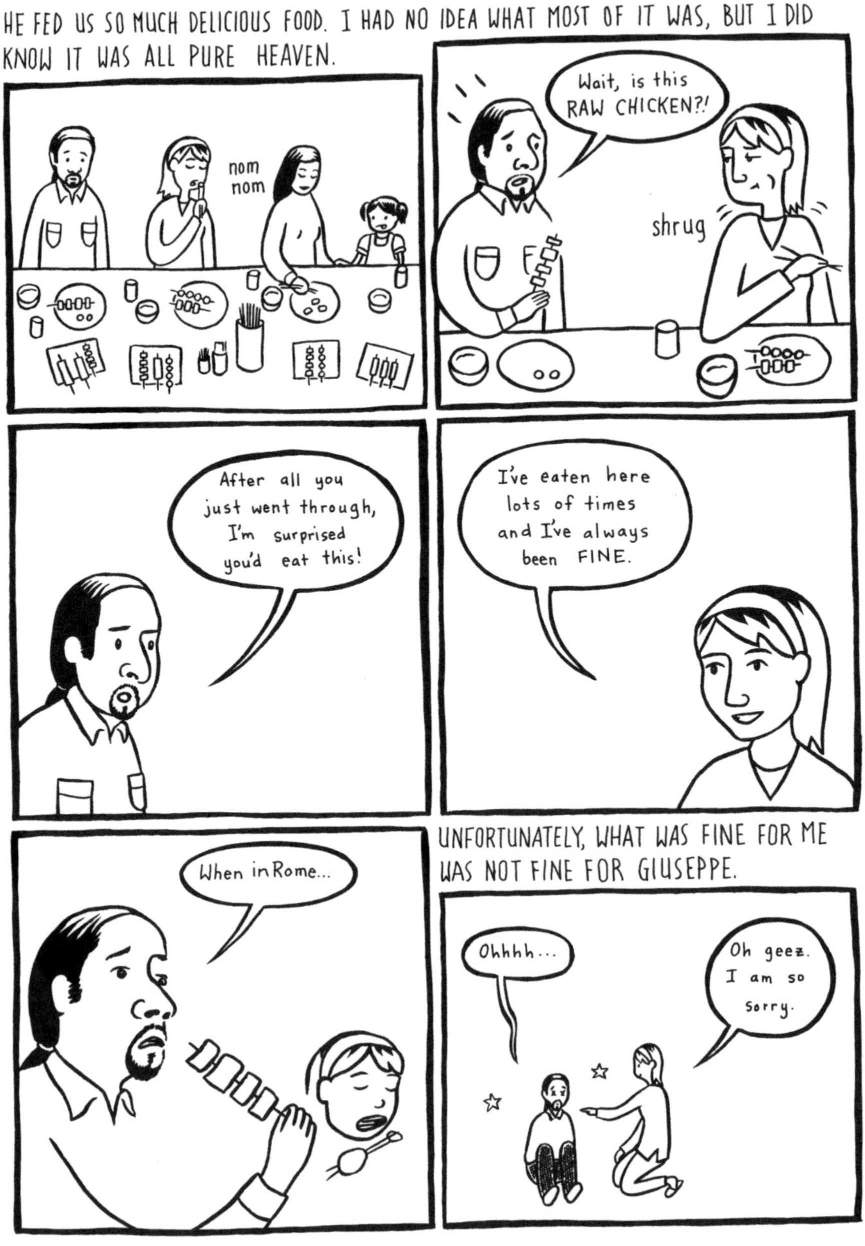
HE FED US SO MUCH DELICIOUS FOOD. I HAD NO IDEA WHAT MOST OF IT WAS, BUT I DID KNOW IT WAS ALL PURE HEAVEN.
nom nom
Wait, is this RAW CHICKEN?!
shrug
After all you just went through, I'm surprised you'd eat this!
I've eaten here lots of times and I've always been FINE.
When in Rome...
UNFORTUNATELY, WHAT WAS FINE FOR ME WAS NOT FINE FOR GIUSEPPE.
Ohhhh...
Oh geez. I am so sorry.

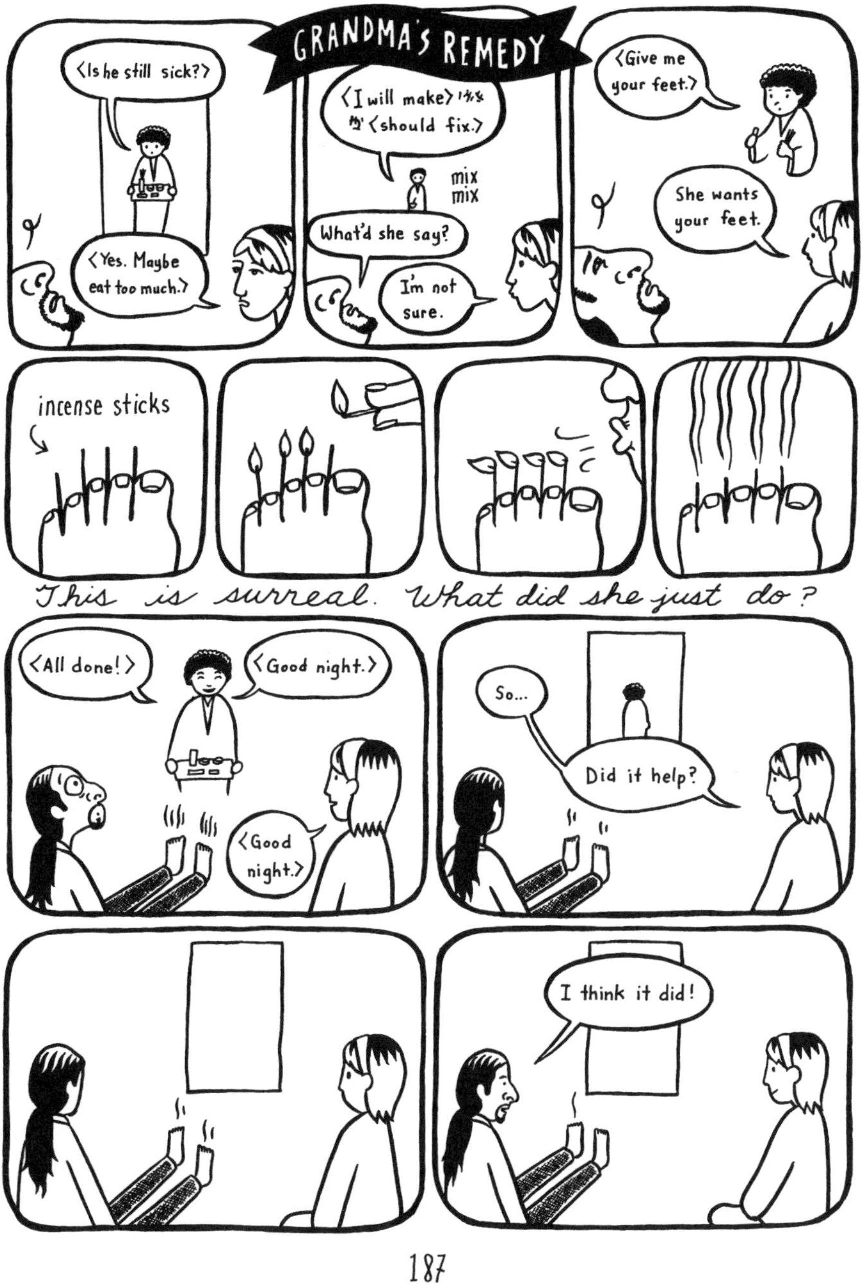
GRANDMA'S REMEDY
⟨Is he still sick?⟩
⟨Yes. Maybe eat too much.⟩
⟨I will make⟩
⟨should fix.⟩
mix mix
What'd she say?
I'm not sure.
⟨Give me your feet.⟩
She wants your feet.
incense sticks
This is surreal. What did she just do?
⟨All done!⟩
⟨Good night.⟩
⟨Good night.⟩
So...
Did it help?
I think it did!

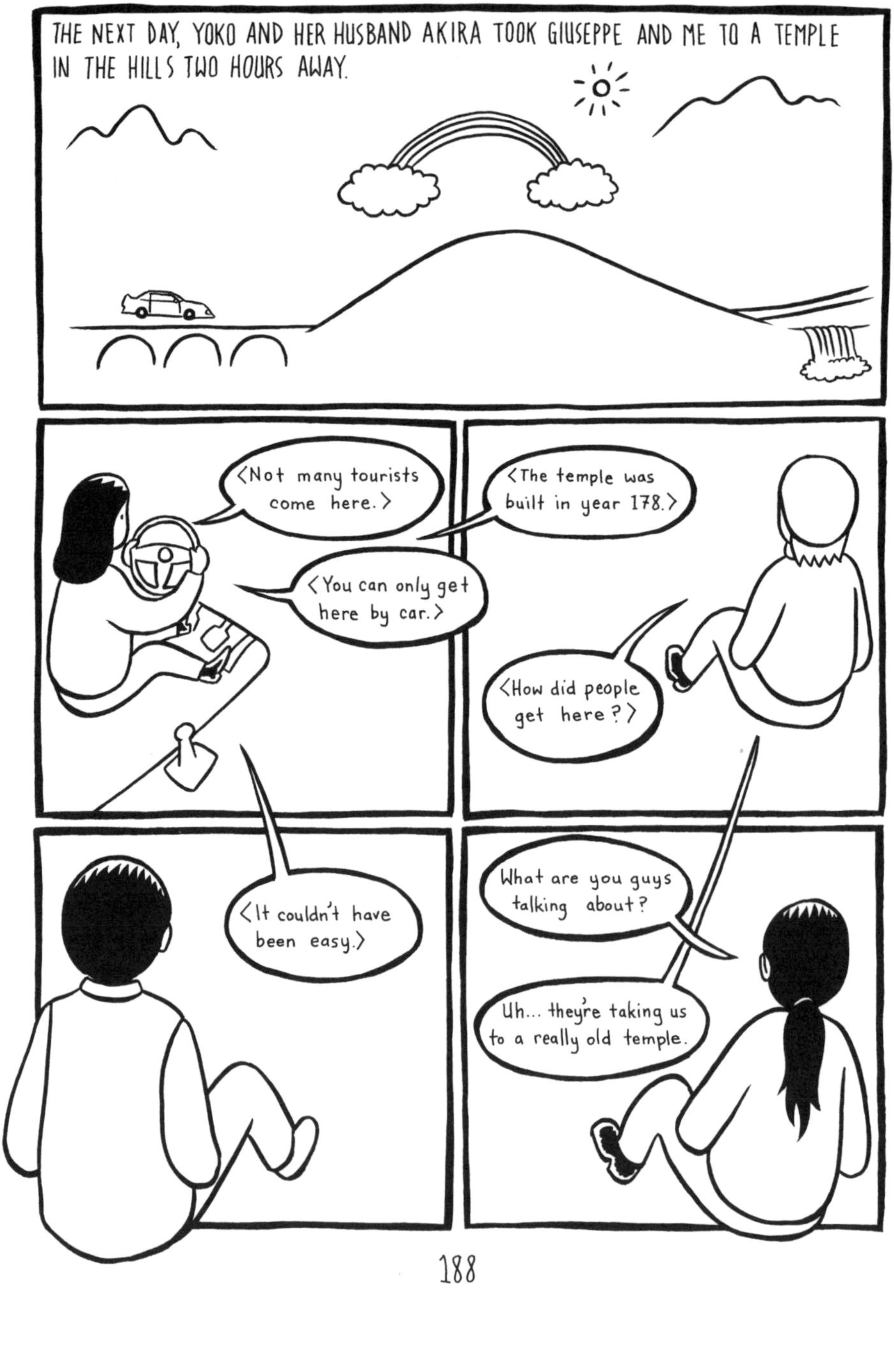
THE NEXT DAY, YOKO AND HER HUSBAND AKIRA TOOK GIUSEPPE AND ME TO A TEMPLE IN THE HILLS TWO HOURS AWAY.
<Not many tourists come here.>
<You can only get here by car.>
<The temple was built in year 178.>
<How did people get here?>
<It couldn't have been easy.>
What are you guys talking about?
Uh... they're taking us to a really old temple.

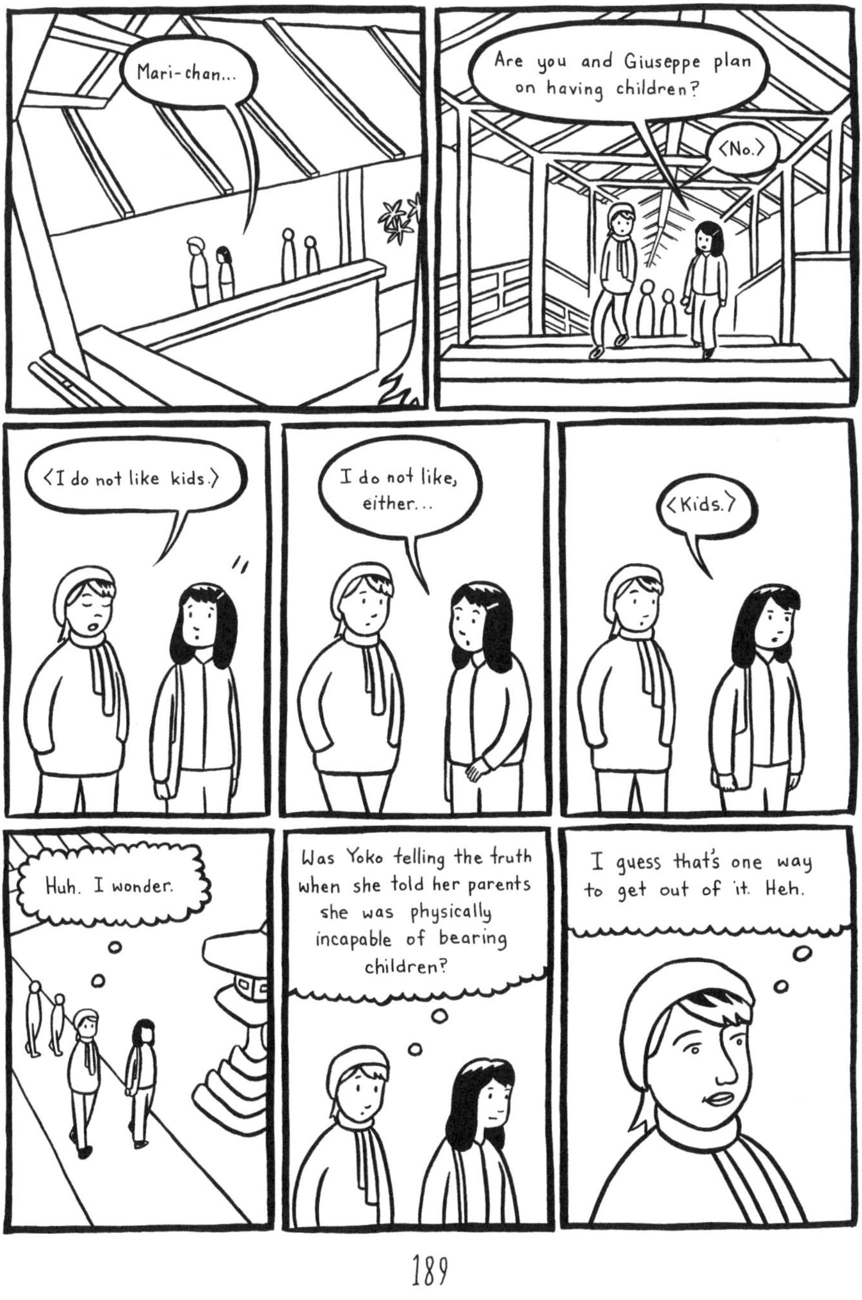
Mari-chan...
Are you and Giuseppe plan on having children?
<No.>
<I do not like kids.>
I do not like, either...
<Kids.>
Huh. I wonder.
Was Yoko telling the truth when she told her parents she was physically incapable of bearing children?
I guess that's one way to get out of it. Heh.

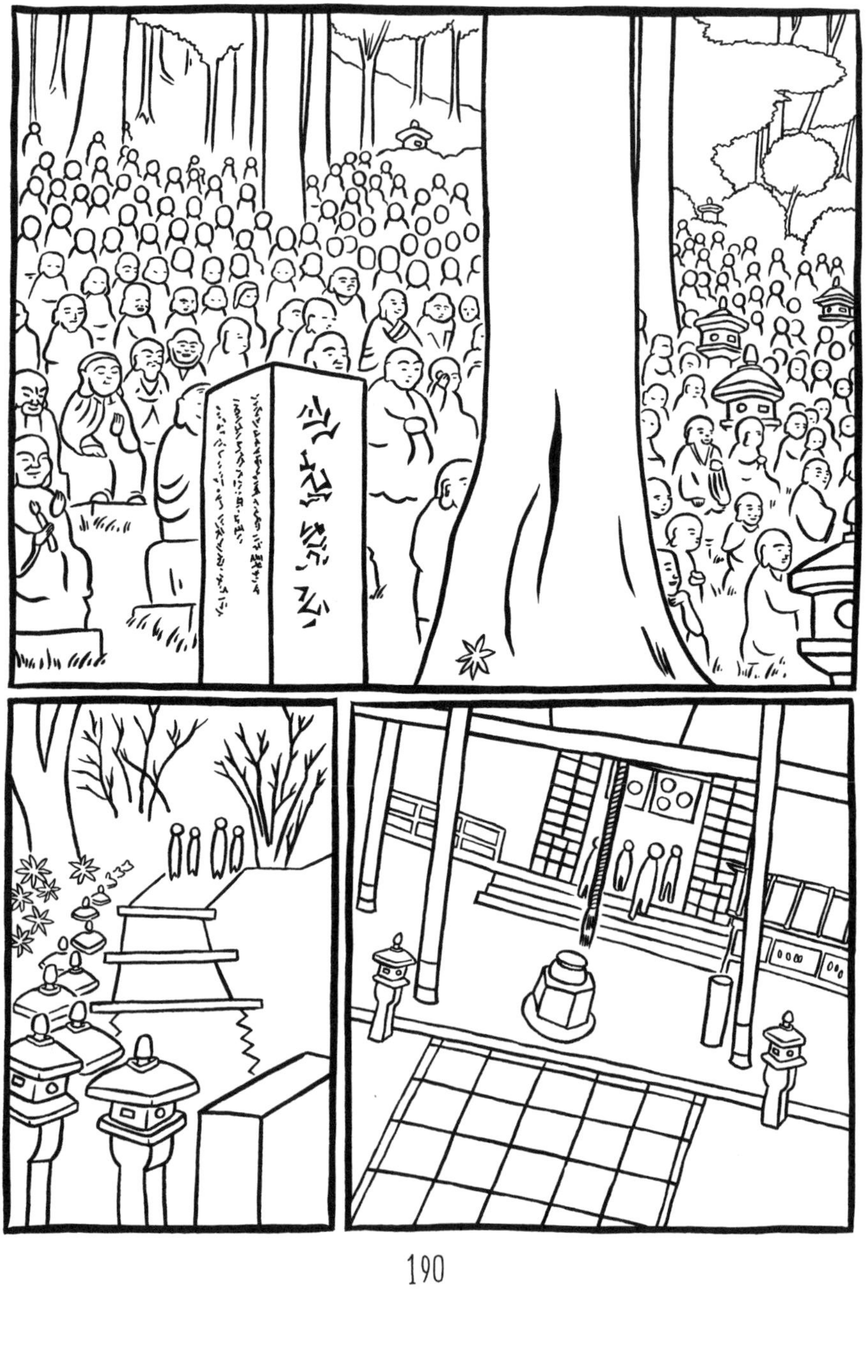

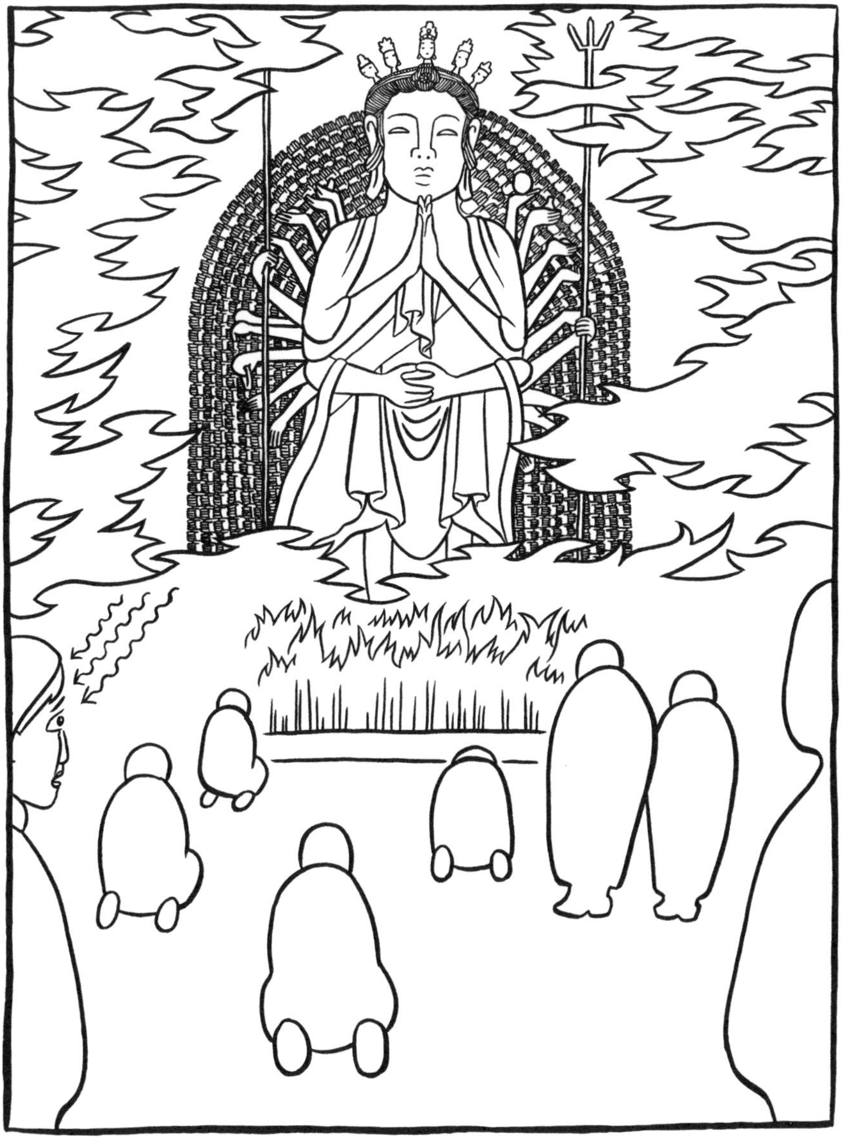

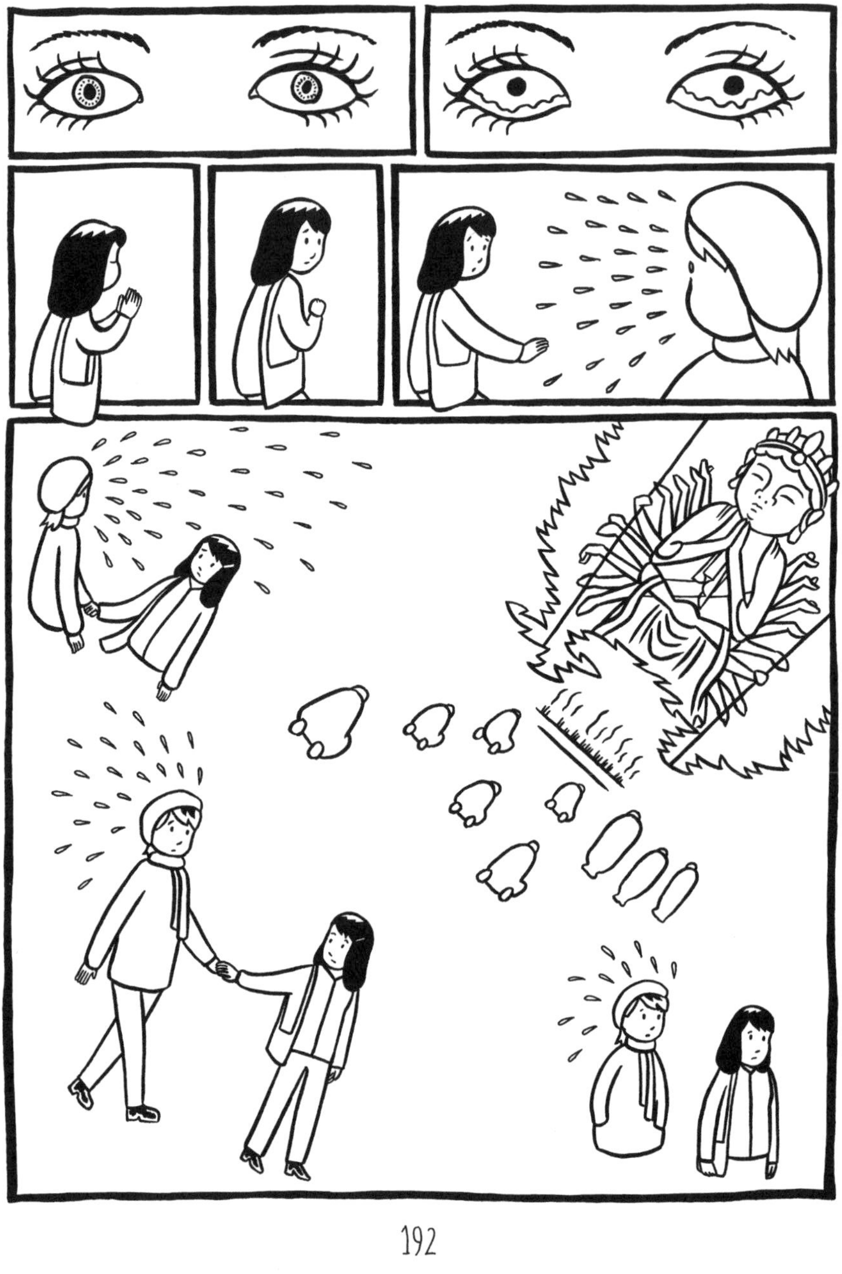

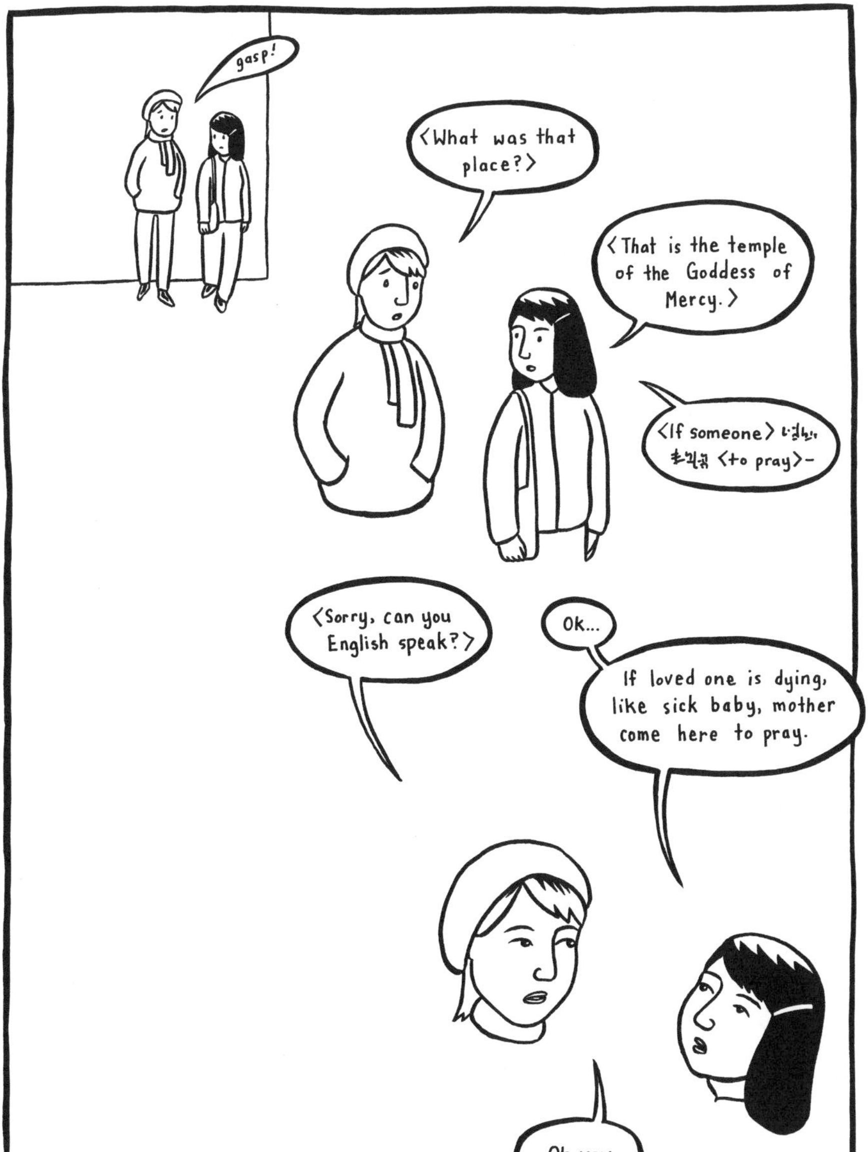
gasp!
<What was that place?>
<That is the temple of the Goddess of Mercy.>
<If someone> <to pray>–
<Sorry, can you English speak?>
Ok...
If loved one is dying, like sick baby, mother come here to pray.
Oh, wow.

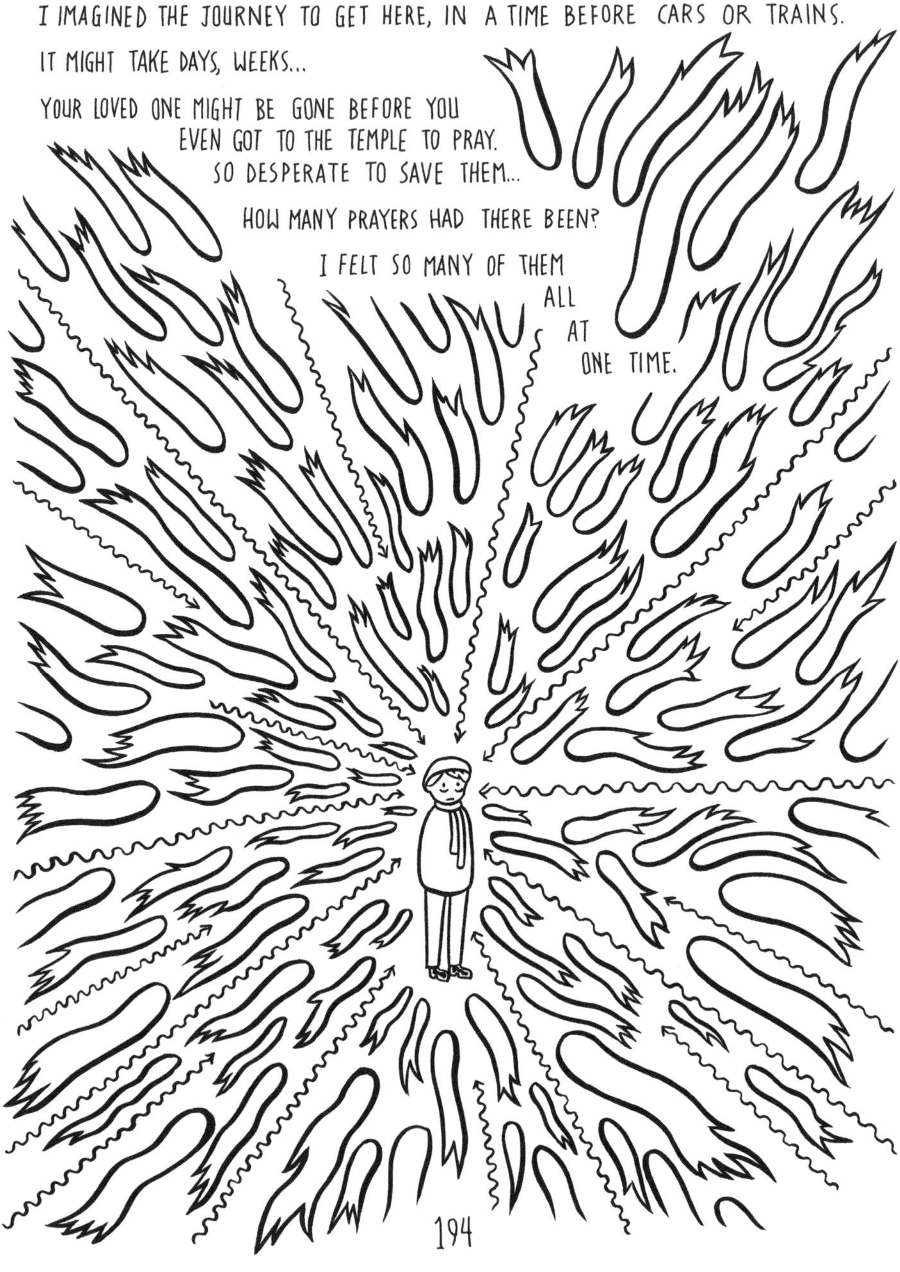
I IMAGINED THE JOURNEY TO GET HERE, IN A TIME BEFORE CARS OR TRAINS.
IT MIGHT TAKE DAYS, WEEKS...
YOUR LOVED ONE MIGHT BE GONE BEFORE YOU EVEN GOT TO THE TEMPLE TO PRAY.
SO DESPERATE TO SAVE THEM...
HOW MANY PRAYERS HAD THERE BEEN?
I FELT SO MANY OF THEM ALL AT ONE TIME.

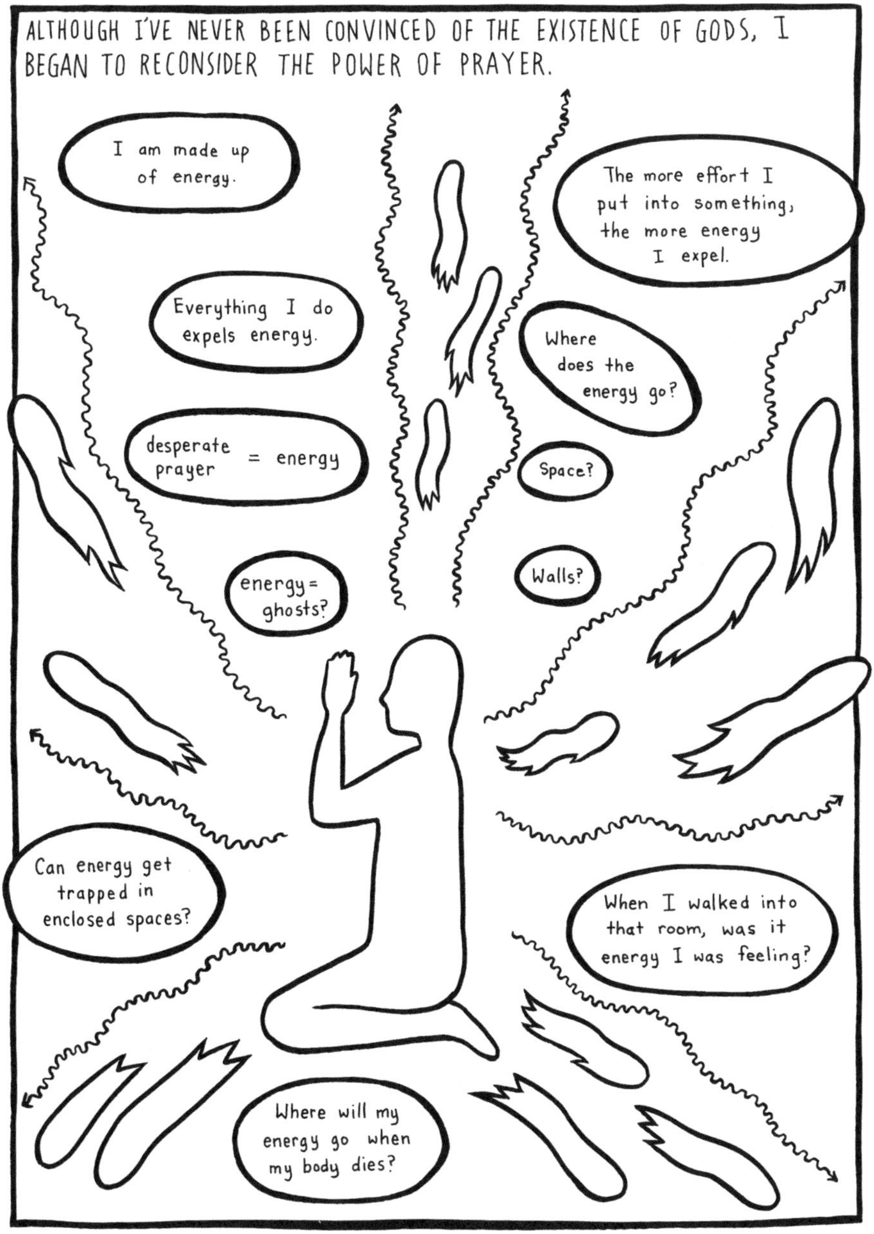
ALTHOUGH I'VE NEVER BEEN CONVINCED OF THE EXISTENCE OF GODS, I BEGAN TO RECONSIDER THE POWER OF PRAYER.
I am made up of energy.
The more effort I put into something, the more energy I expel.
Everything I do expels energy.
Where does the energy go?
desperate prayer = energy
Space?
Walls?
energy = ghosts?
Can energy get trapped in enclosed spaces?
When I walked into that room, was it energy I was feeling?
Where will my energy go when my body dies?

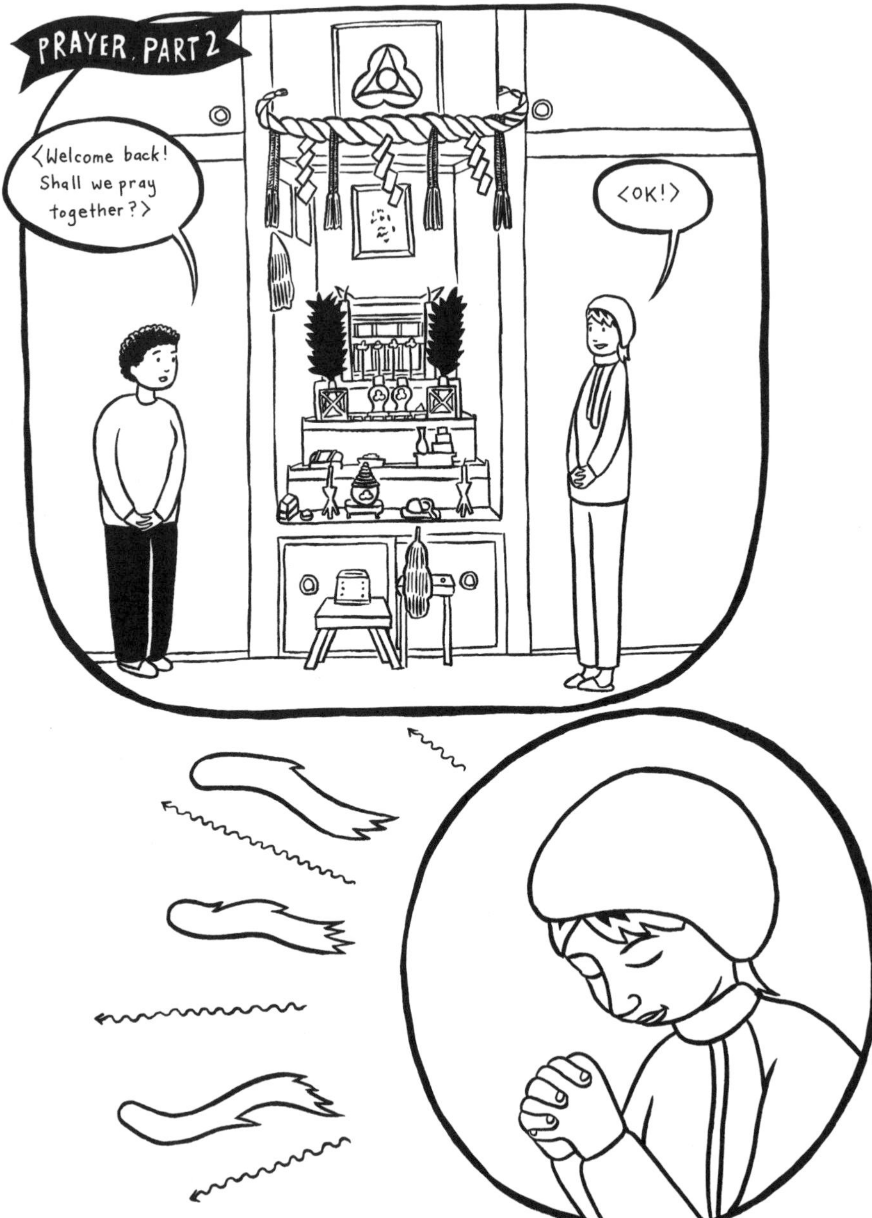
PRAYER, PART 2
<Welcome back! Shall we pray together?>
<OK!>

TOO SOON, IT WAS TIME FOR US TO GO. BUT THERE WERE STILL QUESTIONS.

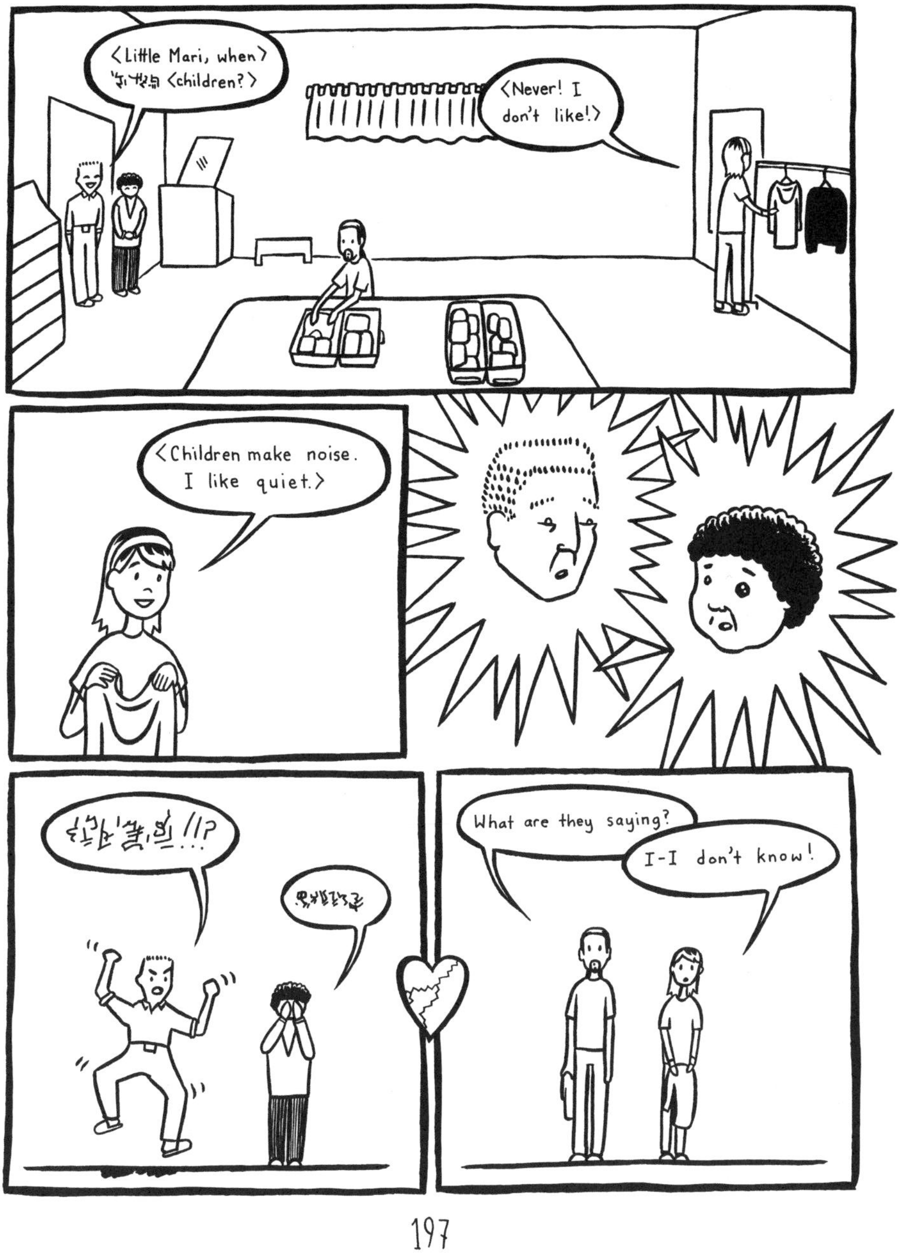

<Little Mari, when>
<children?>
<Never! I don't like!>
<Children make noise. I like quiet.>
What are they saying?
I-I don't know!

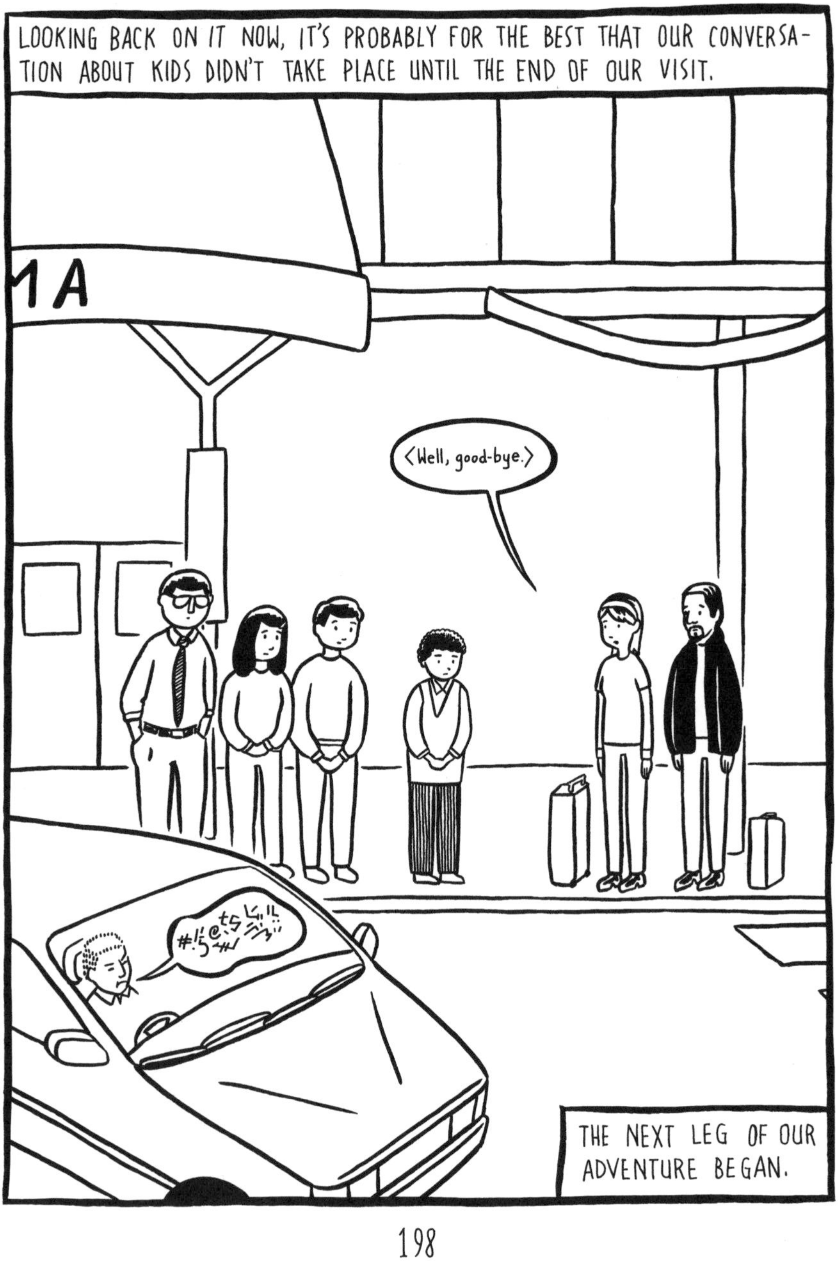
LOOKING BACK ON IT NOW, IT'S PROBABLY FOR THE BEST THAT OUR CONVERSATION ABOUT KIDS DIDN'T TAKE PLACE UNTIL THE END OF OUR VISIT.
MA
⟨Well, good-bye.⟩
THE NEXT LEG OF OUR ADVENTURE BEGAN.

HIROSHIMA

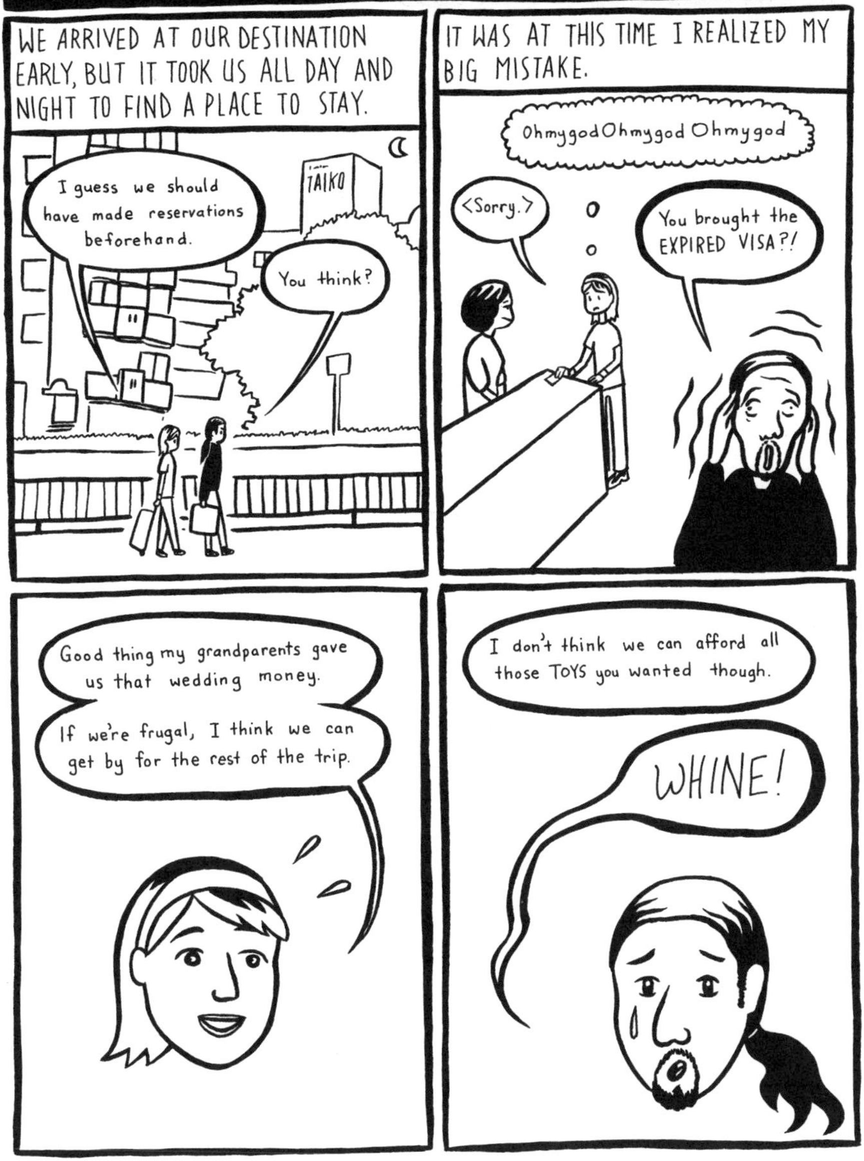
WE ARRIVED AT OUR DESTINATION EARLY, BUT IT TOOK US ALL DAY AND NIGHT TO FIND A PLACE TO STAY.
TAIKO
I guess we should have made reservations beforehand.
You think?
IT WAS AT THIS TIME I REALIZED MY BIG MISTAKE.
OhmygodOhmygod Ohmygod
<Sorry.>
You brought the EXPIRED VISA?!
Good thing my grandparents gave us that wedding money.
If we're frugal, I think we can get by for the rest of the trip.
I don't think we can afford all those TOYS you wanted though.
WHINE!

KYOTO

IT SOON BECAME APPARENT THAT NONE OF OUR DESTINATIONS WERE PREPARED TO ACCOMMODATE SPONTANEOUS VISITORS WITH A LIMITED BUDGET.

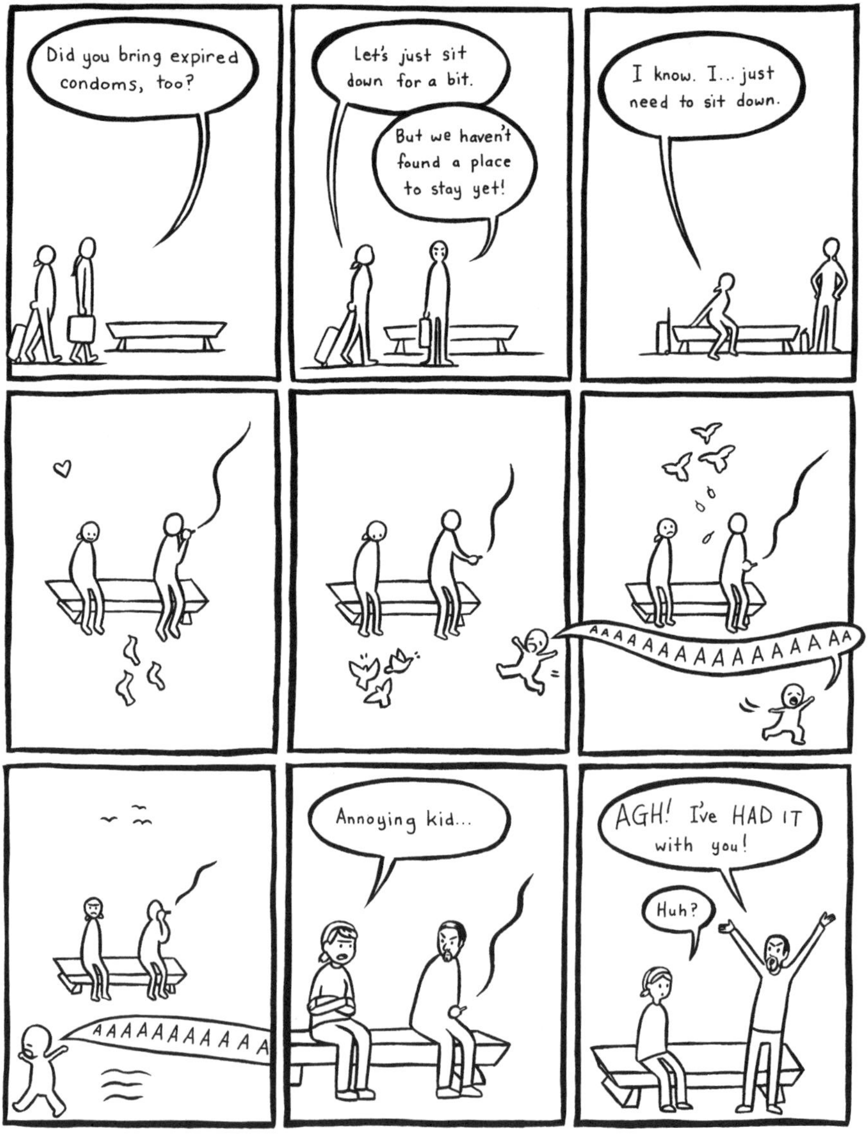

Did you bring expired condoms, too?
Let's just sit down for a bit.
But we haven't found a place to stay yet!
I know. I... just need to sit down.
AAAAAAAAAAAAAAAAA
AAAAAAAAAAAA
Annoying kid...
AGH! I've HAD IT with you!
Huh?

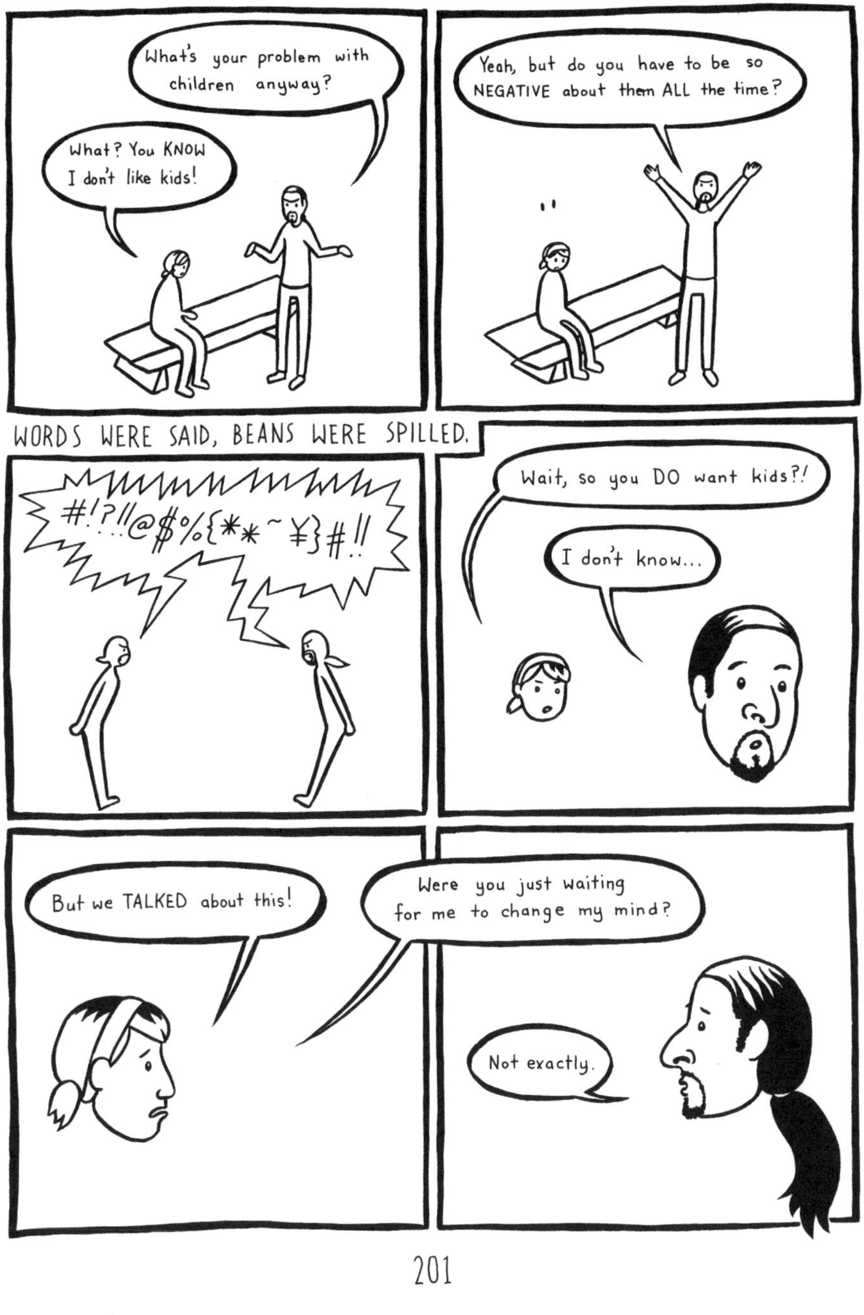
What's your problem with children anyway?
What? You KNOW I don't like kids!
Yeah, but do you have to be so NEGATIVE about them ALL the time?
WORDS WERE SAID, BEANS WERE SPILLED.
#!?!!@$%{**~¥}#!!
Wait, so you DO want kids?!
I don't know...
But we TALKED about this!
Were you just waiting for me to change my mind?
Not exactly.

GIUSEPPE HAD BEEN PRETENDING TO BE MY SOUL MATE.

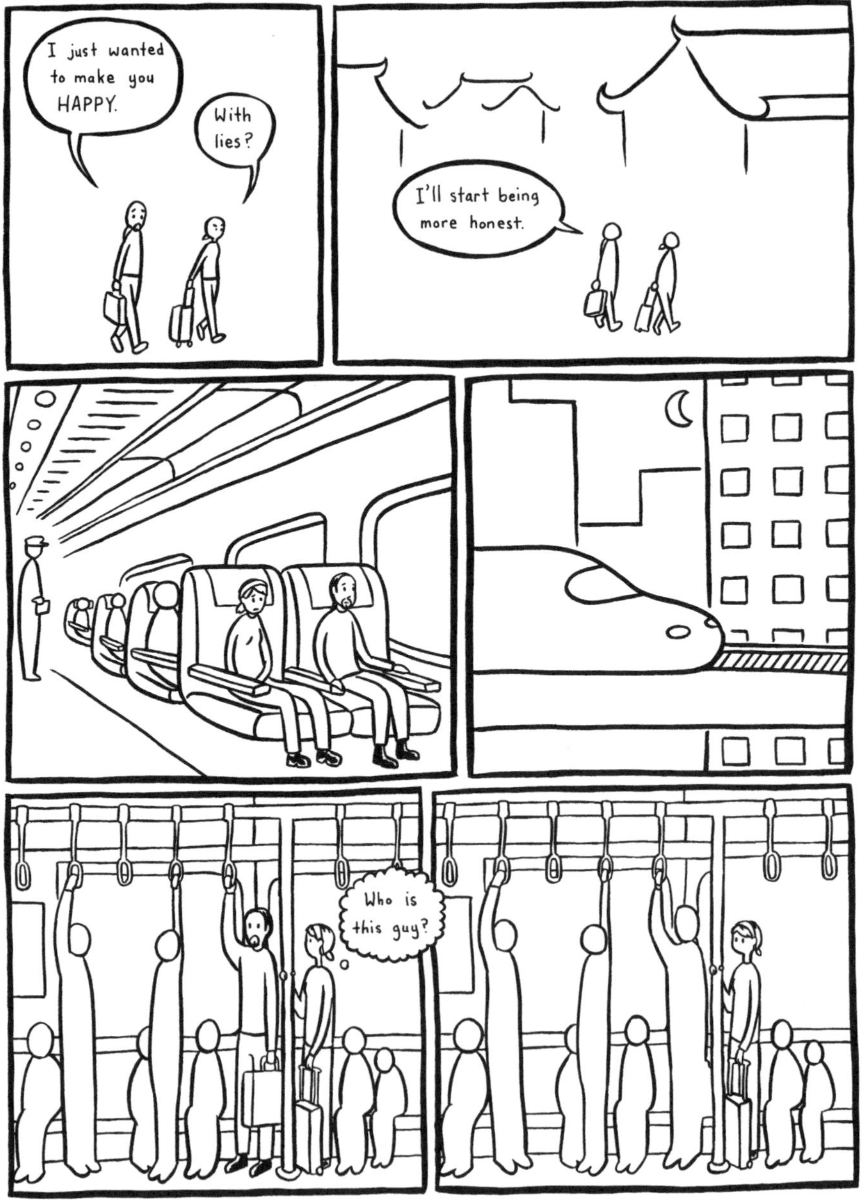
I just wanted to make you HAPPY.
With lies?
I'll start being more honest.
Who is this guy?

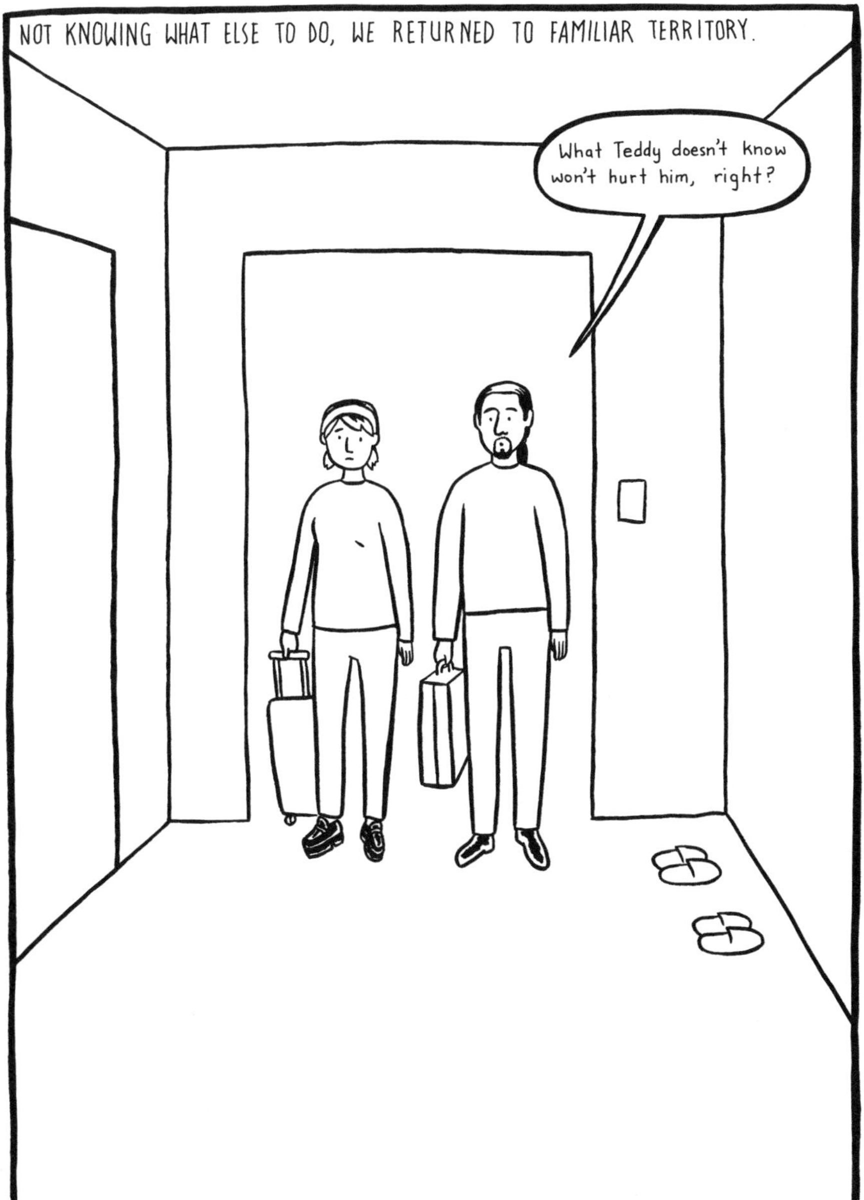
NOT KNOWING WHAT ELSE TO DO, WE RETURNED TO FAMILIAR TERRITORY.
What Teddy doesn't know won't hurt him, right?

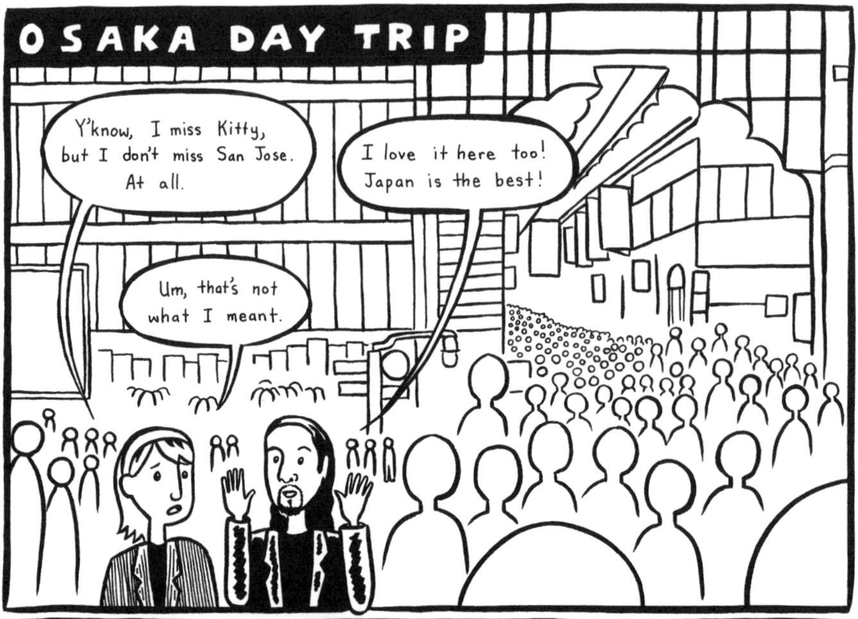
OSAKA DAY TRIP
Y'know, I miss Kitty, but I don't miss San Jose. At all.
I love it here too! Japan is the best!
Um, that's not what I meant.

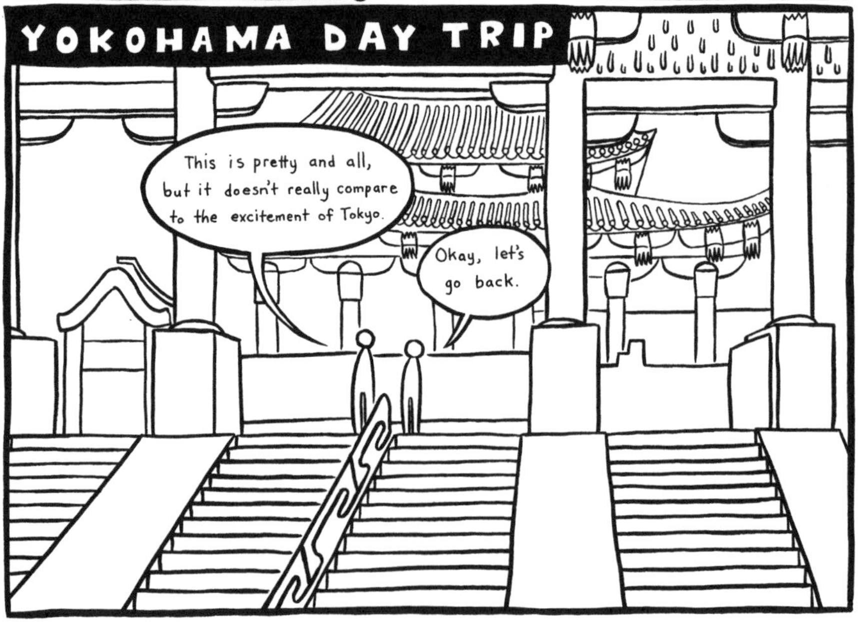
YOKOHAMA DAY TRIP
This is pretty and all, but it doesn't really compare to the excitement of Tokyo.
Okay, let's go back.

I WAS SICK OF LOOKING SO STRAIGHT-EDGE FOR WORK, FOR MY FAMILY.

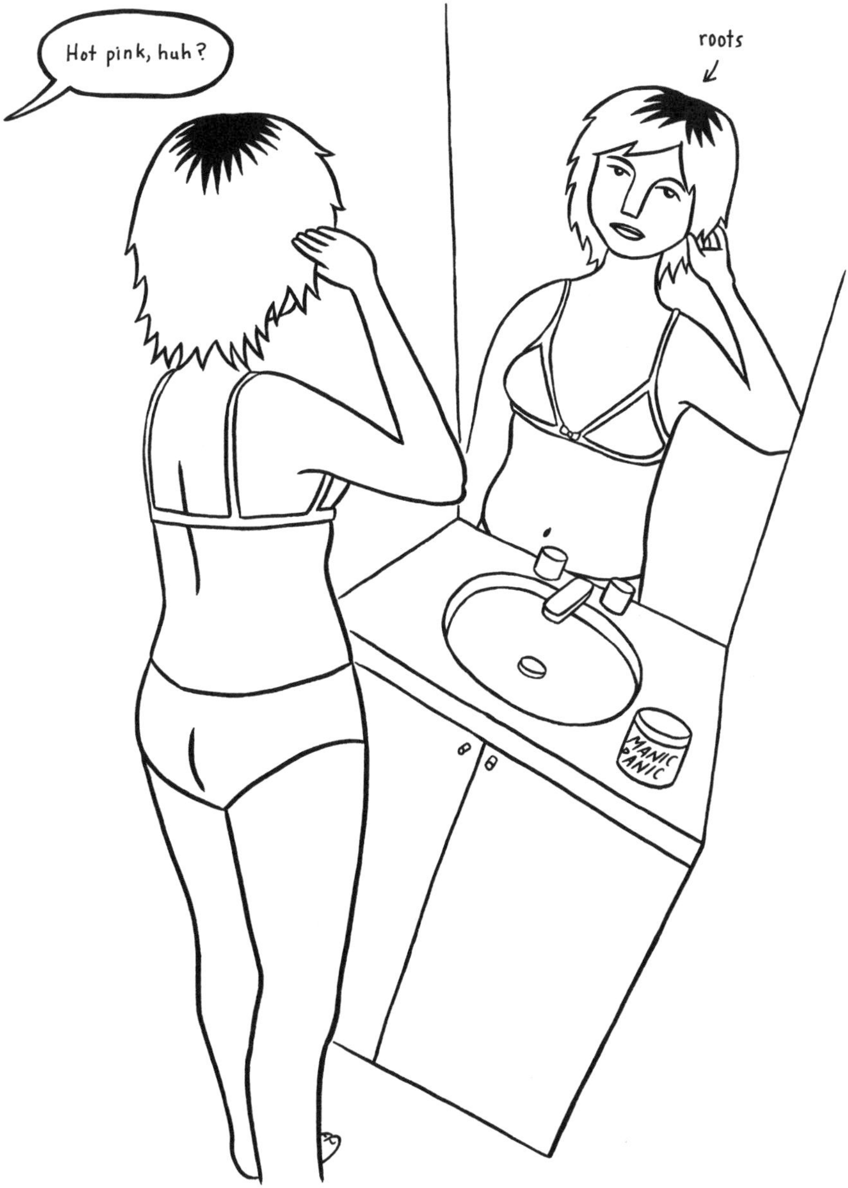
Hot pink, huh?
roots
MANIC PANIC

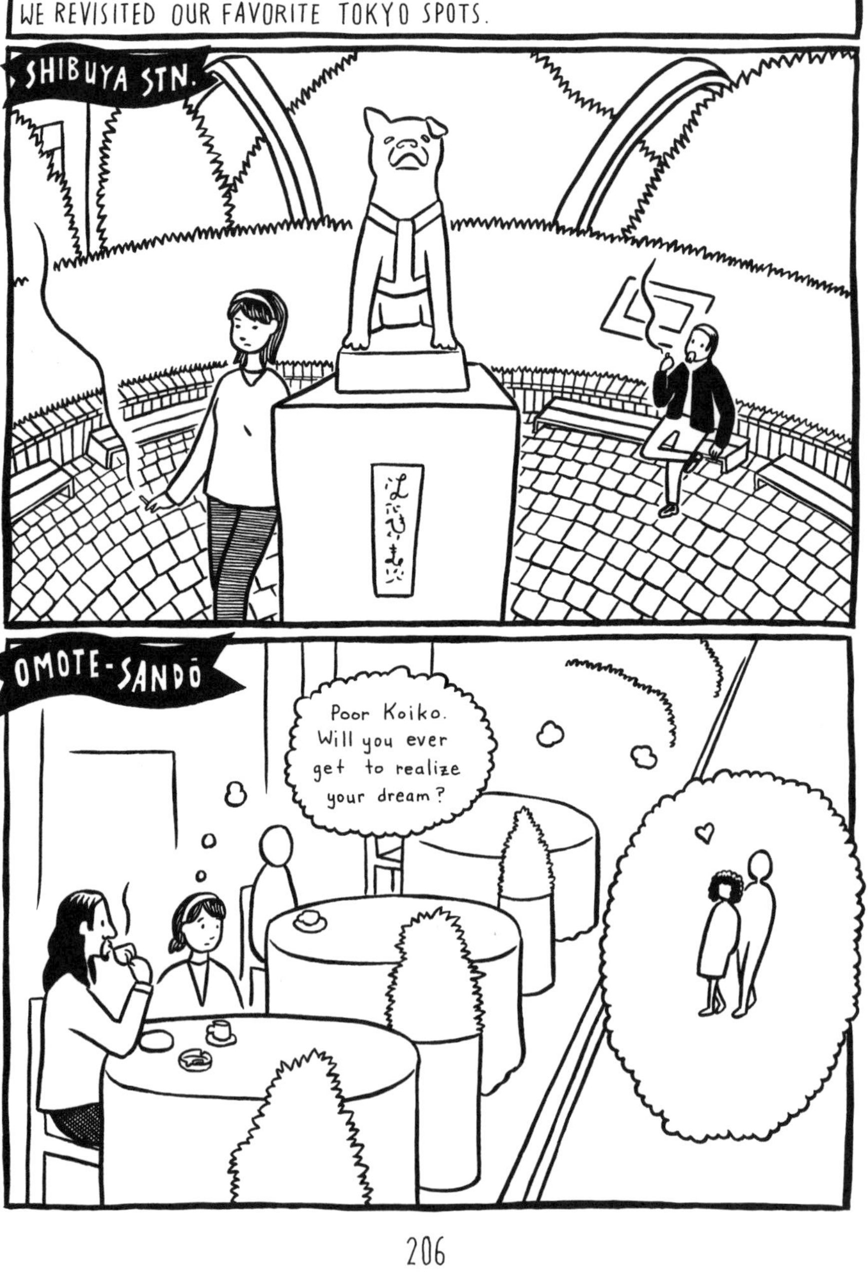
WE REVISITED OUR FAVORITE TOKYO SPOTS.
SHIBUYA STN.
OMOTE-SANDŌ
Poor Koiko. Will you ever get to realize your dream?

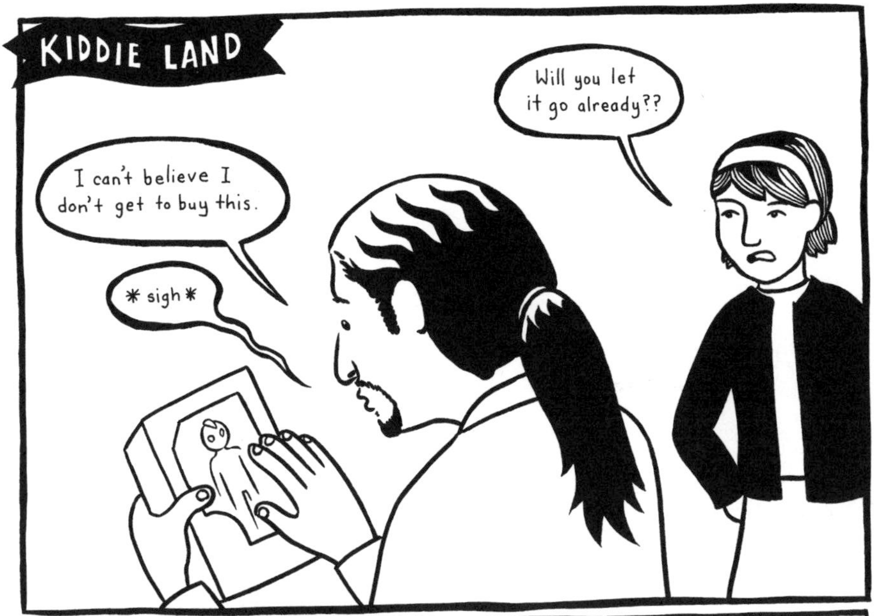
KIDDIE LAND
I can't believe I don't get to buy this.
* sigh *
Will you let it go already??

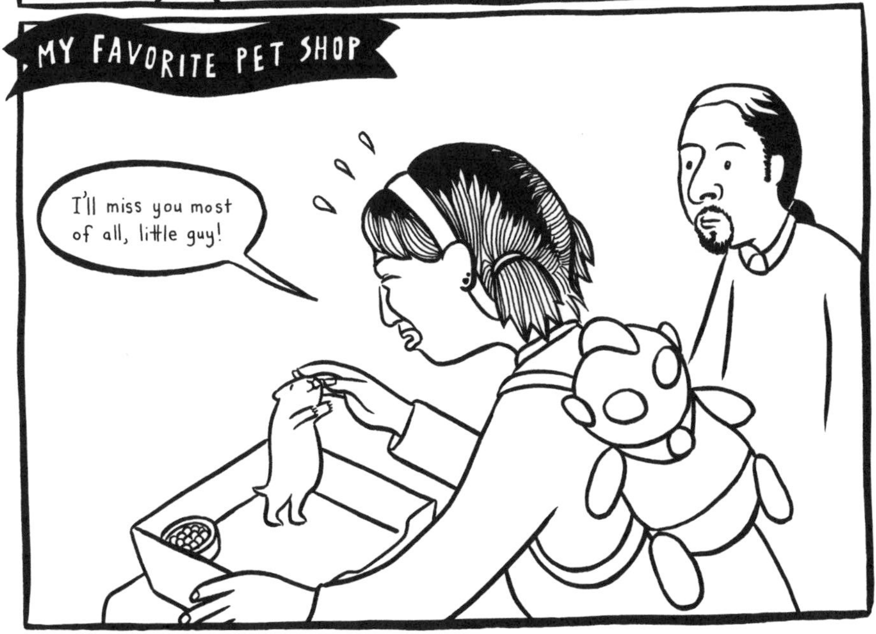
MY FAVORITE PET SHOP
I'll miss you most of all, little guy!

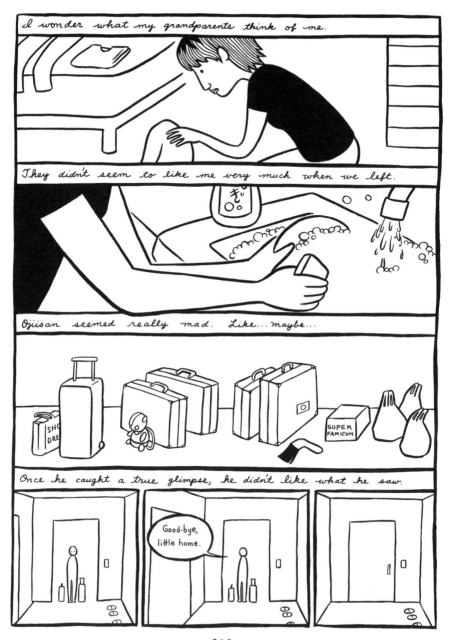

I wonder what my grandparents think of me.

They didn't seem to like me very much when we left.

Ojiisan seemed really mad. Like... maybe...

Once he caught a true glimpse, he didn't like what he saw.

SUPER FAMICOM

Good-bye, little home.

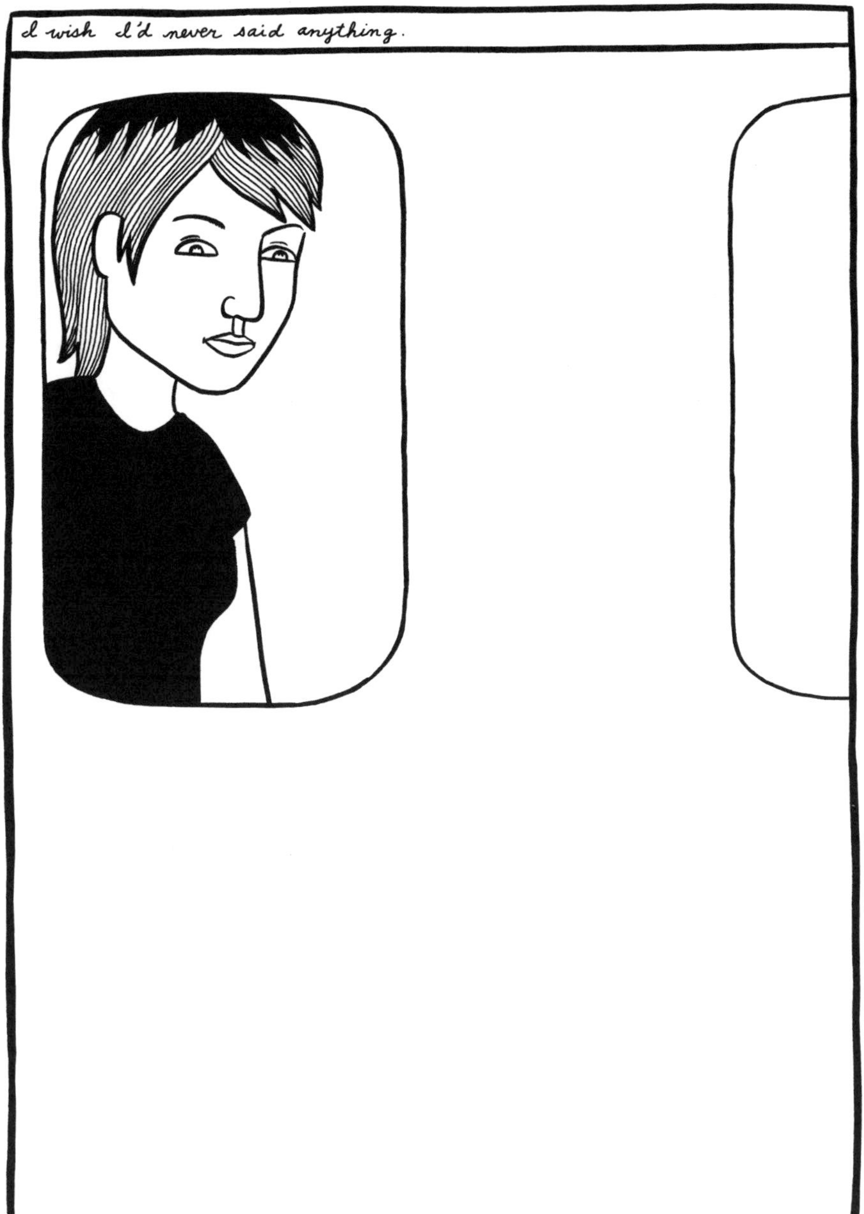
I wish I'd never said anything.

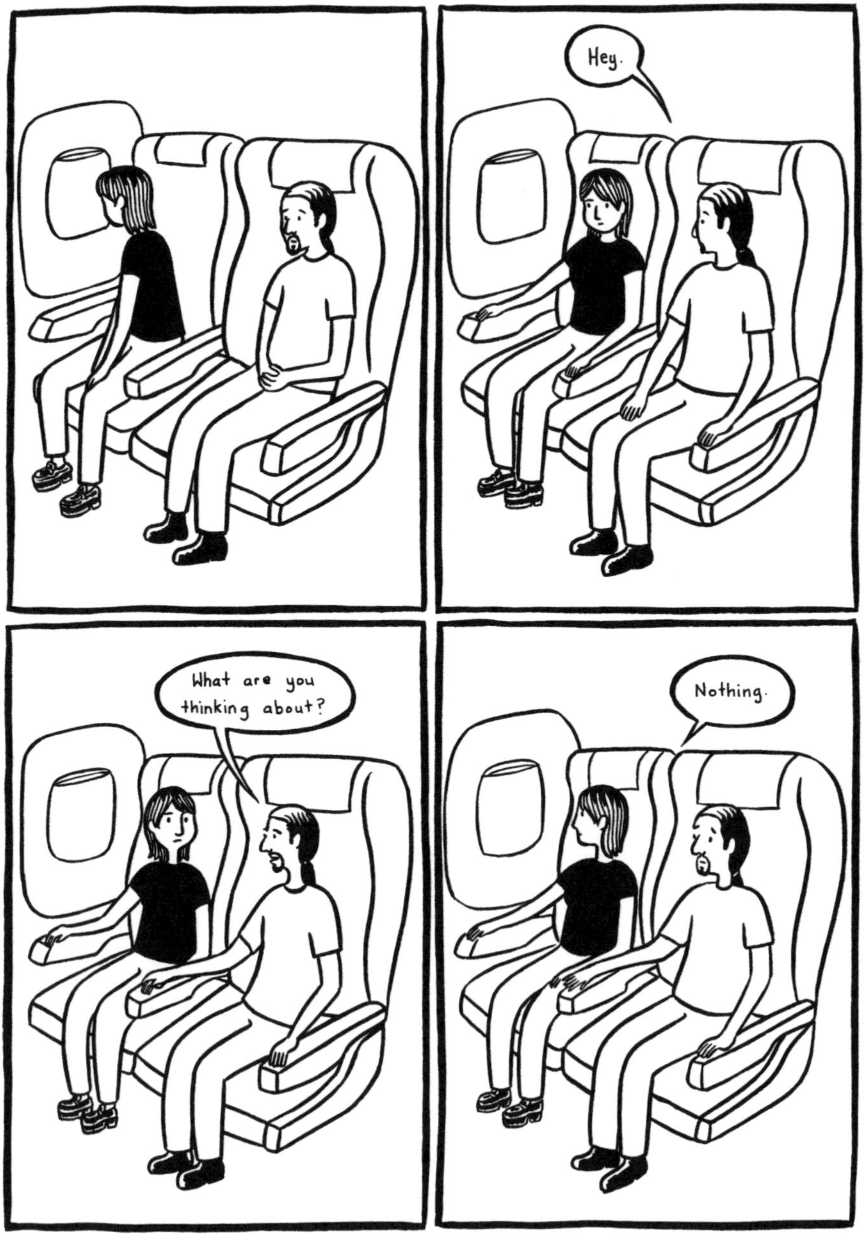
Hey.
What are you thinking about?
Nothing.

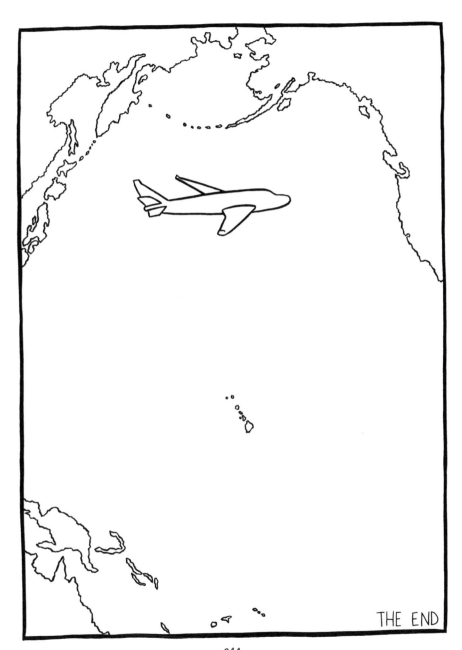

THE END

EPILOGUE

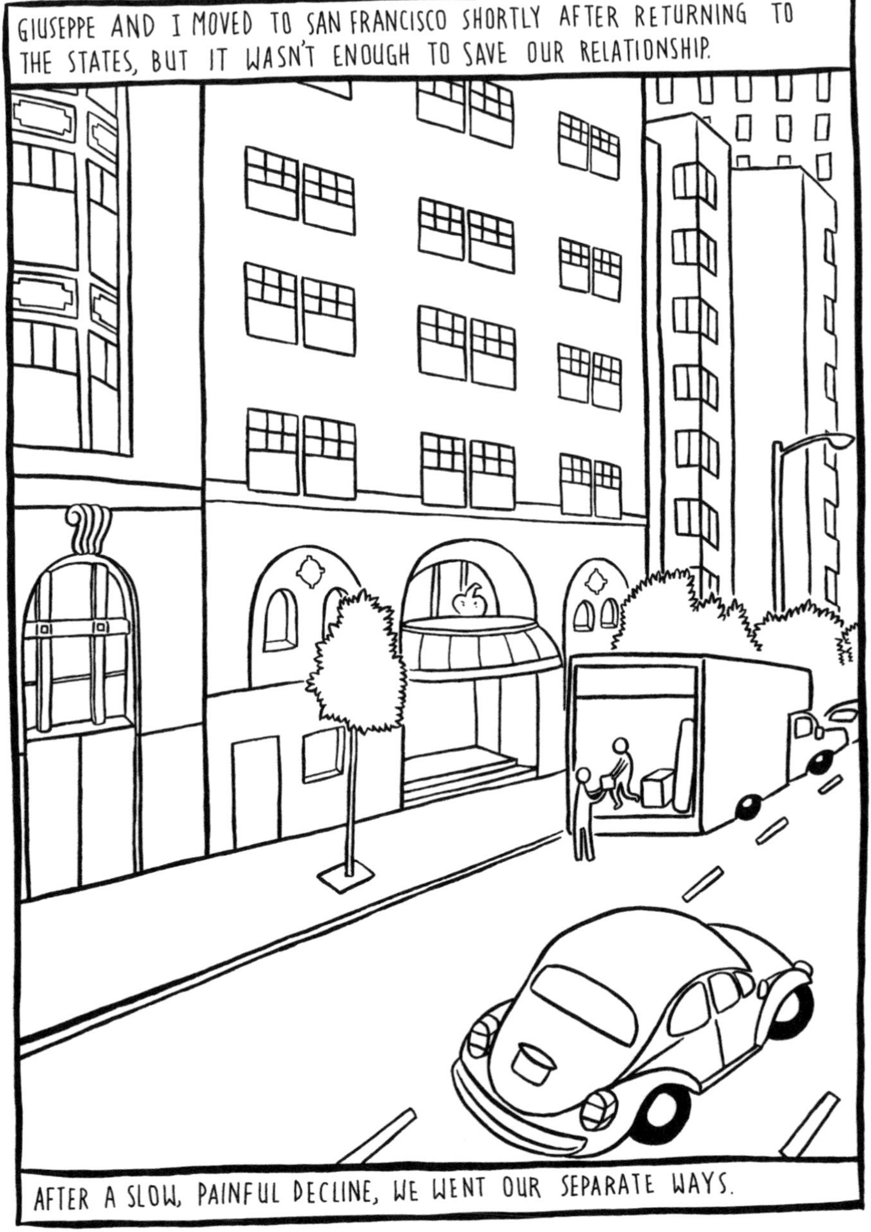
GIUSEPPE AND I MOVED TO SAN FRANCISCO SHORTLY AFTER RETURNING TO THE STATES, BUT IT WASN'T ENOUGH TO SAVE OUR RELATIONSHIP.
AFTER A SLOW, PAINFUL DECLINE, WE WENT OUR SEPARATE WAYS.

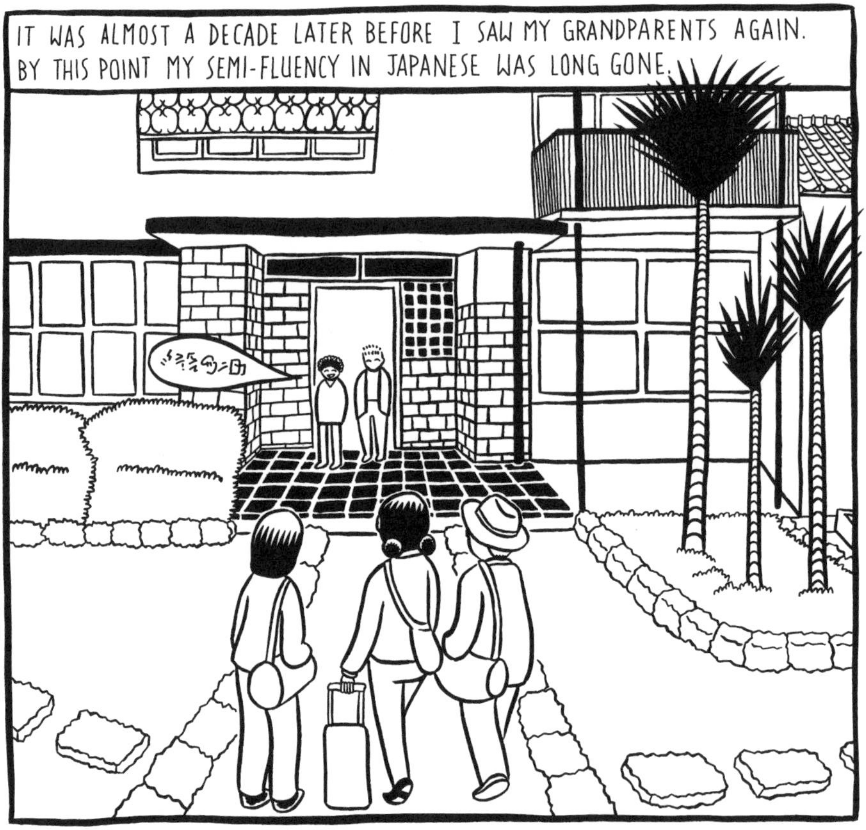
IT WAS ALMOST A DECADE LATER BEFORE I SAW MY GRANDPARENTS AGAIN. BY THIS POINT MY SEMI-FLUENCY IN JAPANESE WAS LONG GONE.

MY MOM HAD TO TRANSLATE FOR US. I WAS OKAY WITH THIS.

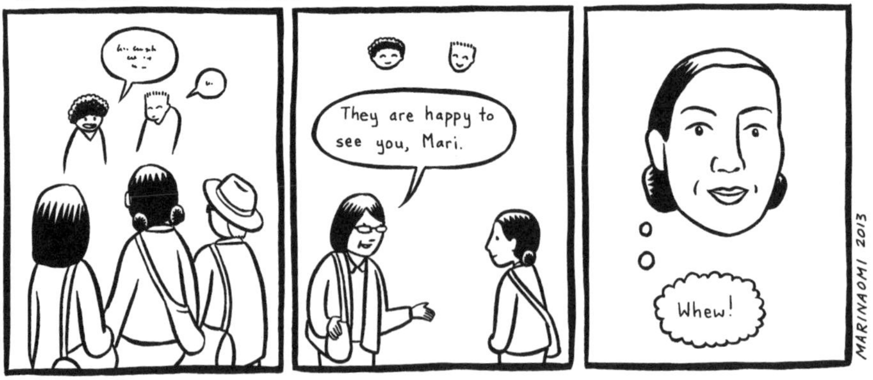
They are happy to see you, Mari.
Whew!
MARINAOMI 2013

Acknowledgements

Big thanks to my brilliant agent, Gordon Warnock of Fuse Literary, and my publishers Raighne Hogan and Justin Skarhus of 2dcloud. These guys went above and beyond to cheer me on and make this happen.

Thanks also to Radar Labs for taking me to paradise to get my shit together.

Shout-outs to TheRumpus.net, SFBay.CA, the CCA MFA in Comics program, the Ladydrawers, and everyone who kept me employed during the making of this book.

I am super-grateful to Osamu Shibamiya for help with cultural editing, and to Lisa Thomson, Rob Kirby, Fiona Taylor, Lainie Baker, Yumi Sakugawa, Nicky Sa-eun Schildkraut and Steph Cha for their professional and moral support.

Super-congratulations to Giuseppe (not his real name) and his amazing wife and new baby.

Most of all, big love to my family (Mom, Dad, Sue, Yoko, and everyone who appeared in this book), especially my muse, my beautiful husband Gary.

Love,

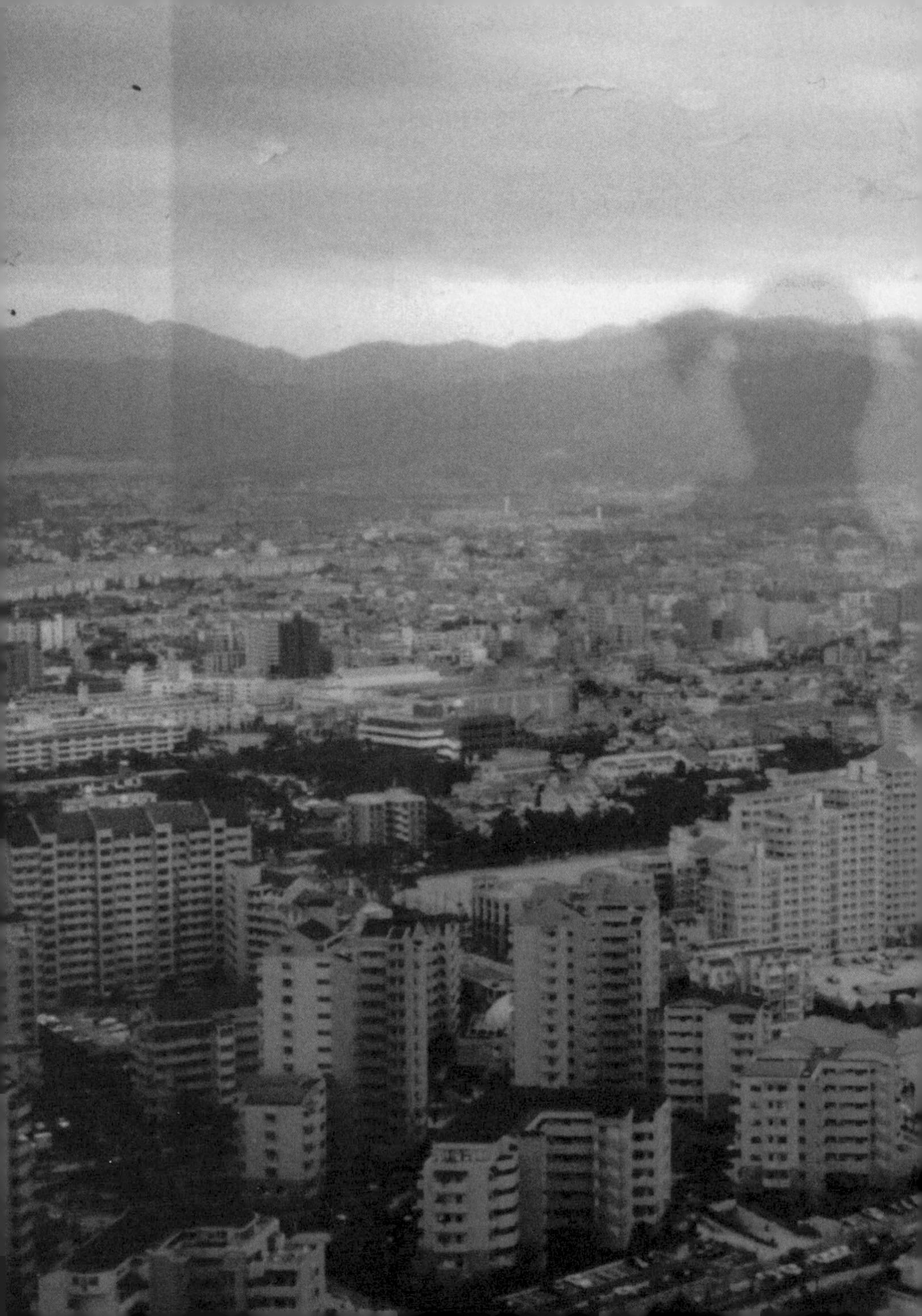

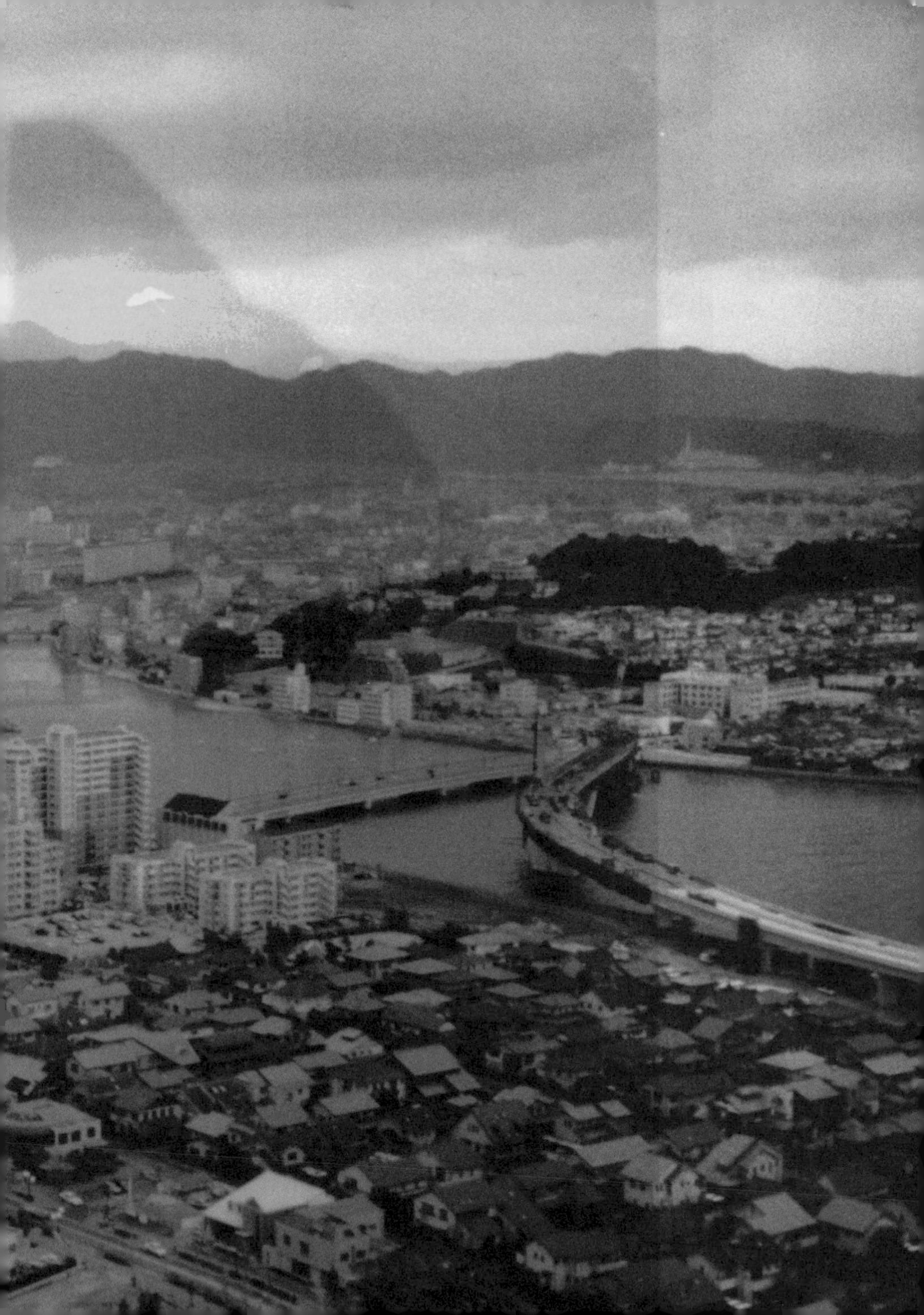

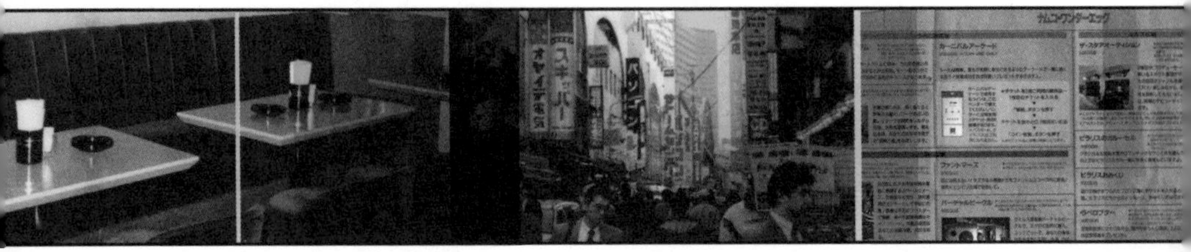
ナムコ・ワンダーエッグ
カーニバルアーケード

MariNaomi has been making autobio comics since 1997. She's the author and illustrator of the SPACE Prize-winning graphic memoir Kiss & Tell: A Romantic Resume, Ages 0 to 22 (Harper Perennial, 2011), the Eisner-nominated Dragon's Breath and Other True Stories (2dcloud/Uncivilized Books, 2014), and her self-published Estrus Comics (1998 to 2009). Her work has appeared in over sixty print publications, and has been featured on numerous websites, such as The Rumpus, The Weeklings, LA Review of Books, Midnight Breakfast, Truth-out, XOJane, Buzzfeed, PEN America and more. Mari's work on the Rumpus won a SPACE Prize and an honorable mention in Houghton Mifflin's Best American Comics 2013.

MariNaomi's comics and paintings have been featured in such institutions as the De Young Museum, Yerba Buena Center for the Arts, the Cartoon Art Museum, San Francisco's Asian American Museum, and the Japanese American Museum in Los Angeles. In 2011, Mari toured with the literary roadshow Sister Spit. She is also the creator and curator of the Cartoonists of Color Database and the LGBTQ Cartoonists Database.

marinaomi.com

Photo by Fiona